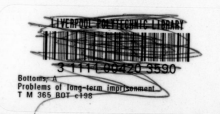

PROBLEMS OF
LONG-TERM IMPRISONMENT

CAMBRIDGE STUDIES IN CRIMINOLOGY

Problems of Long-Term Imprisonment

Edited by
Anthony E. Bottoms and Roy Light

Series Editor: A.E. Bottoms

Gower

Aldershot · Brookfield USA · Hong Kong · Singapore · Sydney

Published by
Gower Publishing Company Limited
Gower House
Croft Road
Aldershot
Hants GU11 3HR
England

Gower Publishing Company
Old Post Road
Brookfield
Vermont 05036
USA

British Library Cataloguing in Publication Data

Problems of long-term imprisonment. —
 (Cambridge studies in criminology; 58).
 1. Long-term imprisonment
 I. Bottoms, Anthony   II. Light, Roy
 III. Series
 365   HV8705

Library of Congress Cataloging-in-Publication Data

Problems of long-term imprisonment.
 (Cambridge studies in criminology; 58)
 Papers from the Eighteenth Cropwood Round-Table Conference held at
 Madingley Hall, Cambridge, March 19–21, 1986, organized by the
 Institute of Criminology, University of Cambridge.
 Bibliography: p.
 Includes indexes.
 1. Imprisonment—Great Britain—Congresses.
 2. Imprisonment—United States—Congresses.
 3. Prisons—Great Britain—Congresses.   4. Prisons— United States—Congresses.
 I. Bottoms, A.E.   II. Light, Roy.   III. Cropwood Round-Table Conference
 (18th: 1986: Cambridge, Cambridgeshire)
 IV. University of Cambridge. Institute of Criminology.   V. Series.
 HV9647.P75 1987   365'.941   87–11852

ISBN 0–566–05427–2

Typeset by Guildford Graphics Limited, Petworth, West Sussex.
Printed and bound in Great Britain by
Billing and Sons Limited, Worcester

Contents

Preface

Cropwood Round-Table Conferences have been organised by the Institute of Criminology, University of Cambridge, since 1968, and are one of the activities made possible by grants from the Cropwood Trust. The conferences are intended to bring together academics, administrators and practitioners to exchange information and constructively debate specific topical issues in penal policy, criminology or law enforcement. Each year an issue is selected for inclusion in the conference series, invitations are sent to those with relevant knowledge and experience to submit papers, and these are circulated in advance to invited participants to form the basis of discussions at the conference. In keeping with the intention of the Cropwood Trust to promote dialogue between the worlds of the universities and of criminal justice practitioners, papers are sought from both academics and those in the relevant criminal justice services.

The conferences aim to be of practical as well as theoretical interest, and thus to be of value for future policy-making. It is intended that participants will take the opportunity to exchange full and frank views and opinions in an atmosphere of confidentiality.

This volume arises from the eighteenth Cropwood Round-Table Conference, on 'Problems of Long-Term Imprisonment', held at Madingley Hall, Cambridge, on 19–21 March 1986. In addition to the Cropwood Trust funding, the organisers were fortunate in receiving a Home Office grant which enabled the traditional conference size to be doubled to 60 participants, representing England and Wales, Scotland, Northern Ireland and the United States. We are deeply grateful to both the Cropwood Trust and the Home Office for making the conference possible.

We would like to express our great appreciation to the staff at Madingley Hall, Cambridge, for providing a splendid venue for the conference; and to Lord Glenarthur, then the Minister of State at the Home Office in charge of prisons, for honouring the conference by attending as the principal guest at the formal conference dinner. Within the Institute of Criminology, we are grateful to Valerie Topsfield, Secretary to the Cropwood Scheme, for much preparatory work on the organisation of the conference; to Brenda McWilliams for extensive assistance with the preparation of the papers and proceedings for publication; and to Kay Foad, Thelma Norman and Pam Paige for help during the conference itself. We are, of course, also most grateful to all those who participated in the conference, especially those who prepared papers.

We would add only one more point. As will be clear from our introduction to the volume (Chapter 1), this conference was seen very much as a follow-up to the 1984 report of the Control Review Committee on the management of the long-term prison system. That report was confined to male prisoners, and it was inevitable that the great majority of the papers at the conference would therefore concern the problems of handling male long-term prisoners. It had nevertheless been our hope that a paper could be presented on the very important issues concerning the future of long-term imprisonment for women in England and Wales, but in the event the presentation of such a paper did not prove possible. We fully recognise that this is a significant omission from the volume, but we hope that the omission will soon be rectified by the publication of relevant material in other contexts.

Anthony Bottoms
Roy Light

Supplementary note

A volume of this kind takes time to process through the various stages of publication, and significant events have occurred in British prisons since the Cropwood Conference of March 1986: for example, the 'Fresh Start' proposals for the revision of the personnel structure of the English Prison Service, and the various disturbances in Scottish prisons in the winter of 1986–7. Most recently, the Home Office Research and Advisory Group on the Long-Term Prison System has published a report (*Special Units for Long-Term Prisoners: Regimes, Management and Research*, London: HMSO, 1987) which will require attention from all those concerned with the future of long-term imprisonment in England and Wales. It has not been practicable to update the chapters in this volume to take account of these various developments, and readers should be aware that most of the chapters were written in the early part of 1986; the introductory chapter was completed in the autumn of 1986.

A.E.B.
R.L.

May 1987

1 Introduction: Problems of long-term imprisonment
Anthony Bottoms and Roy Light

Prison systems exist in all developed countries, but they vary enormously in size, administration, objectives, and so on. Yet all prison systems share certain common problems, chief amongst which are the problems of security (ensuring the secure custody of inmates committed by the courts) and control (ensuring that disorder does not break out within the prison). These problems are perhaps especially important when considering long-term prisoners. Public opinion in most countries becomes disturbed if long-term prisoners, convicted of serious crimes, escape from prisons with any regularity; yet the very length of sentences imposed on long-term prisoners enhances the difficulty of ensuring that their conditions of captivity do not lead to control problems. And beyond the management of the long-term population generally, there is the problem of how best to deal with a relatively small group of inmates often described as being the 'hard core'.

Different countries have different ways of handling their more difficult long-term inmates. In the United States Federal prison system, for example, the notorious Alcatraz Prison, on an island in San Francisco Bay, was once used to 'control the most uncontrollable inmates . . . those who used physical violence against their fellow-convicts, the leaders of strong-arm gangs and riots, the escape artists, the leaders of strikes and organised protests, and those men who assaulted or killed employees' (Ward, Chapter 3).[1] This prison was closed, and a system of dispersing Alcatraz-type prisoners among different prisons was used instead for a short time; but soon the Federal Bureau of Prisons 'began to return to a policy of concentration', based at Marion Penitentiary, Illinois (Ward, Chapter 3) — though, as we shall see, it was concentration of a rather different kind. In Scotland, the small size of the prison system has influenced the prison administration to decide to keep most of its long-term recidivist inmates in one main maximum-security prison (Peterhead), but to augment this provision by the development of small units for control-problem prisoners, including the much-discussed Barlinnie Special Unit (Coyle, Chapter 11; Whatmore, Chapter 12).

In England and Wales,[2] the focus of most of the papers in this collection, the present system can only be understood in the light of its particular history. This history has been well documented elsewhere (Home Office 1984a, Annex C; King and Morgan 1980, Chapter 3), and we shall not elaborate it in detail here. Briefly, however, for those unfamiliar with the story, the main landmarks have been as follows. Several spectacular escapes of nationally notorious long-term prisoners in the 1960s culminated in the ridiculously easy escape of George Blake, a spy serving 42 years, from Wormwood Scrubs in 1966. This precipitated an immediate and swiftly executed inquiry into prison security, led by Lord Mountbatten of Burma, former Viceroy of India. Mountbatten concluded that there was no really secure prison in the country, and recommended a variety of measures to remedy this, most of which were quickly implemented, notably (i) major improvements in physical security in selected prisons (better perimeter security, television cameras, dogs and so on), and (ii) the introduction of a new classification system based on security risk, ranging from Category A ('prisoners whose escape would be highly dangerous to the public or police or to the security of the State') to Category D ('those who can reasonably be trusted to serve their sentences in open conditions') (Home Office 1966). Mountbatten also recommended that Category A prisoners should be concentrated together in a new fortress institution to be built on the Isle of Wight. This proposal was not implemented, however, mainly because of another committee's recommendations two years later; this was the Radzinowicz Committee (a subcommittee of the Advisory Council on the Penal System), which, alarmed *inter alia* at the possibilities of control difficulties within a single fortress prison, recommended instead the dispersal of Category A prisoners among several 'dispersal prisons' (Advisory Council 1968).

Thus was created the English 'dispersal system', which by the early 1980s comprised eight prisons.[3] But this dispersal system has by no means been trouble-free. A series of major riots and disturbances in various prisons from 1969 to 1983 (for details see Home Office 1984a, Annex D) meant that only two established dispersal prisons (Wakefield and Long Lartin) had escaped serious disorder.[4] Moreover, these major disturbances were only the tip of the iceberg of considerable tension in the day-to-day running of most dispersal prisons. The problem of security for long-term prisoners had been essentially solved by the Mountbatten recommendations[5], but the problem of control in dispersal prisons clearly remained a major difficulty.

It was against this background that the Home Office established the Control Review Committee (CRC), an internal working party consisting entirely of Home Office civil servants and prison governors. The setting up of the committee came at what looked like an unpropitious time (September 1983), sandwiched as it was between a major riot in the dispersal prison at Albany, Isle of Wight, in May, and the Home Secretary's announcement, in October 1983, of a distinctly more restrictive policy for the paroling of long-term prisoners in England.[6] Yet the committee's report, published in July 1984 (Home Office 1984a), has been generally welcomed as a wide-ranging and extremely thoughtful review, not only of control problems in dispersal prisons, but of the long-term prison system as a whole. The report has, without any doubt, changed the terms of the debates about long-term imprisonment in England.

One of the comments of the CRC was that insufficient research attention had been paid to the problems of long-term prisons, and it recommended the future involvement of outside academics in developing a programme to meet this need. In November 1984, the Home Secretary announced the setting-up of a Research and Advisory Group on the Long-Term Prison System (RAG), the members of which included Home Office officials and three university academics (see further Norris, Chapter 2). Early on in RAG's deliberations, its then Chairman, Mr A.J. Langdon, suggested that a wide-ranging conference on CRC-related themes, held a couple of years after the publication of the CRC report, would be a useful stimulus to further debate on the general problem of long-term imprisonment in England. The Cambridge Institute of Criminology has, since 1968, promoted a series of 'Cropwood Round-Table Conferences' (see Preface), the purpose of which is to bring together administrators, practitioners and academics in constructive debate on criminal justice topics. The interests of RAG and of the Cambridge Institute were therefore brought together in a Cropwood Conference held in March 1986, the papers for which form the chapters of this book.

In this introduction, we have attempted to provide a background for the chapters which follow, and to offer a framework which may perhaps be found helpful in considering the various complex and interlocking problems of long-term imprisonment. In doing so, we have drawn from time to time upon the extensive discussions which took place at the Cropwood Conference, but we have deliberately not attempted to provide an exhaustive account of the discussions themselves. We have also sometimes injected our own theoretical arguments or value-commitments; we think no apology is needed for this, but in fairness to other contributors and to readers, we have tried to be quite explicit about when we are reporting Cropwood discussions and when we are advancing our own ideas.

Law-jobs theory

The Cropwood Conference covered — as will shortly become apparent — a very wide range of disparate yet interrelated topics. In considering the shape of this introduction, it seemed to us important that we should present the relevant material, if possible, within a coherent framework which would aid readers' understanding of the issues, and of the way in which they relate to each other. We have chosen to attempt this through the 'law-jobs' theory of Karl Llewellyn, the American legal theorist (see Llewellyn 1940). Certain jobs, argued Llewellyn, have to be performed in any human group — be it a family, a bridge club, a university, a country, the United Nations, or a prison system. The 'rules' (formal or informal) and practices developed to deal with these 'jobs' are the law and legal system of that particular group. Four main law-jobs were identified:[7]

(i) *The disposition of the trouble-case.* In any human society, disputes and 'trouble' sometimes arise. A bridge club member accuses another of cheating, others join in on each side, and a major quarrel develops: the issue has to be dealt with before the club can return to normal. One car crashes into another at a crossroads: each driver blames the other and demands payment for the repairs — a solution has to be found. And so on. A characteristic of most developed or large-scale social groups is the existence of special social institutions (courts, arbitrators, etc.) to deal with 'trouble-cases' when they arise.

(ii) *Preventive channelling and the reorientation of conduct and expectations so as to avoid trouble.* This second law-job refers to a society's arrangements for avoiding trouble arising, as opposed to its arrangements for handling trouble when it has arisen. 'Preventive channelling' can take many forms — from, for example, the passing of legislation to try to persuade people not to engage in particular acts (such as acts of racial discrimination); to the installation of traffic lights at a road junction where many crashes have occurred; or the fitting of steering-locks on cars to try to prevent them from being stolen.

(iii) *The allocation of authority and the arrangement of procedures which legitimise action as being authoritative.* This law-job, called 'the say' for short by Llewellyn since it deals with 'who has the say' in a given group, is the 'constitutional law' of each society.

Sometimes who has the say is a clear-cut issue, but sometimes it is not:

> No constitutional question of jurisdiction was ever more delicate or puzzling than that presented when Christmas is at Grandma's, and Grandma has said the lid is off, and Father thinks the children are getting out of hand, and Grandma is not Father's mother (Llewellyn 1940, p. 1387, note 7).

Similarly tricky situations arise regularly in prisons, where the spheres of responsibility of different kinds of prison staff often overlap.

(iv) *The net organisation of the group or society as a whole so as to provide direction or incentive.* This idea, called the 'net drive' by Llewellyn, was also described by him as the 'whither of the totality'; or, in Norman Lewis's (1980) more prosaic phrase, the 'goal orientation' of the group. In a real sense, it provides the normative orientation within which the other law-jobs are performed. It is fundamental to the understanding of any functioning organisation.

Llewellyn's law-jobs theory can be and has been criticised (see, for example, Twining 1973, pp. 175–84) as a total theory of law, not least because it is unclear whether it is an empirical or an a priori theory, and because it has some tautological aspects. As Twining (1973, p. 181) notes, however, and as we know from our own teaching experience, many law students have found it illuminating to analyse groups with which they are acquainted in terms of how the 'law-jobs' are done, bearing in mind that this does not just mean the formal rules of the particular group. In this sense, the theory is a 'rough but useful tool for functional analysis' (Twining 1973, p. 182).

Following this approach, in our view the law-jobs theory does provide a helpful analytical tool (we claim no more for it than that) which assists in clarifying the complexly interlocking issues surrounding the long-term prisons debate. It helps us to see that, within a given prison system, we need to discuss all four main law-jobs (not just one or two, such as 'trouble-case' and 'preventive channelling'), and that we need to understand how the four aspects relate to each other within the system as a whole. It also reminds us, through the fourth law-job, that in a real sense the kind of prison system we develop depends crucially upon its goal orientation.

In the remainder of this introduction, we shall consider the four main law-jobs as they relate to the issues discussed at the Cropwood Conference.

Whither long-term prisons? Net drive and the prison system

We deal first with the 'net drive' because it is so fundamental.

People are sent to prisons for long terms by the courts for a variety of reasons — but mostly the protection of the public, general deterrence, and retribution. One can, of course, agree or disagree with the courts' reasoning in these matters, either generally or in any particular case. But once someone has been sent to prison by the courts, for both prisoner and staff the fact of the sentence is the most important point.[8] For the prisoner, the sentence has some-how to be served; for the staff, the overriding concern must be that the prisoner is kept in safe custody for the period ordered (this is the dimension usually called 'security' in prison language). Yet both prisoner and staff have interests also in the reasonable predictability of prison life during the sentence. Most prisoners like to know where they stand, and few prisoners like to feel that the prison is such a disorderly place that they may be the subject of assaults or threats. Thus prisoners have a certain investment in a degree of day-to-day internal order within the prison, and staff naturally share that concern (this is the dimension of 'social control', or, in prison language, 'control': see Young, Chapter 4).

These goals of security and internal order (or 'control') are generally recognised as basic to any prison system, and there was no disagreement about their importance at the Cropwood Conference. The aims were also explicit in the CRC's terms of reference: 'To review the maintenance of control in the prison system, including the implications for physical security' (Home Office 1984a, para. 1). What was rather more controversial at the conference was the relationship between the two concepts (Fitzgerald, Chapter 6), and the meaning of 'control'. 'Security' as a concept is, at least in its most basic form, easy to understand — prisoners must not be allowed to escape; but the meaning of 'control', and the style of its achievement in a prison system, is much less clear-cut (Young, Chapter 4; and see further below).

Security and control are essentially instrumental concepts. If they were the sole objectives for a prison system, they could perhaps be realised in a highly repressive manner. Thus, the CRC recognised the need to go beyond these aims in its own report, where it advanced a tentative draft of the objectives for a prison system, including *inter alia* 'that prisoners' lawful rights are respected'; that 'the life of a prison should be as close as possible to normal life'; and that prisoners should be given 'the opportunity to participate in a programme of constructive activities' (Home Office 1984a, para. 108).

There was general agreement at the Cropwood Conference about the need for some 'third dimension' in the objectives of long-term imprisonment, beyond security and control. One experienced prison administrator characterised this 'third dimension' in the single word 'dignity'. David Ward reported that in the United States the sentencing of people to prison by the courts for rehabilitative purposes was 'stone cold dead', but within the prisons there was general agreement that there should be 'an array of remedial and psychologically-based services' available to prisoners on a voluntary basis, but not affecting their release prospects either way.

These various formulations are perhaps best regarded as all derived from a more fundamental value-stance which was not explicitly articulated at the conference, though it was implicit at various stages. This value-stance was, in our view, well stated in a 1983 Prison Department Chaplaincy Working Party report on dangerously disruptive prisoners (Home Office 1983). That report commented on two points. First, *the intrinsic worth of persons*. This was attributed by the Working Party to Greco-Roman and Judaeo-Christian traditions (Home Office 1983, para. 20), but is also to be found in the Kantian injunction to treat people (oneself and other persons) 'never simply as a means, but always at the same time as an end' (Paton 1948, p. 91). The Working Party formulated the principle in this way: 'In prison, as in court [the human being] is deserving of respect, whatever his crime; . . . However far [he has] fallen below the human standards expected by society . . . it is morally impossible to deny [his] humanity or the rights which flow from it '(Home Office 1983, paras 21–2). This formulation is, of course, very close also to the views of modern moral philosophers such as Dworkin (1978, p. 272), who speaks of the moral duty of governments to treat those whom they govern with concern and with respect; or of Gewirth (1978) who argues that the 'principle of generic consistency' (as between the rights necessarily claimed for oneself, and the treatment of others), requires that

> the agent must . . . be impartial as between himself and other persons when the latter's freedom and well-being are at stake, so that he ought to respect their freedom and well-being as well as his own. He should therefore treat other persons as well as himself as persons and not as things or objects whose only relation to himself in transactions is that of facilitating his own purpose-fulfilment. (Gewirth 1978, p. 140)

Secondly, building on the above, there is for the Chaplaincy Working Party an additional dimension of *hope for the future of unique individuals*, applied in this case to the prisoner. The first aspect emphasises the present worth of all human beings, and the respect and concern which should flow from that. This second aspect now looks to the future of each human being (here, the prisoner), and concludes that this future must be allowed to contain an element of hope. As the Working Party put it:

> To talk realistically about 'making and keeping human life really human' . . . means taking seriously the essential requirement he has for possibilities of growth. He needs to be understood not simply as a member of the biological category of human beings, but also as having this future dimension of hope, which we can call *human becoming* . . . (Home Office 1983, para. 23, emphasis in original).

Notice that there is no talk here of forced rehabilitation in prison, nor any suggestion that prison has any special properties which can facilitate human growth; rather, there is a statement that a prison system should allow prisoners opportunities for hope and future development. As the Working Party report recognised, such opportunities necessarily involve a risk of abuse, but they should nevertheless be regarded as fundamental to a civilised prison system.

Thus, a civilised long-term prison system has to achieve security and control while recognising the respect and concern due to prisoners, and allowing them possibilities for future hope.

Preventive channelling

With this threefold goal orientation, how should long-term prison systems work? Naturally, in confronting this question, a prison system should look first to issues of preventive channelling, since if the preventive structures of the system work well, 'trouble-cases' (escapes and control difficulties) are minimised.

The Mountbatten physical security and classification developments (see above) already offer a striking example, within the English system, of success in a form of 'preventing channelling' aimed at the security side. The CRC report can then perhaps be regarded as an imaginative rethinking of the preventive channelling issues, especially on the control side; as Pearson (Chapter 2) well put it:

> the central theme running through all the [CRC] proposals was the need to gain control of the arrangements for dealing with long-term prisoners; and by doing this to increase the options available to all who are involved (including prisoners), avoid last-resort situations in which staff and prisoners are uncomfortably boxed in by the system, introduce systematic incentives to good behaviour and give a more coherent shape to long sentences.

In what follows, we shall concentrate attention on four separate 'preventive channelling' matters which were discussed at the conference: the administrative structures of the system; management; the concentration–dispersal debate; and the architectural dimension.

Administrative structures of the system

The administrative structures of the system should be designed and operated to aid the system and lead to achievement of its major goals. Unfortunately at the moment some of the structures of the system in England and Wales appear to do almost the opposite.

One dimension of this, much stressed by the CRC, is that of *sending the right signals:*

> It is ... essential that the whole system which bears on the prisoner should be structured in a way which encourages him to co-operate rather than the reverse and which makes a clear connection between the prisoner's behaviour and the course of his prison career. We doubt if the present system passes this test (Home Office 1984a, para. 22).

Pearson (Chapter 2), a member of the CRC, strongly reinforces this message: at present, often 'the prisoner achieves what for him is an improvement by bucking the system' (for example, a prisoner located in an unpopular Isle of Wight dispersal prison may achieve his desired goal of returning to a prison close to his family in London by committing disciplinary offences, while 'the prisoner who conforms stays where he is, no matter how unwelcome his location').

Members of the conference supported the view that the present system in England often sent the wrong signals, and needed considerable improvement in this respect. The first moves towards a so-called 'family ties' approach, announced by the Home Secretary early in 1986 (see Norris, Chapter 2) were therefore welcomed. This approach is intended to improve contact between lower security prisoners and their families by granting enhanced home leave, correspondence and telephone facilities; thus it hopes to provide incentives for prisoners and 'to make security downgrading and progression through the prison system a consistent and psychologically credible process' (Norris). Nevertheless, doubts were expressed at the conference about whether it is possible to achieve a totally consistent set of signals within the system. For example, given the importance of closeness to home (to facilitate visits) in most prisoners' thinking about choice of prison, and given also the inevitable geographical constraints of a prison system with a limited number of prisons, perhaps some prisons regarded as officially 'worse' within the administrative system would always be regarded as 'better' by some prisoners on geographical grounds. Some participants favoured the offsetting of such 'wrong signals' by dramatic further enhancements of 'family ties' privileges in the lower security categories, but whether this would solve all the problems remains doubtful. In particular, for a prisoner who realistically (given his offence type and length of sentence) faces no possibility of reduction in security category for several years at least, incentives linked to a lower classification will have little immediate point or meaning.

A second dimension of administrative structure is that of *sentence planning*, a matter given some prominence by the CRC (Home Office 1984a, paras 31ff, and p. 100). This idea was well received at the conference, as a way of planning for uncertainties including parole and future opportunities, and in order to ensure that a realistic, open and honest dialogue with the prisoner about the potential structure and content of his sentence could be achieved. It was felt that a well-developed sentence-planning system would enable the prisoner to feel more in control of his situation, and committed (or reconciled) to the plan for his prison career. A system of this kind (though not as well developed as some would wish) operates for life-sentence prisoners (see Home Office 1984a, Annex H); it involves concentration of lifers in three lifer 'main centres' for about the first three years of their sentence, and a career plan followed thereafter. This system is generally regarded as a structural improvement on the previous system for lifers; its main strengths are thought to be that it does not throw the life-sentence prisoner straight into the 'open regime' of the standard dispersal prison during the early part of his sentence when he is likely to be personally distressed (Sapsford 1983), and that it enables a sensible plan for 'doing time' to be established. The CRC suggested extending this system to all long-term prisoners, but recommended that the initial period out of the dispersal regime should be one of 12 months rather than three years, and argued for the placement of the prisoner in a local prison observation, classification and assessment unit (OCA unit) for this period.[9] In fact non-lifer sentence planning has made no practical progress since CRC because of the rapid escalation of the prison population in England in 1985 and the pressures this placed on the local prisons (see Norris, Chapter 2). The conference, while welcoming sentence planning in principle (see above), expressed some doubts about the CRC's view that 'long-term prisoners would generally benefit from a longer period in the calmer, more controlled atmosphere of a local prison in which they could begin to come to terms with their sentence' (Home Office 1984a, para. 24); and about whether 12 months was the right period. The issues were not debated in depth, but in our view there are certainly considerable doubts about whether the local prisons can be properly described as 'calmer' (though the kinds of pressures are certainly different); and also about whether the different OCA units in local prisons all over the country could realistically undertake sentence planning for long-term prisoners. Especially in the light of the current pressures on the local prisons, if sentence planning has a future for determinate sentence prisoners, it is, we think, perhaps more likely to come from a modified version (on a shorter time-scale) of the 'lifer main centre' concept. In saying this, however, we have to recognise that this would have some disadvantages from the point of view of prisoners' proximity to their homes.

Sentence planning is considered by the CRC only in the context of prison itself. Yet, as Coker (Chapter 16) reminds us, towards the end of the sentence there is a very important additional element of planning to be achieved: that of easing the transition from prison to the outside world (for example, through the pre-release employment scheme), and of preparing the prisoner for his life outside and the requirements of post-release supervision (if appropriate). In these tasks, the probation service (including the prison probation officer) plays a special though not exclusive role.

Coker's paper also usefully draws attention to a number of social work research studies (including two of prisoners after release), showing that the perceptions of offenders and of officials on various matters 'central to the purposes of oversight and assistance' do not always coincide, nor is the mismatch always recognised. These findings highlight the importance of a thorough understanding of the prisoner's point of view in all aspects of sentence planning, even if his view ultimately has to be — for one reason or another — overridden or rejected.

The third dimension of administrative structure is that of *categorisation*. Classification of inmates has a long history within prison systems, and has been used at different periods for different purposes. In the days of the rehabilitative ideal, for example, it was possible to regard classification as 'one of the cornerstones of any progressive and scientific system', which was 'an indispensable element of the fundamental idea of individualised treatment' (Mannheim and Spencer 1949), based on the matching of treatment regime to individual need. Subsequently, of course, the Mountbatten Report introduced security at the core of its categorisation system, and this has been used in England for twenty years.

Could categorisation be better developed to aid further the 'preventive channelling' elements of the long-term prison system, especially as they relate to control problems? The CRC reached no definite recommendation on this point, but did believe that the existing English categorisation system should be reviewed (Home Office 1984a, p. 101), and added that 'categorisation is not just something that is relevant to the idea of managed careers for long-term prisoners. It is at the heart of prison management' (Home Office 1984a, para. 85). The CRC also noted the apparent success of the new classification system introduced by the US Federal Bureau of

Prisons in 1979. This, the CRC noted, 'is credited with increasing the population of the lowest security level by 10 per cent and decreasing that of the two highest levels by 18 per cent despite an 8 per cent increase in the number of inmates imprisoned for offences of violence' (Home Office 1984a, para. 84). These claims were strongly supported by Gilbert Ingram (Chapter 9). He noted the cost savings achieved by this downward shift in classification, but also emphasised that the overall escape rate had declined since the adoption of the new system, despite the downward shift. His own conclusion on the importance of classification for preventive channelling was unambiguous: 'Providing different environments for inmates with different security needs is a key to control, and this cannot be accomplished without a valid classification system... a realistic classification system can minimise the number of problems for both staff and inmates.' Notice here that Ingram speaks of both *security* and *control*, reflecting the fact, which became obvious during the conference, that American prison analysts tend to use both ideas conjointly and not to draw the rather sharp conceptual distinctions between the two typically made in England. (In England, the differentiation has undoubtedly been accentuated by the security failures of the 1960s, the success of Mountbatten in security terms, and the control failures of the 1970s.) Hence, when one looks at the components of the classification system in use in the Federal system in the United States (see Ingram, Chapter 9) it is clear that, while some of the components are security-based (for example, severity of current offence, escape history), others are control-based (for example, history of violence, and, at the 'custody' level, number and severity of disciplinary reports).

Another feature of the Federal classification system is its objective, computerised nature. In the conference discussion, it became clear that this was very important, since the responsibility for each inmate's classification level essentially depends on the national scoring system, not on the subjective judgment of the classifying officer. This feature, plus the relatively stringent scoring system used, has produced the downward shift in categories already noted. An advantage claimed for this approach is that the classifying officer is largely relieved of personal responsibility for the classification decision, and hence is not tempted to increase the security level to 'cover his ass', in the American phrase.[10] Everything does depend, however, on a meaningful, reliable and valid scoring system if this 'objective' approach is to work properly, for it is of course intended to be objective only in its implementation, not in its conceptualisation.

How far should these American approaches be adopted in the English context? There are two main issues: the possible addition of a 'control' dimension to the Mountbatten security classification, and a possible move to a more 'objective' approach.

A Home Office Working Party on prison categorisation in the early 1980s (Home Office 1981) raised the possibility of a formal control classification to set alongside the Mountbatten security classification. Thus, just as one has an 'ABCD' security classification, so one might also have a '1234' control classification, and, for example, an inmate might be categorised as 'C1', indicating 'a man with a low escape potential who posed a very serious control problem' (Home Office 1981, para. 25). In the end, the Working Party recommended strongly against such an approach on the grounds 'that it would be subjective, that it would lead to labelling and that it would not help the management of prisoners because it could not lead to allocations to particular kinds of establishments' (Home Office 1984a, para. 87). The CRC shared many of these doubts about a fully-fledged control classification, not least because they felt that not enough was understood about control, and systematic research was needed. (For the beginnings of such systematic research, discussed more fully below, see Williams and Longley, Chapter 14). Nevertheless, the CRC did seem to favour keeping open the idea of adding some control elements to preventive categorisation within the English system (Home Office 1984a, para. 88), and this view was shared by many at the Cropwood Conference.

On the other question of objectivity, it is now clear that the existing English categorisation system is far from satisfactorily objective. A report by the Chief Inspector of Prisons in 1984 (Home Office 1984b) showed that there was considerable variation between the four regions of the Prison Department, and the Chief Inspector commented that 'it is hard to defend having comparable prisoners assigned to different categories in different regions' (Home Office 1984b, para. 3.13).[11] In part, this regional variation was the product of considerable conceptual confusion within the subjectively-based English system. Thus, not only are 'prisoners who are judged to present a *control* problem . . . [sometimes] assigned to a higher *security* category than would otherwise be the case' (emphasis added), there is also confusion between the ideas of *classification* and *allocation*, so that 'on occasions categorisation criteria are "adjusted" in order that a sufficient number of candidates can be found' to fill a prison with a particular security profile (Home Office 1984b, para. 3.2). Indeed these concepts of security, control and allocation seem to be 'so interwoven in the minds of prison staff that they sometimes do not differentiate between the three when carrying out their duties' (Home Office 1984b, para. 3.2). We understand that the Prison Department is currently reconsidering its categorisation procedures in the light of the Chief Inspector's report, the earlier report by the 1981 Working Party, and the views of the CRC. It is likely that a tighter and less subjective approach will be promulgated within the existing Mountbatten framework. It should be clear from the above discussion that this would be a desirable first step in the better use of classification for preventive channelling within the English system, but that other improvements also appear to be possible.

Management

The CRC report speaks in various places about 'managing' (Home Office 1984a, p. 27ff) and about staff (Home Office 1984a, pp. 634–5). The emphasis in these passages is twofold. On the one hand, there is a concern to stress that 'relations between staff and prisoners are at the heart of the whole prison system and that control and security flow from getting that relationship right' (Home Office 1984a, para. 16). On the other hand, there is a concern with managing *the system* (Home Office 1984a, p. 27), including national planning about policy aims, and about objectives and priorities for individual establishments; this includes a helpful reconceptualisation in which the Committee turned away from the broad concept of 'regime activities' toward the more specific and individualised idea of 'prisoner programmes' (Home Office 1984a, para. 97).

Important though much of this is, none of it quite captures some issues about managing long-term prisons which emerged as centrally significant during the Cropwood discussions. Perhaps the easiest way to begin to illustrate these issues is by reference to the paper by Michael Jenkins (Chapter 13) on Long Lartin Prison, one of the two established dispersal prisons in England which have escaped serious disorder (see above). In what he called a 'personal view' of Long Lartin, Jenkins in the oral presentation of his paper emphasised the debt owed to the first governor and his team in 1971. Long Lartin had originally been designated as a Category C prison, but before becoming operational its usage was changed to that of a dispersal prison. A bold decision was taken: within the enhanced perimeter security, a regime as close as possible to the originally-intended Category C regime would be operated. Jenkins claimed that this, properly built upon, has meant that Long Lartin throughout its history has operated as openly and trustingly as it can with inmates. When the CRC team visited Long Lartin, both local management and the local staff associations (including the Prison Officers' Association) stressed the central importance of good relationships between staff and inmates in creating good order within the prison.

Developing this theme further, Jenkins commented in the Cropwood discussions that he thought relationships were the most significant feature of control in prisons, and that 'you may have to lose some control in order to gain control'. Similarly, at the end of his formal paper, he comments: 'Concentration upon control is likely to stimulate resistance; tuning in to prisoners' needs reduces the emphasis upon control and the need for it.' An implication of this was, on occasion, the need for 'informal contracts', several examples of which are given in the paper. In developing these contracts 'all parties will recognise that each has power and no-one has absolute power'.

These views were very well received at the Cropwood Conference. A number of other participants emphasised similarly-based regimes elsewhere, including the Special Unit at Barlinnie Prison (Coyle, Chapter 11; Whatmore, Chapter 12; Fitzgerald, Chapter 6), and the 'personal officer' scheme at Parkhurst 'C' wing (Evershed, Chapter 15). Another well-known example in a larger unit is the regime operated by Warden Frank Wood at Oak Park Heights Prison, Minnesota, a maximum-security prison where the warden spends at least a quarter of his time 'eyeball to eyeball' with inmates and employees, and emphasises to his staff that they 'should treat the inmates as we would want our sons, brothers, or fathers treated' (Ward, Chapter 3).

These are all particular empirical examples of a management style based centrally on relationships. They have, however, perhaps a more far-reaching significance. Mike Fitzgerald (Chapter 6) was concerned to emphasise the need for management to think forward proactively to deal with relevant issues, and not just to react to events as they occurred (when 'the telephone rings'). In his view, the primacy of security over staff–prisoner relations is an unfortunate key feature of the British prison systems at present, though this primacy does not exist everywhere — for example, in the Barlinnie Special Unit, there is a secure perimeter but very constructive relationships.[12] Fitzgerald argues for a reversal of priorities, in which staff–prisoner relationships should be the basis for regimes, and the bedrock of good internal order in prisons; moreover, such relationships should be, in his phrase, 'built up rather than handed down' — that is, there should be an abandonment of hierarchical management models. Fitzgerald also stresses the need for proper grievance procedures and channels of accountability for adequate 'preventive channelling' — we shall return to this later.

There is some resonance between Fitzgerald's view and two of the other papers. Gilbert Ingram (Chapter 9) emphasised that the United States Federal system has since 1973 adopted a 'unit management' concept in all its prisons (of whatever architectural style): 'A key feature of unit management is the decentralisation of the institution's authority structure resulting in a flattening out of the typical hierarchical chain of command.' Ingram emphasises that this system produces a smaller gap between inmates and the warden than the traditional hierarchical management. It is clear from the Platt Report on prison design (discussed more fully below) that such management systems would, if introduced in England, involve far-reaching changes: 'The flexibility required of staff under the particular Unit Management model which has been developed by the Federal Bureau would represent a radical change for the prison system in England and Wales, raising considerations that go far beyond the scope of this report' (Home Office 1985a, p. 74). Additionally, in his theoretical paper, Peter Young (Chapter 4) emphasised, as lessons of sociological theories of social control, first, that 'control' should not be thought of only as the imposition of coercion (and indeed that power has natural limits to its exercise); and secondly, that 'the most effective form of (social) control is that which facilitates the voluntary and rational recognition of rules', that is, where individuals feel an *obligation* to rules rather than feel *obliged* to conform to them. Following these theoretical lessons, he emphasised the need, in his view, for prisoners to feel they have 'a stake in the system'. Discussion of this paper at the conference explored to some extent the limits of this 'voluntary and rational recognition of rules', for example with mentally ill prisoners, those politically committed to an alternative world-view, and so on.

Cropwood Conferences are intended to create an open-ended forum for discussion, not to produce formal resolutions or conclusions. Nevertheless, it was certainly our impression that these various emphases on proactive rather than reactive management, on the centrality of relationships and informal contracts, on the need for prisoners to have a 'stake' in the system, and on the link between these ideas and sociological theories of social control, were a central feature of the conference, and did between them take the discussion to a stage beyond that reached by the CRC. This view was shared by one practitioner-participant, who wrote to us as follows:

> my feeling was that the conference members increasingly emphasised the significance of the quality of staff–inmate relationships in the determination of the prison regime. This was mentioned in discussion quite regularly, and by the time the presentations on small units were given [see below], the importance of leadership style, staff participation and even involvement of prisoners in the institution (at least to a limited extent) seemed established as worthwhile concepts to explore.

Of course, many apparently promising ideas for the running of prisons have in the past not lived up to their initial expectations, so it would be foolish to be too optimistic about this approach. Nevertheless, it seems reasonable to hope that an active exploration of the merits and limitations of the approach will take place, accompanied by some careful research.

Finally, it should not be supposed that the conference's discussion of management issues related solely to the kind of matters raised in the previous paragraphs. Other themes, of a more traditional kind, were also emphasised as being extremely important in preventive channelling terms: these included an absence of capriciousness in management; a sense of predictability about the regime; and the fostering of a sense of confidence and safety among both inmates and basic-grade staff, linked to the broader structures of the prison system.

The concentration–dispersal debate

We have previously outlined the origins of the concentration–dispersal debate in England in the 1960s, at the time of the Mountbatten and Radzinowicz reports. Naturally, the CRC reconsidered this debate, and in doing so it was inevitably influenced by the history of the dispersal system, and by the previous report of the May Committee (Home Office 1979a).

The May Committee was primarily set up to consider pay and conditions of service for prison officers. However, a liberal interpretation of its terms of reference enabled the Committee to produce a wide-ranging review of various aspects of the three United Kingdom prison systems, including (albeit briefly) the concentration–dispersal debate, which the members considered one of the most difficult questions that they had to confront. May recommended a continuation of the dispersal system, at least under present operational conditions; yet at the same time the Committee clearly had substantial doubts about the positive merits of dispersal, and it took the view that 'the issue must be determined not by the strength of the arguments in favour of dispersal, but of those against concentration' (Home Office 1979a, para. 6.72).

The arguments against concentration which impressed the Committee were, first, that of security (one-third of the Category A prisoners were now convicted of terrorist offences, and placing these offenders together in one, or even two, establishments 'would pose unprecedented security problems'); secondly, that of control within one or two Category A prisons (especially because of what terrorists located together could achieve in concert); and thirdly, that of the recruitment, retention and motivation of staff (Home Office 1979a, para. 6.72). These views did not, however, convince all critics: in particular, King and Morgan (1980, Chapter 3), as part of their extensive critique of the May Report, argued strongly in favour of a concentration policy (as indeed Roy King had done in evidence submitted to the May Committee). According to King and Morgan, while there may be some overlap between issues of security and control, generally speaking prisoners causing security and those causing control problems 'are far from forming a unitary group', and, since they are thus 'analytically and empirically separate there is everything to be said for adopting separate policies to deal with each problem' (King and Morgan 1980, p. 80). These separate policies should be, they argued, first, a concentration policy for security problems; and secondly, a policy of handling control problems through classification, allocation and separation.

The only exception to this clear security–control distinction allowed for by King and Morgan was the terrorist group, who, it was conceded, posed problems of both security and control. This group, however, was thought to pose many special problems, and King and Morgan advocated that they should not be placed in the envisaged concentration prison, but should all be accommodated in 'some variant of the special security wings' (King and Morgan 1980, p. 93).[13]

The CRC did not refer explicitly to King and Morgan's views. Their analysis rather bore some similarity to that of the May Committee; in particular, they concluded that: 'For as long as the debate had to be conducted within parameters dictated by the available prison designs . . . we think that it was right and inevitable that the arguments against concentration should have prevailed' (Home Office 1984a, para. 9). In reaching this view, however, the CRC were also sure that the May Committee had been 'right to be sceptical about the positive benefits of the dispersal concept' (Home Office 1984a, para. 7); and they concluded that 'the dispersal system seems a precariously balanced structure to carry our hopes into the next century' (Home Office 1984a, para. 127).

The new dimension introduced into the debate by the CRC was that of architecture. The Committee was impressed by American 'new generation' prison designs, with their self-contained housing units within a secure perimeter (see below). The clear separation of prisoners, and the flexibility of response made possible by these designs 'on the face of it . . . avoid many of the dangers that led the Radzinowicz and May Committees to advise against a policy of concentration' (Home Office 1984a, para. 20). The CRC considered that the population requirement for very high-security accommodation in England and Wales would probably not exceed 400,[14] and that perhaps the new generation designs would allow these prisoners to be held in a concentrated way in two small prisons. They recommended that 'these possibilities are urgently examined' (Home Office 1984a, para. 20). In the meantime, the remainder of their report was geared to an alleviation of the problems of the present dispersal system, though the principles involved were believed to remain valid even if a concentration policy based on new generation prisons were to be established (Home Office 1984a, para. 21).

In response to this and other interest, the Home Office set up a Working Party to study 'new generation' prisons in the United States. We shall return to this topic more fully later, but for the moment we need note only that the Working Party considered that 'the "new generation" approach provides a workable solution and a third option to what has hitherto been assumed to be a straightforward choice between concentration and dispersal', but that nevertheless: 'It is not for us to form a view on whether maximum security prisoners in England and Wales should continue to be dispersed, as at present, or concentrated in a small number of maximum security prisons, as suggested by the Control Review Committee' (Home Office 1985a, p. 93).

The Cropwood Conference did not debate the concentration–dispersal arguments in any sustained way in the English context. It did, however, devote some time to the relevant issues, particularly in the light of American experience. As previously indicated, the United States Federal prison system has moved from former policies of concentration (Alcatraz), through dispersal, and back to a form of concentration (Marion) (Ward, Chapter 3). Experience at Marion was discussed extensively (Ward, Chapter 3; Ingram, Chapter 9). A particular advantage claimed for Marion was that it had helped to reduce violence and other disruptive behaviour in other parts of the Federal system, not only by the removal of assaultive prisoners to Marion, but also by exercising a general deterrent effect on inmates elsewhere through its fearsome 'end-of-the-road' reputation (Ingram, Chapter 9). However, there is so far no clear research evidence for the claimed general deterrent effect. It was also argued that a prison such as Marion was inevitable in the United States Federal context. This is because it houses exceptionally difficult individuals, whose behaviour is thought of, in the American phrase, as being 'off the scale'; and the Federal Bureau of Prisons believes that such individuals will cause problems wherever they are in the system, so that concentrating them in one place 'allows for a tighter and more focused security programme which reduces the havoc they can cause' (Ingram, Chapter 9).

But Marion also has some substantial disadvantages. Its record of institutional violence is most unenviable (Ward, Chapter 3), leading eventually to the creation of 'lockdown' status in 1983. The conditions in Marion since lockdown have shocked some British visitors: they include fully-enclosed exercise cages; 'closed' visits with no physical contact and oral communication only by telephone; and all inmate out-of-cell movements (save in one unit) being taken in legirons and handcuffs behind the back (see Home Office 1985a, pp. 115–16; Ward and Breed 1985). Additionally, there are sub-units, of increasing degrees of restriction, within Marion itself (Ingram, Chapter 9). Hence, although Marion deliberately seeks to 'provide an avenue of hope' to the inmate by enabling responsible conduct over a period of time to earn a transfer back to a less restrictive prison (Ingram, Chapter 9), nevertheless some observers have wondered whether Marion adequately fulfils the dimensions of 'respect and concern' for prisoners, and hope for their future potential, usually regarded as important in the goals of a prison system (see above on 'net drive'). As one British participant who had visited Marion put it in the conference discussion, Marion seemed 'to represent the complete negation of all that is believed in in the rest of the Federal system'.

However, David Ward, in post-conference correspondence with us, has questioned this judgment. He points out that a fundamental concern in the maximum-security institutions of the larger prison systems in the USA is with the 'body count' (the incidence of homicides and serious assaults), and that on this point Marion, since lockdown, is quite successful. Ward also argues that the constitutional rights of all inmates at Marion are, so far as possible, protected by the courts, as indeed they have to be given Marion's high visibility as the Federal system's end-of-the-line institution; further, he observes that inmates are rotated in and out of Marion, with few returning for a second visit.

The central issue in all this is perhaps an ethical one: namely, how far the apparently extreme nature of the Marion population, together with Marion's claimed utilitarian success in maintaining the 'body count' and in reducing disruption in the system, may justify practices and procedures which would be regarded as ethically unacceptable in other countries.

Before leaving Marion, one final point should be made. Although the Radzinowicz Committee in England was apparently influenced by the closure of Alcatraz in moving towards a dispersal policy (Advisory Council 1968, para. 41), it should not be assumed that the existence of Marion implies a return to a concentration policy of the kind envisaged by the Mountbatten Report. Whereas Alcatraz housed both control- and security-problem prisoners (some of the most publicly notorious inmates in the Federal system were placed on 'the Rock', partly for symbolic reasons), in the recent past Federal administrators have become concerned primarily with within-system difficulties, so Marion tends to emphasise the control rather than the security dimension (though, as already noted, this distinction is regarded as of little importance in American discussions). Emphasising control as it does, and seeking to provide a hopeful route back to a normal institution (see above), Marion has now reduced its average length of stay to 27 months (Ward, Chapter 3) out of an average sentence length for Marion inmates of 41 years (Ingram, Chapter 9). Hence, for most inmates Marion 'is viewed as a temporary assignment' (Ingram, Chapter 9), whose role is that of an 'administrative segregation prison' (Ward, Chapter 3).

Drawing on his American experience and on his own previous published views (King and Morgan 1980; King 1985a), Roy King made an important contribution to the conference discussion.[15] He argued as follows: first, there are important historical differences between the English system and the Federal system in the United States. In England, because of the lack of a secure prison before 1966 and the embarrassments caused by escapes in the 1960s, security had been particularly stressed after Mountbatten. In the United States, there had never been a comparable security crisis, and the tendency now was to treat the 'concentration' facility at Marion primarily as a resource to deal with control, not security problems (see above). Secondly, King argued, experience in the two countries since the 1960s suggested that the dispersal of security risks in the English system had been a failure; and the concentration of control problems in the United States Federal system had been a failure. King argued that the correct course was in fact to disperse control-problem prisoners (as suggested by the CRC with its 'small unit' policy — see below), and to concentrate security-risk prisoners as suggested in the Mountbatten Report, and now in a new context within 'new generation architecture' (Home Office 1984a; and see below).

Perhaps surprisingly, the conference never debated this very interesting intervention systematically. King's suggestion is certainly an intriguing one. But our own subsequent reflections on the issues raised by it suggest to us that two matters in particular need to be carefully thought through before one can reach any clear resolution of the concentration–dispersal debate.

The first of these two matters concerns the security–control distinction itself. There are certainly some cases where a prisoner presents a security but not a control problem (the well-socialised spy, for example) and others where an inmate presents a control but not a security problem (the constantly aggressive minor offender). But the key question is, given that a 'Mountbatten' policy would concentrate especially Category A prisoners, how many such prisoners are also likely to cause control problems? We have seen that, at the time of the May Committee, one-third of Category As were convicted of terrorist offences, and King concedes that for a substantial number, though not all, of such prisoners 'the security problem and the control problem would indeed coincide' (King and Morgan 1980, p. 93);[16] he has therefore to exclude this large group from his concentration policy (see above). Additionally, in the research by Williams and Longley reported to the Cropwood Conference (Chapter 14), there are much higher proportions of Category A prisoners in the 'control problem' samples than in the comparison samples (see Tables 14.4 and 14.6). These two data sources, incomplete as they are, suggest to us that a very careful research examination of the extent to which security and control problems are discrete is required before too heavy a policy reliance is placed upon a general distinction between 'security risk' and 'control problem'.[17]

The second matter requiring further reflection arose from some discussions with a group of criminal justice practitioners who were set an assignment on the concentration–dispersal debate during the Institute of Criminology's Senior Course in Criminology in July 1986.[18] This group felt that the CRC had been unduly modest in its approach to the concentration–dispersal issue. According to the CRC, there was a traditional Mountbatten–Radzinowicz debate which now had to be set in a new context by new generation architecture. But, the practitioner group argued, by offering potential solutions to control problems within the existing dispersal system (through sentence planning, classification, small units, and so on), the CRC had itself changed the terms of the debate. It seemed likely to the group that the CRC report, if fully implemented, would indeed largely solve the control problem in dispersals; if this were so, then neither security nor control would remain as a major problem of the dispersal system.

Very possibly this view would be regarded by the CRC members themselves as too optimistic.[19] Nevertheless, the practitioner group's assessment *could* turn out to be right; and if it were right, then the concentration–dispersal debate would have to be thought through in a rather different way. The key question would then become: given that the dispersal system can (hypothetically) operate without major problems of either security or control, what are the arguments for and against concentration? This question has not, to our knowledge, been systematically addressed in the literature. Although the view that the implementation of the CRC's recommendations would solve all the main control problems of the dispersal system may be over-optimistic, we believe that squarely facing the practitioner group's question does help to sharpen the analytical clarity of the debate. In our view, the key issues to be considered in addressing this question are the following:

(i) whether security would be weakened by opting for a concentration solution (as the May Committee evidently thought it would, at least if terrorists were included among the population in the concentration prison — see above);

(ii) whether control problems would be exacerbated by opting for a concentration solution, either in existing buildings or in 'new generation' buildings (the May Committee thought control difficulties would be worse in a concentration prison of conventional design, again assuming terrorists would be part of the population);

(iii) the issue of the huge human and financial costs involved in requiring, within a dispersal system, many aspects of Category A security for *all* prisoners, despite the fact that some five-sixths of the prisoners are in Categories B or C (King and Morgan 1980, Chapter 3; Home Office 1984a, para. 132);

(iv) the probable public notoriety of a concentration prison, if established (this point is based on the analysis by David Ward, in Chapter 3, of Alcatraz and Marion: he argues that 'when two or three hundred men with the most serious records of criminal violence in the country are concentrated in one prison it is not the prisoners but the prison that provokes controversy;

(v) whether it makes sense, as King and Morgan (1980) propose, to separate off the terrorist group from the rest of the Category A population in developing one's policy; and

(vi) how far (if at all) the advent of 'new generation' architecture affects any of the above five arguments.

We would not presume to offer here any definitive solution to this long-running debate.[20] It is perhaps important to remind ourselves, however, that ultimately the key issue is that of preventive channelling — creating structures for the system that will minimise difficulties (security and control especially, but not forgetting the human dimension of prison life, or the financial cost of various options). The primacy of the 'preventive channelling' issue in this context was forcibly and clearly stated by one senior prison administrator at the conference, in a comment with which we strongly agree. The issue, he remarked, is *not*, at the end of the day, simply 'concentration or dispersal'. The issue is, how best can we make arrangements for Category A prisoners? The answer to this question may involve a simple 'concentration' or 'dispersal' solution; but it may, alternatively, involve a solution which is neither fully one of 'concentration' nor one of 'dispersal', but a mixture of solutions for prisoners in different circumstances.[21]

'New generation' architecture

We have seen that the CRC saw American new generation architecture as a way of breaking out of the traditional concentration–dispersal debate; and that the Platt Report (Home Office 1985a) confirmed that this was a 'workable solution and third option', but made no definite recommendation for its adoption in England for maximum-security prisoners.

In this situation, it was clearly important for the Cropwood Conference to consider 'new generation' architecture and its relevance to the English long-term prison system. There is no need here to explain all the main features of 'new generation' architecture, as they are applied in most prisons, for this has been done in the Platt Report (Home Office 1985a and see Platt, Chapter 5). The only new generation prison for maximum–security prisoners considered in the Platt Report does, however, require some special attention, because it featured extensively in the Conference discussions: this is Oak Park Heights Prison, Minnesota, a prison within the Minnesota State prison system (see Ward, Chapter 3; King, Chapter 5; see also Ward and Schoen 1981).

Figures 1.1 and 1.2 show the main features of Oak Park Heights in schematic form. These features include separated housing units, a secure corridor linking the housing units, a separate recreation space for each housing unit, and a wide sterile zone outside the living area. It should also be noted that, for security reasons, the ground level at the back of each living unit is at the roof level of the housing block; thus, all housing units face inwards.

Oak Park Heights is generally regarded as having been successful in the accomplishment of its tasks. Architecturally, the conference was told that it is widely admired by prison administrators, and indeed that one warden of another prison, on seeing Oak Park Heights for the first time, thought that he 'had died and gone to heaven'. On a day-to-day level, the prison apparently works well (Ward, Chapter 3; King, Chapter 5), though in evaluating this it is important to bear in mind: first, that Oak Park Heights, being a state prison facility, does not contain the kind of very difficult inmates housed at Marion (Ward, Chapter 3), though its inmates are broadly comparable to those in the English dispersal system (King, Chapter 5); secondly, that its penological success is thought to be in large part due to the management philosophy of its exceptional Warden, Frank Wood (Ward, Chapter 3; see also

Rutherford 1985). Wood had at an earlier date been successful in 'taming' the older Minnesota state maximum-security prison at Stillwater, which had a history of disorder (see Ward, Chapter 3); indeed, David Ward comments that had the legislators known that control could be re-established in the old prison they might never have voted the money for the building of Oak Park Heights!

It was reported that senior Federal Bureau of Prisons personnel would like a facility such as Oak Park Heights within the Federal system (and some Federal prisoners are placed there on a contracted-out basis). The Federal system has only Marion for its maximum-security (level 6) population, and Marion was built 25 years ago, before new generation architecture was developed. The Federal system is now, however, totally committed to new generation architecture, and *all* new prisons, of all security levels, are being built to new generation specifications.

A governor-grade member of the CRC explained to the conference why the Committee had been attracted to 'new generation architecture' (and specifically Oak Park Heights) in developing its recommendations. In traditional English prisons, he claimed, the 'association' period in particular is often fraught with problems, with many prisoners milling around and little effective staff control over a large number of inmates. These institutions therefore, in his view, needed to be broken down into smaller, more manageable units: this would reduce the possibility and scale of control incidents, make inmates and staff feel more personally secure, and facilitate the development of staff–inmate relationships. The Oak Park Heights design appeared to the CRC members to make all this much more feasible than did traditional designs. It would also facilitate the development of some kind of devolved unit-management style, and would permit the placement of inmates into hopefully compatible groups, with possibly different regimes developed in different housing units. Hence, in the CRC's view, it did seem possible to move to a smaller number of maximum-security prisons (more of a 'concentration' solution) if this new architecture were available.

It was for reasons of this kind that Roy King (Chapter 5) described new generation prisons as taking a proactive stance towards the kinds of problems of control identified in the CRC report. He also considered that nothing 'has been as successful in marrying design to purpose as either the radial prison of the early nineteenth century or the new generation prison of the late twentieth century'. Despite opinions of this kind, a number of observers consider that much more research evidence is needed on 'new generation' design, and its advantages and disadvantages in day-to-day prison use, before policy conclusions can be reached. Unfortunately the Platt Report

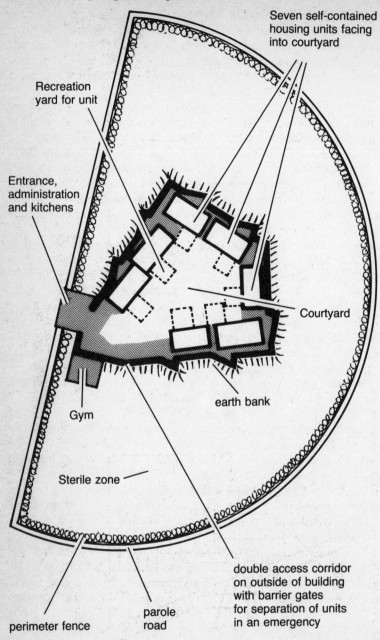

Seven self-contained
housing units facing
into courtyard

Recreation
yard for unit

Entrance,
administration
and kitchens

Courtyard

Gym

earth bank

Sterile zone

double access corridor
on outside of building
with barrier gates
for separation of units
in an emergency

perimeter fence

parole
road

Figure 1.1 Layout of Oak Park Heights Prison

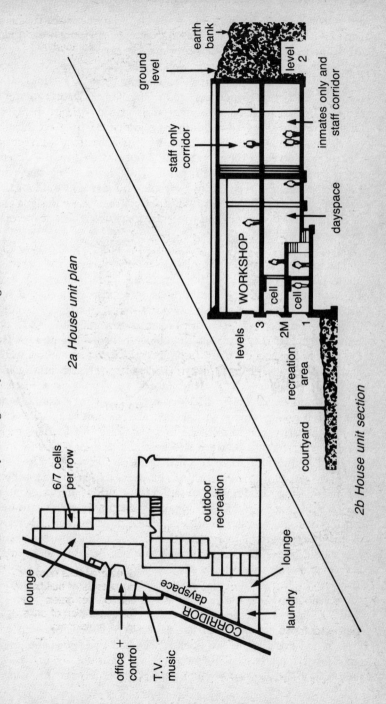

Figure 1.2 *Schematic plan and section of housing units, Oak Park Heights Prison*

2a *House unit plan*

6/7 cells per row

lounge

office + control

T.V. music

CORRIDOR dayspace

outdoor recreation

lounge

laundry

2b *House unit section*

earth bank

ground level

level 2

staff only corridor

inmates only and staff corridor

dayspace

WORKSHOP

cell

cell

levels 3

2M

1

recreation area

courtyard

did not utilise all the available research, relatively scanty as it is; David Canter (Chapter 10) fills in some of the gaps, and places the available research in its appropriate context.

Should we grasp the nettle, follow the CRC's lead, and build one or two high-security new generation prisons in England to replace the existing dispersal system? Roy King (Chapter 5) argued the case for including one or two such prisons within the Home Office's already agreed building programme. In reaching this conclusion, King was influenced by considerations of security, control and overcrowding; and he was not deterred by the absence of research on new generation prisons, taking the view that while research evaluation is certainly desirable, 'hundreds of millions have been spent, and will be spent, on other prisons whose designs were never properly evaluated, and which we know from bitter experience to be gravely faulty'.

Andrew Rutherford (Chapter 2) opposed King's proposal to build a new prison of this kind, just as he had previously expressed opposition to the CRC on this particular issue (Rutherford 1985). For Rutherford, management is much more important than design: he pointed particularly to Frank Wood's management style in considering the success of Oak Park Heights, and quoted Wood's own remark that: 'If they gave me the choice between having Oak Park Heights and an incompetent, dishonest staff or a tent and competent and honest staff I'll take the tent and the competent, honest staff' (Rutherford 1985, p. 410). Rutherford (1985) also drew attention to the dramatic events at Mecklenburg Prison in Virginia, a new generation prison which twice gained national notoriety in 1984 for serious security and control failures (see also Ward, Chapter 3). The main difference between Mecklenburg and Oak Park Heights, asserted Rutherford, is in the management stance: Mecklenburg's style is one of minimum contact between prisoners and officers. In considering the English situation, Rutherford indicated at the conference that he was in favour of prison design being improved, but he believed it was essential to avoid the view that architecture is the basic solution to prison problems. In England, he argued, we should place management considerations before new buildings, and in particular we should do everything we can to ensure that the system learns from the relative success, in control terms, of Wakefield and Long Lartin (see above).

King's reply to these points has been twofold. First, he has argued that 'it just is not the case that we have to choose between good design and good administration ... we need both good design and good staff, and both will have to be fought for' (King 1985b). Secondly, King argued at the Cropwood Conference that a better management system within the existing dispersal system would still leave us with far too many prisoners unnecessarily placed in maximum-security establishments. This second point is a useful reminder that for King (as for the CRC) the 'new generation' architecture debate is ultimately inextricably intermingled with the concentration–dispersal debate.

Since this is the case, one additional point, not raised at the conference, is worth making. The Platt Report notes that the Warden of Oak Park Heights 'feels that long-term incarceration in self-contained modules could lead to mental deterioration', and that at present the average stay at Oak Park Heights is not expected to be more than five years (Home Office 1985a, p. 66). While the 'mental deterioration' effects may not be as severe as Wood believes (see the research on the effects of long-term imprisonment discussed by Walker, Chapter 8), nevertheless if, for one reason or another, five years is considered the longest tolerable stay at a prison like Oak Park Heights for the average inmate, its usefulness as a long-term maximum-security prison in the sense intended by Mountbatten would obviously be limited. It should be borne in mind, however, that the Platt Committee, despite reporting these observations about Oak Park Heights, nevertheless considered that the experience of this prison did constitute a viable 'third option' in the context of the English dispersal–concentration debate (see above; also Home Office 1985a, p. 93).

It should finally be made clear that, though King and Rutherford are divided on the issue of whether to build a new maximum-security prison in this country, they are both committed to a reduction in the overall prison population, and to the view that much of the Prison Department's present building programme is unnecessary (King and Morgan 1980; King, Chapter 5; Rutherford 1984; and Rutherford, Chapter 2). In this connection, the Minnesota experience perhaps contains one important warning, whatever the success of Oak Park Heights in its own terms: for Stillwater, once to be closed, remains open for business as a maximum-security institution despite the building of Oak Park Heights, which was intended to be its replacement.

'Trouble-case' and small units in the long-term prison system

The 'trouble-case' law-job is concerned with the handling of disputes and social disturbances after they have arisen in any social group (see above). In the context of long-term prisons, this means, especially, dealing with control breakdowns of one kind or another, but doing so within the overall 'net drive', including the dimension of humaneness (see above).

In most prison systems, immediate or short-term responses to 'trouble' within an institution include:[22]

(i) discussion or negotiation (two inmates fighting may be stopped by a prison officer and dealt with informally; or there may be more individualised discussion with a perceived recurrent trouble-maker about ways in which that individual and staff can more amicably live together);

(ii) use of the punishment system (including loss of privileges or earnings or forfeiture of remission, aimed to be an individual deterrent to the inmate and a general deterrent to others);

(iii) use of segregation facilities (this may be within or outside the punishment system, and is used mainly to protect the inmate from others, as an intended deterrent, or for incapacitation);

(iv) specialist intervention (referral to medical, psychological or probation specialists in an attempt to ease the perceived difficulties);

(v) transfer to another institution (for a variety of reasons including 'cooling off', a belief that the inmate will function better in a different environment, separating members of groups from each other, and so on).

All these kinds of intervention take place regularly in English dispersal prisons, and will continue to do so.[23] However, the CRC reported that 'the management and staff of long-term prisons consider that the existing facilities for dealing with those who present *serious* control problems are inadequate' (Home Office 1984a, para. 46, emphasis added). More graphically, Pearson (Chapter 2), a member of the CRC, described the existing situation as one where 'a quite small stage army' of persistently disruptive inmates 'was rotating round the dispersal prison network, spending varying periods of time in ordinary location and segregation at each, with occasional diversion to prison hospitals or local prisons by way of relief'. To break into this cycle, the CRC proposed the establishment of a number of small units in varying locations specifically to handle persistently troublesome inmates. The CRC did not attempt to specify what regimes should operate in such units, though they did write that 'different prisoners will obviously have different require-ments' (Home Office 1984a, para. 65). One of the main tasks of the Research and Advisory Group (RAG) which was subsequently established (see above) has been to advise the Home Office on the development of a strategy for these small units (see Norris, Chapter 2). The Home Office has so far established a unit at Parkhurst Prison for prisoners with a history of troublesome behaviour *and* who have a history or present symptoms of mental abnormality (see

Evershed, Chapter 15); and it is setting up another unit at Lincoln Prison, not involving any specialist intervention by doctors or psychologists, but designed 'to encourage a change of behaviour using the traditional skills of prison officers working with small numbers of prisoners' (Lord Glenarthur, Minister of State at the Home Office, 2 October 1985). Other small units will follow. Full details of the exact nature of all these units is not publicly available at the time of writing, but an advisory report from RAG on this topic is scheduled (Norris, Chapter 2). The preliminary paper by Evershed on the regime of the Parkhurst Unit (Chapter 15) was well received by members of the Cropwood Conference, who regarded the development of the Unit so far as sensible and constructive.

One central issue in considering small units of this kind is of course the selection of suitable candidates. This raises the issue of whether it is possible to identify particular *individuals* who are 'troublesome', or whether, at the other extreme, 'trouble' is really created not by individuals but by the system, so that particular inmates may be very 'troublesome' in one context, but not at all in another. (For a graphic individual illustration of this point see the case of Jimmy Boyle: Boyle 1977; 1984.)

Research is being conducted in England to try to throw more light on this issue. The first stage of this research is reported by Williams and Longley of the Prison Department's Adult Offender Psychology Unit (AOPU) (Chapter 14). They have found, on the one hand, that there is much less than total agreement between different sources within the prison system about which long-term prisoners can be described as 'troublesome'; but, on the other hand, taking together all candidates for the 'troublesome' label (from all nominating sources), the nominated inmates differ significantly from the normal dispersal prison population on a number of variables, including the score on a modified version of the (US) National Institute of Correction's custody rating scale, and the number of transfers within the prison system during the current sentence. Further research from the AOPU, pursuing these themes, is anticipated; and the Home Office, advised by RAG, is also developing other research including a more qualitative examination of the nature of control problems in dispersal prisons, and the way in which such problems emerge (see Home Office 1986, pp. 6, 25–8). At this interim stage, clearly no very hard-and-fast conclusions should be drawn; but tentatively, the Williams and Longley research perhaps leads one to think that some prisoners *are* more difficult than others (it is not totally a matter of reaction to particular environments), but nevertheless, the lack of agreement between nominating sources perhaps reflects the fact that prisoners respond very differently to different environments and are thus differentially perceived as 'troublesome' in different contexts. Both these points, but especially the second, have important implications for the prison system, and for the projected small units strategy.

The Scottish prison system has run small units for troublesome prisoners for a number of years; the various units, and their philosophies, are spelt out by Andrew Coyle (Chapter 11). Coyle concludes by saying that, in the Scottish experience, there are two matters of paramount importance in approaching the handling of difficult prisoners: first, the separation into small groups; and secondly, the development and fostering of intensive staff involvement. As an important additional point, Coyle emphasises the importance of staff training, and he reports that the Scottish prison administration now recognises it was wrong initially to assume that a special unit for disruptive prisoners could be set up in Inverness Prison (a small establishment primarily intended for short-term local inmates) without special training for the staff. In the discussion following Coyle's paper, Scottish participants also emphasised the importance of staff involvement not only in the manning of small unit regimes, but also in the period prior to the establishment of units. It was indicated that the support and involvement of the Scottish Prison Officers' Association in the period leading to the setting up of the Barlinnie unit was vital in ensuring the subsequent viability of that unit.

Although the Scottish prison system has a variety of units, Scottish participants indicated that perhaps the units had not been developed into a complementary *system* as well as they might have been. (By contrast, the Home Office in England is hoping to develop complementary units formally linked within a system, though with what success remains to be seen.) Some of the Scottish units are located within Peterhead Prison, the main prison for long-term recidivist prisoners in Scotland, although with the exception of the rather special 'own-protection unit' and the 'individual unit',[24] these Peterhead units have only been in use since the end of 1984 (Coyle, Chapter 11). Outside Peterhead, the only units are those at Inverness and Barlinnie, and these are described by Coyle as being 'at the extreme ends of a spectrum'. They are indeed very different. The Inverness Unit is spartan, and, save in exceptional circumstances, prisoners are not held there for more than three months. It could perhaps be regarded as a less severe and much more temporary version of Marion, and, like Marion, it can reasonably be described as a temporary 'administrative segregation prison'. By contrast, conditions at the Barlinnie Special Unit are certainly not spartan in prison terms, and the length of stay has been very considerable (the unit opened in 1973, and in the 13 years since then has admitted only 24 prisoners; see Whatmore, Chapter 12).

The Barlinnie Special Unit has become famous all over the world, and the conference was naturally anxious to learn about it (Coyle, Chapter 11; Whatmore, Chapter 12; see also Boyle 1984; Carrell and Laing 1982). Key features of the regime were felt to be: the importance, for both inmates and staff, of the small size and secure perimeter of the unit, leading to a feeling of personal security even in emotionally turbulent meetings such as take place regularly at Barlinnie; the advantages of 'community meetings' as a form of peer social control, yet always in a spirit of fairness (Whatmore, Chapter 12); the 'normalisation' of life within the walls that is able to take place, in which the free flow of visitors into the unit is seen as particularly important (this includes inmates' personal visitors, visiting art teachers, and so on, as well as visitors interested in penology and prisons).[25]

Two problems raised about the Barlinnie Unit at the conference were those of *siltage* and *slippage*. By 'siltage' was meant the long average stay of the inmates leading to very few vacancies in the Special Unit, which has perhaps helped to foster a growing sense of the irrelevance of the unit to the rest of the Scottish system.[26] This matter raises genuinely difficult issues. On the one hand, the object of special units is to place difficult prisoners where they are best located within the system, and this might indicate a long stay in a particular unit; on the other hand, given a limited number of units, if a unit is to pull its weight within the prison system as a whole, there is a natural tendency to argue that there has to be a regular turnover of inmates and the creation of vacancies so that other inmates needing that kind of regime can be accommodated. This latter pressure could be alleviated by building more units, but in practice what can happen instead is that the staff of a unit come to define its purpose as 'to return prisoners to normal location' rather than 'to reduce control difficulties' (or whatever was the original purpose of the unit).

By 'slippage', in the Barlinnie context, was meant slippage from the original purpose of the unit, perceived as being for violently disruptive inmates; it was claimed that the present inmates were not a really difficult disruptive group, as were the first prisoners in the Unit. In reply, however, it was said that although the first three inmates in the Special Unit were of this type, the next one was not (he was regarded as institutionalised, and had spent 13 years in prison with no history of violence); hence the unit has always had a 'mix' of prisoners, which is considered desirable in fostering a working democratic community, and is in line with the original remit of 'known violent inmates, those considered potentially violent and selected long-term inmates' (Scottish Home and Health Department 1971).

In considering the Scottish experience as a whole, some participants noted the advantages of a very small prison system where many of the governors and inmates know each other well. There was some speculation as to whether the four prison regions in England and Wales could be given much greater autonomy, and thus achieve the perceived advantages of small scale. On the other hand, it was noted that in England the small unit strategy recommended by the CRC and being developed by the Home Office was being run on a centralised basis, and there may be some advantages in this in allowing for uniform, centralised selection and a more heterogeneous and complementary system of units than could be achieved within a smaller prison service.

It will be noted that both England and Scotland have in different ways opted for some *dispersal* of control-problem prisoners, by contrast to the United States Federal system's policy of concentrating such prisoners at Marion. Gilbert Ingram was asked, in his session, how far he was attracted by this 'dispersed-control' option (see above on King's conference intervention). Ingram replied that he found the concept attractive, but thought perhaps the Marion inmates presented such extreme difficulties that such a solution might not work for them; one also had to consider the possible deterrent effect of Marion on other prisoners elsewhere in the system.[27]

Clearly there remain many unsolved issues in this 'trouble-case' area. It was noted, with some regret, that the fascinating experience at Barlinnie Special Unit had not been properly researched, and the determination of the Home Office and RAG to build in evaluation from the outset in the English small units was welcomed (see Norris, Chapter 2).

As a final point, it should be said that, although we have dealt with small units as part of the 'trouble-case' law-job — and rightly so since these units form an additional resource for governors when faced with control difficulties in their prisons — nevertheless a successful small unit can be regarded also as a kind of 'preventive channelling', helping to avoid future difficulties by and for its inmates as and when they return to the mainstream prison system (or perhaps to the outside world). On the other hand, this does presuppose that the mainstream prison system (or 'normal location', in prison terms) will not exacerbate the prisoner's difficulties of adjustment when he returns, and this may not be a correct assumption. In any event, the transition from a special unit back to a mainstream prison is always likely to present some problems for the individuals concerned.

'The say' and prison accountability

In one sense, it is obvious who has 'the say' in prisons — ultimately, the staff do, on behalf of the State (Mathiesen 1974; cf. Sykes 1958). However, the issue is, of course, much more complex than this. We need to know which staff have the say (and why); how they exercise the say; and the extent to which they feel obliged to, or wish to, share the say with inmates. These are large questions, well beyond the scope of this introduction.

Of particular importance to our subject is the issue of accountability, since long-term prisoners are clearly potentially subject to a whole series of decisions made about them which may crucially affect them, yet in which they may have little or no say (categorisation, allocation, transfer, work placements, and parole, to name only some of the most obvious ones). The Chaplaincy Working Party report, which we cited earlier when discussing 'net drive', was explicit on the importance of accountability (Home Office 1983, Chapter 5). For this Working Party:

> An important aspect of keeping 'human life really human' is the practical recognition that responsibility and accountability for one's decisions are of the very essence of the moral stature of men and women. No-one, be he prisoner or prison official, is exempt from the moral obligation of having to account for his actions (Home Office 1983, para. 61).

The Working Party went on to note that decision-making in any organisation is easily flawed, 'for any number of reasons — organisational, personal and moral'. It thought, therefore, that there was a need for three things: a readiness, within limits, to share prison decision-making with lay colleagues; the creation of a framework of *openness* which 'both supports those who make decisions and enhances the likelihood that the decisions made will be wise ones' (Home Office 1983, para. 62); and a willingness to temper executive power by a series of checks and balances. It seems to us that this Working Party approach has much to offer as a set of guiding principles.

The CRC said little about accountability as such, but did advocate that the prison service 'should be completely open about the establishment of the [new small units] and the way they operate' (Home Office 1984a, para. 70). There is perhaps an implied contrast here with the ill-fated Control Unit experiment in England in 1974–5, since that unit not only mounted an impossibly difficult regime for its inmates (Home Office 1984a, para. 52), but was set up in a way that was certainly not 'completely open' (Thomas 1975; see also Leigh 1980, pp. 120–7).

Additionally, the CRC argued that Boards of Visitors in prisons with small units would have an important part to play 'as friendly but critical watchdogs' (Home Office 1984a, para. 70); and that outside academics should play a part in the construction and implementation of a research programme on control-related issues in prisons (Home Office 1984a, para. 120) (this is now part of the role of RAG: see above).

At the Cropwood Conference, the issues of openness, and of accountability in the strict sense, were raised somewhat separately. As regards *openness*, many non-Prison Department participants urged a greater general openness upon the Prison Department, by which they meant both more physical access and greater information made available about the system; and American participants and those with experience of the United States noted the typically greater openness of prison systems across the Atlantic. Some lively debates ensued. *Accountability* was discussed especially in the context of Morgan and Richardson's paper (Chapter 7). They argued strongly, with detailed reference to existing law and practice, that the English system falls far short of the ideal so far as accountability is concerned. This is so, they claim, because the rights of English prisoners are poorly protected at law and are vulnerable to claims of administrative convenience, while the system as a whole is subject to 'only the most superficial degree of general accountability'. Fitzgerald (Chapter 6) also argues for greater accountability, which he sees as being linked to management style (see above); for him, the system needs to be both *externally* accountable (to outside observers) and *internally* accountable (to staff and inmates of that institution). He claims that the latter dimension is not a 'simple-minded recipe for "prisoner power"', but follows from the recognition of the centrality of staff–prisoner relations in prisons.

If there is to be greater accountability, how is this to be achieved? Two issues are perhaps specially important here. The first is the issue of *standards*. Morgan and Richardson discuss this matter, and note the general absence of clearly worked-out standards against which the adequacy of particular aspects of institutional life can be judged. This is particularly relevant to the work of the Inspectorate of Prisons (see note 11), since some kind of standard (clearly worked out or otherwise) obviously has to be applied when the Inspectorate makes judgments about particular institutions or topics. As noted by Morgan and Richardson (Chapter 7), the Inspectorate is beginning to develop a more systematic code of standards, but this will inevitably take a long time to bring to fruition. (On standards generally, see also Maguire *et al.* 1985, part 2).

It is one thing to develop clear standards, and another to ensure that those standards are complied with. An administrator made the valid point that, in trying to attain adequate standards of provision, the Prison Department is to an extent at the mercy of the courts (in relation to the number of people they send to prison) and of Parliament (in relation to how much money is made available to the Prison Department).

The second general issue concerning accountability is that of *structures*. This was not fully discussed at the conference (see generally Maguire *et al.* 1985; Home Office 1985b; Morgan and Richardson, Chapter 7), but one key question which was raised was whether or not it is desirable for the courts to be involved. One administrator suggested that accountability is already adequately achieved through Parliament,[28] and questioned whether the involvement of the courts is desirable; whether in fact the community would gain anything by the courts (domestic or European) taking a more interventionist stance. Could it not be, he argued, that much court time would be consumed, life made more difficult for governors and staff, and all for no discernible benefit to the community in general?

Morgan and Richardson's reply to this was essentially twofold. One was to invoke the 'golden rule' in ethics, namely that 'an act is morally right if and only if, in performing it, the agent refrains from treating others in ways in which he would not want the others to treat him' (Feldman 1978, p. 105), and to argue that we, if we were prisoners, would in fact want to test administrators' and governors' decisions in an outside tribunal, so this right should not be denied to prisoners.[29] The second point made was that someone has to take the ultimate decision in individual cases, and that, as Parliament is unsuitable for this role, it was important that there should be an ultimate arbiter outside the prison system itself. In arguing for a greater involvement of the courts, however, Morgan and Richardson emphasised that they were not envisaging instant or repeated access to the courts, which could clearly make the day-to-day running of prison systems impossible; rather, they saw the courts as the ultimate arbiters in a grievance procedure which would have many prior steps, and hopefully most grievances would be amicably settled well before the court stage. Their general approach was supported by a prison governor who thought that, while prisoners' recourse to the courts was sometimes uncomfortable for senior management in a prison, nevertheless it was helpful, in creating order within a prison, for prisoners to know that they could take grievances beyond the prison itself. This governor added, however, that in his position he did not have to provide the resources to enforce court decisions.

In the United States the courts have in recent years played a major role in intervening in prison life, sometimes even declaring a whole State prison system unconstitutional. David Ward indicated that court intervention had produced very significant changes in the most basic prison procedures in many states, yet legislatures would, in most cases, have been reluctant to intervene because of the cost implications. Moreover, courts' intervention could benefit staff as well as prisoners; for example, the improvement of prison procedures could lead to a significant reduction of danger, or better working conditions, for prison guards.

One issue relevant to accountability, and centrally involved in the question of 'the say', is the issue of *control of staff*. Several academic participants, following the lead given by Rutherford (Chapter 2) and Fitzgerald (Chapter 6), raised this matter, and argued that it was just as important as the control of inmates, a view which was disputed by others.

From our point of view, the most important dimension of this question concerns how far basic-grade staff may help or hinder the development of desirable regimes and practices in long-term prisons. We have already seen, for example in the discussion of the regimes of Long Lartin, Parkhurst 'C' wing and the Barlinnie Special Unit, how basic-grade staff can make an invaluable contribution to the development of a relationship-based regime; and we think it is very important to recognise fully the good work which is often done in this way in many prisons. In such situations, to speak of 'the control of staff' is happily not necessary. Nevertheless there can be no serious dispute that on certain occasions in the last decade some staff in long-term prisons in England have acted not only improperly, but in a way which has arrogated to themselves a 'say' to which they were not constitutionally entitled. The two most dramatic documented instances of this are, first, the aftermath of the Hull riot of 1976, when some prison officers effectively took over a wing of the prison the day after the prisoners' surrender, and subjected some inmates to degrading treatment (Thomas and Pooley 1980), and secondly, the Wormwood Scrubs incident of 1979, when, in the weeks following the incident,

> the indications are that members of the POA [Prison Officers' Association] committee played a more intrusive role in the operational decision-making process [of the prison] than is appropriate, ... [and] the Governor's personal inclination and desire ... to return D Wing to a normal dispersal

prison regime as soon as possible ... [was effectively thwarted by] the implacable opposition of the POA (Home Office 1982, paras 113, 136).

The scale and nature of these examples is, of course, exceptional; but the incidents in question nevertheless emphasise the importance of governors being allowed to govern, and they reinforce arguments about a proper system of accountability in running prisons for long-term inmates.

A final point linked to acountability is that of the effects of long-term imprisonment, considered by Walker (Chapter 8). This paper is rather different from many of the others, in that it is not primarily concerned with policy issues relating to long-term imprisonment; yet, as conference organisers, we felt it was very important to include this subject in the conference's deliberations, since it is so vital an issue when considering the long-term prisoner's point of view, or that of the prison system in promoting respect, concern and hope for the future for long-term inmates (see above on 'net drive'). As can be seen from Walker's review, the research evidence is far from complete or definitive, but the apparent effects of long-term imprisonment appear not to be as adverse as many have claimed, believed or feared. Nevertheless, as he points out, some adverse effects do seem to exist ('there are live babies in the bath-water', as Walker puts it), and, in so far as this is the case, any prison system which is properly accountable to its inmates and to the general public has a duty to discover and to minimise such effects wherever possible. In some aspects of the performance of this duty, the role of the prison probation officer is vital, though best fulfilled in collaboration with other staff (see Coker, Chapter 16).

Effects were also briefly mentioned by David Ward (Chapter 3). Interestingly, Ward reports that studies of ex-Alcatraz inmates show, as an interim result, that inmates with a moderate number of disciplinary reports in Alcatraz, while being more likely to succeed in the post-release period than those with many disciplinary infractions, were also more likely to succeed than those who conformed in prison. Hence 'resistance through a number of forms, including rule violations, may have a positive psychological function for inmates both in prison and after release'. This finding intriguingly suggests that, while for administrators the establishment of control in prison is necessary, nevertheless in the longer term inmate conformity within prison may not be an unqualified good. This links up with many of the issues about the nature of power and of social control raised in the paper by Young (Chapter 4), and is perhaps a fitting point on which to conclude our introduction to the issues raised by the Cropwood Conference.

Notes

1 In this introduction, undated references to an author and chapter number refer to the chapters of this book.

2 There are three different legal jurisdictions within the United Kingdom — England and Wales, Scotland, and Northern Ireland. Each has its own prison system, and these systems operate independently of one another.

3 These were Albany, Frankland, Gartree, Hull, Long Lartin, Parkhurst, Wakefield, and 'D' wing at Wormwood Scrubs.

4 Frankland has also escaped serious disorder, but it did not join the dispersal system until 1983.

5 In the years 1968–73, only nine Category A prisoners escaped from dispersal prisons or from one of the special security wings (on which see note 13 below). Since January 1974, there have been no escapes of Category A prisoners from normal dispersal prisons, though three Category A prisoners escaped from Parkhurst special security wing in 1976 (all were recaptured within 24 hours). Additionally, three provisionally-classified Category A prisoners escaped from a local prison (Brixton) in 1979 (information supplied by the Home Office Prison Department).

6 This announcement, which took place at the Conservative Party Conference in October 1983, indicated, first, that certain classes of murderer would not normally be released from their life sentences until they had served at least 20 years in custody, and second, that prisoners serving determinate sentences of over five years for offences of violence or drug trafficking would be granted parole only in exceptional circumstances, or to allow supervision for a few months before the end of the sentence (for details, see Home Office 1984c, Chapter 1).

7 In some formulations, there are six law-jobs, the second one listed here being divided into 'preventive channelling' and 'rechannelling', and the 'job of juristic method' being added (Twining 1973, p. 175). Additionally, Llewellyn did not intend the list of six law-jobs to be exhaustive, and on occasion 'dealt rather perfunctorily with others' (Twining 1973, p. 182). We are following Lewis (1980) in focusing only upon four main law-jobs.

8 Fitzgerald (Chapter 6) argues that this point was not adequately understood by the CRC, and provides a very different starting-point for analysis than that contained in the CRC report.

9 For reasons of security, the CRC argued that Category A prisoners should not go to local prison OCA units, but that instead two induction units of 15 to 20 prisoners each should be opened within the dispersal system for them (Home Office 1984a, para. 79).

10 There is, however, the possibility of 'manual override' in the system, allowing a classifying officer to depart from the objective score if he deems it appropriate. But such departures from the objective standards have to be individually justified. It is claimed that this approach allows staff still to feel in control, while also (through the computerised system) giving them the confidence to be more liberal.

11 The Inspectorate of Prisons for England and Wales was set up from the beginning of 1981, following a recommendation in the May Report (Home Office 1979a). The Inspectorate was later put on a statutory footing by the Criminal Justice Act 1982. The Chief Inspector is a Crown appointee answering directly to the Home Secretary, but he and his supporting staff are independent of the Home Office Prison Department.

12 Note that the Mountbatten Report had argued that 'a constructive liberal prison regime and secure prisons are not necessarily incompatible' (Home Office 1966, para. 202), and this point was a central feature of the Radzinowicz Report (Advisory Council 1968).

13 The English prison system contains two 'special security wings' (at Parkhurst and Leicester), each containing a very small number of Category A prisoners

who, on security grounds, are thought to require special conditions.

14 It is interesting to note that this estimate by the CRC exactly corresponds with Roy King's earlier estimate in his evidence to the May Committee, though that evidence was, at the time, strongly disputed by the Home Office (1979b, volume II, part III, Discussion Paper 9, paras 10–30).

15 A general rule of Cropwood discussions is that oral remarks made are unattributable to specific individuals, except in the case of speakers in relation to their own papers. Here and in one or two other places in this introduction we have thought it necessary to depart from this rule; in such instances, we have done so only with the consent of the individual concerned.

16 King and Morgan (1980, p. 93) add, however, that for terrorist prisoners ' "being disruptive" must take on a quite different meaning from that understood by other, non-politically motivated, prisoners'.

17 It is known that some prisoners are placed in a higher *security* category because they are a *control* problem (Home Office 1984b, para. 3.2), and this could be thought to be affecting these figures. But, though there is no research evidence on the point, our understanding is that this kind of effect is much less likely to occur at Category A than at Category B level, because of the centralised and rigorous nature of the Category A procedures.

18 This is a two-week course held biennially for practitioners in various services relevant to criminal justice (police, prison service, probation service, prosecutors, judges and magistrates, and so on). The group in question contained a cross-section of people from various services.

19 It should be recalled that the CRC said: 'there are real operational problems in mixing Category A prisoners among a much larger number of inmates with lower security requirements... This means, to put it crudely, that the inherent tension in prisons between security and control is accentuated in dispersals. A level of security dictated by the requirements of the Category A prisoners is resented by the rest of the population' (Home Office 1984a, para. 7).

20 For the record it should perhaps be added that the Senior Course group, after weighing these issues, opted in favour of a dispersal policy run within a much smaller number of prisons than at present (that is, the proportion of Category As in each prison would be substantially higher than the present 10–15 per cent).

21 It is worth noting in this connection that the present system is not one of pure dispersal, because of the special security wings (see note 13); and King and Morgan's (1980) proposals were not those of pure concentration, because of their special suggestions for the terrorist group (see above).

22 This refers to day-to-day (small-scale) control difficulties rather than to major control breakdowns (riots, hostage-taking, and so on) where different conditions apply.

23 It should be noted that these 'trouble-case' responses do not always lead to a diminution of trouble; they can and have exacerbated situations where they have been perceived as unfair, oppressive or arbitrary responses.

24 These are described by Coyle (Chapter 11). There are equivalent facilities in the English system; the equivalent to the 'individual unit' is the 'High Security Cell Unit' at Wakefield, which is described in Home Office (1984a, p. 21).

25 These visiting privileges in particular have led over the years to a number of criticisms of the laxness of the Special Unit regime. Against this it is usually argued that the emotional demands made on unit members through the style of the regime make the 'pains of imprisonment' greater, not less, within the unit.

26 As one participant put it, apart from the very occasional vacancy at Barlinnie, 'all there really is in Scotland for difficult prisoners is a bus between Peterhead and Inverness'.

27 The Platt Report (Home Office 1985a, p. 93) rather similarly argued that 'the

provision of one or two specialised establishments for maximum security and disruptive prisoners could serve, as does the existence of Marion in the United States Federal system, to relieve tensions in our Category B prisons and enable them to operate in a more constructive way'.

28   The Prison Department is part of the Home Office, of which the Home Secretary is the head; he therefore can be (and is) asked questions in Parliament about the running of the system.

29   There is a problem with the 'golden rule' in the case of persons with unusual desires (for example masochists); later ethical formulations, such as those by Kant and Gewirth cited earlier, attempt to overcome this difficulty while maintaining the important principle of consistency of ethical treatment of oneself and others.

References

Advisory Council on the Penal System (1968), *The Regime for Long-Term Prisoners in Conditions of Maximum Security* (Radzinowicz Report), London: HMSO

Boyle, J. (1977), *A Sense of Freedom*, London: Canongate.

Boyle, J. (1984), *The Pain of Confinement*, London: Canongate.

Carrell, C. and Laing, J. (eds) (1982), *The Special Unit, Barlinnie Prison: Its Evolution through its Art*, Glasgow: Third Eye Centre.

Dworkin, R. (1978), *Taking Rights Seriously*, London: Duckworth.

Feldman, F. (1978), *Introductory Ethics*, Englewood Cliffs, NJ: Prentice Hall.

Gewirth, A. (1978), *Reason and Morality*, Chicago: University of Chicago Press.

Home Office (1966), *Report of the Inquiry into Prison Escapes and Security* (Mountbatten Report), Cmnd. 3175, London: HMSO.

Home Office (1979a), *Report of the Committee of Inquiry into the United Kingdom Prison Services* (May Report), Cmnd. 7673, London, HMSO.

Home Office (1979b), *Inquiry into the United Kingdom Prison Services: Evidence by the Home Office, the Scottish Home and Health Department and the Northern Ireland Office* (3 vols), London: HMSO.

Home Office (1981), *Working Party on Categorisation Report*, London: Home Office Prison Department.

Home Office (1982), *Home Office Statement on the Background, Circumstances and Action Subsequently Taken Relative to the Disturbance in 'D' Wing at H.M. Prison Wormwood Scrubs on 31 August 1979; Together with the Report of an Inquiry by the Regional Director of the South East Region of the Prison Department*, HC 199, London: HMSO.

Home Office (1983), *Working Party on Regimes for Dangerously Disruptive Prisoners Report*, London: Home Office Prison Department, Chaplain-General's Office.

Home Office (1984a), *Managing the Long-Term Prison System: The Report of the Control Review Committee*, London: HMSO.

Home Office (1984b), *Prison Categorisation Procedures: Report by H.M. Chief Inspector of Prisons*, London: Home Office.

Home Office (1984c), *Criminal Justice: A Working Paper*, London: Home Office.

Home Office (1985a), *New Directions in Prison Design: Report of a Home Office Working Party on American New Generation Prisons* (Platt Report), London: HMSO.

Home Office (1985b), *Report of the Committee on the Prison Disciplinary System* (Prior Report), Cmnd. 9641, London: HMSO.

Home Office (1986), *Research Programme 1986–87*, London: Home Office Research and Planning Unit.

King, R.D. (1985a), 'Control in Prisons' in M. Maguire, *et al.* (eds), *Accountability and Prisons*, London: Tavistock.

King, R.D. (1985b), 'New Generation Prisons' (letter), *The Listener*, 9 May, pp. 19–20.

King, R.D. and Morgan, R. (1980), *The Future of the Prison System*, Farnborough: Gower.

Leigh, D. (1980), *The Frontiers of Secrecy: Closed Government in Britain*, London: Junction Books.

Lewis, N. (1980), 'Every man should have his own Karl Llewellyn', Inaugural Lecture, University of Sheffield (unpublished, copy lodged in Crookesmoor Library, University of Sheffield).

Llewellyn, K. (1940), 'The Normative, the Legal and the Law-jobs: the Problem of Juristic Method', *Yale Law Journal*, vol. 49, pp. 1355–1400.

Maguire, M., Vagg, J. and Morgan, R. (eds) (1985), *Accountability and Prisons*, London: Tavistock.

Mannheim, H. and Spencer, J.C. (1949), *Problems of Classification in the English Penal and Reformatory System*, London: Institute for the Study and Treatment of Delinquency.

Mathiesen, T. (1974), *The Politics of Abolition*, London: Martin Robertson.

Paton, H.J. (1948), *The Categorical Imperative: A Study in Kant's Moral Philosophy*, London: Hutchinson.

Rutherford, A. (1984), *Prisons and the Process of Justice*, London: Heinemann (republished by Oxford University Press, 1986).

Rutherford, A. (1985), 'The New Generation of Prisons', *New Society*, 20 September, pp. 408–10.

Sapsford, R. (1983), *Life Sentence Prisoners*, Milton Keynes: Open University Press.

Scottish Home and Health Department (1971), *Report of a Departmental Working Party on the Treatment of Certain Male Long Term Prisoners and Potentially Violent Prisoners*, Edinburgh: SHHD.

Sykes, G. (1958), *The Society of Captives*, Princeton, NJ: Princeton University Press.

Thomas, J.E. (1975), 'Special Units in Prisons', in K. Jones (ed.), *The Yearbook of Social Policy, 1974*, London: Routledge and Kegan Paul.

Thomas, J.E. and Pooley, R. (1980), *The Exploding Prison*, London: Junction Books.

Twining, W. (1973), *Karl Llewellyn and the Realist Movement*, London: Weidenfeld and Nicolson.

Ward, D.A. and Breed, A.F. (1985), *The United States Penitentiary, Marion, Illinois: Consultants' Report Submitted to Committee on the Judiciary, U.S. House of Representatives* (Ser. no. 21) Washington, DC: US Government Printing Office.

Ward, D.A. and Schoen, K.R. (eds) (1981), *Confinement in Maximum Custody*, Lexington, MA: D.C. Heath.

PART I
GENERAL ISSUES

2 The Control Review Committee report

THE REPORT: *A.J. PEARSON*

This paper seeks to sketch in the immediate background against which the Control Review Committee (CRC) was established; set the CRC task in the context of earlier efforts to grapple with the management of the long-term system; identify the major themes that emerged from the Committee's analysis of the problem; and comment on the key proposals for change.

Formation of the Control Review Committee

The CRC set up by the then Home Secretary in September 1983, was created between the riot at Albany in May 1983 and the announcement in October 1983 by the government of its firmer policy towards parole for serious, violent offenders. The Committee's task, 'to review the maintenance of control in the prison system, including the implications for physical security, with particular reference to the dispersal system, and to make recommendations' (Home Office 1984, para. 1), put it right at the heart of current developments. These terms of reference focused on the dispersal system but were not confined only to this area. It provided an opportunity for some very necessary things to be said, and at a time when notice would be taken. A measure of the Committee's achievement in discharging their task was the widespread support given both to diagnosis and prescription for making better sense of the care of long-term prisoners. It proposed an enormous agenda for action.

Composition of the CRC

A brief word about the Committee's membership is appropriate at the outset, because the way they contributed together to the report was central to whatever achievements may flow from its work. Membership was drawn from senior officials in Prison Department headquarters, with Anthony Langdon (the then Director of Operational Policy) as Chairman, a Regional Director, the Director of Psychological Services and four serving governors, each with a variety of experience working in dispersal prisons. On the face of it, a fairly conventional mixture for a departmental committee, though not one necessarily guaranteed to achieve the most harmonious of working relationships. But on this occasion the balance was excellent. From the start the group had a joint purpose and mutual respect. It had other qualities, too: a sense of urgency, a recognition that the questions it was addressing went to the very heart of the system, and a realisation that it was unlikely that a comparable opportunity to contribute to the direction which the Service should take would present itself again during the working lives of most members. The conclusions reached were genuinely unanimous. They were a careful distillation of the enormous contributions made by a whole range of people with an interest in the system, as well as reflecting the deeply-held views of members of the Committee.

Background to the CRC task

The CRC task should be set in the context of the attention paid to the handling of long-term prisoners over the last 20 years. It is unnecessary to rehearse in detail the events of the mid-1960s which sharpened political and professional concern about the prison system's ability to cope with long-term prisoners. The imposition of long fixed sentences in a few well-publicised cases, concern about indeterminate life sentences following the abolition of the death penalty and, most significantly, the spate of escapes (Wilson, Biggs, Blake) which led to the setting-up of special security wings in four prisons and ultimately to the Mountbatten inquiry, are all matters of record. The Mountbatten Report (Home Office 1966) is perhaps most widely remembered for its account of the physical deficiencies of the prison estate in countering determined escape attempts and for the remedies prescribed to rectify these faults.

Given the reasons for the Mountbatten inquiry it was hardly surprising that attention centred on the security dimension, and this in turn sparked off the concentration–dispersal debate which has continued as an underlying theme ever since, surfacing each time a major breakdown in control occurs in one of the prisons holding long-termers.

But Mountbatten also exposed a much more difficult issue, and one which has been at the heart of all subsequent thinking about long-term prisoners: the dilemma facing policy-makers and practitioners in achieving an acceptable balance between the undoubted need for effective security and the much more elusive goal of creating a viable quality of life for staff and prisoners working and living in very secure institutions.

The Home Secretary of the day accepted many of Mountbatten's proposals but was not immediately convinced of the case for concentrating high-risk prisoners in a fortress-type prison. The Advisory Council on the Penal System (ACPS) was invited to consider the nature of the regime under which long-term prisoners might be held in conditions of maximum security; a subcommittee of the ACPS, under the chairmanship of Professor Radzinowicz, conducted this review. In the report (Advisory Council on the Penal System 1968), the Radzinowicz Committee came down strongly against Mountbatten's preferred solution of concentration, largely because it would be extremely difficult to operate such a regime in a fortress prison. Instead, Radzinowicz advocated, and the Home Secretary accepted, that high-risk long-term prisoners be dispersed between three or four prisons which would be made very secure. Within a secure perimeter a liberal and constructive regime was to operate and special provision be made in each prison for a discrete unit (segregation unit) to house the small minority of disruptive prisoners who would have to be removed at least for a time if a liberal regime for the majority was to be maintained.

Events, however, moved on rapidly whilst the Radzinowicz proposals were being thought through and given effect. The riot at Parkhurst (October 1969), the widely reported disorders during the summer of 1972 and the riot at Gartree later in 1972 all served to underline the fact that, whilst notable improvements had been made to physical security, much less success had been achieved in articulating and implementing satisfactory control measures *within* institutions.

In the wake of the widespread prisoner disorders of 1972 (not confined to long-term prisons and not all of a very damaging nature, save for ugly episodes at Albany in August) a departmental working party under the chairmanship of the then Director General was charged with examining 'the operation of the dispersal policy with particular reference to its effect on control within prisons; and to make recommendations' (Home Office 1973). The two significant recommendations — for control units to house the most disruptive prisoners to be found in the dispersal system, and for a small number of cells in local prisons to be set aside to house troublesome prisoners from dispersal prisons for a limited time — each reflected the widely held view that within the long-term population of dispersal prisons there is a small minority of prisoners bent on disrupting the routine by personal acts of violence towards others, by perpetrating serious damage to buildings or by so intimidating fellow prisoners that their lives are made unbearable. The short, turbulent history of the one control unit ever used (at Wakefield) has been thoroughly examined elsewhere. Using cells in local prisons for short-term 'cooling off' periods remains an option for dispersal prison governors.

Throughout the 1970s the fledgling dispersal system was beset by a series of extensively publicised major incidents (at Gartree in 1972 and 1978; at Hull in 1976; at Parkhurst in 1979; and at Wormwood Scrubs also in 1979). All highlighted the apparent fragility of the system and its inability to cope adequately with the damaging behaviour of the minority. The House of Commons Expenditure Committee made a vivid comment on the situation in which many prisoners found themselves, and thus the circumstances in which staff had to work:

> The true harshness of prison life does not stem solely from the deprivation of liberty and limited choice, nor from the actual physical conditions but from the daily or hourly pressure which prisoners inflict on each other. One must recognise the element of personal insecurity involved in a situation where the weakest are exposed to the strongest, the vilest and most violent, where the most powerful dominate and constantly intimidate (House of Commons 1978, para. 42).

Following the Chief Inspector of Prisons' inquiry into the riot at Hull in 1976 (Home Office 1977), he proposed that a regular forum be established to enable those most closely involved with the dispersal system to share thinking and standardise practice so far as was practicable. This group — the Dispersal Prison Steering Group (DPSG) began to meet in 1977. It comprised Prison Department officials with responsibility for policy and operational matters, all regional directors and the governors of each dispersal prison. In practice the group was caught up in a long, and seemingly never-ending, search for uniformity with regard to the range and the number of personal items prisoners were allowed to have in possession. The discrepancies as between one prison and another created persistent irritation both for staff and prisoners. The failure of the DPSG to address fundamental issues was recognised in 1979 by the creation of a small working party charged with considering major issues. This group, the Working Party on Control in Dispersals (WPCD) continued to meet until reconstituted with a different membership and revised terms of reference as the CRC in mid-1983.

At the end of the 1970s — a traumatic decade for dispersal prisons by any reckoning — the May Committee (Home Office 1979) entered the debate and examined once again the fundamental question of concentration versus dispersal. Whilst the dispersal system *per se* was not their primary concern, the Committee acknowledged that the basic argument addressed earlier by Mountbatten and Radzinowicz was one of the most difficult they had had to consider. They concluded on balance in favour of dispersal not so much on the basic arguments in support of it as on the strength of argument against concentration.

The CRC diagnosis

The CRC's diagnosis of the problems facing the long-term prison system, and by extension the whole adult prison system, is spelled out in Chapter 2 of the report (Home Office 1984). What emerged from the evidence was a set of interrelated criticisms which went to the very heart of the assumptions and practices that formed the framework of the system.

A system?

It was abundantly clear to members of the CRC from their own observations during visits to prisons and from the evidence submitted, that what was described as a 'long-term system' was not in fact a system; rather it was a loose confederation of institutions, each doing its best to survive and make sense of what it was doing without a sustainable, clearly thought-out strategy that reflected the needs and aspirations of both prisoners and staff. And because of the way in which dispersal prisons had developed, the malaise in those prisons was especially acute. In essence, the criticism that emerged was that dispersal prisons had become relatively stagnant pools of high privilege *into which* the most difficult prisoners were thrown soon after sentence, *out of which* there was little incentive for them to progress and *within which* there was a limited range of responses available to deal with disruptive behaviour.

The costs of disruption

The Committee tried to identify how this unhappy state of affairs had come about. The struggle to effect an acceptable balance between security, on the one hand, and control, on the other, has been a feature of life since the dispersal policy was introduced. There is an ever-present tension between the two, and it has to be said that success in improving security, and so greatly reducing the damaging escapes of prisoners who are a potential danger, has not been matched by equal success in control. Serious disturbances and major riots occurred at five of the eight dispersal prisons in use at the time of the CRC review. Many millions of pounds of structural damage occurred and prisoner accommodation was put out of use. But the cost in terms of loss of confidence in the system by staff and increased anxiety among prisoners about their own safety, though not easily quantifiable, was none the less a real and significant factor.

Prison design

Criticism of prison design was registered by many witnesses, and supported by the personal experience of CRC members. The group of prisons designated for use in the dispersal system was arbitrarily selected. Each had to be extensively and expensively modified, principally to provide the necessary perimeter defence. Each had a different range of facilities within the perimeter, experience in handling long-termers which varied from extensive (for example, Parkhurst and Wakefield) to nil (Albany and Gartree) and presented peculiarities for ease of control because of different designs, which included traditional radial-style, old-style galleried wings and new-style 'hotel corridor' units.

'Open' regime for all

Each of the prisons was striving to achieve some sort of uniformity of practice. All were charged with providing an 'open regime' along the lines outlined by Radzinowicz when he proposed a liberal regime. This meant that prisoners were allowed free association out of their cells for most of the day, access to workshops, education and recreation. More to the point, all were operating undifferentiated regimes for all prisoners and so not surprisingly were vulnerable to disruption. Moreover, the prisons did not lend themselves to dealing with prisoners in small, and thus more manageable, groups, save in the limited circumstances of segregation units and occasionally the prison hospital.

Given this somewhat unpromising scenario, it was hardly surprising that the overwhelming bulk of the evidence submitted pointed to the fact that control in dispersal prisons was achieved against the grain of the system rather than with its support.

Dispersal prisons unsuitable for all long-termers

It was clear that the open dispersal regime was neither appropriate nor necessarily desirable for all long-term prisoners. For a great many reasons some prisoners are unable to cope with considerable free association, perhaps by reason of their unstable personalities and behaviour, perhaps by reason of the nature of their offence in attracting odium from others, perhaps by being unable to channel their considerable energies into acceptable channels. But for whatever reason, a proportion of the long-term population clearly exert a disproportionate influence on the life of the institution to the detriment of the majority.

Timing of entry to dispersal prisons

This fundamental weakness was exacerbated by other features. Entry into the dispersal system generally occurred too early after conviction and sentence, and was regarded as a prescriptive right by long-termers. For perfectly valid security reasons some prisoners move quickly from the relative privation of the local prison in which they have spent their time awaiting trial to the relative high privilege of long-term prisons. But for the majority, there is no such overriding need for speed of transfer.

Allocation

The division of responsibility for allocation was also a source of concern. At the time of the CRC work this task was split three ways. Separate divisions in Prison Department headquarters dealt with the allocation of life-sentence prisoners and Category A prisoners, whilst each of the four Prison Department regional offices handled the allocation of long-term, determinate-sentence prisoners in Category B. The outlets available to each region were different. Even though strenuous efforts were made to avoid, for example, the build-up of potentially disruptive groups of long-term prisoners in each prison, the difficulties experienced by the receiving prisons in maintaining an acceptable balance in their populations were magnified because of the allocation from different sources.

The persistently disruptive

The facilities for dealing with prisoners who disrupted the system persistently were unsatisfactory. Radzinowicz's proposal that each dispersal prison should have its own segregation unit within the perimeter but physically separate from the main prisoner living areas had been fully implemented in only one prison (Wakefield). But there had grown up a considerable belief in dispersal prisons that the provision of discrete segregation units would not necessarily meet the needs. Disruptive prisoners, it was argued, were capable of continuing to exercise a destructive influence even when segregated within the institution, but this invariably disappeared when they were sent elsewhere. Alternative arrangements for short-term transfer to local prisons for a 28-day 'cooling-off' period as provided for by Circular Instruction 10/1974 were regarded as helpful to a limited degree. Otherwise dispersal prison governors engaged in horse trading with colleagues, with headquarters and regional offices to offload particularly troublesome prisoners. The reality was that a quite small stage army of prisoners was rotating round the dispersal prison network, spending varying periods of time in ordinary location and segregation at each, with occasional diversion to prison hospitals or local prisons by way of relief. Prisoners' behaviour varied according to where they found themselves and the ability of each prison to cope with the problems they presented. It was clear that some means had to be found of breaking into this destructive cycle, and that the task could not be performed by the dispersal prisons operating in isolation from the remainder of the adult system.

Incentives and disincentives

The mechanisms for providing incentives to good behaviour and disincentives to bad behaviour were somehow out of kilter. Two simple examples illustrate the point. Allocating a long-term prisoner to a prison in which accommodation by prison standards is well above average, and where work and recreational opportunities are good, may appear to be a reward. Yet if he is far from home and visits are difficult, he will not regard it as a desirable location, especially if his chances of a move to a more acceptable location are remote. In these circumstances, he may conclude that misbehaviour is the only way to achieve what for him is an improvement. And the system had become accustomed to respond precisely as the prisoner wished. This is well illustrated by the number of prisoners being returned from the uncrowded relatively good conditions of prisons on the Isle of Wight to crowded London prisons on disciplinary grounds. Quite simply, the prisoner achieves what for him is an improvement by bucking the system. The prisoner who conforms stays where he is, no matter how unwelcome his location. At the other end of the scale, the prisoner who has responded well in dispersal conditions and been downgraded in security rating may be 'rewarded' by finding himself in a Category B or C prison lacking the range of facilities to which he has been accustomed, where living accommodation may be worse and restrictions on freedom of movement within the establishment greater. Lacking any prospect of improving his circumstances by legitimate means, the prisoner resorts to illegal behaviour and is invariably 'rewarded' by being returned to more secure conditions. In each case the system responds in a way that is at odds with its avowed aims.

CRC proposals

The central theme running through all the proposals was the need to gain control of the arrangements for dealing with long-term prisoners; and by doing this to increase the options available to all involved (including prisoners), avoid last resort situations in which staff and prisoners are uncomfortably boxed in by the system, introduce systematic incentives to good behaviour and give a more coherent shape to long sentences. In sum, the proposals were designed to provide a 'package of practical improvements that will be readily understood' (Home Office 1984, para. 15).

Time-scale for implementation

The lead time and resource implications in giving effect to the ideas will vary. In the long run, for example, major modifications to the buildings housing long-term prisoners will be very important. The 'new generation' prisons, which so impressed those members of the CRC who visited the United States, appear to offer significant improvements on the present plant. They clearly offer greater flexibility in use, do not replicate the unsatisfactory features of the 'hotel corridor' design of newer British prisons, and make possible the care and containment of prisoners in small groups. All this is some way in the future and clearly needs more detailed consideration than the CRC was able to give it. But there was no doubt in the minds of members that in principle it would be right to go down the road of building new generation prisons, adapted and modified as may be best for our circumstances.

Other proposals are capable of more immediate action. Reducing the size of the dispersal prison estate, putting in place improved rewards for good behaviour by enhancing the range of facilities available to long-termers in prisons at the lower end of the security range, and recreating units for the better care of disturbed prisoners have all been pressed forward. A third cluster of proposals, including the creation of sentence-planning units for all long-termers and long-term prisoner units for the persistently disruptive, fall to be dealt with in the medium term.

The staff dimension

The central importance of prison staff was a thread running through everything the Committee had to say. The following extract from the report (Home Office 1984, para. 16) encapsulates the CRC view:

> nothing else that we can say will be as important as the general proposition that relations between staff and prisoners are at the heart of the whole prison system and that control and security flow from getting that relationship right. Prisons cannot be run by coercion; they depend on staff having a firm, confident and humane approach that enables them to maintain close contact with inmates without abrasive confrontation. Nothing can be allowed to qualify the need for staff to be in control at all times, but we are sure that the great majority will agree with us that this is best achieved by the unobtrusive use of their professional skill at involvement with prisoners. This is the foundation on which we want to build.

In the report there is therefore a renewed statement of the importance of adequate training for staff in areas related to human interaction as well as the necessary skills required on occasion for using physical restraints (control and restraint techniques and 'MUFTI' — minimum use of force tactical intervention). There is also a plea for a more vigorous approach to career development for staff and for dealing with the stress inevitably experienced by those involved day by day in dealing with prisoners.

Radical changes in present practice

The Committee was convinced that essential change could be achieved in a number of ways. Centralising the allocation of long-term prisoners (lifers and those serving fixed sentences of five years and over) is certainly one way of doing this by removing the anomalies in divided allocation referred to earlier. The speed of entry to the dispersal system should also be slowed down. Long-termers spend on average six months in a local prison after sentence and generally believe that transfer to a long-term prison will occur irrespective of their behaviour. The CRC concluded that it would be right to aim to allocate long-termers about 12 months after sentence. Special consideration would apply in the case of life-sentence prisoners who now spend the first three years of their sentence at one of the lifer main centres, where they are assessed and a rudimentary career plan devised. The proposal is that they spend about 12 months in a local prison and two years in the main centre. To accommodate long-termers awaiting allocation it was proposed that sentence planning units (SPUs) should be set up in selected local prisons. The tasks of the SPUs would be to formulate with the prisoner a career plan at the start of the sentence and to discuss with the prisoner the probable shape of the sentence, that is, the sort of establishment in which he might be held, a likely time-scale for security downgrading and transfer, and the range of opportunities to which he might be exposed. In this way a dialogue would be begun between staff and prisoners and some commitment obtained as to how the prisoner should be handled. It would be designed to give a more orderly shape to the prisoner's progress through the system, not least in offering appropriate rewards for acceptable behaviour.

Incentives for good behaviour

To achieve this objective some remedial action is called for in the provision of facilities available in prisons at the lower end of the security range. Such things as extension of home leave periods, relaxation in censorship and freer access to telephones are all accepted as important to prisoners and means by which they can maintain contact with families and friends. For suitable long-term prisoners in the middle and later stages of sentence they are very important and should be used as rewards for good behaviour. The rewards hitherto available in lower security prisons have been insufficiently attractive to outweigh those disincentives referred to earlier. The package proposed, which has come to be known as the 'family ties package', is being actively pursued.

A staging system?

The proposals to do with prisoner career planning, creation of special units and the provision of incentives and disincentives were felt by the CRC to add up to a more coherent strategy without the pitfalls of the old stage system. A number of those who gave evidence supported the reintroduction of a staging system (abolished in adult prisons in 1967) and their proposals were very carefully examined. The decision to reject staging was taken for two reasons; first, that there appeared to be an inevitable tendency for progress to become automatic, and second, for delays in moving forward to become exceptional. These weaknesses ran counter to the positive system the CRC wished to commend.

Special provision for serious control problems

Getting the long-term system into better shape will create a more purposeful and stable environment for the majority. Special provision is, however, needed for the minority who present serious and persistent control problems. This group comprises those who behave in a disorderly way themselves, those who encourage others to misbehave and those who suffer from some form of mental disturbance. This crude description is not comprehensive, the groupings are not mutually exclusive and they are constantly changing in composition. The options available to prison managers in dealing with the problem were damagingly limited. They boiled down to three choices: living with the problems and running the risks involved, closing down regimes to an unacceptable level for the majority because of the behaviour of the minority, and passing the problem on to others.

Three initiatives were proposed. Prisoners who suffer from some form of mental disorder which leads them to behave in an aggressive and/or unstable fashion clearly need to be separately catered for. Few qualify for transfer to hospital under section 47 of the Mental Health Act 1983 because they fail to meet the tightly drawn criteria with regard to treatment and the prevention of further deterioration. This group, for which the prison system remains the only place of secure detention, includes those with long institutional careers already behind them, often including periods is psychiatric hospitals;

inadequate personalities who respond to institutional stress by resorting to violence, including self-injury; and overtly aggressive prisoners who may be both immature and inadequate and who erupt into frequent and unpredictable bouts of violence against other people, against property and often against themselves. Their bizarre behaviour creates stress for staff and other prisoners which can in turn give rise to control problems. The present state of knowledge offers limited prospects of successful treatment. The need, therefore, is to reduce the risk they present within prisons by caring for them in a suitably modified regime which takes account of their condition and offers enhanced psychiatric support.

'C' wing, Parkhurst

The unit set up in 'C' wing, Parkhurst, which operated between 1970 and 1979 was one attempt to deal with these seemingly intractable problem prisoners. The test for admission was not so much a sharp psychiatric diagnosis but rather the practical one that the prisoner had persistently demonstrated over a period of time disturbed behaviour of a kind which could not be managed in an ordinary prison regime. The factors taken into account were violence towards staff, inmates or property; attempted suicide, self-mutilation or regular hunger strikes; repeated disciplinary offences; chronic sick reporting; and mental illness. The aim was to devise as constructive a way as possible of managing such prisoners so that they could achieve an optimum level of behaviour consistent with their make-up. The unit was small (35–40 prisoners), run by a multidisciplinary staff team, had space in which prisoners could move freely and a routine flexible enough to cope with day-to-day swings in prisoner behaviour. No claims were made that long-term, lasting improvements in behaviour would necessarily result from exposure to the 'C' wing regime. A more limited, but none the less valuable, aim was in view, namely to offer an alternative method of managing difficult and disturbed prisoners for periods when they could not be managed in a normal prison wing. The CRC was convinced that this unit should be reopened as soon as possible and indeed it is now in operation once again (see Evershed, Chapter 15). The Committee further argued that a second unit of this type should be considered in the light of experience gained with the reconstituted 'C' wing, Parkhurst.

Grendon

Grendon Prison has dealt with the psychiatrically disturbed for over 20 years. But the criteria for admission and the regime have always been quite different from those used at Parkhurst. The crucial differences are that prisoners at Grendon have been participants in a personally demanding programme, that the prospects for sustained improvement in behaviour should be good, and that release into the community in the foreseeable future should be likely. These requirements thus ruled out the less mature, less articulate and less resilient amongst the disturbed prisoner population. There is no doubt that Grendon has achieved notable success within the limits of the most careful selection, with banishment for those who become or seriously threaten violence. But the CRC believed that there would be substantial advantage in using Grendon's experience in managing a rather broader section of the disturbed prisoner population without compromising its already distinctive contribution to the prison system. Indeed, when the CRC report was published the Director of Prison Medical Services had already set up a committee to advise on the best ways of achieving this aim and that work continues.

Long-term prisoner units
Another group for whom special provision was felt to be essential was that composed of those who do not necessarily suffer from psychiatric disabililty but who nevertheless are persistently at odds with the system — in physical confrontation with staff and prisoners, in exploiting weaker prisoners and in activity generally calculated to dislocate orderly institutional life. The proposal here was to set up three or four small units (long-term prisoner units) operating closely supervised but relatively open regimes. The units would preferably be housed outside dispersal prisons in local or Category B training prisons. The thinking behind this proposal was to break the vicious circle either of segregation within dispersal prisons with all the attendant drawbacks outlined earlier; or temporary transfer to a local prison for a 28-day period during which prisoners experienced a very spartan regime; or the wasteful merry-go-round of regular transfer between dispersal prisons with prisoners retaining access to all the facilities and opportunities with which they' have been demonstrably unable to live in an acceptable fashion elsewhere.

In proposing long-term prisoner units, the CRC was quite definitely not seeking to revive the ill-fated control units, for which a purely punitive purpose was envisaged. Paragraph 14 of Prison Department Circular Instruction 35/1974 left no room for doubt on this score: 'the regime of the unit is not directed towards providing "treatment", there is no expectation that it will cure prisoners of wanting to stir up trouble; only demonstrate to them that it does not pay to do so'. The CRC saw the units as a positive initiative offering a facility midway between traditional segregation and ordinary location in which programmes should be developed relating to prisoner needs. The common features in mind are small size and close staff supervision so that opportunities for indulging in excesses of behaviour are severely limited. The Committee did not have time to set out a detailed prospectus for each such unit, but did identify the broad parameters within which they should operate. The primary aim is the safe and humane containment of those unsuited to normal prison life. The units should not be regarded as places of last resort from which no transfer can be sensibly secured. The units must complement each other and not be an *ad hoc* collection of aims and regimes. Finally, the prison service should be completely open about the aims and objectives of the units and the way they operate because there is nothing to hide in trying to develop better ways of caring for an important minority of the long-term prisoner population.

Protection under Rule 43

A third group presenting special difficulties is the long-term Rule 43 population who seek protection for their own safety. They do not normally present control problems themselves, but are unable to live easily in mainstream prison life, often because their offence provokes hostility from others. Traditionally they have been housed in segregation units. This has serious disadvantages in taking up space needed for others, but just as importantly in reducing the quality of life of those prisoners to a very poor level: little or no association, and limited work, educational or recreational activities. All this reduces their ability to develop the very social skills which might enable them to end their self-imposed isolation. Accordingly, the Committee recommended that work be put in hand to set up units specifically designed to provide a better quality of life for Rule 43 protection cases. Such units need not be in the most secure prisons, though there is a need to cater for those who are both security risks *and* held under Rule 43. The handful of prisoners (eight in 1984) who have killed in prison or who present a real and continued threat that they will kill clearly need special attention. The special high-security cells at Wakefield presently meet part of that need, and the Committee were satisfied that they should stay in use. A small addition to the stock may be needed.

Prisoner programmes

Another thread running through the entire CRC package was the desire to move away from the vague concept of the 'regime'. In its place the Committee proposed that a bundle of prisoner-orientated activities amenable to objective performance-setting and efficiency audit should be identified and given the simple, accurate title 'prisoner programmes'. Such programmes would offer a range of activities — work, education, recreation, therapy — geared to personal need instead of being dictated by disproportionate emphasis on any one activity which may or may not engage prisoners' interest. The notion of constructing individual programmes is certainly not a soft option for prisoners. If properly organised the reverse will be true by requiring prisoners to co-operate in determining the shape and content of particular parts of the sentence. And this applies not only to those in mainstream long-term prisons but equally to those in the separate special units. The whole is in keeping with the style of managing prisoners' careers, from their involvement in the sentence-planning phase onwards.

Research, information systems and monitoring
The lack of research conducted in so many of the areas examined by the CRC was very apparent. A number of subjects seemed to offer scope for the involvement of outside help and in setting up specific research programmes: for example, in planning the small long-term prisoner units and evaluating their operation; for evaluating the efficacy of centralised long-term allocation; in reassessing security classification and the interaction between security and control; in the behavioural science implications of pursuing a 'new generation' set of prison buildings; and in assessing the control aspects of implementing a prisoner programme approach. And in the system generally refinement is needed in the assembly, analysis and use of basic data. But quite apart from the intrinsic value of sharpening up the research input, the CRC was absolutely convinced that the prison system must tap into the fund of knowledge and skills available outside, and particularly in the academic community. The first step along this road has been taken by the setting up of a Research and Advisory Group (RAG):

> to provide the Prison Department, on request, with a source of advice on the research needs arising from the report of the Control Review Committee, and how they may be met, and, in particular, to advise on the planning, co-ordination and evaluation of the proposed long-term prisoner units (Home Office News Release, 5 November 1984).

Three academics are members of this group.

Conclusion
On a narrow interpretation of its terms of reference, the CRC could be said to have been charged with looking at a small part of the

prison system (dispersal prisons) in which only a small proportion of the total prison population is contained — around 3,000 out of a total prison population of 45,000; concentrating attention on the handful of prisons which made up the dispersal network; and seeking to deliver neat solutions on this relatively narrow though important front.

Yet it quickly became clear that a much broader review of the system was needed, and this of necessity meant looking at the adult system as a whole because the issues addressed were so wide-ranging. What all this added up to was an attempt to produce a practical and humane prospectus in a form that is intellectually and politically sustainable now and for years to come. It meant, for example, hazarding a revised set of objectives for the prison service as a whole (Home Office 1984, para. 108), tapping into and articulating the hidden consensus of views within and outside the service about measures needed to improve the service, deliberately ceasing to draw a wholly artificial distinction between looking after prisoners and efficiency, and reinforcing the need to look after prisoners efficiently.

Two complementary sets of initiatives were proposed. First, to improve the basic structure and gain control of the system by centralising allocation, sentence planning at the outset, and individualising prisoner programmes which are regularly reviewed. The second line of development proposes special measures for managing those whose behaviour does not respond to the inbuilt incentives of a better-structured system. Resources will be needed to achieve major improvement. But additional costs could be partly offset by the interplay of two factors — reducing the size of the highly expensive dispersal prisons by taking out of use two units; and taking positive action to reduce the likelihood of costly breakdown and consequent loss of accommodation by setting up units designed to manage constructively those most likely to engage in damaging behaviour.

The CRC was given a rare opportunity to speak out about the achievement of a saner, more clearly managed and more competent prison system, in which firmness and humanity genuinely do go hand in hand. The report offers a prospectus with which most can identify and within which the prison service and outsiders can work together in practical and hopeful ways. Much remains to be done and the far-reaching nature of the task was clearly acknowledged by the Director General of the Prison Service:

> what has also emerged, almost more strongly than the Committee itself had signalled, is the way in which implementation of their proposals, especially on managing the careers of long term prisoners and on the development of a fuller and more coherent set of privileges, will ultimately permeate the whole system and not merely those prisons that have to

handle the difficult and dangerous prisoner. This is indeed a positive agenda and a stimulating prospect (Home Office 1985, para. 17).

References

Advisory Council on the Penal System (1968), *The Regime for Long-Term Prisoners in Conditions of Maximum Security* (Radzinowicz Report), London: HMSO.

Home Office (1966), *Report of the Inquiry into Prison Escapes and Security* (Mountbatten Report), Cmnd. 3175, London: HMSO.

Home Office (1973), 'Report of the Working Party on Dispersal and Control' (Cox Report), London: Home Office (unpublished).

Home Office (1977), *Report of an Inquiry by the Chief Inspector of the Prison Service into the Cause and Circumstances of the Events at H.M. Prison, Hull, During the Period 31st August to 3rd September, 1976*, HC 453 (Fowler Report), London: HMSO.

Home Office (1979), *Report of the Committee of Inquiry into the United Kingdom Prison Services* (May Report), Cmnd. 7673, London: HMSO.

Home Office (1984), *Managing the Long-Term Prison System: The Report of the Control Review Committee*, London: HMSO.

Home Office (1985), *Report of the Work of the Prison Department 1984/85*, Cmnd. 9699, London: HMSO.

House of Commons (1978), *Fifteenth Report of the Expenditure Committee: The Reduction of Pressure on the Prison System*, London: HMSO.

DISCUSSANT: *ANDREW RUTHERFORD*

It is a pleasant task to respond to such an excellent paper which succinctly sets out the context to the report of the Control Review Committee (Home Office 1984) and examines several implications for policy. In one sense my role is difficult, given that there is much in the report and in Tony Pearson's paper with which I agree. The report after all was put together by several of the most liberal senior officials in the Prison Department and there can be little argument that it is one of the most sensible and sensitive documents to have emerged from the Home Office in recent years.

Tony Pearson neatly articulates the key dilemma confronting policy-makers and practitioners as being to achieve, 'an acceptable balance between the undoubted need for effective security and the much more elusive goal of creating a viable quality of life for staff and prisoners working and living in very secure institutions'. Throughout the report there is an insistence that prisons for persons serving long sentences be seen in relation to the prison system as a whole, and that 'control in dispersals is achieved against the grain of the system rather than with its support' (Home Office 1984, para. 14). With this I agree, but I will be suggesting that it is useful to widen the context further so as to take fully into account the nature of the rapidly expanding prison system. Furthermore, I will be suggesting that we do not confine the term 'control' to problems posed by particular prisoners. Tony Pearson goes some way in this direction when he writes of the Control Review Committee's determination to 'gain control' of the system by centralising allocation, sentence planning and other issues relating to long-term prisoners.

Before exploring aspects of control within this context, I would like to refer briefly to three specific issues which arise in the paper.

Issues in Pearson's paper

The concentration–dispersal debate

Tony Pearson refers to this debate as being an underlying theme since Mountbatten, but it remains unclear as to whether opinion within the Home Office has recently shifted. Certainly, the report argues for some reduction in the number of dispersal prisons. With the opening of Frankland in 1983 the number of dispersal prisons had grown to eight (2,930 places). By taking out Wormwood Scrubs and Hull, the six dispersal prisions left will provide 2,324 places or 6 per cent of total capacity (as at 31 March 1985). When Full Sutton is opened there will be 2,766 places.

Whether or not on the back of 'new generation' prison architecture, the Committee clearly envisage the need for a smaller maximum-security system. At least one commentator, Roy King (*Guardian,* 13 February 1985) suggests that the 'new generation' architectural possibilities strengthen the case for concentration, and in his paper to this conference (Chapter 5) he makes an explicit call for at least one non-local prison to be so constructed.

The use of transfer for control or punishment purposes

The converse side is the so-called 'home ties package'. It is worth quoting rather fully from the CRC report:

> From the point of view of prison managers, one of the most effective ways of increasing the options of dealing with difficult individuals or groups would simply be to widen the allocation of determinate sentence prisoners so that it extended outside regional boundaries. This would extend both the number and the nature of the options. Some training prisons run more controlled regimes than others, but no one region has more than a very narrow part of the range at its disposal. Furthermore, a deliberate transfer to a prison in a part of the country that is a long way from a prisoner's choice is itself a sanction which we should not lose sight of. We put a lot of weight on the importance of helping home contacts and we realise that transfers far from home can be said to punish a prisoner's family rather than the prisoner himself. We therefore think that transfers of this kind should not be done lightly or without warning. But in our view the present extreme difficulty of arranging them is a

quite excessive self-imposed restriction of the room for manoeuvre in running the long term system (Home Office 1984, para. 38).

The Home Office in its evidence to the Prior Committee (Home Office 1985, vol. 2, p. 13) on the prison disciplinary system, stated:

> The allocation of inmates is an entirely administrative procedure . . . The preferences of the inmate and the location of his family are normally taken into account, but these factors are liable to be outweighed by other considerations when a transfer is effected in the interests of maintaining good order.

It will be recalled that the Prior Committee, although instinctively feeling there ought to be safeguards on this matter, made no recommendations other than saying there may be a case for some more extensive independent monitoring of the use of such powers (Home Office 1985, vol. 1, paras 2.42–2.43). If transfer is to be an even more crucial aspect of the control of long-term prisoners, matters cannot be left there.

Institutional 'ethos'

My third point can be put as a question. Are there special features associated with the regimes at Wakefield and Long Lartin that account for the absence of serious incidents at those two prisons? Some years ago a senior Prison Department official described Gartree as being 'a sick institution'. How can we better articulate or indeed begin to measure characteristics of this kind? Michael Jenkins makes several useful observations on this (Chapter 13). The real significance of Oak Park Heights (described by Roy King in Chapter 5) seems to me to be located less in its architectural features than within its institutional ethos (see Rutherford 1985).

Aspects of control

Three broad control issues must be highlighted. These are prison population; conditions within the prison system; and staff.

The prison population

Questions about long-term imprisonment have to be viewed in the context of a rapidly expanding prison system, as shown in Table 2.1. In brief, it can be said that with reference to growth, the prison system is increasingly out of control. The present crisis situation consists of:

(i) The abandonment of the effort throughout the 1970s by Home Office ministers to hold or reduce prison population size. The signal of change of policy was given first by William Whitelaw

Table 2.1 Prison overpopulation

		Prison Population	Capacity
Mountbatten Inquiry	1966	33,086	31,000
Dept. Working Party	1972	38,328	36,000
May Committee	1979	42,220	38,000
CRC	1984	43,295	39,000
Home Office projections	1994	53,000–59,0000	51,000

on 15 March 1982 when he told the House of Commons: 'We are determined to ensure that there will be room in the prison system for every person whom the judges and magistrates decide should go there, and we will continue to do whatever is necessary for that purpose'.

(ii) The doubling of Mr Whitelaw's prison building programme. The Whitelaw plan was for ten new prisons. If we include Lindholme, published plans are now, four years later, for 19 new prisons. The capacity of the penal estate is to grow by the early 1990s from approximately 39,000 to 51,000.

With this expansionist mood in full gear it would not be surprising if the Prison Department were planning for further prison building through the 1990s.

The trade-off between expansion and conditions

Sometimes overlooked in the present prisons spending bonanza are the hard realities of the trade-off between relentless expansion of the penal estate and the conditions experienced by prisoners and staff within prisons. There is every indication that the high-cost squalor which characterises many prisons is becoming more pronounced. Education, workshops, remand centre provision are among the casualties. It makes understandable, but it does not justify, Leon Brittan's decision announced on 12 April 1984 to go back on a commitment made two years earlier that the government would bring forward proposals on minimum standards for prisons. The trade-off appears to be working in favour of expansion at the expense of conditions, casting an ironic shadow over Mr Brittan's claim (at the Prison Officers' Association Conference in 1985) that the building programme 'means a major improvement, not only in the conditions in which staff have to live, but also in the conditions in which staff of the service have to work'. Similarly repeated reassurances by Home Office ministers that 'we are on course' to eliminate

overcrowding by the end of the decade are both hollow and misleading. This has recently been acknowledged by the Home Office. Let
the Comptroller and Auditor General explain:

> It seems to me, that unless the Home Office take special operational
> measures, the programme will fail to achieve their broad objective of
> matching total available places with total prison population by the end
> of the decade. *The Home Office have explained that this is what was meant
> by the phrase 'eliminating overcrowding by the end of the decade', first used
> by the Home Secretary in November 1983 and often since repeated, for
> example in the Government Expenditure White Paper of January 1985*
> (Cmnd. 9428 II). They have also told me that, although through their
> strategic planning they hope to minimise local mis-matching, they do
> not have the more detailed objective of providing adequate prison places
> of the right categories and in the right locations, partly because of the
> inherent uncertainties involved and also because to aim for eliminating
> all overcrowding in every establishment would require a major overpro-
> vision of accommodation. However, at the end of the decade there may
> well still be overcrowding in some prisons and under-occupation in others
> (National Audit Office 1985, p. 6, emphasis added).

Staff

It is interesting that the focus should now be on the control of
prisoners. Certainly a few years ago for Home Office mandarins
it was staff that presented the key control challenge (see, for example,
'The growth of industrial action: an historical account', in Home
Office evidence to the May Committee, Home Office 1979, pp. 115–
25, which includes 50 examples of action taken by local branches
of the Prison Officers' Association which interfered with the administration of justice, prison administration or with the prison
regimes). One governor wrote: 'The control of prisons had by the
mid-seventies to a very large extent passed into the hands of the
Prison Officers' Association' (see Rutherford 1984, pp. 83–7, which
includes examples of staff control problems at two dispersal prisons).

But it would be unfair to focus exclusively on uniformed staff.
The control unit saga of the early 1970s contains severe warnings
(it is interesting that the Home Secretary in welcoming the CRC
report on 17 July 1984 referred to them as being 'discredited' given
that Roy King had his knuckles rapped by the Home Office five
years earlier for calling them 'infamous' (see Home Office 1979,
pp. 193–4). Only portions of the story have been published, and
for these we are in debt to Harriet Harman, David Leigh and the
Guardian. The extracts from documents considered by the High
Court in *Williams* v *Home Office*[1] and published in the *Guardian*
in 1980 make salutary reading. The constructive ideas put forward
by the unpublished (indeed uncirculated) Director General's Work-

ing Party Report (Home Office 1973) were during the next 12 months
perverted. By March 1973 an official at Prison Department headquarters was writing that the new units should be 'short-stay with
only the essentials provided'. The *Guardian's* (8 April 1980) summary
continues: 'Dismissing fears that the ventilation envisaged for the
cells was inadequate, he said that it would let the prisoner realize
what normal "delights he had forfeited by his bad behaviour"'.
Although others in the Home Office, including the Home Secretary
(Robert Carr) and the Permanent Secretary (Sir Arthur Peterson)
stressed positive features of the regime, an official from P5 (security)
advocated 'sterility . . . seclusion and anonymity'. Indeed, 'a barren
existence more likely to persuade him to behave . . . largely ignored
by the staff. Such a regime strictly followed would prove successful
in most cases in a matter of months'. The resulting documents
showed a victory by P5 over P2 (medium and long-term security).
Under pressure from P5 for example, the maximum period of confinement was increased from one to six months. My favourite
quotation, however, is not the head of P5 on the circular to governors
setting up the control unit regime ('only circular instructions which
modify standing orders are sent to the House of Commons Library.
This one will not therefore go to the House of Commons.') but
is a memo which emerged from P3 (sentenced adult offenders) in
the autumn of 1975 just prior to Roy Jenkins' announcement that
the Wakefield Control Unit was to be closed. This memo, refresh-
ingly states: 'One of the ways out of our present situation may be
to lay it all open, both to get public support . . . and to persuade
the staff that we will not get what we need by pretending that
we do not live in a democracy' (*Guardian*, 8 April 1980).

Enough has been said to remind ourselves of the regressive tendencies within prisons and prison systems. The proposal to establish
three or four small long-term prisoner units must, and rightly, raise
doubts as to their regime. But it is at this point that the CRC
report and Tony Pearson's paper depart in tone from the Home
Secretary's announcement of 17 July 1984. The report (Home Office
1984, para. 66) notes that, 'the long-term units are not punitive
in purpose. The primary aim will be the safe and humane containment of those who are unsuited to normal prison life, and although
very controlled conditions may sometimes be required to achieve
that end, every effort should be made to ensure that the regime
is as positive and supportive as possible.' Both the report and Tony
Pearson contrast the new units with the control unit (the 'regime
that the unit operated was a blind alley for the prison service and
not really in keeping with the values that we now try to instill
in our training. We therefore want to make it absolutely plain that

the units we advocate will be of a totally different kind': Home Office 1984, para. 52). However, Mr Brittan in his welcome of the CRC report struck a different note on some of the long-term prisoner units: 'the regime will be sparse and highly regulated; and whose existence should have a welcome deterrent effect.'

One can only speculate on why and how the Home Secretary's announcement of 17 July 1984 was drafted in this way. The dismal and disturbing control unit saga was in part the product of secrecy, even within the Prison Department. Openness within and beyond the prison system would seem to be a pre-requisite of decency in conditions of confinement, a point to which the Control Review Committee (Home Office 1984, para. 70) gives some emphasis.

Note

1 Michael Williams was a prisoner in the Wakefield Control Unit who, after his release on parole in 1980, sued the Home Office for false imprisonment in respect of the time he spent in the unit: see *Williams* v *Home Office* [1981] 1 All ER 1151 and *Williams* v *Home Office (No. 2)* [1981] 1 All ER 1211.

References

Home Office (1973), 'Report of the Working Party on Dispersal and Control' (Cox Report), London: Home Office (unpublished).

Home Office (1979), *Report of the Committee of Inquiry into the United Kingdom Prison Services* (May Report), Vol. 2, Cmnd. 7673, London: HMSO.

Home Office (1984), *Managing the Long-Term Prison System: The Report of the Control Review Committee*, London: HMSO.

Home Office (1985), *Report of the Committee on the Prison Disciplinary System* (Prior Report), Cmnd. 9641, London: HMSO.

National Audit Office (1985), *Report by the Comptroller and Auditor General, Home Office and Property Services Agency: Programme for the Provision of Prison Places*, London: HMSO.

Rutherford, A. (1984), *Prisons and the Process of Justice*, London: Heinemann (republished by Oxford University Press, 1986).

Rutherford, A. (1985), 'The New Generation of Prisons', *New Society*, 20 September, pp. 408–10.

IMPLEMENTATION: *S.G. NORRIS*

When the Control Review Committee (CRC) report (Home Office 1984) was published in July 1984 the then Home Secretary welcomed it as 'a positive agenda for establishing a better framework of control in our long-term prison system'. The report avoided simplistic solutions and offered a wide-ranging and complex package of recommendations. The implementation of some elements will necessarily extend over several years. The following provides a brief account of the progress that has been made in implementing the report's recommendations since its publication.

The Research and Advisory Group on the long-term prison system

The CRC recommended that the Prison Department should establish closer links with the academic world in order to bring a wider perspective to the task of implementing and evaluating the recommendations. This recommendation has been accepted, and one of the first actions of the then Home Secretary following the report's publication was to set up a Research and Advisory Group (RAG) on the long-term prison system with the following terms of reference:

> To provide the Prison Department, on request, with a source of advice on the research needs arising from the Report of the Control Review Committee, and how they may be met, and, in particular, to advise on the planning, co-ordination and evaluation of the proposed long-term prisoner units (Home Office News Release, 5 November 1984).

This group is chaired by the Director of Operational Policy and its members include three outside academics: Professor Anthony Bottoms of the Cambridge Institute of Criminology; Professor John Gunn of the Institute of Psychiatry, University of London; and Professor Roy King of the University College of North Wales. To date the RAG has concerned itself mainly with the development of a strategy for special units and the compilation of a research programme (both subjects are dealt with later in this paper); it is intended, however, that the group should widen its areas of involvement in the year ahead.

Special units

One of the CRC's major recommendations was that a number of small units should be established for long-term prisoners who, for one reason or another, present severe control problems in our long-term prisons. The Prison Department has attached priority to establishing these special facilities in order to provide relief for the long-term prisons.

The first of the special units was opened at 'C' wing, Parkhurst, on 30 December 1985 and now provides a facility for long-term prisoners who have a history of both troublesome prison behaviour *and* psychiatric illness or abnormality. A more detailed account of the unit's admission criteria and its operation so far is given in Evershed (Chapter 15).

A second special unit is scheduled to open later in 1986 catering for prisoners who do not require psychiatric oversight, and three or four further units are being planned for subsequent years. Each of the units will operate a different regime, but they will all have certain important characteristics in common. They will not be punitive in purpose and transfer to the units will not be imposed as a punishment. The various regimes will all be designed to be positive and supportive, and staff working in the units will be specially trained and have the time to give inmates individual attention. Although some units will provide a more structured environment than others, it is intended that all will offer prisoners the opportunity to spend the majority of the day out of their cells engaged in purposeful programmes such as work, education, PE and recreation.

The development of the special units' strategy is being taken forward with the assistance of the Research and Advisory Group. It is hoped to publish a report giving an account of the thinking underlying the group's approach.

Grendon

Grendon Prison currently provides a facility for those prisoners who are suffering from some form of mental disturbance or disability which makes them unsuited to normal prison life but who are not eligible for transfer to a special hospital. The CRC hoped that as a result of the work of the recently established Advisory Committee on the Therapeutic Regime at Grendon (ACTRAG), Grendon's regime might be broadened and developed in order to enable it to take a wider range of prisoners. The first report of ACTRAG (Home Office 1985a) was published in July 1985. The report recommended that Grendon should continue to concentrate on group psychotherapy, but it also proposed that a 'rescue unit' should be established at the prison to cater for prisoners in acute need of psychiatric care and support. The proposal for the establishment of a 'rescue unit' has been accepted in principle.

Family ties

The CRC drew attention to the need to provide long-term prisoners with incentives to good behaviour. They recommend that incentives should be developed in Category C and D prisons in order to make security downgrading and progression through the prison system a consistent and psychologically credible process, mentioning specifically extension of opportunities for home leave, relaxation of censorship and use of telephones. Acknowledging the force of these arguments for providing incentives, the present Home Secretary decided to begin with the provision of additional privileges in open prisons (from 1 April 1986) that will make it easier for prisoners to strengthen and retain their contacts with family and friends. These additional privileges are: no limit on the number of letters prisoners may send and receive; earlier and more frequent home leave; and access to payphones.

Research

The CRC identified a lack of research into prison control issues. With the assistance of the Research and Advisory Group, the Home Office Prison Department has drawn up a research programme designed to fill that gap. The Department has commissioned a literature survey into those aspects of prison regimes (including the composition of an establishment's population) that appear to be associated with the promotion of control. In addition, it will shortly be commissioning an examination of the nature of control problems among long-term prisoners and of their emergence, including a study of the circumstances in which prisoners are transferred from normal location.

It will be particularly important to evaluate the operation and effectiveness of the special units. The intention is that a descriptive and evaluative account should be prepared of each unit. Work has already begun in respect of 'C' wing, Parkhurst, and the Institute of Psychiatry (University of London) will be playing a major part in the evaluation of the unit. In addition, an attempt will be made to evaluate the effect that the existence of the special units has on the level of control incidents in the long-term prison system. The special units' allocation process will be monitored, and, in due course, once several units are in operation, the cost effectiveness of the special units will be studied in the context of the long-term prison system as a whole.

Planning long-term prisoners' sentences

Since the CRC reported, the prison population has risen sharply and the local prisons in particular are now harder pressed than ever. In these circumstances we have concluded that it is not practical to require the locals to take on the additional burden of holding and assessing all long-term prisoners for 12 months after sentencing as the CRC proposed. During 1986 we shall be reassessing the merits, practicality and resource implications of the CRC's recommendations on sentence planning and central allocation of long-term prisoners.

The size of the dispersal system

The CRC envisaged that the opening of special units would gradually relieve dispersal prisons of those prisoners who present the most serious control problems, and that it might then be possible to reduce the size of the dispersal system. When the new dispersal prison, Full Sutton, opens in 1987 there will be a total of eight dispersal prisons. In February 1986 Hull was converted from a dispersal to a local prison, providing relief for Leeds, which was the most overcrowded prison in the country. About 30 dispersal prisoners, including Category As, will remain in 'A' wing at Hull until Full Sutton opens. The number of dispersal prisons will be kept under review with particular reference to the CRC's recommendation that Wormwood Scrubs 'D' Hall should cease to have a dispersal role.

'New generation' designs

The CRC recommended an urgent examination of the possibilities of 'new generation' prison designs now current in the United States. They concluded that by enabling separation of groups of prisoners in self-contained units such prisons avoided many of the dangers that led the Radzinowicz and May Committees (Advisory Council on the Penal System 1968; Home Office 1979) to advise against a policy of concentration of high-security prisoners (Home Office 1984, para. 20). The CRC considered that if new generation designs were successful, two such prisons would be sufficient to meet the likely future need for high security accommodation. Following publication of the CRC report, the then Home Secretary set up a working party and commissioned a detailed study of the American designs and their relevance to the Prison Service in England and Wales. The working party's report (Home Office 1985b) was published in December 1985. Its conclusions are summarised by Terence Platt (Chapter 5).

References

Advisory Council on the Penal System (1968), *The Regime for Long-Term Prisoners in Conditions of Maximum Security* (Radzinowicz Report), London: HMSO.

Home Office (1979), *Report of the Committee of Inquiry into the United Kingdom Prison Services* (May Report), Cmnd. 7673, London: HMSO.

Home Office (1984), *Managing the Long-Term Prison System: The Report of the Control Review Committee*, London: HMSO.

Home Office (1985a), *First Report of the Advisory Committee on the Therapeutic Regime at Grendon*, London: Home Office.

Home Office (1985b), *New Directions in Prison Design: Report of a Home Office Working Party on American New Generation Prisons* (Platt Report), London: HMSO.

3 Control strategies for problem prisoners in American penal systems
David A. Ward

This paper is a brief review of changes in American penal policy since the early 1960s which is intended to provide readers with a basis for understanding current issues related to the control of those prisoners labelled 'violent' or 'dangerous'. Several limitations should be noted at the outset of this discussion. Most obvious is the fact that this description does not pretend to do justice to the welter of social, economic and political forces that have shaped government policy, even in a specifically defined area such as 'corrections'. A consideration of American history from the rebellious, protest-studded, optimistic period of social engineering of the 1960s, through the days of despair and disillusionment about foreign and domestic policy that followed the Vietnam War and the failure of plans for the 'Great Society', to the re-emergence of the more traditional and conservative values expressed by the Reagan administration, would underlie a complete understanding of the current state of affairs in American penal policy. Another limitation is that one paper cannot review the penal policies of the 50 state governments which, together with the Federal government, comprise the political structure of the United States. Similarities in policy and practice come about because the states are united by a Federal constitution, by a Federal governmental superstructure, by language, and by certain shared social, cultural, economic, and political traditions. However, in contrast to England and most Western European countries, there is in the United States no centralised, unified prison system which determines which policy options will be adopted and how they will be operationalised throughout the nation. Each state, within the bounds of its membership as part of the republic, and within the interpretation of the Federal constitution, devises its own penal policies and the bureaucratic structure to implement them. Since the states differ from each other in terms of their cultural traditions, their economic resources, the size and variety of racial and ethnic groups that comprise their populations and the degree to which they are urbanised and industrialised, their crime rates as well as their penal policies vary. Rates of violent crime are higher in the South and West, drug-related law violations are higher in the border states, organised crime and gang activities are generally absent from the north central states, and rates of commitment to jail and prisons vary profoundly; some states, like Minnesota and Massachusetts, have jail and imprisonment rates per 100,000 population similar to those of England and Canada while other states, such as South Carolina and Georgia, have rates three or four times higher. Having 50 states and the Federal government operating separate penal systems that reflect 51 sets of values and strategies may appear to be a blueprint for disorganisation, but this division of authority does allow for different approaches to the same problems to be employed in different states of the union. The experiment in Massachusetts to close all youth prisons could not, for example, have been attempted on a national scale; the experiment to encourage the development of alternatives to incarceration through a programme of subsidies to the counties was a Californian invention which became the model for community corrections legislation in other states; the sentencing guidelines system developed in Minnesota, which specifies which offenders go to prison and for how long, while placing a cap on the state prison population, has become the model for similar sentencing systems in other states as well as for the Federal government. Innovative practices developed in one state — or in one prison for that matter — provide models which other jurisdictions may adopt or adapt, but inclinations to experiment in corrections policy or to learn from other systems are greater among the northern-tier states than among the southern states.

The American Federal government does attempt to influence state and county government policy through conferences and publications, by legislation, by example or model, by the provision of sets of standards, and by the provision of extra funds to state and county corrections agencies which follow Federal strategies or guidelines. But in the area of penal policy the most important Federal influence comes as a result of the requirement that all states and counties abide by Federal court decisions which protect the rights of all citizens which are articulated in the United States Constitution — including those citizens who are in prison or jail.

Through court-ordered actions, and in some states, through the court-appointed 'special masters' (generally former corrections officials regarded as progressive) minimum standards of operation have been established for every prison in the United States, with special attention having been given to maximum-security prisons where inmate rights are most severely limited.

It should also be noted that the maximum-security prisons of the United States — San Quentin and Folsom in California, Attica in New York, Stateville and Joliet in Illinois and the Federal prisons at Leavenworth, Kansas and Alcatraz in California — constitute the image Americans have of what a penitentiary is, and for many of them, what it should be. Sherman and Hawkins (1981) describe what they call the 'monomanie of the penitentiary' that characterises the thinking of so many Americans about the appropriate response to criminal law violations. These well-known prisons are what citizens have in mind when they urge their political representatives and criminal justice agency heads to 'lock them up and throw away the key'. In the discussion concerning problem prisoners which follows, our focus will also be on three prisons in three penal systems selected not only because they are among the most visible in the United States, but also because they are moving along different strategic routes in the effort to cope with this problem.

The final section of this paper provides a brief description of recent research on the effects of long-term confinement in several high-security prisons, including one of the best known penitentiaries in America, the former Federal prison at Alcatraz, California.

The Federal Bureau of Prisons: from concentration to dispersion and back to concentration

During the 1920s and 1930s crime became an important and very visible social problem in the United States. The unhappy national experiment in prohibiting the sale of alcoholic beverages provided the basis for local, then state-wide, and finally regional organisation of illegal alcohol production, distribution and consumption activities. During this same era social and economic conditions, including what is known in the United States as 'the Great Depression', prompted some citizens to turn to bank and post office robbery and the kidnapping of wealthy businessmen or their children for ransom. The gangs of bank robbers, the purveyors of illegal alcohol and other forbidden substances and services, and the kidnappers, engaged in activities which crossed state lines, and it soon became apparent that local police departments were not organised to deal with these forms of crime in terms of training, intelligence gathering, communication and inter-state co-ordination of efforts. The concern of most citizens over the increases in violent crime and the special concerns of the wealthy, who were being held for ransom and whose banks were being robbed, provided the basis for a rapid and substantial expansion of Federal police powers. In the early 1930s the Federal Bureau of Investigation (FBI) was established and the Federal Bureau of Prisons was formed.

J. Edgar Hoover, the new director of the FBI, convinced the

Attorney-General that the United States needed a prison which would serve as a symbol of the Federal government's power and determination to punish serious offenders That symbol became the Federal penitentiary on Alcatraz Island in San Francisco Bay. When it opened in 1934, Alcatraz was intended by Department of Justice officials to establish a new standard for the punishment and incapacitation of the country's most notorious criminals, and the Federal prison system's most accomplished escape artists and trouble-makers. Alcatraz became the prototype of the 'last resort' prison based upon the contention that if prison officials locked up those with most serious behaviour problems in one prison with a high degree of control, not only could these inmates be managed but normal programmes and security procedures could be continued in the other prisons of the Federal system. To achieve the extraordinary degree of control required at a super maximum-security prison the regimen at Alcatraz contained the following elements:

(i) Compared to all other American prisons, there would be a small inmate population (275) supervised by a large custodial force (150).
(ii) No direct commitments from the courts would be allowed; inmates would come only on transfer from other prisons, with all transfers in and out of the prison controlled by Bureau headquarters.
(iii) No effort at rehabilitation would be attempted, no positions for social workers, teachers, vocational instructors, psychologists or psychiatrists would be allotted to the staff roster. Education, vocational training, religious instruction, recreational and counselling programmes found in other penitentiaries would not be offered.
(iv) As a maximum-custody, minimum-privilege prison, no commissary would be established, mail and visiting privileges would be limited to a letter or two a week and one visit a month with blood relatives only. No newspapers would be allowed and certain magazines would be permitted but none containing any news about crime or criminals. No radio was allowed until the mid-1950s (two channels controlled by staff) and no television was permitted. The silent system was imposed during the 1930s.
(v) The 'programme' was to consist of work (which would be a privilege because, although no pay was provided, extra good time could be earned and work was the only activity to fill the days), two hours of yard recreation at weekends, reading library books and several individual activities such as painting and taking correspondence courses. All programme elements were subject to removal when inmates were sent to disciplinary segregation which would be for indefinite periods of time. Disciplinary

isolation called for restricted diets and confinement in darkened strip cells.

(vi) Since inmates would be sent to Alcatraz as punishment for bad conduct a period of good conduct — about four years for the average inmate — was necessary to convince the staff that an inmate merited transfer back to other prisons. The other incentive for inmates to improve their conduct was that no inmate would be paroled from Alcatraz; parole was to be considered only when the inmate had earned a transfer back to other prisons.

The mission of Alcatraz, then, was to control the most uncontrollable inmates in the Federal prison population — those inmates who used physical violence against their fellow convicts, the leaders of strong-arm gangs and riots, the escape artists, the leaders of strikes and organised protests and those men who assaulted or killed employees. (Alcatraz also housed certain celebrity prisoners who were sent to 'The Rock' as a symbolic gesture of the government's most severe punishment outside of the death penalty. Included in this latter category were prominent gangsters such as Al Capone and Machine Gun Kelly, a number of organised crime bosses, several high-visibility 'traitors' including Morton Sobel of the Rosenberg spy case, and the Federal prison system's most notorious prisoner, Robert Stroud, who killed a prison officer in the dining hall at Leavenworth Penitentiary and later became known as 'The Birdman of Alcatraz'.)

While the Department of Justice hoped that by sending to Alcatraz less than 1 per cent of the Federal prison population the other 99 per cent could serve their sentences in relative peace and quite, the Department clearly did not expect Alcatraz to become the highest-profile prison in American history. Alcatraz came to be the standard by which all high-security prisons in America are measured, in part because of its dramatic location — a rocky island, often fog-shrouded and looking quite forbidding, yet in full view of the citizens of one of the country's major cities. In addition, the Bureau of Prisons put into place, before Alcatraz received its first prisoners, a policy which denied all newspaper reporters, magazine writers, journalists and media representatives access to the island, the prison and the inmates. To lock up the country's most notorious gangsters, bank robbers, kidnappers, escape artists, and prison hell-raisers in one small prison called 'The Rock' and to then deny the press and the public any information about how Capone, Kelly, 'The Birdman', and all the rest were getting along, created a public relations problem which occupied the time and attention of the Bureau of Prisons' officials for 30 years.

It is a commentary on the complexities of the interaction between government policies and the perceptions of those policies by the public, the press and some criminal justice professionals that when two or three hundred men with the most serious records of criminal violence in the country are concentrated in one prison it is not the prisoners but the prison that provokes controversy. During the past five decades, first at Alcatraz and now at its replacement, USP Marion, representatives of the news media appear to shift from an interest in what the inmates in these prisons have done to the citizens, their fellow prisoners or to prison employees and concentrate more on what the staff and regimen of these prisons are doing to the inmates. There are a number of reasons for this shift, including the drama reported in the press and portrayed in films and on television that is associated with life in end-of-the-road penitentiaries such as San Quentin, Stateville and Attica. But Alcatraz and Marion receive even more critical attention than the well-known state prisons because the Federal government is perceived to represent the state-of-the-art in penal policy and practice while at the same time taking care to protect the constitutional rights of the prisoners. The Bureau of Prisons, by virtue of taking on the responsibility of managing the nation's most recalcitrant prisoners, has thus taken on a special obligation to succeed where others have failed.

Alcatraz, from the day it opened with the dramatic transfer of the nation's gang lords and desperadoes by special armoured trains, from which the prisoners never disembarked until they were loaded on barges and deposited at the dock on the island, generated a massive number of rumours, unending speculation and always sensational reporting. Escape attempts, inmate protests, prison killings, suicides, and the famous 'Battle of Alcatraz', which brought guards from other prisons and military forces to the island in 1946, produced dramatic press reports and trial testimony about the rigours of doing time on 'The Rock'. Alcatraz convicts were always happy to tell all when they were finally transferred to other prisons and then released on parole or discharged and Alcatraz quickly became known as 'Hellcatraz', 'The Rock of Despair', and 'America's Devil's Island'. According to court testimony and inmate accounts, the spartan regimen on the island was turning the most hardened convicts into 'the living dead', with many prisoners becoming candidates for mental hospitals. From the day it opened Alcatraz was always under attack, but as the medical model of corrections emerged during the 1950s the pressure on the Bureau of Prisons to discontinue its policy of concentrating all of its rotten apples in one barrel rapidly increased. Finally, in the early 1960s the critics found the ally they needed in a new Attorney-General, Robert F. Kennedy. With the most visible and controversial prison in America sitting in the middle of California, the state in which the new treatment philosophy was most completely implemented, and with the senior official of the Department of Justice opposed to the image of Federal 'corrections' presented by 'The Rock', the Bureau of Prisons returned to the policy of dispersing its problem prisoners. By the end of March 1963, all of the Alcatraz inmates had gone back to Leavenworth, Atlanta, and other Federal penitentiaries.

During the late 1950s and early 1960s, however, racial violence had been building in Federal prisons. Because violence and escape attempts were still a reality, as Alcatraz was emptied, a new maximum-security prison located on a wildlife refuge in rural Marion, Illinois, came on-line. Initially USP Marion was intended to house the most disruptive young prisoners from throughout the Federal system, not the older, seasoned convicts who had been sent to Alcatraz. Additionally, the Alcatraz inmates were regarded as representing too severe a test for a new prison — the security system, new staff and operational procedures needed to be broken in with a more tractable group of prisoners. Thus when the first inmates were transferred to Marion in 1964, only ten men from Alcatraz were included. Most of the Alcatraz inmates adapted without serious problems to life in Leavenworth and Atlanta, prompting the Alcatraz staff to point out that although some of the inmates had not spent the usual time on the island, even a partial dose of the regimen there had had beneficial effects. By the late 1960s however, the Bureau of Prisons began to transfer to Marion some of the Alcatraz inmates who did not 'adjust' elsewhere.

Marion began to receive older and more sophisticated prisoners with records of violence in and out of prison, and in 1973 the Bureau began to return to the policy of concentration not by placing the most disruptive inmates in just one prison but in a special unit, or Control Unit, at Marion. The purpose of the Control Unit was 'to separate those offenders whose behaviour seriously disrupted the orderly operation of an institution from the vast majority of offenders who wish to participate in regular institutional programs' (Bureau of Prisons Policy Statement 5212-1, June 1983). In 1978 the Bureau began to implement a new inmate classification system which called for the addition of a new higher security classification level to the levels already in place, and in 1979 Marion became the Bureau's only 'level 6' penitentiary. Marion's purpose was now to provide long-term segregation within a highly controlled setting for inmates from throughout the Federal system who:

(i) threatened or injured other inmates or staff;
(ii) possessed deadly weapons or dangerous drugs;
(iii) disrupted 'the orderly operation of a prison';

(iv) escaped or attempted to escape in those instances in which the escape involved injury, threat of life or use of deadly weapons.

The decision to establish Marion as a super-maximum-security penitentiary was influenced by a number of events including a series of gang-related killings at the Atlanta Penitentiary, the growing power of gangs in other prisons including the creation of 'assassination squads', an increased number of assaults upon inmates and staff at levels 4 and 5 prisons, the violent deaths of three inmates at Marion in a one-year period, a series of escape attempts at Marion involving the use of weapons, explosives, and outside assistance (in one case a hijacked helicopter and in another a hijacked aeroplane), and the stabbing of the Associate Warden and the Food Service Steward in the inmate dining room at Marion. Furthermore, during the late 1970s, years in which the inmate population in the Federal system had been declining, the rate of assaults, particularly upon staff, was increasing. In the period between January 1978 and June 1979 there were 25 homicides, 536 inmate-on-inmate assaults and 344 assaults upon staff.

A 1979 Federal Bureau task force on Marion concluded that the need to reduce violence in the Federal prison system superseded all other considerations:

> It is of paramount importance to note that this proposal, proactive in approach, is designed to greatly reduce incidents such as those above, both at Marion and other facilities. All other considerations at this point are secondary. Once implemented, other factors relating to programs or work would be considered. A distinct advantage of creating a closed-unit operation at Marion is that other institutions would be able to remove from their populations the violent, assaultive, and disruptive inmates who require the stringent controls that Marion would possess. This should enhance programming capabilities at other institutions (Henderson 1979, pp. 6–7).

When the Bureau concluded that placing the most recalcitrant and difficult inmates in the Federal system in one place would allow other prisons to operate more openly, and that the new 'strictly controlled movement procedures' at Marion should produce a safer environment for inmates in that prison, the return to the Alcatraz model was complete, a fact recognised by newspaper reporters and journalists whose articles about Marion were inevitably titled, 'The New Alcatraz'. The Bureau's team reviewing this policy change was aware, however, that having changed the function of Marion at a time when the Bureau's population of violence-prone offenders was climbing, and as more of the states gave up on their efforts to control their most unruly prisoners and sent them on to the Federal system, serious problems might well develop in the future:

> The leadership of the Federal Prison System — at Marion, at the Regional level, and in the Central Office — will never accept violence and intimi-

dation as a norm for Marion, or any other facility. However, there must be a realistic acknowledgement that the type of inmates now confined there can, through a variety of ingenious methods, still perpetrate assaults, attempt escapes, and otherwise disrupt institutional operations under even the most stringently monitored circumstances. These problems can be anticipated as a result of the decision to concentrate this population at one facility; Marion will not be violence free, simply because of the type of inmate housed there. In fact, unless properly managed on a day-to-day basis Marion contends with a population which presents the potential for the most serious prison disturbance in our System's history. (Program and Procedure Review, USP Marion, 2-5 November 1981, pp. 6-7).

In the early 1980s Marion did in fact experience the difficulties that had been anticipated. During the period from February 1980 to June 1983, along with 14 attempted escapes and ten group disturbances, there were 54 serious inmate-on-inmate assaults, eight inmates were killed by other prisoners, and there were 28 serious assaults on staff members.

The frequency and seriousness of assaults on inmates and employees at Marion accelerated during the summer and autumn of 1983. In July an institution-wide search following an assault on an officer turned up 79 home-made knives. In September an inmate was killed and others were stabbed; two officers were taken hostage in the disciplinary segregation unit and one of them was stabbed; two officers were attacked as they escorted a group of inmates in the prison's main corridor, one of the officers was stabbed 12 times; in other incidents an officer was assaulted by an inmate wielding a mop-wringer and a chair and another was attacked as he went to the aid of an inmate being assaulted by three other prisoners. On 22 October 1983, in two separate incidents in the Control Unit, two officers were stabbed to death and several others were injured. Four days later another inmate was killed and four inmates attacked several officers in the prison's main corridor. Six days later a state of emergency was declared and USP Marion was placed on lockdown status — a status which continues to the present.

The Bureau of Prisons has reported a decrease in assaults in other prisons which it attributes to the deterrent effect of Marion. It should be noted that of the 373 inmates present at Marion on 28 October 1983, 236 have subsequently been transferred to other prisons; only eight of these inmates have engaged in misconduct serious enough to warrant their return to Marion. As Marion has assumed its special role as the administrative segregation prison for the Federal system, the average time served at the prison has dropped from four years in the early 1980s to some 27 months. Confinement in USP Marion should thus be seen as occupying only a small segment of the rather long sentences most of the inmates will be serving in the Federal prison system. But if confinement at USP Marion is, in fact, so unpleasant that it actually exercises a deterrent influence on other inmates, the Bureau is likely to continue to have public relations problems and continuing litigation over conditions in 'the new Alcatraz'.

Prisoner's rights under a lockdown regimen

A review of the events that followed the imposition of the lockdown at Marion is beyond the scope of this paper (see Ward and Breed 1986), but it is important that readers outside the United States understand the significant role that the American Federal courts play in listening to complaints from prisoners and their lawyers and then specifying basic living conditions and the rights of inmates in all prisons, including high-security prisons and the Control Units within those prisons. For five decades level 6 inmates have been suing the Bureau of Prisons. The inmates at Alcatraz had filed some 1,900 petitions, appeals, motions, writs of mandamus, and other legal challenges *before* the Federal courts decided that prisoners' constitutional rights followed them into prison. When the Federal courts moved away in the mid 1960s from the 'hands off' doctrine by which judges left all matters of prison management to the judgment and discretion of wardens and Department of Corrections officials, a body of case law began to accumulate which has specified for state and Federal prison administrators the basic rights of prisoners as the courts have interpreted those rights ensured by various sections of the United States Constitution. Particularly relevant are those sections which prohibit 'cruel and unusual' punishment and specify that 'due process' procedures must govern decision-making processes such as the determination of guilt or innocence, the granting and revocation of parole, disciplinary actions, the assignment of custody levels, and transfers between prisons. At USP Marion, for example, the Federal District Court of Southern Illinois had, prior to the October 1983 lockdown, prohibited windowless doors in the disciplinary segregation unit and mandated at least one hour of exercise per day for each inmate. Since inmates at Marion and at all other prisons already have constitutionally protected rights which cover basic living conditions from health services to diet, the most recent complaints by the prisoners have related to staff actions during and following the imposition of the lockdown. Recent complaints have alleged unfair and improper restrictions on inmates' visiting privileges, their right to have access to lawyers and to legal materials and to religious counsel and religious rituals. Cases alleging violations of inmates' rights reach the Federal courts as a result of suits or petitions filed by individual inmates or by groups of inmates, by legal actions filed by inmates' privately-retained attorneys, and by legal aid groups such as the Marion Prisoners' Rights Group, and the National Prison Project of the American Civil Liberties Union. In addition, oversight authority over prisoners' civil liberties is maintained by the Civil Rights Division of the US Department of Justice and the Committees on the Judiciary of the United States Senate and the House of Representatives.

Although litigation over the past two decades has specified most of the basic elements of confinement for all American prisons, some 37 states are currently either operating under judicial decrees or are in the Federal courts contesting such issues as overcrowding, the presence of women officers (inmate privacy), and the responsibility of prison administrations to protect inmates from physical and sexual assault. With most aspects of confinement, including confinement in the Control Unit, already litigated and with the lockdown in place for more than two years, it is not surprising that inmates at Marion and their lawyers have sought to alter the conditions of confinement on a new basis, namely the contention that negative mental health consequences accrue to the lockdown regimen. This avenue had already been opened through a series of cases involving Marion inmates dating back to 1978 in which the local Federal Distict Court itself evidenced concern about the mental health consequences of long-term confinement in the Control Unit. In this complicated area where one must distinguish between mental health problems brought to a prison or the Control Unit by an inmate as distinct from problems precipitated by the conditions of confinement, judges, lawyers, and prison administrators are at present basing their judgments on their instincts, their own life experiences and their own values, not upon any body of empirical evidence which speaks to this issue. It is remarkable that for one of the most serious problems confronting correctional system managers, prison staff and inmates in the United States so little is known about any of the effects of long-term confinement in high-security prisons. In a later section we shall take note of several recent studies which have addressed this important topic, and we will link psychological adaptation to long-term confinement to the ready access prisoners at Marion and other high-security prisons have to lawyers and legal actions as a means of protesting against the actions of those who seek to control them. Before this issue is addressed, however, the directions in which two state prison systems are moving along the concentration–dispersion dimension merit attention.

California: back to dispersal

During the early 1960s a spirit of optimism pervaded the California

Department of Corrections. Influenced by experimental programmes developed for the military to deal with a range of psychological problems from combat fatigue to the effects of confinement in prisoner-of-war camps, and by new approaches to the treatment of the mentally ill (particularly the therapeutic community concept pioneered by Dr Maxwell Jones at Belmont Hospital in London) the field of 'corrections' emerged from the field of penology. As prisons became 'correctional institutions', as prisoners became 'residents', and as guards became 'correctional officers', the new purpose of imprisonment became the rehabilitation of offenders. California officials embraced the theory that psychologically based treatment programmes such as group counselling and 'community living' could 'correct' deficiencies in educaton and job training as well as impairments in psychosexual and superego development. Criminal law violators would have their problems diagnosed by mental health experts, treatment would be applied and the experts, through intermediate sentences, would allow 'residents' to be released when rehabilitation had occurred. So great was the optimism about the positive functions of imprisonment that most of the major remedial and psychologically based intervention programmes were subjected to evaluation by outside researchers invited in to study departmental programmes. As the results of these treatment evaluation studies in California and in other parts of the country began to gain attention, and as minority prisoners defined themselves not as persons who had problems with authority figures but as persons whose problems emanated from discriminatory practices imposed by an oppressive majority, a sense, first, of disappointment, and then of despair, became attached to the concept of rehabilitation. Legislators and other elected officials began to pay serious attention to the argument that it was not only naive but dangerous to assume that confinement in any penitentiary could be a positive experience for the 'residents'. Furthermore, the treatment programme evaluation studies conducted in California and elsewhere, and summarised in Robert Martinson (1974), were cited by elected officials as evidence that the costs clearly exceeded the benefits derived from hiring large numbers of expensive prison staff — psychiatrists, psychologists, and social workers — and running expensive programmes. Imprisonment, it was argued, would always be a negative experience and it should therefore be the penal sanction of last resort for those whose law violations involved crimes against persons, persistent criminality or involvement in organised criminal groups and organisations; the majority of offenders, that is, property offenders, should be diverted from the prisons to alternative programmes. California pioneered the implementation of the concept of 'community corrections' by establishing a 'probation subsidy' programme which paid counties to keep all but the violent and repetitive offenders in local institutions, organisations and programmes. The effect of this change in penal policy on the population of the state prisons was of course profound. A comparison of the commitment offences of prisoners in the California prison population in 1963 and in 1980 shows that the proportion convicted of crimes against persons — homicide, assault, rape and robbery — increased from 37 per cent to 61 per cent, while property and drug-law commitments dropped accordingly. With a higher proportion of person offenders came an increase in the proportion of minority inmates (from 45 per cent in 1963 to 60 per cent in 1980) and prisoners serving longer sentences. As the state prison population dropped sharply from 28,600 in 1969 to 21,000 in 1971, violence in the prisons increased sharply. A special 'Report to Governor Ronald Reagan on violence in California prisons' was prepared by the Board of Corrections in 1971 after four prison officers were killed in separate incidents at Soledad Prison and four officers were killed at San Quentin (three inmates were also killed at Soledad and three were killed at San Quentin). Of particular concern to California officials was the increase in violence directed towards prison staff. From 1953 to 1970 only four employees had been killed by inmates, but during 1970 and the first nine months of 1971 nine staff members were killed. California constructed four high-security 'adjustment centres' within the prisons at Soledad, San Quentin, Folsom and at a youth prison. In 1980 a new classification system went into effect which concentrated the most serious management problems in the system at San Quentin and Folsom. When violence continued, lockdowns of the entire prison for months at a time were implemented for the 3,000 inmates at San Quentin and a new 'Security Housing Unit' (SHU) was established at Folsom in which upwards of 600 of the prison's 3,000 inmates were continually 'locked down', with lockdowns sometimes ordered for the entire prison.

Despite these measures, the rate of assaults on staff per 100 average institution population doubled from 0.89 in 1978 to 1.73 in 1984. The number of 'incidents' (assaults by inmates on other inmates and staff, possesion of weapons, narcotics use and/or possession, sex between inmates, sexual assaults by inmates on staff, successful and unsuccessful suicides and miscellaneous actions) increased from 366 in 1970 to 2,060 in 1978 and to 5,105 in 1984, with the rate per 100 average institution population increasing from 1.36 to 10.07 and 12.73 for the same years. Sixteen California prisoners were killed in 1984, 91 attempted suicide and 18 succeeded.

In June 1985 legislative hearings were held to investigate the factors behind the 120 stabbings that had occurred during the first six months of that year at Folsom Prison, a prison referred to as the 'Beirut of California' because of the warfare involving various factions and gangs. The report on the hearings (Joint Legislative Committee on Prison Construction and Operations 1985) recommended that gang members be separated from the rest of the inmate population and then 'dispersed throughout the prison system rather than concentrating them in one or two institutions' (p. iii). Other security-orientated recommendations included changing or eliminating the classification system which produced the overcrowding and concentration of problem inmates in San Quentin and Folsom, hastening the construction of new prisons, instituting more effective searches of visitors for drugs and other contraband (including 'random searches of visitors' autos') and limiting lockdowns to targeted segments rather than locking down entire prison populations. On the other hand, the gravity of the situation at Folsom prompted the Joint Legislative Committee (1985, pp. iii-vii) to propose some new and rather different approaches to the problem including the following:

— Establishing inmate participation policies; these could include:
    (a) a degree of inmate self-government;
    (b) inmate-owned and operated industries;
— Discontinuing double celling;
— Building inmate-designed and constructed facilities in order to cut construction costs and to provide inmates with jobs;
— Establishing better inmate–administration communication;
— Conducting 'face-to-face' grievance inquiries since many prisoners have difficulty expressing their complaints in writing;
— Promoting frequent contact between staff, wardens, and inmates through shared meals, dormitory meetings, and 'logged in' cell block visits by wardens;
— Including inmates in the grievance review process;
— Establishing new policies which would allow inmates to make the transition from prison life to community life; these policies could include:
    (a) allowing families to live with inmates at work camps;
    (b) permitting conjugal visits;
    (c) authorizing inmate-owned and operated industries with parolees acting as outside sales representatives;
    (d) giving inmates a measure of self-government in order to foster responsibility.

Because legislators could not get answers from the Department of Corrections representatives or other witnesses to basic questions about the relationship between rehabilitation and recidivism; the comparative quality of life in different penal institutions; whether older inmates have a 'moderating influence' on younger prisoners; the impact of inmates on the communities to which they return; and the relationship between prison-based and community-based gangs, the Joint Committee urged the establishment of a research institute within the University of California to study such issues so that policies could be based upon empirical data.

The Folsom report (Joint Legislative Committee 1985, p. A17) concluded:

> Folsom Prison is operating under chaotic conditions. The greater the security measures imposed, the greater the amount of violence.
>
> Housing warring inmates of different races and gangs in the same cell blocks and on the same cell tiers is not a rational approach. It is akin to forcing integration among the Catholics and Protestants in Northern Ireland, or the Christians and the Moslems in Lebanon.
>
> Reducing the population does not seem to be a workable solution. For example, since January 1, 1985, the prison's population has been reduced by over *400* inmates, yet violence has continued to sky rocket.
>
> Institution lockdowns over extended time periods appear equally fruitless.
>
> Without question, the time to develop and employ more effective management methods at Folsom is long overdue. To continue to utilize the same failed means of more restricted lockdowns and ever greater security controls will only make matters worse.

As California officials consider dispersing problem prisoners and Federal Bureau of Prisons officials contend that concentration, with all of its attendant difficulties, is bringing violence in Federal prisons under control, the state of Minnesota has recently opened a new maximum-security prison which allows for concentration and dispersion within the same prison.

Minnesota: new generation management in a new generation prison

In February 1976 a Joint House–Senate Committee of the Minnesota Legislature released a report, *The Minnesota State Prison*, which was the product of a year-long investigation of killings, suicides and other violence at the state prison at Stillwater. Between 1968 and 1973 no homicides were reported at the prison, then one occurred in 1974 and three in 1975; there were no suicides at the prison between 1968 and 1970 but there was one in 1971, two in 1972 along with two deaths from drug overdoses; there were four suicides in 1973 and four more in 1974. Between October 1973 and October 1975 there were 91 assaults by inmates on staff members, 43 reported inmate-on-inmate assaults, 75 inmates charged with possession of weapons and three attempted escapes. Inmates told investigators that they were fearful of homosexual rape and that they were subject to shakedowns for money, commissary and personal items. The power of the prison gangs was demonstrated by the murder of an inmate about to inform on drug trafficking while he was locked up for 'protection' in the prison's disciplinary segregation unit. The legislative inquiry concluded that the prison was unsafe for both staff and inmates; that employees, as well as most inmates, were afraid to go into certain areas of the prison; that low staff morale accounted for the high turnover of employees; and that the state could no longer control all of its adult male felons in an antiquated fortress prison. (With most of the Stillwater's 800 inmates living in two huge five-storey cell blocks, staff supervision could never be sufficient and when only a segment of the inmate population was to be punished all the inmates had to be similarly punished because there were no alternative housing units.) The Joint Committee concluded that the state needed at least two new facilities to allow the adult felon population to be divided up in terms of both criminal record and prison conduct. It was ultimately concluded that a new high-security prison should be constructed, with Stillwater Prison to be remodelled into a medium-security facility. It should be noted, however, that in 1976 a new Commissioner of Corrections placed a new warden in charge of Stillwater Prison with a mandate to take control of the prison. Within the next several years, systematic, random lockups and shakedowns of the prison and a new management philosophy succeeded in making the prison a much safer place for inmates and employees (see Ward *et al.* 1979). If the legislators had known that control could be re-established in the old prison they might not have appropriated $31 million for a new prison, but funds had already been appropriated and construction was under way by 1978. A new classification system to sort out the state's population of male felons into four prisons became operational and, in 1983, the new high-security facility at Oak Park Heights began to receive prisoners. (Stillwater was remodelled but continues to be a maximum-security prison.)

The new prison should, however, be seen in the context of other key correctional policy initiatives undertaken by the Commissioner of Corrections, Kenneth Schoen, who moved on a number of fronts that impacted on the state prison population including the implementation of a Community Corrections Act that diverted all but violent and persistent offenders into county facilities and programmes. A new system, called 'sentencing guidelines', replaced the indeterminate sentencing system, specified who would go to prison and for how long, and placed a cap on the number of persons who could be committed to the state prison system. (If the population began to reach a stated number sentence lengths would be reduced so that crowding beyond 'programme capacity' would not occur.) As in California, these policies have had a profound effect on the state prison population in terms of the commitment offences of the inmates (few property offenders), the fact that longer terms are to be served, and the increased proportion of minority offenders.

The population at Oak Park Heights is comprised of some 350 inmates including 30 'management problems' transferred from the overcrowded Wisconsin state prison system, ten inmates who were control problems in other states and some 25 'level 5 and 6' Federal prisoners, most of whom have been at USP Marion. Almost all of the Minnesota state prisoners at Oak Park Heights have been convicted of crimes against persons: 33 per cent are serving time for homicide, 16 per cent for robbery, 9 per cent for assault, 23 per cent for sex offences and 3 per cent for kidnapping; the Minnesota prisoners are 55 per cent white, 33 per cent black, 8 per cent Indian and 4 per cent Hispanic. Since the prison began receiving inmates in March 1983, no inmates or employees have been killed, no assaults on staff have required hospitalisation, and there have been only superficial injuries to inmates in four incidents in which weapons were used. Less serious assaults involving inmates, meaning physical altercations, average about five per month and about three incidents per month involve staff. There have been no Federal court orders issued in regard to any aspect of confinement at Oak Park Heights, there have been no investigations by the Minnesota Civil Liberties Union, by the National Prison Project or by two other organisations which represent inmates, Legal Aid to Minnesota Prisoners and the Legal Aid Center.

The physical setting and physical plant at Oak Park Heights reflect the mandate of Commissioner Schoen that the new prison should not be offensive to the environment or to nearby residents, that it allow for a variety of programme options (including the possibility that one of the units might house long-term women offenders and that some inmates might have private, that is conjugal, visiting privileges), and that it not replicate the traditional symbols of state prisons such as high walls and gun towers. A creative architect and the fortuitous location of a tract of state-owned land located on the river bluffs overlooking Stillwater produced a unique, earth-sheltered, modular design in which up to 400 prisoners can be housed in seven completely separate and self-contained units.[1]

While visitors are impressed by the obviously different physical appearance of Oak Park Heights, what is also significant is the management style and philosophy of Frank Wood, the same warden who brought order and control to Stillwater Prison in spite of its antiquated physical plant. Oak Park Heights operates with a variety of programme components for inmates housed in its various units — there are industries units in which some inmates can make up to $400 per month, there is an education unit for those going to school, a mental health unit, a unit with treatment programmes for those sex offenders and chemically dependent inmates who wish to participate in them (participation has no effect on length of time served under the fixed sentence system) and a control unit with specific periods of confinement for those inmates who are assaultive or found to be engaging in drug trafficking or in violation of other prison rules.

The Joint Committee report on Folsom Prison included the recommendation that the Warden make routine tours of the prison rather than staying in his office. At Oak Park Heights, the Warden spends 25 per cent or more of his time 'eyeball-to-eyeball' with inmates and employees. Most new inmates transferred in for disciplinary reasons are first greeted by the Warden when they are in holding cells prior to being sent to one of the units. The Warden personally conducts the last meeting of the orientation for new inmates so that they understand their responsibilities and the prison's responsibilities to them. Staff members involved in physical confrontations with inmates must meet and talk out the hostility that naturally accrues to these events. Other elements of the Wood policy are that 'staff should treat the inmates as we would want our sons, brothers, or fathers treated'; that inmates who do not go to work or school will not be left free to watch television and 'roam around their units' but will be locked in their cells; that the response to inmate trouble-making will be individualised rather than punishing groups of inmates; that units will be locked up on a random but regular basis for three to four days to purge contraband; that every lock will be tested every day; that inmates will be kept very busy — that is, the staff will plan how the inmates spend their time; that staff always deliver promptly on inmate requests no matter how inconsequential the requests may appear; and that inmates in the Control Unit be periodically rotated into the Mental Health Unit for observation and a change of physical environment, as well as for a period of relief from nearby inmates and staff. While this description provides only a few examples of a rather different operating philosophy than would be expressed by the wardens of prisons in other states, it is intended to make the point that 'new generation' policies must accompany 'new generation' prison designs if safer and more positive environments are to be established in high-security prisons. Experience in another new generation prison in the state of Virginia demonstrates that physical environment, even the new modular construction, is no guarantee against violence, property destruction, and escape.

Oak Park Heights, it should be emphasised, does not contain the same type of inmate population as is housed at USP Marion. The Minnesota prisoners have committed violent offences but, with a few exceptions, they have not killed other inmates or prison staff, they do not have organised crime, major drug-ring or street-gang connections, and their escape records do not compare in frequency of attempts or degree of sophistication. Thirty-five per cent of the Marion prisoners have killed one or more inmates or employees in prison. Marion houses the leaders of major national and state prison and street gangs, as well as members of national and international drug rings which commit so much violence that a new term, 'narco-terrorism' has been coined to characterise their activities. While operations at USP Marion might be facilitated by the Oak Park Heights design, the management strategy at Oak Park Heights has not been tested on a Marion-type population. However, since the great majority of state prisons also do not contain Marion-type prisoners, Oak Park Heights offers a new model for most of the high-security prisons in America at a time when new models are badly needed. The challenge for the Federal Bureau of Prisons at USP Marion is to continue to try to experiment with programmes and procedures in the very prison where experimentation is most dangerous.[2]

Recent studies of the effects of imprisonment

A review by Bukstel and Kilmann (1980) of 90 experimental studies of the psychological effects of imprisonment (including solitary confinement) on performance, personality, and attitudinal variables concluded, as usual, that methodological flaws were found in many of the studies. Nevertheless, some notable findings appeared, including the following: 'Inmates in solitary confinement may not desire that time pass quickly, in that they may enjoy a break from the noisy, overcrowded main population environment' (Bukstel and Kilmann 1980, p. 474). 'An inmate's adjustment to prison may vary according to sentence phase and release date' (Bukstel and Kilmann 1980, p. 476). Also:

> Each individual who experiences prolonged confinement reacts to this situation in an idiosyncratic manner: some individuals show deterioration in response to confinement, and others show improved functioning, whereas others show no appreciable change. Intrainstitutional factors, such as institutional orientation, degree of crowding, and peer group

affiliation, may affect personal functioning during imprisonment. In addition, an inmate's psychological functioning may vary according to which phase of the sentence is being served and the time until the anticipated release date. Although this review was primarily concerned with the effects of intrainstitutional variables, such extraprison factors such as the degree of contact with the outside world and expectations concerning one's life after release also may influence one's adaptation. Overall, the evidence suggests that an inmate's response to confinement is determined by a complex interaction of variables. *Thus the findings do not unequivocally support the popular notion that correctional confinement is harmful to most individuals* (Bukstel and Kilmann 1980, p. 487, emphasis added).

After reviewing the research literature in connection with his own study of long-term offenders in New York state prisons, Flanagan (1982, p.116) concludes that efforts to document the presumed negative effects of long-term confinement have not yielded convincing supportive evidence: 'Regardless of the life area studied — whether physical degeneration, development of psychopathology, negative attitudinal change, or cognitive impairment — the portrait offered by these recent investigations is that long term confinement per se does not necessarily lead to damage to the person.'

In an important study conducted in three prisons for adult males in two north-eastern states, Goodstein (1979) examined the relationship between four inmate adaptations to imprisonment, including being rebellious and becoming institutionalised, and post-release adjustment. Goodstein (1979, pp. 265–6) concluded:

These results lend no credence to the widely held assumption that poor prison adjustment leads to difficulties after release. On the contrary, they indicate that the inmates who adjusted most successfully to a prison environment actually encountered the most difficulty making the transition from institutional life to freedom. Furthermore, it appears that the inmates who adjusted least to the formal institutional culture may have made the smoothest transition to community life. These findings raise questions about the validity of the conventional assumptions about the relationship between prisonization and post-release outcome.

Although these findings do not confirm predictions in the correctional literature, they parallel the conclusions of a number of studies of adjustment patterns of former mental patients released to community life. It appears that the prison, like the traditional mental hospital, does not prepare inmates for a successful transition to freedom through its routine administration of rewards and punishments. It is ironic that institutionalized inmates who accepted the basic structure of the prison, who were well adjusted to the routine, and who held more desirable prison jobs — in essence, those whom some might call model prisoners — had most difficulty adjusting to the outside world. Even more ironic is the fact that inmates who might have been called the troublemakers in prison seemed to have the fewest problems after release. Taken together, these findings provide a picture of the correctional institution as a place which reinforces the wrong kinds of behaviour if its goal is the successful future adjustment of its inmates. In the process of rewarding acquiescent and compliant behavior, the prison may, in fact, be reinforcing institutional dependence . . . It is possible that the rebellious inmates, the group scoring highest on the prisonization scale, adapted more easily to the outside world because they had maintained their autonomy and decision-making ability throughout their prison terms; this might account for the positive relationship found between prisonization and post-release success. One could argue that rebellious inmates, hostile to authorities in general, will eventually resume antisocial behaviors and thus will manifest higher recidivism rates in the long run. However, this study suggests that for a short time, at least, prisonization definitely is not a liability and may, indeed, be an asset in post-release adjustment.

The conclusions of these studies have been confirmed in a follow-up study conducted by the present author of 500 of the 1,550 inmates who served time at USP Alcatraz. Given the rigours of doing time on 'The Rock' and the almost unanimous judgment of criminologists, prison reformers, inmates, and many prison officials that the consequences of long-term confinement in this super-maximum-security prison would surely be negative, the results are surprising. Despite the fact that Alcatraz inmates were classified as 'habitual, intractable', that they served an average of 14 years on sentences that included approximately four years at Alcatraz, and that they had very extensive criminal careers, 49 per cent of the Alcatraz inmates did not return to prison and some 22 per cent were never reported for another arrest after release. An analysis of a wide variety of factors associated with post-release success and failure (return to prison as a parole violator or with a new term) indicated that, as expected, increased age was associated with post-release survival, although the return-to-prison rate increased for inmates who were over the age of 45 when released. Another significant correlation was found between the number of escape attempts and post-release adjustment — the more attempts, the less likely the success. Single factor correlations as well as regression and discriminant analyses indicate that a significant predictor of post-release success is the number of prison rules violations — but the direction of the prediction is unexpected — inmates with a moderate number of disciplinary reports (between five and ten) are more likely to succeed than inmates with under five reports or those with more than ten reports. Further analysis of the relationship between prison (mis)conduct throughout the inmate's entire prison sentence, that is pre- and post-Alcatraz time, as well as time spent at Alcatraz, and construction of a rate of prison rule violations that takes the seriousness of the infractions into account is under way. At this point, however, these findings, along with the analysis of mental health problems which indicate that the rate of transfer from Alcatraz for pyschiatric reasons to Federal medical centres (about 7 per cent), is the same rate found for a comparison group of Leavenworth inmates, suggest that contentions that long-term confinement, particularly in super-maximum-security prisons, will make inmates unfit for life in the free world and that serious mental health problems are likely to accompany this experience, must be questioned. The Alcatraz study indicates that resistance through a number of forms, including rule violations, may have a positive psychological function for inmates both in prison and after release. Good conduct in prison for this special group of prisoners is not an accurate predictor of successful adjustment in the free world. This finding will not be welcomed by prison officials, but a number of Federal prison wardens briefed on the Alcatraz study findings commented that they were not surprised when 'model prisoners' failed on the streets. The form of resistance at USP Marion in which inmates continually generate legal challenges to the Bureau of Prisons as well as to the courts on their convictions may satisfy, in a lawful way, the need for inmates to fight the regimen and control over them. Legal challenges stimulate thinking and reasoning, take up large amounts of time in an institution with limited activities, give inmates the satisfaction of challenging every aspect of confinement, and occasionally the satisfaction of convincing the courts that prison policies and individual sentences should be changed.

This research reaffirms the complexity of human behaviour and the need to examine empirically our criminal policy assumptions; it should also challenge correctional administrators and policy-makers to be creative in that area of prison administration when the stakes are highest because, in so many American prisons, the lives of inmates and employees and the safety of the citizens is on the line.

Notes

1 The planning process and key elements of this programme upon which the design of Oak Park Heights was based is described in a series of papers in Ward and Schoen (1981).

2 There are two models for innovative management being applied in Minnesota and the Federal Bureau of Prisons which also emphasise the difference in size of the two systems. There are some 2,500 inmates in five Minnesota prisons and more than 35,000 inmates in 46 Federal facilities. The Oak Park Heights management philosophy is a reflection of one person, Warden Frank Wood; the programme and policy at USP Marion reflect not only the management style of Warden Jerry Williford but also the significant and direct involvement of Director Norman Carlson, Assistant Director Gilbert Ingram, Regional Director George Wilkenson (a former warden at Marion) and other top management officials in Federal Bureau of Prisons headquarters.

References

Bukstel, L.H. and Kilmann, P.R. (1980), 'Psychological Effects of Imprisonment on Confined Individuals', *Psychological Bulletin*, vol. 88, pp. 469–93.

Flanagan, T.J. (1982), 'Lifers and Long-termers: Doing Big Time' in R. Johnson and H. Toch (eds), *The Pains of Imprisonment*, Beverly Hills, CA: Sage.

Goodstein, L. (1979), 'Inmate Adjustment to Prison and the Transition to Community Life', *Journal of Research in Crime and Delinquency*, vol. 16, pp. 246–72.

Henderson, J.D. (1979), *Marion Task Force Report*, (Internal report for the Federal Bureau of Prisons).

Martinson, R. (1974), 'What Works? Questions and Answers about Prison Reform', *The Public Interest*, vol. 36, pp. 22–54.

Sherman, M. and Hawkins, G. (1981), *Imprisonment in America*, Chicago: University of Chicago Press.

Joint Legislative Committee on Prison Construction and Operations (1985), *Violence at Folsom Prison: Causes, Possible Solutions*, Sacramento, CA: Joint Publications Office.

Ward, D.A. and Breed, A.F. (1986), 'The United States Penitentiary, Marion, Illinois' in *Marion Penitentiary 1985. Oversight Hearing Before the Subcommittee on Courts, Civil Liberties and the Administration of Justice of the Committee on the Judiciary, House of Representatives* (Ser. no. 26), Washington, DC: US Government Printing Office.

Ward, D.A., Milligan, H., Milligan, C.O. and Calabrese, A. (1979), *Technical Report, National Institute of Justice: Preliminary Study, Stillwater Prison. 1979: A Survey of Inmate and Staff Views of Personal Safety and Other Aspects of Living and Working in the Minnesota State Prison*, Washington, DC: US Department of Justice.

Ward, D.A. and Schoen, K.F. (eds) (1981), *Confinement in Maximum Custody*, Lexington, MA: D.C. Heath.

4 The concept of social control and its relevance to the prisons debate
Peter Young

The publication of the report of the Control Review Committee (CRC) (Home Office 1984) raises once again what has been called 'the hardy perennial' (Sykes 1958, p. vii) problem of the nature of the prison. If the Committee's recommendations are accepted, they would appear to be, for the policy-maker and the prison manager, the first steps in a transformation of the prison regime, indeed of the very architecture and fabric of the prison itself. For the academic penologist it raises an equally fundamental set of issues: for example, the report marks the final and clear end of the rehabilitative era. No direct appeal is made to the concept of rehabilitation as a possible justification of imprisonment and this alone makes the report of considerable interest. However, the most important set of issues touched upon concern the very subject-matter of the exercise — the problem of how to achieve and maintain control and order in the prison. Although the remit of the Committee limited its deliberations to a particular section of the population — long-term, adult males in the dispersal prison — the arguments advanced and the recommendations made are, as the report suggests, relevant to any penal establishment. In many ways we seem to be at what may be a turning point in prison management and history.

My task in this paper is not to examine in detail the policy recommendations the Committee make, for example, the feasibility of sentence-planning units; such an exercise is better left to those more experienced in the practical problems of administering the penal system. Rather, I wish to focus on the concepts which lie at the heart of the report — in particular that of control — and subject them to analysis; to question what is meant by them and how they are used. Although this involves stepping back from the immediacy of the debate surrounding the report, some of the things I say I do believe to be practical and therefore relevant to it.

This wider sort of analysis is important not only for further clarification but also, I intend to argue, because the meaning given to terms and the way in which they are used are bounded by preceding contexts. It is too easy to miss this point, with the consequence that we may ascribe to concepts 'common-sense' attributes which once examined turn out neither to make the sense we thought they did, nor this sense to be shared in common. To put this a different way, there may exist in any argument concepts which from our point of view (our context) seem to be unproblematic and clear in meaning but which others see as neither clear nor unproblematic. It becomes important, therefore, always to examine the relationship between contexts and concepts. One way of examining this inherent contextual limitation is to attempt to recover the intended meaning given it by the author. This does not involve our guessing at what the personal foibles of the author were or are, but rather in investigating the way in which a particular concept is used in the text; how it fits into its structure and the function it serves. By doing this we not only gain some idea of what is meant by the concept as it is used, but also the limitations of this usage. And, as a result, we end up with a better notion of the problem the author faced and we can also note what was included and what was left out.

My first task, therefore, becomes that of investigating what the CRC meant by control; how they used the term and the sense in which their usage restricts other possible ways of describing the problem. I will argue that the Committee worked with a restricted conception of control. This would not matter particularly if nothing hinged on it. However, it does matter because their conception of control leads, I will argue, to a limited idea of what can be achieved in prison; of how order can be maintained by control and therefore of how we can improve prisons both for those who work and those detained in them. To support this argument, I will use a wide body of sociological literature that discusses and describes social control and social order. This will mean looking at other institutions as well as the prison to see how order and control work in them. This is a justifiable explanatory strategy as one of the lessons of the existing body of sociological literature on the prison (most of which, it is worth pointing out, the Committee do not make reference to, for example, Clemmer 1940; Sykes 1958; Cressey 1961) is that prisons are not unique but share in common many features with other organisations and bureaucracies.

Before I begin this argument, two further qualifications. First, within sociology, the concepts of order and control are necessarily tied together in the sense that any type of order presupposes some form of control and vice versa. If follows therefore that making reference to one of these concepts invokes reference to the other — they are twinned. This seems to be implicit in the CRC report, although they rarely mention both at once. This is the reason why, in my introduction, it is argued that the CRC report raises the hardy perennial issue of how to achieve both in the prison. Second, although these concepts are twinned they are not to be confused or substituted one for the other. Order can be achieved by a variety of different means of control and, similarly, the use of a specific means of control does not mechanically result in the maintenance of a particular type of order. Thus, although there is a necessary conceptual linkage between the two, the actual empirical or real-world relationship is various and contingent. Unfortunately, as Gurvitch (1945) noted, this distinction between conceptual linkage and empirical contingency is often not made. This can lead to an exaggerated emphasis on the applied mechanics of social control, without any or very little attention being given to what control is for — what type of order one is seeking.

What does the CRC mean by control and order?

It is surprising in a report devoted to the problems of achieving better control and order in the prison that no explicit definition of these terms is offered. This may well be because the Committee reasoned that all those who read the report, or who are interested in the problem, will share a very similar view of it, so the need for explicit discussion and definition was beside the point. While, in some ways, this may be a reasonable assumption to make, it does carry with it certain risks. The 'reasonableness' of the assumption depends upon whether one views it from the practical or socio-logical point of view (not that there is necessarily a gap between them). From the practical point of view it is probably the case that the immediate audience at which the report was aimed — policy-makers and prison managers — would take the same view of the problem. Indeed, the method by which this report, like most govern-mental ones, was produced — the gathering of evidence from inter-ested witnesses — guarantees this to be the case. This is especially true when the majority of the witnesses who submitted written or gave oral evidence (see Home Office 1984, Appendices 1 and 2 to Annex B, pp. 46–8) were prison governors or prison officers. Also, because it is precisely this type of audience that will implement its recommendations if they are accepted, then again it can be seen as 'reasonable' that the Committee did not feel the need to define explicitly what they meant by control.

From the sociological point of view there are problems with approaching the issue in this way which make it seem less reasonable. First, the report does not reflect, because it did not take into account, evidence from the inmate population. As the Committee recognises at various points in their report (Home Office 1984, paras 16, 22–35, 89–108), inmates have a legitimate interest or 'stake' in the maintenance of a peaceful, orderly prison. In many ways their 'stake' is as great, if not greater, than the staff's as they have to live within it more intensively for the period of their incarceration. Yet their view is not represented, nor, from the list of witnesses, was it a category of evidence after which the Committee sought. It is quite fundamental, from the perspective of a sociological analysis of order and control, that one investigates it from all 'sides'. One result of this may be to press home the need to recognise the argument made above, that order can be achieved in a variety of ways by a variety of different controls; control, even in the prison, as I think the Committee recognises (see especially, Home Office 1984, para. 16), is a negotiable thing. The Committee has produced, as it were, a blueprint for industrial relations without recognising one side of the bargain.

It would not be a legitimate defence either to argue that the Committee was not engaged in a research project or that it is impractical and naive to suggest that inmates be 'polled' about how they wish prisons to be run and this to be represented in an official report. The first response would not be accurate because by taking evidence from governors and other officials the Committee was, albeit in a rudimentary sense, 'researching' the issue. All that is being suggested is that their 'population' should have been extended. The second response may reflect a political reality but it does so at the expense of denying the problem both conceptually and on the ground. It also misrepresents the case. One is not suggesting a plebiscite in prisons, rather the point is an analytical one about the nature of control and order and should be recognised as that and that alone.

As it stands, the CRC report did not, for understandable, if somewhat shaky, reasons see it as either necessary to take into account inmates' views on order and control or to offer an explicit definition of control. These two are related because, it is suggested, if the first of these tasks had been undertaken then the second might also have been. Staff and inmates may well share, in principle, similar ideas of an orderly prison as a peaceful, harmonious place, but could well differ on how this is best achieved (that is, on methods of control). With this as their context, the Committee might have seen a case to exist for more explicitly defining and discussing what is meant by control. My argument is that it did neither of these things and I propose therefore to call its implicit description of control a 'managerial' one. By this it is meant that it describes control from a managerial perspective. It is this perspective that forms the contextual limitation of its usage of the concepts of control and order.

The 'managerial' perspective

The CRC offers an analysis of order and control stressing three components:

> (i) Disorder and breakdowns in control are caused by the structure and organisation of the present dispersal system; the system sends contradictory messages to inmates, there is a clash between security and control requirements, there is inadequate sentence planning, and the architecture of existing prisons is seen to box in the debate.
>
> (ii) There exists a certain category of mentally disturbed inmates who, presumably, will always pose a problem and therefore there is a need for units to exist to handle them.
>
> (iii) At the heart of the problem, order and control depend upon staff–inmate relationships. All is seen to 'flow from getting that relationship right. Prisons cannot be run by a coercion' (Home Office 1984, para. 16).

If we examine these as categories then it is clear that they are quite different from one another. The second, referring to disturbed inmates, is in some ways extrinsic to the question of how an improvement in management or in resource allocation can lead to a more orderly prison. This should not be taken to mean that these types of inmate could not be better handled by the system so as to lessen their potentially problematic impact on the prison, but rather that the reasons for their sometimes disorderly behaviour lie outwith the prison. The prison receives this type of inmate and responds reactively to them. Presumably these inmates will be a potential source of disorder under any regime, however it is managed, short of continually isolating and segregating them, which I think the Committee rejects.

The other two categories do have certain things in common, but, it is suggested, are also different. Where they are similar is that they both see the maintenance and breakdown of control and order as being generated by pressure within the prison. The first stresses, broadly speaking, the organisational and resource criteria that are tied up with order and control; the third, the human and social context. What the Committee suggests is that mismanagement of either or both can 'cause' disorder and a breakdown in control. Inasmuch as these are coloured by pressures arising purely within the prison, then the solution to mismanagement is to restructure them within the prison walls.

In its recommendations, the Committee places by far the greatest weight on restructuring within the first category, that is, the restructuring of organisation and resources. The scope covered is immense, ranging, as we noted, from what they see as the immediately achievable, such as the setting up of sentence-planning units, or the reopening of a Parkhurst 'C' wing type of unit, to the more long term, such as the building of 'new generation' prisons, which it hopes will be the beginning of the end of the dispersal system.

There are two points to be made. It is because of the weight placed upon restructuring organisation and resources, in addition to those reasons mentioned earlier, that this perspective on control and order is called managerial. Although the Committee's analysis of control recognises staff–inmate relationships to be the irreducible foundation upon which all rests, it nevertheless gives priority to the manipulation of the physical environment of the prison (its organisation and resources). This I see as a species of managerialism.

My second observation is that, while there is a connection between resources and human and social relationships, the nature of this connection is far from clear. What needs to be further spelt out is how the manipulation of resources will lead to the improvement of human and social relationships in the prison. This question is raised not to deny that there is a connection between the two — there is, for example, a substantial body of research literature that shows 'environment', the organisation of physical space, to be crucial. Rather, my point is that it would take a very brave (some may say foolhardy) social scientist to claim that we know enough to be sure that *a* certain change in environment *necessarily* leads to a *particular* desired result. Now this is not simply because we 'do not know enough'; it is not just a problem of the state of our knowledge. What our knowledge of organisations does tell us is that it is insufficient to analyse them only from the point of view of resource management.

For example, one of the findings of the earlier sociological studies of the prison (Clemmer 1940; Sykes 1958; Cressey 1961) was that one cannot hope to reach an understanding of these institutions 'if the researcher confines his attention to organisational charts and official lines of command' (Cressey 1961, p. v). The formal aspects of the organisation (its declared purpose, its lines of command, and so on) were seen as an insufficient basis upon which to describe how order is maintained. All organisations, not just prisons, give rise to various informal practices that can modify or even displace (goal displacement, as it was sometimes called) the formal aspects. With regard to the prisons, the most notorious of these informal aspects was the discovery of the 'inmate subculture', and the collusive role of the staff in recognising and helping to maintain it (Sykes 1958; Cressey 1961).

The significance of these observations is that they lead to the

conclusions that order in the prison depends upon the social relationships (the inmate subculture; staff–inmate relationships) which arise,
as much if not more than it does upon their formal structure. Disturbances and riots occur when for some reason the precarious balance
which these informal social relationships establish becomes disturbed
(Sykes 1958; King and Elliott 1977).

While it may be argued that these early studies of the prison
laid too much emphasis on the informal aspects of prison at the
expense of the formal, they nevertheless can be seen to have highlighted two fundamentally important considerations. First, no matter
what the proper balance between formal and informal aspects is,
any account of how order and control are achieved and maintained
must investigate these informal patterns of behaviour. Without them,
the account is incomplete and partial because the concepts of order
and control are partial. Second, these studies established the need
to see the prison as a 'total social system'. By this it is meant that
one must look at the prison as a sort of small-scale society in itself.
Each part must be related to the whole if a proper understanding
of the institution is to be achieved. It follows that undue concentration on either the problem of resource allocation and organisational
restructuring, or on what we have called the informal aspects of
staff–inmate and inmate subcultural relationships, is inadequate. To
understand and explain the nature of order and control we must
work at all these different analytical levels. Now it does not follow
that any policy recommendations must similarly operate at all of
these levels at once, but what is clear is that these levels form the
context within which proposed solutions are constrained.

There are, of course, different ways of dealing with and reacting
to these necessarily imposed constraints. The policy-maker and
prison manager could well intervene at any one or more levels. Most
likely, and as the CRC chose, the level of intervention will be at
what is seen as the one most immediately capable of being manipu-
lated, this being the level of resources, organisational and physical.
Individuals and their relationships are both more elusive and more
recalcitrant — they easily slip from the focused lenses of the practitioner. Moreover, policies that deal directly with the individual quite
rightly raise immediate moral and political issues. This is especially
the case with the prison, where the question of the justified use
of power has always been contested, not least by the inmates themselves. To put this in the terms of a very influential recent social
theorist, every exercise of power creates a resistance (Foucault 1977).

That the CRC should have put forward a managerial conception
of control and order is understandable. The Commitee was composed
of managers and, in a very important sense, its report was written

for managers. It is this which forms the contextual limitation to its analysis. Because there is no investigation of the inmates' point of view, because the Committee's analysis of the formal and informal aspects of the prison seems not to pay adequate attention to either how they are interrelated or more specifically to the contribution of the informal aspects to the maintenance of order and control, then their analysis of both, it is suggested, is partial and incomplete. If this is accepted, then it puts in doubt the efficacy of their proposed reforms. While their reforms may improve, in a technical sense, the allocation of resources by using staff and space more efficiently, we may question, because of the reasons outlined above, whether this will result in an improvement in control. The CRC's proposals may not achieve their objectives.

Criticising the CRC report in the way that I have does create an obligation to offer an alternative. I shall endeavour to discharge this obligation by outlining in greater detail how a sociologist might analyse the concepts of control and order and how this is relevant to the debate on prisons.

Sociology, social order and social control
There are considerable difficulties in achieving the objectives I have set. These are both conceptual and expositional. The concepts of order and control, what has been meant by them and how they have been used, are central to the very project of sociology. Indeed, it has been claimed that these concepts constitute *the* problem of sociology. All the major sociological theorists can be seen to have attempted to answer the question of how social order is possible. In many ways this question is simply another way of asking how society is possible. How is it that individuals come to live together in units and groups, the totality of which we call society? Why do there exist orderly patterns of behaviour?

Different sociologists have, of course, given very different answers to this question. For Marx, the answer lay in how individuals relate to the productive, material forces that are seen to constitute the basis of all social behaviour. For Durkheim, the answer lay in conceiving society as a form of collective morality, which constitutes a regulatory whole, greater than the sum of its parts. Yet again, for Weber, the question was even more complex as he seems sceptical, like many of the more recent social theorists, of talking about society as a whole, as a totality, at all. Rather, for Weber, the question was one of how individuals create meaning, how meanings are related to actions, and how actions build up into patterns.

My difficulties are exacerbated because the central concept of this paper, social control, is not one which the European sociological tradition uses. Rather, as a 'term of art', and as a technical concept, social control is a creation of the more pragmatic American tradition. This does not mean that European and American sociology were talking about different things, rather the framework of analysis is different. In the European tradition, the analysis of how social order is achieved and maintained was conducted by using extremely broad, general concepts, such as social class, collective consciousness, and the state. Within the context of different descriptions of society these were seen as components of social order, of what makes society possible. The American tradition did not, and this continues, use these broad inclusive concepts, rather its focus was more pragmatic and narrow. Gurvitch (1945, p. 269) puts the difference this way: while in the European sociological tradition, the notion of control, if it is used explicitly, means something like supervision, inspection or surveillance, in American sociology its meaning veers much closer to the literal English language sense of the term as power and domination.

The differences between these two traditions can probably be explained by reference to different intellectual contexts and histories. At the risk of gross over-generalisation, the early American sociologists perceived their emerging society in a very different way from their European counterparts. Working at the turn of the century, American sociologists set out to explain a quickly changing society, characterised by rapid expansion, waves of immigration from Europe and the emergence of new urban centres such as New York and Chicago. Their work is not infused with the historical consciousness which so characterises European thought. While the primary aim of the classical, European sociologists was to account for the emergence of one type of society — capitalism — against the backcloth of a long history of other types of social order (for example, feudalism), the American sociologists faced the apparently ahistorical issue of how America could be perceived as a society, a social order, at all. This lent to American thought an immediacy and pragmatism, which, although present also in European thought, did not form its focus. The concept of social control developed out of this social and historical context as a way of explaining how, out of change, a stable American type of society existed.

The very general nature of the 'potted' history I have given demonstrates the problem of exposition I face. To give a full and proper account of how sociologists use the concepts of order and control would require me to write a detailed history of both European and American sociology. Even if I were capable of such a task — which I am not — its relevance to our present proceeding would be questionable. What I will do, therefore, is to extract from the discipline what I see to be of particular relevance. This necessarily means that what I write is incomplete, but I can do no more than ask that this qualification be recognised.

Social order and social control

Convention requires expositions to begin with a formal definition of terms. While there is no wish to fly in the face of convention, it is suggested that too much can be made of this particular one in social science. As Philip Selznick (1969, p. 4) has observed: 'Social science is best served when definitions are "weak" and concepts are strong.' What Selznick means is that too much energy devoted towards providing 'tight' formal definitions reduces the potential of social science to get on with description and explanation. This is because social science, especially sociology, is open-ended; it is subject to continual debate and revision as empirical findings force us to think again. Selznick recommends, therefore, that we characterise concepts rather than define them, by describing the 'problem' they endeavour to encapsulate.

We have already characterised the concepts of order and control. By order is meant that pattern of social relationships that forms a whole; by social control is meant those mechanisms that create and maintain this pattern. What is common to both these concepts is their generality and inclusiveness. As we have said, very often social order is used as a synonym for society and similarly social control has been used in such a way as to refer to any mechanism, practice or institution that binds people into social relationships.

The nebulous character of these concepts has advantages and disadvantages. The primary advantage is that it allows commentators to indicate that the particular object being studied, be it crime, prisons or the family, is part of a larger whole and accordingly ought to be studied in the broadest of ways. To miss out this relationship between particular and general thus becomes to limit sociological understanding. Perhaps one of the best examples of the power of these types of explanation is to be found in Durkheim's analysis of the normality of crime.

Durkheim (1895) argued, convincingly, that far from being pathological, crime and deviance were in fact positively functional to the maintenance of social order. To use his words, crime is a 'normal social fact' that performs the important functions of, through the reactions to it (that is, punishment), reinforcing the collective consciousness of society. Also, crime and deviance stimulate social change.

The great advance made by Durkheim's work was to challenge prevailing and common-sense conceptions of crime and punishment.

By contending that crime and punishment have positive functions, Durkheim shows they are essential features of social order. Punishment's 'true functions' are not to be found in the justifications of retribution, deterrence or social defence. Rather its true functions are as a form of social control, contributing to the maintenance of our common moral values.

The primary disadvantage of the nebulous nature of the concepts of control and order is that their very generality lowers their analytical usefulness. Because they can be made to include so much and exclude so little, their usefulness can be limited. One often feels that the concept of control is used as a sort of conceptual shorthand to reduce complex situations by claiming to have discerned a common purpose or function, that is, that of social control. To use a hypothetical example, it is sometimes claimed that the family or law are types of social control. While this may point to certain characteristics that are not ordinarily thought of, it in fact says very little. It does not tell us what the family or law are like, why they do operate as controls, and so on. Of course, these details can be filled in, but there is a tendency to stop short and for commentators to seem to think that the investigation is complete simply by invoking the notion of control. Indeed, what appears to be sought after in these circumstances is a demonstration that society does not work in a straightforward way but has a 'devious' side to it; that institutions we thought were benign or supportive are in fact as much a medium for power and repression as are those we ordinarily think of in terms of power (like the prison).

This type of work can be made into a powerful form of analysis but it requires that these 'additional' functions or purposes be demonstrated in detail. If they are not, then all that is done is to confront commonsense with what is purported to be sociological sense.

It has been argued (Parsons 1937), that at the heart of the problem denoted by the concepts of order and control is a concern with the question of how the individual relates to society. How and why do individuals come together and live in the inclusive social grouping we conventionally call society? It is to be expected that different theories in answer to this question have been advanced. For some, there exists an essential duality; society and the individual are separable entities, although not necessarily opposed. For others, there is no duality; individuals are entirely social beings, so no essential distinction between them can be made. While any particular theory may well embrace both these conceptions, there is usually a stress on one or the other of these possibilities.

These broad conceptions of the relationship between society and the individual can influence the more specialised theory of social control. If, for example, the dualist position is advocated then it becomes necessary to characterise precisely how individuals are bound to the social order. Is the basis of the binding to be described as a process of coercion, constraint or consensus? Does an ascendant society coerce recalcitrant individuals into certain socially defined roles, such as criminal, prison governor, civil servant; or is society an extension of certain attributes of human nature and thus potentially in harmony and equilibrium with the individual (as is the case with academics)? The answers given to these questions have a direct bearing on a theory of control. For instance in the work of the American sociologist normally seen as the first great populariser of control theory, Edward Alsworth Ross (1901), social control is explicitly described as a study in 'social ascendancy'. By this, Ross meant that social control is to be understood as that process by which society attains a superordinate position over the individual. For Ross, control was a purposive, intended form of social action designed to subject individuals to social rules they did not themselves make. Although this may seem to push Ross towards a coercion-based theory of control, he was adamant that it did not. Rather, coercive (external) social control was only one possibility. Other theorectically and practically important possibilities existed. According to Ross, conformity to rules can be promoted also by sentiments and motivations 'internal' to the individual (internal social control); yet again, rule-following may result from rational appraisal of rewards or penalties or non-rational commitments inculcated through the processes of socialisation. For Ross, the most effective type of social control was that which was rational and internal. It was the most effective because it resulted in the individual choosing to obey rules rather than being forced by external pressures. Social order is guaranteed because the individual feels obligated to obey rules. Conformity becomes voluntary and 'spontaneous'.

The example of Ross's work is important for a number of reasons. First, it shows that any theory of control necessarily rests upon certain assumptions we make about how the individual relates to society. These 'deep' questions thus are not purely 'academic' in the pejorative sense of the term, but are answered implicitly whenever control is considered. This applies, of course, to the CRC report.

Second, Ross's work was of great historical importance in the history of the sociological theory of social control. It set the agenda against which subsequent researchers reacted, both in support and criticism. One of the more unfortunate aspects of this reaction was that, because Ross described social control as a study of social *ascendancy*, researchers have linked control with only one of the possibilities he outlines. The concept of control has become tied to coercion, ignoring the richness of Ross's original formulations. As a result, as Gurvitch (1945) has noted, in American sociology and social psychology control theories have on occasion seemed little else than elaborate manuals detailing strategies to be followed by 'controllers'. When this occurs, another important side of Ross's work is diminished. Ross argued forcefully that the study of social control always involves questions of value; an analysis of control necessitates, he said, some evaluation of the goal for which one is aiming. In Ross's case, his principle of evaluation was liberal; he was concerned to evaluate methods of control according to whether they extend or limit the powers and freedom of individuals. If a particular method of control limited individual freedom then it was suspect and another was to be preferred. The problem with much of the technical social control literature is that it appears to play down the 'open' nature of Ross's analysis and to substitute for it an impoverished study of what could be called the social psychology of conformity. As a result, the 'critical' edge, so manifest in Ross's analysis, is blunted; the analyst of social control comes close to being a technologist unable or unwilling to deal with the very far-reaching moral and political issues that a study of control necessarily invokes.

The third reason why Ross's work is important follows on directly from this. The tendency to define control in terms of coercion is due also to the meaning we normally take the concept to have in ordinary everyday language. 'To control' means to impose our power or will on another individual to limit his actions or to make him do something. A similar normative component attaches to the concept of order ('I order you to.'). This creates a problem for sociological theories of control and order. While our everyday understanding of the terms ties them necessarily to power and coercion, the sociologist sees this as only one empirical possibility; as only one way in which social control works. For the sociologist, control does not necessarily mean coercion. Indeed, if we understand coercion to be what control theorists would call external social control, then, as we said above, it is not in the long term regarded as effective. As Sykes (1958) argued in relation to the prison, 'total systems of power' have inbuilt defects; there exist very real sociological limits to them. Total systems of power are unstable, they can only guarantee conformity to rules in the most short-term and minimal of ways. It is to Ross's credit that his work raises these intriguing and important theoretical and practical issues. By pointing out that coercion is only one means of control, he opened up a range of possibilities that still have to be explored. One of these concerns is how social control and power are related more generally.

Although there is a tendency to see power as only a negative, repressive force, it need not be conceived only in this way. We sometimes use the term in a positive manner to indicate that power creates as well as places limits. For example, we sometimes talk of the 'power of creation' or the 'power of love', ascribing in both cases a positive role to power. Of these two views, it is the negative conception of power that predominates. It has dominated modern political theory as in the 'negative conception of liberty' (Berlin 1969, Chapter 3) (the idea that liberty is best defined in terms of the absence of intervention; power is always to be limited in its effects on the individual) and it certainly dominates in most modern social science. Social control theories are no exception to this. Within social control theory, power is generally seen in a negative way as a force which places limits on action. This is true even though control theory, as we have seen, separates control from coercion.

Recently, the adequacy of this negative conception of power has been challenged by the work of Michel Foucault. In a series of important works (most of which I find exceedingly obscure) Foucault outlines both a new theory of the nature of social knowledge and a version of a positive view of power. Foucault's work is rich and complex and I cannot possibly do justice to it in this paper. Rather, I shall concentrate on what I see as relevant to our present concerns.

The starting point of Foucault's theory is that power has both a negative and positive side to it. Power limits, but power also creates. In his account of the emergence of the prison, Foucault analyses the jail as an exemplification of power in modern society. He argues that the organisation of regimes and the architecture of the prison are intimately related to power. Architecture is related because the physical design of the prison is an expression of how power separates out and defines. For Foucault, power and architecture came together in Bentham's Panopticon. Within the Panopticon inmates are incarcerated in cells, under the constant surveillance of the guard. The cells are arranged in tiers with the guard in such a position that he can view all inmates at all times. The structure is built within a dome (perhaps 'the new generation' prisons are simply a modern, triangular panopticon).

This organisation of physical space represents power in both its negative and positive forms. The negative aspects are clear. The Panopticon offers complete control over the physical and social relations of its inmates. The positive aspects are more indirect. The 'disciplinary' regime of the prison, its attempt to change inmates through rehabilitation, is one example of its positive side. Furthermore, because Foucault argues that power is always met with resistance, the emergence of what the more traditional prison literature calls the inmate subculture can be seen as an example of power positively creating new possibilities.

The relationship between power and resistance is important for two reasons. First, it shows the limits to power. Power is never illimitable. Secondly, Foucault argues that because power is thus limited, no single institution or person can ever monopolise it. Rather, power works through what he calls 'micro-physics', the capillaries of social life. Power in both its negative and positive forms infuses all social life.

This rendition of Foucault is somewhat crude, and it must be made clear that according to him every exercise of power carries with it both negative and positive consequences. Power works along both its dimensions at once.

Foucault's theory of power is a corrective to the negative conception of it that dominates social control theory. It reinforces the argument that control and coercion are separable, but also extends the conception of power, opening up new possibilities of how we can think of the relationship between social control and power. Foucault's work also accords with the common-sense way in which we experience power. I do not think some of it would necessarily surprise any experienced prison officer.

Social control, the CRC report and long-term prisoners
In the light of these observations, what can we learn about control and order in the prison? The following seem to me to be important implications:

(i) That we should not only think of control as the imposition of coercion. According to social control theories, the most effective form of control is that which facilitates the voluntary and rational recognition of rules. The most stable forms of order are those in which individuals feel an obligation to rules, not ones in which conformity to rules is imposed by pressures external to them.
(ii) That power is not a purely negative force and that there exist natural limits to its exercise. 'Total systems of power', as Sykes (1958) calls them, are illusions. Consequently, attempts to enforce 'total power' are self-defeating (as the CRC recognises).
(iii) That to understand how prisons operate, how control and order are achieved and maintained, we need to view them in both their informal and formal aspects. This, of course, is more of an analytical than an empirical point.

The CRC report recognises some of these implications but does not, I suggest, follow them through to their logical conclusions, because of their managerial perspective. While it would be quite wrong to see their managerial perspective as embracing a purely coercive view of control, the emphasis on resources which I have claimed exists within the report does lead them into a conception of control which ignores the implications of my first two points above. If the most effective forms of control are those in which individuals voluntarily feel obliged to conform to the rules, then those are the types of regime we should, from the humanitarian and a 'value for money' point of view, encourage.

The problem with this suggestion is that we are prone to think of the prison only as a coercive institution, thus apparently ruling out in principle the possibility of implementing the type of regime suggested. People are, after all, it will be pointed out, retained within prison walls against their will. This I could not and would not deny; but does it follow from this that the only sort of regime we can have inside the walls is premised on coercion? I am sceptical of this conclusion.

If power is limited in the way described and if the most effective form of control is voluntary obligation, then it is only sensible to recognise this. We should not see these observations as creating problems for prison managers but as the foundation upon which a realistic regime that will achieve the objective of an orderly prison can be built. This regime would make the prison a better place for both staff and inmates. How could such a regime be constructed?

The Special Unit at Barlinnie Prison in Glasgow offers one example of how it is possible to create such regimes for long-term prisoners within the constraints of the present system. The key to the unit is the process of decision-making. Inmates are actively involved in making decisions on how the regime of the unit should work, and as a result are under obligation to it. Inmates seem to be involved in decisions about the day-to-day operations and about what forms of behaviour are seen as acceptable. Although not all the inmates sent to the unit find they can live within it, some do and have prospered. The control problems faced by the Scottish prison system at the end of the 1960s and the beginning of the 1970s have diminished significantly. It is too easy to be too romantic about the Barlinnie Special Unit, but my point is that its regime makes good sociological sense. It is consistent with the points made above. It is a good example, I contend, of an 'open' regime, and I would like to think that this is what the CRC had in mind when they use this term in their report. Michael Jenkins (Chapter 13) also provides good evidence of how such a regime works in Long Lartin. Jenkins writes of an 'unwritten contract' between prisoners and staff and lists some of the rules by which it works. What is interesting about these rules is that they all work only if both 'sides', staff and inmates, feel under obligation to the contract. If this obligation were not there, then Long Lartin could not, in my view, run the open regime that Jenkins describes so well.

I worry that the new generation prisons could create an environment that is not at all conducive to the type of regime proposed. The new generation prisons appear to be, as was pointed out before, a modern version of the Panopticon, the major difference simply being their triangular shape. It should be remembered that the very purpose of the Panopticon was to achieve total surveillance over inmates through the control of physical space and a disciplinary type of regime. Controlling space in this way does seem to push the regime in the direction of coercion. If the new generation prisons are aimed at this, then it is difficult to see how they could nurture the growth of the more open regime that is much more likely to result in an orderly, harmonious prison (see again, for example, Chapter 13). At the very least much more ought to be known about how these new generation prisons work before the expense of constructing them is assumed.

If my arguments are accepted, this would necessitate considerable changes in the traditional attitudes of both staff and inmates. It would require staff, at all levels, to perceive their authority in a new and more open way. The *de facto* negotiations that already take place between staff and inmates would have to become *de jure*, in the sense that officers would no longer see them as a concession. It is always extremely difficult to get individuals voluntarily to recognise apparently self-denying edicts, but the advantages in terms of a better working environment would be considerable. Any such edicts would have first, in the nature of the exercise, to be issued by the staff but would have to be matched by one from the inmates.

Several objections to this proposal could be made, and I shall conclude by anticipating three of them. It could be objected, first, that these regimes could not provide a working model for the whole prison system; second, that they are more labour-intensive and therefore costly, and third, that the relaxed regime may constitute a security risk. In response to these points, I argue, first, that we are not proposing the regime as a model for the whole system but only for a relatively small portion of it, namely long-term adult prisoners. The question of what sort of regime is suitable for the whole system is beyond the scope of this paper. But if it is argued that one limitation to my suggestion is size (that it can only work with small numbers) then we must critically examine the prison population as a whole and assess once again whether so many need to be imprisoned. (But, any objector to what I say would be required to demonstrate both *conceptual* and practical limits to my suggestion.

Normally, the objections focus on the practical only.) This raises the issue of sentencing policy, but it is wrong to think that we can discuss general strategies for the prison unless we do look at it. To the second possible objection, I would reply that it may well prove more expensive to build new prisons than to promote the regime I have outlined, which could work within the existing system. And to the third objection, there is no evidence to suggest that this regime constitutes a security risk greater than that experienced now in prisons.

Theories of social control lead us to believe that the most stable and harmonious types of order are those in which individuals feel they have a 'stake'. As is obvious, I believe much can be done to construct these types of order within the prison. Not only would the proposed regime make the prison a better place, but the demands placed upon all to accept responsibility may well result in what one criminologist has perceived to be the main justification of the prison in this post-rehabilitative era, the 'facilitated change' (Morris 1974) of the inmate.

References
Berlin, I. (1969), *Four Essays on Liberty*, London: Oxford University Press.
Clemmer, D. (1940), *The Prison Community*, New York: Holt, Rinehart and Winston.
Cressey, D. (ed.) (1961), *The Prison: Studies in Institutional Organisation and Change*, New York: Holt, Rinehart and Winston.
Durkheim, E. (1895), *Rules of Sociological Method*, Eng. trans. (1938), New York: Free Press.
Foucault, M. (1977), *Discipline and Punish*, London: Allen Lane.
Gurvitch, G. (1945), 'Social control', in G. Gurvitch and W. Moore (eds), *Twentieth Century Sociology*, New York: Philosophical Library Inc.
Home Office (1984), *Managing the Long-Term Prison System: The Report of the Control Review Committee*, London: HMSO.
King, R.D. and Elliott, K. (1977), *Albany: Birth of a Prison — End of an Era?*, London: Routledge and Kegan Paul.
Morris, N. (1974), *The Future of Imprisonment*, Chicago and London: University of Chicago Press.
Parsons, T. (1937), *The Structure of Social Action*, New York: The Free Press; London: Collier Macmillan.
Ross, E.L. (1901), *Social Control*, New York: Macmillan.
Selznick, P. (1969), *Law, Society and Industrial Justice*, New York: Russell Sage Foundation.
Sykes, G. (1958), *The Society of Captives*, Princeton, NJ: Princeton University Press.

5 New generation prisons

NEW GENERATION PRISONS, THE PRISON BUILDING
PROGRAMME, AND THE FUTURE OF THE DISPERSAL
POLICY: *ROY D. KING*

The Control Review Committee report (Home Office 1984) provided
a devastating indictment of dispersal policy. Adopted by the
government in 1968, following the advice of the Radzinowicz Sub-
Committee (Advisory Council on the Penal System 1968) in preference to that of Lord Mountbatten's Inquiry (Home Office 1966),
the policy of dispersing high security-risk prisoners among a number
of very secure prisons had, by then, evolved over a period of some
15 years. It had been reviewed at least three times before: first
in 1973, after the Albany and Gartree riots, by an internal working
party under W.R. Cox, then Director-General of the Prison Service
(Home Office 1973); next by G.W. Fowler, the Chief Inspector of
Prisons, in the context of the Hull riot (Home Office 1977); and
then by the May Committee, as part of their general deliberations
into the prison service, but coincidentally after the second Gartree
riot of 1978 and contemporaneously with the incidents at Parkhurst,
Hull and Wormwood Scrubs in 1979 (Home Office 1979).

The Cox and Fowler reviews acknowledged differences between
the rhetoric of Radzinowicz and the problems of implementing policy
on the ground, but advocated a general strengthening of that approach
(not to mention the prisons themselves) because they felt it to be
right. The May Committee were frankly critical of many aspects
of dispersal policy, but were prepared to see its continuance not
because of any intrinsic benefits real or supposed but simply because
they could see no viable alternative in existing operational conditions
(see King 1985). By contrast, the Control Review Committee,
appointed in the aftermath of further incidents at Albany and
Wormwood Scrubs and in the tough law and order climate symbolised
by Leon Brittan's revised package on parole, provided both a radical
critique of dispersal policy and an alternative strategy for the future.

The Control Review Committee endorsed the May Committee's
scepticism about the positive benefits of the dispersal concept. 'It
is a very expensive business,' they declared, 'to run eight prisons
at the highest possible level of security. And there are real operational

problems in mixing Category A prisoners among a much larger number of inmates with lower security requirements'. Moreover, design difficulties of the 'existing plant' make it 'impossible to devise any workable arrangements' to compartmentalise the population: as a result 'the inherent tension in prisons between security and control is accentuated in dispersals' (Home Office 1984, para. 7). The Committee noted that: 'The dispersal system has indeed been successful in preventing escapes, but the maintenance of control has been another matter: of the eight existing dispersal prisons, five have experienced serious disturbances or major riots' (Home Office 1984, para. 8). The Committee gave an account of the main incidents in an annex to the report, though that was far from the full catalogue of woe that has beset the institutions over the years. Nevertheless the Committee observed: 'These losses of control have caused structural damage costing millions of pounds. And that is not the only damage. All experience indicates that it is a very difficult business to restore confidence and a healthy atmosphere to a prison that has known serious disorder. It can be a very long time before such a prison can again pull its full weight in the system' (Home Office 1984, para. 8).

A major problem of the dispersal system was that Albany, Gartree, Hull, Parkhurst, Long Lartin, Wakefield, and 'D' Hall Wormwood Scrubs had all been more or less hastily adapted or redesigned, albeit at great cost. These 'arbitrarily selected prisons' of 'different strengths, weaknesses and constraints' all aspired to provide 'the same kind of open regime' (Home Office 1984, paras 10–11). Any success they had in maintaining control was 'achieved against the grain of the system rather than with its support' (Home Office 1984, para. 14). Only Frankland, added to the system in 1983, and Full Sutton, due to be completed in 1986, were designed as dispersal prisons — but more about them later. The dispersal prisons, moreover, were neither well sited nor well integrated into the system as a whole. Regional variations — North Region with four of the nine sites earmarked for dispersal 'has no Category B training establishments that are not dispersal prisons' — conditioned the shape and composition of the dispersal population (Home Office 1984, para. 37). And, it was said, some prisoners engaged in disruptive behaviour in order to be 'rewarded' by a transfer out of Albany or Parkhurst on the Isle of Wight to more accessible prisons on the mainland; while those who behaved well enough to earn a lower security categorisation were 'rewarded' by transfers to prisons with less open regimes and fewer facilities (Home Office 1984, para. 26). Ironically, then the dispersal policy, intended as a device for diluting control problems in high-security prisons, not only had no institutional machinery for dealing with them (Home Office 1984, para. 12), it actually made them more likely to arise.

In the course of its many recommendations for the better management of the long-term prison population — alongside its proposals for more objective categorisation, central allocation, planning of prisoners' careers with individual programmes, a clear system of rewards and punishments, and the provision of special units for when things go wrong — the Control Review Committee gave the strongest advocacy to the possibility of replacing the existing dispersal system as we know it by a much smaller system based on the 'new generation' prison designs current in the United States. These designs, together with a system of decentralised unit management, offer the possibility of separating groups of prisoners into self-contained units with differentiated regimes within a single prison. The Committee noted that very high-security prisons of new generation design are in use in the United States, and went on as follows:

> On the face of it these designs avoid many of the dangers that led the Radzinowicz and May committees to advise against a policy of concentration. We think that our requirement for very high security accommodation is unlikely to be more than 300–400, and it would appear that, if 'new generation' prison designs are indeed successful, this number could be held in two small prisons of the new kind without incurring the disadvantages that we have noted as being inherent in dispersal policy. We therefore recommend that these possibilities are urgently examined (Home Office 1984, para. 20).

The Committee recognised that the changes it wanted could not all be introduced at once (Home Office 1984, para. 137). But they were agreed that 'allocation to dispersal prisons is not done with such discrimination or clarity of objective as to justify a claim that the Category B population of dispersal prisons warrants an enhanced level of security' (Home Office 1984, para. 132). If the rule-of-thumb allocation of a certain percentage of Category A prisoners, which did not have 'much force', was dropped and in the light of their other proposals to deal with control problems, then the dispersal system could be significantly reduced by taking out 'D' Hall at Wormwood Scrubs and one other prison (subsequently identified as Hull) from the dispersal system (Home Office 1984, para. 136).

The CRC looked forward to the 'end of the dispersal system in its present style, which applies such a very high and expensive level of security to so many prisoners and so many prisons' (Home Office 1984, para. 132). It did not 'flatly recommend the replacement of the dispersal system by a small number of "new generation" prisons', but only because 'that concept of prison design has still to be evaluated in the UK.' Nevertheless, the Committee continued:

we do not conceal our hope that this is the way in which the matter will develop. We cannot put a cost on one or two 'new generation' prisons in x years' time, nor can we say how room might be made for such projects in the building programme. What we can say is that the dispersal system seems a precariously balanced structure to carry our hopes into the next century, and that a small maximum security system must surely be cheaper than a large one (Home Office 1984, para. 127).

In welcoming the CRC report the then Home Secretary, Leon Brittan, said that it provided a 'positive agenda for action' and that the proposals would be 'vigorously pursued'. The urgent examination of new generation prison design has indeed been carried out with great despatch, and the report of the Working Party on American New Generation Prisons (Home Office 1985a) was published in December 1985. In their terms of reference the Working Party were charged with 'considering any lessons to be learned in relation to the design of establishments in England and Wales, particularly those used to accommodate prisoners in the higher security classifications' (Home Office 1985a, p. 1). In their conclusions, the Working Party indicated that it was not for them

> to form a view on whether maximum security prisoners in England and Wales should continue to be dispersed, as at present, or concentrated in a small number of maximum security prisons, as suggested by the Control Review Committee. But we consider that the 'new generation' approach provides a workable solution and a third option to what has hitherto been assumed to be a straightforward choice between concentration and dispersal. In this context, we consider that the method of operation of the State Correctional Facility at Oak Park Heights, Minnesota, offers a valuable model of the application of new generation concepts to a maximum security establishment (Home Office 1985a, p. 93).

But the Working Party did also take the view that 'the physical designs of the "new generation" concept are also likely to be of particular application in local prisons' (Home Office 1985a, p. 94). And whereas the Working Party did not recommend that the workable solution along the Oak Park Heights model should be incorporated into the building programme — presumably on grounds that this was a policy decision outside their remit — they did suggest that 'new generation' design solutions 'should be explored in connection with the remaining local prisons in the current prison building programme' (Home Office 1985a, p. 94), the need for which had already been agreed. And that appears to be where matters stand at the moment. The new Home Secretary, Douglas Hurd, made no reference whatever to maximum security in his Written Answer on the day of publication of the Working Party's report though he did refer to feasibility studies at the proposed local prisons at Doncaster and Milton Keynes. No position has yet been taken on the longer-term situation for dispersal policy, nor has the question been explored of how 'new generation' maximum-security prisons could fit into the building programme. At least not in public.

In this paper I propose to try to fill those gaps. I first consider the appropriateness of 'new generation' prison design for maximum-security accommodation in England and Wales and its linkage to the other CRC recommendations. I then try to show what the implications would be for the building programme, the capacity of the system to cope with overcrowding, and the concern for the effective use of resources if priority were given to one or two such prisons.

New generation prisons: in theory ...

The first thing to be said about new generation prisons — if only for the benefit of the press who always get it wrong — is that not all new prisons are new generation prisons. The term refers to a number of design features, which, taken together, amount to the first systematic rethinking of the prison environment in relation to prison aims and objectives that has taken place since the earliest days of the separate system and the designs of Havilland and Jebb. It could be argued that there have been numerous attempts to design prisons for the purpose of treatment and training — the Blundeston series in this country, for example — or for security — Kumla in Sweden and Marion in the United States; but none has been as successful in marrying design to purpose as either the radial prison of the early nineteenth century or the new generation prison of the late twentieth century. There are plenty of new prisons today — both in this country and elsewhere — which are being built and will be built to old designs that suit nobody's purposes. New prisons they will be: new generation most certainly not.

The second thing to be said about new generation prisons, or at least the response to them, is that it is slightly odd that so much concern should be expressed about the need to evaluate them. Not that anything should be said against evaluation. It is just that hundreds of millions of pounds have been spent, and will be spent, on other prisons, whose designs were never properly evaluated, and which we know from bitter experience to be gravely faulty. Of course much depends on just what is meant by evaluation. There does not appear to have been any evaluation study between, say, William Crawford's (1834) report on the penitentiaries of the United States (to which the Platt Report (Home Office 1985a) should perhaps be compared) and the actual building of the new model prison at Pentonville and Jebb's (1844) report on its construction. Though there was much debate, the proof of the pudding was largely in the eating.

In fact the only research study that explicitly addresses prison design in the United Kingdom is that carried out by Canter and Ambrose (1980) from the University of Surrey. Such is the sad history of prison research in this country, that although this study was financed by the Home Office, and completed as recently as 1980, there is no mention of it or any of its findings in either the CRC report or the Working Party report, even though Canter had been able to refer to some research evidence, of just the sort which the Working Party requested, relating to the effectiveness of the design of the New York and Chicago Metropolitan Correctional Centers by Wener and Olsen (1978) and of Butner Federal Correctional Institution by Giber (1979). This is particularly ironic given the welcome aspirations of CRC for 'closer and more understanding relations between the prison system and the academic communities' (Home Office 1984, para. 120).

Canter and his colleagues collected basic data on 16 institutions representing the full range of prison designs then in use; and then proceeded to in-depth case studies of six establishments: Coldingley (nuclear design); Featherstone (satellite design); Gartree (nuclear); Hollesley Bay (campus); Pentonville (radial) and Rochester (block design). They concluded that: 'In general, no existing design solutions emerged as successful across the full range of issues ... There is, as a consequence, certainly scope for developments in design which go beyond the design solutions currently available' (Canter and Ambrose 1980, p. 4). They found that the design of the prison did indeed carry significance for both staff and prisoners, and while this varied from prison to prison, there were certain areas of common agreement. Prisoners conceptualised the design in terms of 'regions' for personal activities, informal association activities and larger places for more formal gatherings — paralleling the 'divisions between the cell, the wing and areas beyond the wing' (Canter and Ambrose 1980, p. 229). Staff conceptualisations related to thoroughfares through which prisoners passed according to a timetable, areas where prisoners congregated in associated groups, and areas for the personal privacy of prisoners or individual contact with prisoners. These 'regions' corresponded with staff goals 'a) to move prisoners easily, b) to be able to see and control them when they are in groups, and c) for prisoners to have adequate facilities for their personal activities' (Canter and Ambrose 1980, p. 227).

Perhaps the most germane finding, at least from the point of view of the present discussion, is that the significance of design became more important as the security level of the prison increased. For both staff and prisoners this was reflected in their concern for personal safety, which both perceived to be threatened by other prisoners. 'In general, staff fear being with groups of prisoners in a context where they cannot be seen by other staff. Prisoners, especially in high-security prisons, are more likely to think of the cell as a place where there may be violence' (Canter and Ambrose 1980, p. 5). Staff at Gartree, which had recently experienced a riot, apparently exhibited 'a "siege" perspective, a defensive conceptualisation which places even greater distance between staff and inmates than is normally present' (Canter and Ambrose 1980, p. 228). Two other points, of considerable relevance to new generation prison design, are worth noting from this study. First 'the designated use of any particular location is not necessarily an effective guide to the role it plays in the life of staff and inmates'. Secondly that 'certain areas are typically under provided for', for example the canteen; and 'others over provided', for example the hospital (Canter and Ambrose 1980, pp. 5–6).

The essence of the new generation prison concept is that it takes a *proactive* stance towards just the kind of problems identified in Canter and Ambrose (1980) and in the CRC report, attempting as far as possible to 'design them out' instead of leaving prison administrators, prison staff and indeed prisoners themselves to develop *reactive* solutions.

Originally developed by the US Federal prison system, when it was first faced with the need to accommodate jail populations in its Metropolitan Correctional Centers, the new generation concept has since been revised and applied to prisons across the full range of security levels. In its ideal form the concept depends upon a *combination* of what in the United States are non-traditional management practices and styles of supervision with a physical structure designed to facilitate those managerial and supervisory styles. In the Federal new generation prisons this involves multi-disciplinary unit management teams, which have delegated responsibility for groups of 50–100 prisoners in discrete living units. The unit staff exercise direct supervision of the prisoners with minimal reliance on structural barriers or technological devices. Structure and technology are employed indirectly in the design of the units themselves, and throughout the institution as a whole, to facilitate supervision whilst providing a pleasant and wholesome environment that commands respect, rather than inviting vandalism and abuse. As the Control Review Committee noted, the designs 'do away with cell corridors — with all their problems — and instead arrange the cells around a central multi-use area in each unit. Since each cell opens directly on to the central area, staff can observe all the cells without having to move about in a consciously patrolling manner' (Home Office 1984, para. 19).

Although the concept can be developed to very high standards of security it remains the intention within any unit that staff do not retreat behind physical and technological barriers but remain in direct contact with prisoners, keeping negative behaviour to a minimum and reducing tension. In American correctional jargon this is known as 'podular/direct supervision' with 'non-barrier architecture' (National Institute of Corrections, n.d.). But jargon apart, it is a far cry indeed from the clanging gates and doors that define staff territory, prisoner territory, and no-go areas in too many traditional prisons, or indeed the elaborate and intrusive electronics, metal detectors and closed circuit television of the more recent past. It should be apparent that in a properly staffed unit of this kind, even at the highest security level, the staff fears about their safety when they cannot be seen by other staff, and prisoners' anxieties about violence in cells, which were identified by Canter, should be reduced to a minimum.

The Working Party report sets out with great clarity the many design features of the new generation prisons they visited and it would be pointless to review them all here. It will be sufficient to draw attention to three issues now. First, that in new generation design great care is given to circulation principles to facilitate movement. Second, much higher proportions of space are devoted to inmate living areas, and much less to workshops, chapels and so on. These were of great concern to staff and prisoners respectively in the Canter and Ambrose (1980) study. Third, there seems to be no particular limit to the number of decentralised unit structures that could be operated within a single institution, but a typical prison containing 400–500 prisoners might comprise six to eight self-contained units. This was seized upon by the Control Review Committee because it offered an inbuilt capacity to separate groups of prisoners, whereas the most critical problem that faces our dispersal prisons is the virtually complete impossibility of separating out the population into more manageable and compatible groups. New generation prisons offer great flexibility, argued the Control Review Committee, 'since the units need not all be run in the same way and may be operated in as separate or concerted a manner as the operational situation requires' (Home Office 1984, para. 20). Certainly, at its best, new generation design can facilitate much more rewarding regimes with better and more convenient dining and working situations, and give a real choice between privacy and associated activity.

In a period when it is no longer the basis of prisons' philosophy that they should fulfil a 'therapeutic' role; and when, it is hoped, there can be no return to an explicitly punitive model of corrections, other than what is involved in the loss of liberty itself; it seems likely that prison systems in democratic societies will increasingly follow the Federal model if they have not already done so. The Federal system now aims to provide safe, humane institutions which offer prisoners the opportunity for change and improvement through their own efforts and through the services and facilities which are provided without being imposed. As far as is possible, within the necessarily artificial environment of enforced confinement, the intention is to provide more 'normal' conditions of life — to reduce, through a combination of good staffing and good design, what David Downes (1987) has recently called the 'depth of imprisonment'.

... and in practice

My ability to speak about the operation of new generation prisons in practice is based upon a period of four months' fieldwork at the Minnesota Correctional Facility at Oak Park Heights in 1984, and on much briefer observational visits of a few days each at the Federal Correctional Institutions at Otisville and Butner. I was also able to spend shorter periods at MCF Stillwater, and the Federal penitentiaries at Leavenworth, Lewisburg, Terre Haute and Marion which offered some bases for comparisons. I shall confine myself here to a few observations based on my research at the maximum-security prison Oak Park Heights, since my concern is specifically with the application of new generation design concepts as a potential alternative to dispersal policy.

Oak Park Heights comes at the extreme high-security end of prison design, although some features are built to lower standards than is currently the case in Britain — for example the use of painted blockwork in cells instead of reinforced concrete (Home Office 1985a, p. 63). Nevertheless Oak Park Heights relies more on vandal-proof fixtures, electronic and physical barriers than either Butner or Otisville, which cater for lower-risk prisoners. In particular, each housing complex has a security 'bubble' which is staffed at all times (often by a woman officer) and from which visual surveillance may be maintained over the whole living area. 'Bubble' staff control access to and from the complex and report all movements to master control. Movement is necessarily restricted: work, education and outside recreation usually involves only movement within the complex: movement to the gymnasium, due process, visits, and so on, are along prescribed corridor routes under remote surveillance or accompanied by staff.

In some respects, then, Oak Park Heights merges the podular/direct supervision described above with the podular/remote surveillance beloved of guard unions because it can minimise staff contact with prisoners (National Institute of Corrections, n.d.). But it must be emphasised that the two styles work in *combination* at Oak Park Heights, the one backing up the other. Thus each complex is typically staffed by three officers — 'one in the bubble and two on the floor' (again including women officers). Supervisory staff also have their offices inside the complex. Moreover the job specifications for staff stress that they are required to behave proactively and not just reactively, and that in their behaviour they must have due regard for the human worth and dignity of prisoners.

Questions have understandably been asked about whether Minnesota, with one of the lowest incarceration rates in the United States should have built a super-maximum-security last-resort prison (Schoen 1981). It was intended as a replacement for Stillwater, but Minnesota now has both even though it has better-controlled prison population growth than many other states. Arguably there are too few Minnesotan prisoners of such security or control risk to warrant such a sophisticated facility. Periodically it is suggested that the Federal Bureau of Prisons should take it over, and certainly Federal wardens who visited Oak Park Heights were both impressed and covetous. In fact Minnesota now boards in high-risk prisoners from other states and the Federal system to make better use of the facility. Ken Schoen, who was the Commissioner of Corrections for Minnesota during the planning stage, now criticises it as 'overbuilt'. He has been quoted as regarding Oak Park Heights as 'a major disappointment' because, late in the day, more and more security features were added. 'What was lost' he argues 'was an important opportunity for inmates and staff to mingle as human beings' (quoted in Edna McConnell Clark Foundation 1984). There may be some truth in such judgments — though it is fair to say that Schoen (1981) himself notes how some standard high-security features were avoided, as does Silver (1981), one of the responsible architects. Silver (1981, p. 128) also makes the fascinating point that Oak Park Heights seeks to leave the public impression that it might be a dungeon, whilst mitigating those very characteristics for prisoners: a timely reminder that prison administrations have to please several publics.

In any case the point I wish to address here is not the suitability of Oak Park Heights for Minnesota, with all its particular history and context, but rather its suitability as a potential model for the high-security prison population in England and Wales with the kind of history described earlier.

At the time of my study, Oak Park Heights had been open for about 18 months and, after a gradual build-up, all complexes were operational. Complex 1 provided sex-offender and drug-dependency programmes; complexes 2, 3 and 4 provided industrial work; 5 comprised the segregation unit; 6 the education unit; and 7 the services

Table 5.1   *Current offence classification (per cent)*

Offence	Albany (n = 380)	Frankland (n = 325)	Gartree (n = 310)	Oak Park Heights (n = 359)
Murder, manslaughter	10	18	40	33
GBH, ABH, assault	8	11	8	10*
Sex	12	8	6	21†
Robbery	45	31	29	21
Other	25	32	17	15
Total	100	100	100	100

Notes: *includes 4% kidnap
      †includes 10% rape
Source: Home Office Adult Offender Psychology Unit Statistics, 1
       November 1984, for UK prisons; research data 1 April 1984
       for Oak Park Heights

unit (housing cleaners, known as 'swampers' and kitchen workers and so on). All of these were 52-bed units. Complex 8 was smaller, with a 32-bed Mental Health Unit and a ten-bed infirmary. In addition to numerous informal discussions, I tape-recorded interviews with 27 prisoners and seven staff. I also administered a self-recording questionnaire to the entire population of 365 prisoners in custody on 19 April 1984. More than 70 per cent returned their questionnaires. Access to official documentary and computer-stored data was also negotiated. What follows is based on a very preliminary and partial inspection of some of these data and on impressionistic field notes.

There are many hazards involved in making cross-national comparisons. But it is important to see whether Oak Park Heights deals with a significantly different type of population from English dispersal prisons. I shall take as comparators Albany and Gartree, new prisons converted for dispersal use, and Frankland, the only purpose-built high-security prison in the UK. All are roughly the same size.

As can be seen from Table 5.1, Oak Park Heights has a higher proportion of offenders convicted of serious violence, especially homicides, than either Albany or Frankland, though a lower proportion than Gartree. The English prisons have proportionately more robbers and other offenders (mostly burglars?) than Oak Park Heights, which by contrast had two or three times as many sex

Table 5.2   Length of sentence (per cent)

Years	Albany (n = 380)	Frankland (n = 325)	Gartree (n = 310)	Oak Park Heights (n = 359)
1–4	21	16	8	36
5–6	26	43	22	10
7–8	18	15	13	7
9–10	13	6	8	8
11–15	11	3	12	11
16+	3	2	4	16*
Life	8	14	34	13†
Total	100	100	100	100

Notes: *(16–40 years)
        †(99+ years)
Source: as Table 5.1

offenders — especially rapists. In terms of length of sentence, Oak Park Heights has proportionately more prisoners serving *both* comparatively short *and* very long sentences than any of the English prisons except Gartree with its substantial life sentence population. Table 5.2 gives the details and shows that some Oak Park Heights prisoners expect to serve very long terms indeed. From Table 5.3 it can be seen that Oak Park Heights has a greater proportion of prisoners below the age of 25 years, whereas the English prisons have more in the age range of 30–39 years. In other respects the distributions are quite similar.

Racially, as can be seen from Table 5.4, Oak Park Heights is much more mixed than any of the English prisons — though in this respect Oak Park Heights is untypical of American prisons many of which have much higher black and Hispanic populations.

Impressionistically there may seem to be fewer prisoners in Oak Park Heights likely to engage in instrumental violence to further criminal and political objectives, although there was a sprinkling of such prisoners from other jurisdictions, including the Federal system. On the other hand, the population contained many prisoners thought to be highly volatile and with a history of considerable, and sometimes random, violence against strangers and the police. Compared to other American maximum-security prisons there was

Table 5.3 Age (per cent)

Years	Albany (n = 380)	Frankland (n = 325)	Gartree (n = 310)	Oak Park Heights (n = 359)
Under 25	20	22	16	34
25–29	32	25	30	27
30–39	37	38	32	28
40–49	10	11	18	8
50+	2	4	4	3
Total	100	100	100	100

Source: as Table 5.1

Table 5.4 Ethnicity (per cent)

	Albany (n = 380)	Frankland (n = 325)	Gartree (n = 310)	Oak Park Heights (n = 359)
White	70	87	81	57
Black	22	6	13	30
Other	7	7	7	13*
Total	100	100	100	100

Note: * includes 9% Native American Indians and 3% Hispanics
Source: as Table 5.1

an absence of the worst gangs — the 'Mexican Mafia' or the 'Aryan Brotherhood' — and many prisoners objected to the high number of sex offenders present, or felt that they had only been sent to Oak Park Heights to fill up the accommodation. But, on the face of it, there is little here to suggest that the Oak Park Heights population is significantly less of a security risk, or likely to be less problematic in control terms, than the population in English dispersals. To the extent that this is the case, however, any 'overbuilding' at Oak Park Heights might be thought more appropriate in the English context.

In preparing this paper I have been able to look at only four of the eight complexes in Oak Park Heights, namely Complex 2 (Industry), Complex 6 (Education), Complex 7 (Services) and Complex 8 (Mental Health Unit). Below are given some very provisional findings: they really require much further analysis — but they go some way towards illustrating Oak Park Heights in use.

New generation prisons are intended to promote the safety of prisoners and their property, and of staff. Prisoners were asked about their experiences and their perceptions. In these four complexes prisoners reported only half the number of incidents of abuse by other prisoners (abuse of property, sexual or other assault) in Oak Park Heights compared to that reported in other prisons they had been in during the current sentence. The reduction was most marked in the Mental Health Unit whose prisoners had perhaps been more at risk in other institutions. They reported only one-quarter of the number of incidents they had previously experienced.

In rather stark contrast to English prisons (recall that Canter and Ambrose (1980) found that both staff and prisoners perceived threats to their safety to come from other prisoners), the prisoners in these four complexes reported between three and six times as many incidents of abuse by staff as by other prisoners. But here too there was a reduction at Oak Park Heights, with three-quarters of the number of incidents reported there compared with other prisons during the current sentence.

Again, one-third fewer prisoners had felt threatened by the behaviour of others since coming to Oak Park Heights than had been the case earlier in sentence; and one-fifth fewer had felt the need to threaten others in order to protect themselves. It is presumably a comment on the pressures obtaining in American prisons that both in Oak Park Heights and in other prisons they had experienced, more prisoners felt the need to threaten others than had actually felt threatened by others.

When asked how safe or otherwise Oak Park Heights was, about two-thirds saw it as very safe or quite safe for staff, and four-fifths as very safe or quite safe for prisoners. Interestingly, prisoners in Industry and Education perceived the environment as more dangerous, especially for staff, than did prisoners in Services or the Mental Health Unit. This may well reflect real differences in relationships and attitudes in the various complexes: those in Services were obviously trusted more and those in Mental Health felt themselves to be benefiting from professional attention, whereas those in Industry were regarded as tougher characters and some at least of those in Education felt they had been 'sent back to school' as a humiliating, informal punishment.

There can be no doubt that movement in Oak Park Heights was tightly controlled, and supervision was close. Indeed, to this observer, it was plain that staff were as closely observed, perhaps more so, than prisoners — a factor which may provide an in-built protection against staff abuses. Not surprisingly, nearly three-quarters of the prisoners regarded the control of prisoner movement as being very close. This, of course, is precisely what English prison staff wished to see, according to the Canter and Ambrose (1980) study discussed above. It is perhaps some measure of the unobtrusiveness of the supervision that only about three-fifths felt it to be very close, and indeed a sixth seemed hardly to notice it at all. The trusted prisoners in Services found fewer problems with both movement and supervision as would be expected.

Taken overall the prisoners in these units were not very impressed with the way in which programmes had been developed in Oak Park Heights: two to three times as many prisoners thought education, treatment and industry programmes to be only fair, poor or very poor as thought them to be good, very good or excellent. However it was noticeable that those who had actually experienced the sex-offender and drug-dependency programmes thought treatment to be much better than those who had not. On the other hand, and just as markedly, those who had been in Industry thought that to be worse than those who had not. Between three and four times as many prisoners thought that the indoor and outdoor recreation facilities were fair, poor or very poor as thought them to be good, very good or excellent. One wonders what the ratings would be in English prisons.

It is right to say that management recognised there was still much to do to improve programmes. And that in design terms, at least to this observer, there were problems of adequate access to the central facilities such as the gymnasium and the sports field, given the limits of the timetable and the need to maintain separation between the complexes. Both prisoners and some staff felt these to be problems.

Prisoner views of staff are notoriously ungenerous. In Oak Park Heights, two out of five prisoners in these four complexes felt that staff behaviour generally was professional or very professional. On more specific questions, however, only one in three thought that staff were helpful in handling inmate problems, and about one in four that staff exercised a fair discipline and a consistent application of the rules. About half the prisoners felt the staff not to be racially prejudiced (and as often as not when prejudice was alleged it was for favouring blacks over whites). It is difficult to interpret these findings without some basis for comparison. It may turn out that these are quite favourable responses given the negative stereotyping that is commonly used. Certainly in the Services Complex and the Mental Health Unit views of staff were more favourable and the majority there saw the staff as professional.

Impressionistically, while some Oak Park Heights staff expressed privately the same kind of views that one hears in many prisons, in public, and, as far as I could see, in their direct relationships with prisoners, they were well presented, courteous, respectful and efficient. Perhaps it is significant that one-third of the 'correctional counsellors' had four-year college degrees. At this level at least they created a more professional impression than I have found in any other prison of any security level. That did not mean, of course, that prisoners had no stories to tell.

Most prisoners in these units found Oak Park Heights neither a particularly hard place nor an easy place to do time. When given an open-ended opportunity to say what was good or bad about the prison two-thirds of the responses related to the architecture, the staff or the regime. This reinforces the point made throughout the literature about new generation prisons, emphasised by the Warden at Oak Park Heights, and repeated by the Working Party in its report — the success of new generation prisons depends upon a combination of good design, competent and professional staffing, and the implementation of fair and effective operational policies.

One further point is worth making. The podular/direct supervisory style, which is seen as comparatively novel in the United States, is historically no newcomer to Britain, which has traditionally placed much greater stress on staff-prisoner interaction. With this in mind, and on this admittedly limited and provisional evidence, something like the Oak Park Heights model would go a very long way towards resolving the problems identified in Canter and Ambrose (1980) and in the Control Review Committee report. As presently functioning it seems to offer a secure, well-controlled and safe environment for separate groups of prisoners, but one in which it is possible to deliver a variety of programmes and to maintain a civilised and humane quality of life.

The building programme and the way ahead
It is beyond the scope of this paper to undertake a detailed appraisal of the various projects in the present prison building programme in England and Wales and to show what contribution they will make towards meeting the continuing crisis of overcrowding. What I can do is to argue the case for including one or two new generation

high-security prisons in the present building programme, to indicate what the likely consequences would be, and to anticipate some of the objections to such a proposal.

I should make it clear that there is nothing inconsistent between advocating the building of a new maximum-security prison and my previously expressed preferences for the minimum use of custody with its explicit reductionist strategy for the prison system, and the minimum use of security (King and Morgan 1980). I still believe that more sensible policies should prevail, and that we had no real need for a building programme on the scale we now have. Circumstances may yet change to bring about new endeavours to control the size of the prison population and to review the expansionist building programme. In that event it may be more appropriate to consider alternative strategies for curbing the excesses of the dispersal system. But in so far as the present building programme will go ahead anyway it is surely better to use this opportunity to get the long-term strategy right for the system as a whole. Building a new generation high-security prison would not only be an appropriate way of dealing with the security and control problems as they are now understood, it would also, as the Control Review Committee suggests, *reduce* the level of high-security provision in the system. Paradoxically it could, and certainly should, also make a greater contribution to solving the overcrowding problem than any other project. In my view, then, urgent consideration should now be given to changing the planned use of at least one of the prisons in the design stage — even bearing in mind the undoubted costs which that would involve immediately. These costs would be recouped later many times over — just as we are now paying many times over for failing to change designs in the past.

The present building programme was designed to bring the total number of prison places into line with the projected prison population by the end of the decade. Even if the population did not rise as expected the programme was justified as a modernisation of the prison estate. In the recent speeches of Lord Glenarthur to the Annual Conference of Boards of Visitors (2 October 1985) and Douglas Hurd to the Governors' Conference (5 November 1985) it has been made clear that the growth of prison population has meant that, unless operational policies change, there is no realistic prospect of that balance between places and population being achieved. It is, to say the least, very difficult to be certain what the picture will look like during the 1990s but given Mr Hurd's current endorsement of the positions taken by his predecessor over parole and executive release, and given the trends in cases coming before the Crown Court, it is more likely than not that the population will grow, and that it will become increasingly skewed towards longer sentences. Leaving larger issues on one side, that makes it more important than ever that the best value is extracted from what is being built.

As at January 1986, of the eight prisons in the detailed and early design stage, four are intended as local prisons at Bicester, Woolwich, Milton Keynes and Doncaster (of which the last two are earmarked for incorporating new generation design features). Two others are intended as Category C prisons at Brinsford (with some under-21 remand accommodation) and Morton Hall; one as a Category B non-dispersal prison at March in Cambridgeshire; and one as a closed youth custody centre (YCC) at Lancaster Farms. In addition, three further possibilities are at the feasibility stage: two of these are locals, one at Ashford and the other at a site in North Region, and the third would be a further Category C prison, also in North Region. This part of the building programme is markedly different from all that has gone before, including those currently under construction. It focuses directly on tackling the overcrowding where it is worst by adding to the local prison stock, rather than indirectly by building training prisons in the hope of syphoning prisoners out of the locals. The older strategy, which has been tried ever since *Penal Practice in a Changing Society* (Home Office 1959) was a demonstrable failure. While it is more difficult to argue against the building of local prisons — knowing the deplorable conditions that currently prevail in so many of them — there is, in fact, no reason to suppose that the newer strategy will be any more successful at resolving the overcrowding problem without major policy changes to control the size of the prison population and further changes in tactical management to control its distribution.

Incidentally, there is one important consideration that should be addressed here. If the building programme fails to solve the accommodation equation, as seems likely, and if the Home Office continues its strategy of keeping the overcrowding in the locals, then it might well be folly to put new generation design into the local prisons because that design is probably less able to cope with overcrowding than the ones we have at present. Such an argument would emphatically *not* apply to high-security accommodation, because such prisons are the most protected from crowding — indeed historically that has been so to the point of profligate and indefensible waste.

Without a great deal more information it would be idle for me to specify a site for a new generation prison to play the high-security role: Brinsford, March and Morton Hall, even though the first two are in the detailed design stage, would leave the local prison programme untouched. But I personally would not rule out one of the sites for a local prison, such as Doncaster, because with some

ingenuity in tactical management the local role could be accommodated elsewhere (after all it is now).

I recognise that the Home Office is under pressure from the Property Services Agency, the Treasury and the National Audit Office
(NAO) not to change the design of prisons once the design work
has commenced. It wastes time and money to do so (NAO 1985,
para. 16). But the reality is that design changes are by no means
uncommon, and it is frequently the case that buildings designed
and built for one purpose are brought into use for quite another.
Much more importantly, any costs through wasted time or design
will be only a small fraction of building costs, and these in turn
are likely to pale into insignificance alongside the costs of living
with mistakes over the useful life of a prison. There can be no
clearer example of this than Frankland and Full Sutton — the two
purpose-built dispersal prisons. In his recent report the Comptroller
and Auditor-General has drawn attention, in the strongest possible
terms, to the problems:

> Frankland prison, for example, is expected to need nearly 400 staff to
> run it, compared with 290 originally estimated in 1976; and Full Sutton
> is being built to the same basic design as a result of a Home Office
> decision in 1978, aimed at saving time in the design stage, despite their
> awareness that the design was manpower intensive and would not
> minimise running costs. (NAO 1985, para. 3.9).

The problems with Frankland are not simply that the 'hollow square'
design is 'manpower intensive due largely to poor sight lines' but
also that existing staff facilities are 'inadequate' and that the segregation unit . . . is too small and is presenting operational difficulties'
(NAO 1985, p. 42). The same problems, of course, apply at Full
Sutton, except that there the segregation unit is even smaller (NAO
1985, p. 32). Although Frankland and Full Sutton were designed
as dispersals, it is ironic that they are likely to be even more expensive
to run than those which were not so designed — only Parkhurst
had higher staff costs than Frankland in 1984–5, and then for special
reasons (Home Office 1985b, Appendix 2). This is the more important given the May Committee's strictures that new building should
be as economical of staffing as possible. And these costs of 40 per
cent more staff than intended, unlike once-and-for-all design or delay
costs, will go on for ever. They could, of course, be substantially
reduced if these prisons were to take a lower security role.

It is instructive at this point to draw some comparisons between
the dramatically high costs of keeping prisoners in maximum security
in England and the relative cheapness of Oak Park Heights. Table
5.5 provides details of the average weekly costs in Albany, Frankland
and Gartree compared to Oak Park Heights.

Table 5.5   Running costs

	Albany (1984–5)	Frankland (1984–5)	Gartree (1984–5)	Oak Park Heights (1985)
Design capacity	480	447	408	406
CNA	309	331	314	406
ADP	312	307	298	355
Total staff*	405.5	441.5	342	300
Unif. staff*	319	360	257	195
Average weekly cost†	620	592	475	409
Average staff cost†	470	510	390	299

Notes: *Staff figures for the UK are for staff in post as at February 1986 (approved manning levels are much higher). Staff figures for Oak Park Heights are taken from Home Office (1985a, p. 57)

† Average cost figures for the UK prisons are taken from Home Office (1985b, Appendix 2, Table D), and are admitted to be somewhat notional because of inadequate accounting procedures. Average cost figures for Oak Park Heights supplied by the Minnesota Department of Corrections for fiscal year 1985. An exchange rate of £1 = $1.50 has been used

For all these reasons it seems more important for the Home Office to take a long-term strategic decision to build at least one prison that *is* appropriate for the purpose and to take that decision *now* without too much concern for the short-term consequences.

The gains to be had from taking such a decision far exceed the limited objectives of getting a proper policy for long-term high-security and control-risk prisoners along the lines suggested by the Control Review Committee — important as they are. For the fact is that reducing the size of the dispersal system would not just release some of the existing dispersal stock for lower security use. It could actually bring back into use several hundred cells which have already been built as part of the post-war prison building programme to relieve overcrowding but which have been 'ghosted' out of existence almost as though they were troublesome prisoners. In fact reclaiming these cells through the building of a new high-security prison would be like getting two new prisons for the price of one.

Over the 16 years of dispersal policy operation the average reported certified normal accommodation (CNA) has been 3,205 (counting only 'D' Hall at Wormwood Scrubs). It has been a matter of some concern that the average daily population (ADP) has been only 2,752 for any number of operational reasons to do with riots, and manning levels given poor design. In effect one whole prison of 450 places has been lying idle. But that considerably understates the underuse of space because for many of these prisons the quoted CNA is far below the original design capacity of the prisons or the quoted CNA immediately before dispersal use. In fact the 'true' or 'original' capacity of these prisons is 3,619 places — in effect a further prison of some 400 cells is just ignored before the CNA is calculated. The data are given in Tables 5.6 and 5.7. These are average figures. If looked at on a year-on-year basis the first four years of the dispersal policy, until 1972, were not too bad. During that period extra cells were brought into use at Wakefield and Hull so that CNA actually exceeded original capacity, and the ADP was nearly 93 per cent of designed places which is a reasonable operating margin. But since then things have become dramatically worse. Over the period 1973 to 1984–5, as the problems with control in the dispersal system took their toll, CNA has operated at 87.5 per cent of original capacity and ADP has operated at 86.4 per cent of CNA. Over the last decade then, a quarter of all the cells originally available to the dispersal prisons have been out of use.

The picture has varied from prison to prison. Wakefield and Hull — in spite of the riot in the latter — have generally made a very full use of the accommodation over the period. No separate figures are published for 'D' Hall at Wormwood Scrubs — I have assumed for these calculations that both design capacity and CNA have been identical at 288 and that ADP has been constant at 282, which were the figures given in the CRC report. This almost certainly gives a more favourable picture than the reality. But Albany, Gartree, Long Lartin and Parkhurst, on the other hand, have had a far worse record: 504 cells which were there at the beginning have been written out of use, and of those that are acknowledged in CNA 302 on average have been empty. The probability must be that Frankland and Full Sutton, in view of their design problems, will go the same way.

Such an underuse of accommodation cannot, I think, be tolerated. I do not wish to exaggerate the problem. Of course there must be an operating margin of empty cells — and the more complex the system the larger that margin must be. But it is nevertheless the case that most of these unused cells are in prisons that have been built since the mid-1960s as part of the building programme designed to end overcrowding. Even allowing for an operating margin, it is tantamount to building a prison the size of March

Table 5.6 Dispersal prisons: accommodation and population, 1969–85

	Albany		Gartree		Long Lartin		Parkhurst		Wakefield		Hull		'D' Hall, Wormwood Scrubs		Frankland		Totals	
	CNA	ADP	CNA	ADP	CNA	ADP	CNA	ADP	CNA	ADP	CNA	ADP	CNA	ADP	CNA	ADP	CNA	ADP
1969	–	–	–	–	–	–	613	469	742	716	261	260	288	282	–	–	1904	1727
1970	479	377	374	327	–	–	557	398	774	751	293	273	288	282	–	–	2765	2408
1971	360	355	374	359	–	–	691	425	891	789	308	291	288	282	–	–	2912	2501
1972	360	349	382	363	–	–	687	419	876	774	302	302	288	282	–	–	2895	2489
1973	360	377	374	269	328	147	685	402	796	726	302	299	288	282	–	–	3133	2502
1974	360	344	180	179	250	188	681	396	783	702	300	294	288	282	–	–	2842	2385
1975	344	333	289	219	410	254	675	371	783	694	318	292	288	282	–	–	3107	2445
1976	303	288	289	239	410	310	480	384	781	733	520	476	288	282	–	–	3071	2712
1977	294	294	391	250	402	337	480	411	781	724	136	120	288	282	–	–	2772	2418
1978	294	283	149	240	350	337	480	333	790	717	318	196	288	282	–	–	2669	2388
1979	294	295	149	129	350	337	480	270	798	681	318	253	288	282	–	–	2677	2247
1980	294	297	215	131	420	336	341	262	798	693	318	274	288	282	–	–	2674	2275
1981	294	208	200	133	420	383	270	244	798	689	318	282	288	282	–	–	2588	2221
1982	294	292	276	177	420	387	270	269	754	701	318	297	288	282	–	–	2620	2405
1983	136	193	310	224	406	387	261	267	746	709	318	294	288	282	318	260	2783	2616
1984/85	399	299	315	295	432	387	328	260	737	708	320	292	288	282	337	307	3156	2830

Source: Annual Reports on the work of the Prison Department, 1969 to 1984–5

Table 5.7 Dispersal prisons' design and use, 1969–85

	Albany	Gartree	Long Lartin	Parkhurst	Wakefield	Hull	'D' Hall, Wormwood Scrubs	Frankland	Totals
Design capacity or CNA before dispersal use	480	408	492	613	631	260	288	447	3619
Average CNA since dispersal use	324	284	383	498	789	311	288	328	3205
Average ADP since dispersal use	288	235	315	349	719	280	282	284	2752

Source: as Table 5.6

or Swaleside — and then leaving it empty like Centre Point. Put in this light, the cost of building one new high-security prison in the present programme becomes a workable proposition.

I can no more say which prisons should come out of the dispersal system, if and when such a new prison is built, than I can say which one of the prisons in the building programme should be sacrificed to make way for it. But the hardware associated with the existing dispersals has a limited life and it is surely necessary now to take a more *strategic* view of the future rather than the tactical response which is currently adopted. It is, after all, the essence of 'new generation' philosophy to be proactive rather than reactive.[1]

Note

1   The research described in this paper was made possible by a grant from the Economic and Social Research Council and by a Social Science Fellowship from the Nuffield Foundation. I am grateful to David Ward for his help in negotiating access to Oak Park Heights and for his generosity during the conduct of the research — though I alone am responsible for the contents. I am also grateful to the Minnesota Department of Corrections, and to Warden Frank Wood, the staff and prisoners in Oak Park Heights for all their help.

References

Advisory Council on the Penal System (1968), *The Regime for Long-Term Prisoners in Conditions of Maximum Security*. (Radzinowicz Report), London: HMSO.

Canter, D. and Ambrose, I. (1980), 'Prison Design and Use Study, Final Report', Guildford: Department of Psychology, University of Surrey (mimeo.).

Crawford, W. (1834), *Report of William Crawford, Esq., on the Penitentiaries of the United States, addressed to His Majesty's Principal Secretary of State for the Home Department*, Parliamentary Papers, 1834 (593), vol. XVI.

Downes, D. (1987), *Contrasts in Tolerance: Post-War Penal Policies in the Netherlands and England and Wales*, London: Oxford University Press.

Edna McConnell Clark Foundation (1984), 'Building for the future' in *Time to Build? The Realities of Prison Construction*, New York: Edna McConnell Clark Foundation.

Giber, D. (1979), *The Psychological Effects of Correctional Architecture and Environment*, Durham, NC: Department of Psychology, Duke University.

Home Office (1959), *Penal Practice in a Changing Society*, Cmnd. 645, London: HMSO.

Home Office (1966), *Report of the Inquiry into Prison Escapes and Security* (Mountbatten Report), Cmnd. 3175, London: HMSO.

Home Office (1973), 'Report of the Working Party on Dispersal and Control' (Cox Report), London: Home Office (unpublished).

Home Office (1977), *Report of an Inquiry by the Chief Inspector of the Prison Service into the Cause and Circumstances of the Events at H.M. Prison Hull During the Period 31st August to 3rd September, 1976*, HC 453 (Fowler Report), London: HMSO.

Home Office (1979), *Report of the Committee of Inquiry into the United Kingdom Prison Services* (May Report), Cmnd. 7673, London: HMSO.

Home Office (1984), *Managing the Long-Term Prison System: The Report of the Control Review Committee*, London: HMSO.

Home Office (1985a), *New Directions in Prison Design: Report of a Home Office Working Party on American New Generation Prisons* (Platt Report), London: HMSO.

Home Office (1985b), *Report on the Work of the Prison Department, 1984/85,* Cmnd. 9699, London: HMSO.

Jebb, J. (1844), *Report of the Surveyor-General of Prisons on the Construction, Ventilation and Details of Pentonville Prison,* London: HMSO.

King, R. D. (1985), 'Control in Prisons' in M. Maguire *et al.* (eds), *Accountability and Prisons,* London: Tavistock.

King, R. D. and Morgan, R. (1980), *The Future of the Prison System,* Farnborough: Gower.

National Audit Office (1985), *Report by the Comptroller and Auditor General, Home Office and Property Services Agency: Programme for the Provision of Prison Places,* London: HMSO.

National Institute of Corrections (n.d.) *New Generation Jails* (Corrections Information Series), Boulder, CO: National Institute of Corrections.

Schoen, K.F. (1981), 'New Prison Construction in Minnesota: Why a New Prison for a State which is Near the Bottom of the Fifty States in Prisoners per 100,000 Population?' in D.A. Ward and K.F. Schoen (eds), *Confinement in Maximum Custody: New Last Resort Prisons in the US and Western Europe,* Lexington, MA: Lexington Books.

Silver, P. (1981) 'The Architects' Response to Minnesota's Proposal for a New Prison' in D.A. Ward and K.F. Schoen (eds), *Confinement in Maximum Custody: New Last Resort Prisons in the US and Western Europe,* Lexington, MA: Lexington Books.

Wener, R.E. and Olsen, R. (1978) *User Based Assessment of the Federal Metropolitan Correctional Centers: Final Report,* New York: Department of Social Sciences, Polytechnic Institute of New York.

NEW DIRECTIONS IN PRISON DESIGN: *TERENCE C. PLATT*

This paper is a factual summary of the report of a Home Office Working Party (1985) on American New Generation Prisons.

Background

The CRC report (Home Office 1984) drew attention to recent developments in the design and management of prisons in the United States, and argued that the designs had been 'very successful in simultaneously improving surveillance and encouraging control of inmates through the development of good inter-personal relations' (Home Office 1984, para. 19). The Working Party was set up to evaluate these claims. Its terms of reference were: 'To examine and evaluate current United States concepts of prison design with a view to considering any lessons to be learned in relation to the design of establishments in England and Wales, particularly those used to accommodate prisoners in the higher security classifications' (Home Office 1985, p. 1).

The method of work

The Working Party set out to evaluate 'new generation' prisons by an examination of the available research material and by visits to selected penal establishments in the United States. In the event they discovered an almost complete absence of relevant research reports or other analytical material. Members of the Working Party visited eight 'new generation' prisons in the United States and five other prisons of more traditional design. The report describes with photographs the 'new generation' prisons visited, and goes on to describe their design, layout and management principles.

Conclusions

The Working Party concluded that the new generation approach provided a workable solution and a third option to what had hitherto been assumed to be a straightforward choice between the concentration and dispersal of maximum-security prisoners. They also recommended that 'new generation' design solutions be explored in connection with local prisons, taking management concepts into account.

The Working Party pointed out that the 'new generation' concept had been developed in response to the particular management philosophies of the Federal Bureau of Prisons, and that the design of individual institutions reflected the Bureau's approaches to management and regimes. They argued that any prison design had necessarily to be based on and to follow from a clear statement of management aims providing a view of how the institution was intended to function. A design developed in the context of one system could not therefore simply be transposed to a different system with the expectation that it would be equally appropriate. The Working Party therefore thought it right in general to limit themselves in the report to pointing up the particular ways in which the 'new generation' approach differed significantly from Prison Department design thinking at that time without attempting to reach final views on the extent to which the Department should in future take on board specific elements of the new approach. It singled out the following design elements:

(i) the campus type layout;
(ii) separation of vehicle and pedestrian access;
(iii) provision of separate house units for about 50–75 inmates, with cells giving directly on to a central multi-use area, and offering good sight lines for easy supervision, while encouraging staff–inmate interaction;
(iv) central dining for some or all of the inmates;
(v) integrated approach to furnishing and decoration to achieve a non-institutional environment, reduction of noise levels and optimum use of space;

(vi) maximum use of multipurpose facilities;
(vii) more generous provision of internal circulation areas;
(viii) the possibility of stacking accommodation vertically in a high-rise design solution.

The Working Party emphasised, however, the importance of key management principles, in particular:

(i) the provision of a suitable range of incentives and disincentives to prisoners, operated in the context of clearly articulated individual career plans;
(ii) an effective transfer system both within and between individual establishments;
(iii) unit management based on decentralised and dedicated teams within individual housing units;
(iv) relatively low levels of staffing.

The Working Party did not consider that the advantages of 'new generation' design thinking would accrue only if these principles were accepted in the precise way they had been formulated by the Federal Bureau. But they said that they were in no doubt that a comparable clear management philosophy was fundamental to the smooth and effective operation of any prison system. They concluded that unless this key point was grasped no amount of design innovation would of itself serve to fill the resultant vacuum.

References

Home Office (1984), *Managing the Long-Term Prison System: The Report of the Control Review Committee*, London: HMSO.

Home Office (1985), *New Directions in Prison Design: Report of a Home Office Working Party on American New Generation Prisons* (Platt Report), London: HMSO.

6 The telephone rings: long-term imprisonment
Mike Fitzgerald

Reflecting on the problems posed by the long-term prison system, a senior Prison Department official commented gloomily that a 'successful day' was one in which the telephone had not rung to announce some incident or disorder at one of the country's penal establishments.

The rise in the long-term prison population has been paralleled by an increasing number of major disorders and incidents, with subsequent official reviews, inquiries, and policy papers on the problems associated with long-term imprisonment. The Control Review Committee (Home Office 1984b), the subsequent Platt Report (Home Office 1985) and the report of the Review Team on the *Management Structure in Prison Department Establishments* (Home Office 1984a) are among the latest published responses to the gathering storm-clouds over long-term imprisonment. Together, they provide an instructive picture of contemporary prison authority thinking about the future of penal policy.

In this paper, I want to begin to trace the principles which would underscore an alternative proposal for long-term imprisonment. I will do this by looking at the *general orientation* of the Control Review Committee, and examining in some detail the basis on which it makes its recommendations. I then want to look at some of these recommendations, before moving on to make explicit some of the principles of an alternative model.

The Control Review Committee
In looking at the CRC, I want to focus on three broad areas: the definition of the conceptual problem; the problem on the ground; and the theory of management which the report endorses.

The conceptual problem
The CRC was set up in September 1983. As the Chair of the Committee has pointed out elsewhere, the CRC was established 'between the Albany riot and the announcement of the Government's

firmer policy towards parole for serious violent offenders — and we were asked to work as fast as possible. Our terms of reference focussed on the dispersal system, but did not confine us to it' (Langdon 1985, p. 8).

At the beginning of their report, the CRC outline 'the conceptual problem' they were to investigate (Home Office 1984b, paras 5–9). The report refers to the 'concentration vs dispersal' debate, and concludes that 'it is easy to state the conceptual and operational problems of the dispersal system' (Home Office 1984b, para. 9).

In order to help establish the basis for an alternative model of long-term imprisonment, I want to spend a little time unpacking the Committee's definition of the conceptual problem they were investigating. This is not an easy task. The problem has been defined in terms of 'concentration' and 'dispersal', 'Mountbatten vs Radzinowicz', 'security and control' for so long, by so many both inside and outside the prison service, that it is firmly entrenched in discussions around policies and practices of long-term imprisonment. But it is none the less important to try to redefine this conceptualisation which both defines the agenda, delimits the issues, and regulates the ways in which they are discussed.

In looking at the problems with the CRC's definition, it is worth reminding ourselves that the problems of long-term imprisonment did not begin with the immediate events leading up to the establishment of the Mountbatten Inquiry (Home Office 1966) and the debate subsequently sparked off by the later Radzinowicz report (Advisory Council on the Penal System 1968).

There have always been long-term prisoners, and the emphasis on security and control dominated penal policy long before the centralisation of the prison system towards the end of the nineteenth century. The work of Howard and Bentham are probably the most often-cited pre-nationalisation formulations of concern about security and control. 'Concentration vs dispersal', then, is a modern starting point for analysing issues which have been, and will always be at the heart of a prison system.

But there are difficulties facing those wishing to take a longer-term view of the modern starting point. One curious problem we face in tracing the development of concerns about security and control strategies is the relative paucity of material available on the prison system post-1914, a period in which the contemporary prison system was shaped. This stands in marked contrast to the exhaustive (and occasionally exhausting) studies of nineteenth-century imprisonment, and the *relative* availability of material on the period from the mid-1960s. Without access to that material, it is difficult to trace and analyse the growth of the long-term prison population in detail, and its impact on the rest of the prison system. The basis for the close marriage of 'security', on the one hand, and 'control' on the other remains uncertain, but is clearly well established by the time of the Mountbatten Inquiry.

'Security' and 'control' are not the same, nor are they necessarily or inevitably related in the ways assumed by the CRC. Tight security does not necessarily guarantee control, and nor do they, separately or together, inevitably produce good order and discipline in the prison system.

Indeed, prison literature has demonstrated how, across time, attempts to generate the tightest security have produced major problems of control, and serious internal disorders. King and Eliott (1977), Cohen and Taylor's (1981) study of 'E' Maximum Security Wing at Durham, and volumes of research conducted in British and non-British prison systems have demonstrated how overarching searches for the tightest security have provoked major problems of control, and provoked serious instances of individual and collective prisoners' disturbances. Annex D of the CRC report identifies eight out of the ten serious disorders listed as challenges to control, rather than attempts to breach security. The report itself acknowledges that the dispersal system 'has indeed been successful in preventing escapes, but the maintenance of control has been another matter' (Home Office 1984b, para. 8).

But despite this conclusion, the Committee apparently see no reason to examine the relationship between security and control more closely. I want to insist that the relationship deserves and needs the closest examination. For the ways in which 'security' and 'control' have been inextricably linked in current British penal policies were not, and are not, inevitable. These linkages are crucial because they establish key features and establish the driving forces of contemporary penal policies and practices. It is only by breaking the links, and re-establishing the relationship between security and control that we can begin to identify a different model of long-term imprisonment. I will return to this later.

By not re-examining the relationship between security and control, the Committee lock themselves into a reassertion of the received wisdoms of the definition of the problem they were charged to investigate.

I want to examine a further set of issues arising from the CRC's definition of the conceptual problem. These issues are clustered around their definition of 'control', and its relationship to 'good order and discipline'. Throughout the report, and Annex D, the Committee insist that there is only one problem of control in dispersal prisons — that of controlling prisoners. This is somewhat remarkable particularly as the Committee refer approvingly to the May Inquiry

(Home Office 1979) into the prisons system in their discussions of control.

The CRC might have defined their conceptual problem of control somewhat differently if they had reread the terms of reference of the May Inquiry, looked at the Home Office evidence submitted to it, and reminded themselves of the circumstances in which it was established, and later published.

The May Inquiry was set up by the Home Secretary (Merlyn Rees) faced with what he called 'the anarchy in the prisons'. In the weeks prior to the announcement of the setting up of this 'urgent and independent' inquiry, the extent and depth of the crisis of control in British prisons had been made manifest, not only by prisoner-related problems (overcrowding, disturbances), but also, more directly, by those of prison staff. In particular, the Inquiry was a response to prison officers' demands for improved pay and conditions, in pursuit of which they had been engaged in a long and increasingly bitter campaign of industrial action over several years. Home Office evidence to the May Inquiry revealed the nature and extent of that campaign. In 1976, prison officers took action on 34 occasions; in 1977, 42; and in 1978, 114. Over 50 different types of action were taken, and every penal establishment was directly affected.

The Home Secretary insisted that the campaign was about more than pay and conditions — it was about who controls the prisons. At the end of October 1978, governors warned that 'total breakdown is imminent in the prison system', a response to the campaign of the prison officers who the governors had told the House of Commons Expenditure Committee were 'probably presenting more difficulties than the prisoners' (Fitzgerald and Sim 1982, p. 138).

The reaction of uniformed staff to the May Report hardly gave grounds for reassurance. They reacted with an overwhelming sense of disappointment, anger and betrayal, with some arguing that it was 'irrelevant' to the problems in the prison service (Fitzgerald and Sim 1980).

There is little evidence to suggest that the control problems associated with prison staff have suddenly disappeared. Recent events at Styal, for example, show how the long-term problems identified in the May Report persist.

However it is defined, then, 'control' cannot be defined solely as a problem of handling prisoners. Rather, questions about control, and strategies for establishing and managing it, have to be addressed not only to the keepers' relations with the kept, but also to relationships between and among different categories of staff. It is a fundamental flaw in their conceptualisation of the problem of control, that the CRC fails to acknowledge, let alone attempt to deal with, the staff dimension of control. This failure is even more surprising given the Committee's view (Home Office 1984b, paras 16–17) of the likely impact of its proposals:

> At the end of the day, nothing else that we can say will be as important as the general proposition that relations between staff and prisoners are at the heart of the whole prison system and that control and security flow from getting that relationship right. Prisons cannot be run by coercion: they depend on staff having a firm, confident and humane approach that enables them to maintain close contact with inmates without abrasive confrontation. Nothing can be allowed to qualify the need for staff to be in control at all times, but we are sure that the very great majority will agree with us that this is best achieved by the unobtrusive use of their professional skill at involvement with prisoners. This is the foundation on which we want to build.
>
> We have not tried to analyse matters like the grievance procedures and the discipline system (which is, in any event, under review by a departmental committee). It is clear, however, that they have an important bearing on prisoners' perceptions of the fairness with which they are treated, and we are naturally aware that unanswered grievances and a sense of unfairness have often been found at the root of disorders in many countries and at many periods. All that we would say is that it is most important that both staff and inmates should feel that they are getting a fair deal, and that all who live and work in a prison should have a stake in preserving its orderly management. We are not suggesting that there should be collusion with prisoners for the sake of a quiet life, but that it should be recognised that prisons function on humane personal relations between staff and inmates, and that there should be sensible reasons for rules and routines.

I have quoted these paragraphs in full, because, taken with the 'definition of the conceptual problem', they form the clearest picture of the general orientation of the Committee. I want to spend a little time examining them.

My first concern is that these paragraphs illustrate yet again the Committee's confusion of 'security' and 'control'. 'Security' does not *necessarily* flow from getting right the relationship between prisoners and staff. I will argue later that it should. But the converse can also be true. Security can also be based on physical and technological architectures and systems and used not only to dominate, but also to *determine* relationships between prisoners and staff. Indeed, it is precisely this which has happened, most visibly in the post-Mountbatten era, in the British prison system. The *primacy of security* over staff–prisoner relations is the key feature of the British prison system.

It also helps us to understand the Committee's own preferred solution to the problems it faced — new prison designs. One need not go to the United States to understand the importance of design to the primacy of security. A visit to the Home Office library and a quick rereading of any books on prison architecture will suffice. One might begin with Bentham, for whom the importance of prison design was paramount. His 'Panopticon' was designed physically to structure the principles and philosophy of his proposed regimes. Thus, the Panopticon was designed to facilitate the maximum observation of prisoners by guards, and to ensure that prisoners, whether or not they were actually being observed, should at all times feel that they were observed:

> A plan was devised in which no part of the prison would be free from the potential observation of an inspector and in which the inspector's view of prisoners would be optimized. The prison was to be circular or polygonal. The cells were to be placed around the inside of the circumference; in the centre of the circle was to be placed the inspection-house in which the inspector or guard was to be situated. From the inspection house the cells were to be visible. The front of the cells were to be secured through an iron grid which would allow for total visibility of the inside of the cell by the inspector (quoted in Fitzgerald and Sim 1982, p. 163).

In identifying its preferred solution as the building of 'new generation' prisons, the Committee has sought to reassert the primacy of security over staff–prisoner relationships, and the determining role of the former over the latter.

My second major concern with paragraphs 16–17 of the CRC report stems from the proposition that 'nothing can be allowed to qualify the need for staff to be in control at all times'. Once again, this demonstrates the Committee's failure to understand the nature of 'control'. As I indicated above, to take no account of relationships between different categories of staff in looking at the problems of control in prisons is seriously misleading.

Moreover, the notion that staff can be in control at all times is, to be quiet blunt, ludicrous. The very considerable first-hand experience of individuals members of the Committee makes this assertion all the more surprising. There is also an array of research, both in this country and elsewhere, which demonstrates that such a proposition is untenable, even in the most extreme circumstances.

That such a proposition can be advanced leads me to a third concern. It is precisely the refusal openly to acknowledge the significance of 'negotiations' between staff and prisoners — both individual and collective — which most seriously undermines the potential impact of the Committee's recommendations. Let me illustrate this.

When members of the Committee visited the Barlinnie Special Unit, they would have arrived at a building housing this unit which was *not* purpose-built. If they had read the original papers which set out the principles on which the unit was to be based, they would have realised how those principles had *not* been operationalised. If they had talked to prison staff involved in the setting up of the unit, for example, the former principal officer, Ken Murray, and read Jimmy Boyle's account of the unit (or even talked to him), they would have realised that the success of the unit was not based on establishing the primacy of security, getting the design right, or establishing a regime in which officers had control at all times. Rather, the success of the unit was in the ways in which relationships between prisoners, between prisoners and staff, and among staff were the primary determining feature of the unit, and these relationships were themselves based on 'negotiation'. As MacDonald and Sim (1977, pp. 26–7) concluded:

> Due mainly to the efforts of its staff and prisoners the Special Unit has evolved over its five years into a self-styled therapeutic community. In terms of physical conditions and personal relationships between prisoners and staff the Unit has progressed away from the traditional authoritarian non-relationships and spartan conditions that the majority of long-term prisoners in Scotland face. There is a great deal of freedom, responsibility and personal choice given to prisoners within the confines of the Unit.
>
> The men wear their own clothes rather than prison uniform. They can decorate their own cells and keep books and record players. They can cook their own food, supplementing prison rations with food bought with their own money. Their mail, unlike that of prisoners in the traditional system, is unrestricted and uncensored. Access to visitors is also unrestricted except when the men are locked up at night.
>
> Each prisoner plans his own routine for the day and democratic community meetings take place weekly to discuss any issues that may have arisen. Any member of the community — either staff or prisoner — who 'lets the side down' by breaking the rules, can end up in the 'hot-seat' where his actions are discussed, criticized and chastised by the other members of the community, again whether staff or prisoner.
>
> These weekly meetings function as a place where people learn to talk out any problems they might have in an open and objective way — something which is impossible in the traditional system. When a decision affecting domestic issues has to be made, each man, staff or prisoner, has one vote. One of the earliest and most symbolic taken was to remove the door of the punishment cell, which meant that reliance on the old method of punishing an individual by locking him up in solitary confinement was abandoned in favour of the new community based 'hot-seat'. This, according to both the staff and the inmates, is a much more effective means of control than the measures used in the traditional system, measures which, in the majority of cases, serve only to make the prisoner more resentful and bitter.
>
> Ultimately, it is this ability to make democratic decisions and the positive staff-prisoner relationships, together with the physical environment far removed from the obsolete conditions of the majority of prison buildings, which makes the Special Unit unique.

The significance of the early years of the Special Unit in the context of this paper is that it *demonstrated* the general proposition that 'relations between staff and prisoners are at the heart of the whole prison system and that control and security flow from getting that relationship right' (Home Office 1984b, para. 16).

The Special Unit is a maximum-security unit, but security once established was not allowed to determine strategies of control, which in turn did not determine staff–prisoner relationships. Thus the Special Unit provided a clear alternative to the Committee's conceptualisation of the problem and its proposals for change. (In the reaction to it by other members of the prison staff, it also provided evidence of the complexities of control which I discussed earlier.)

Let me make clear my reasons for using the example of the Special Unit. I do not wish to romanticise it, not do I wish to underestimate the problems it continues to face both from within the prison service and from the outside world. My purpose in using it is that it provides the clearest attempt to manage the problems associated with long-term imprisonment on the foundation which the CRC itself endorses.

But the problem with the CRC report is that the Committee does not seem to want to build on its own foundation stone of staff–prisoner relations. Thus, in advocating 'open regimes', the CRC not only asserts that staff must be in control at all times, it also insists that by an 'open regime'

> we certainly do not mean one that allows prisoners to decide what to do from day to day, but one that offers a range of constructive activities, the opportunity of association, and supervision by staff who have the time and training to take a personal interest in each inmate as an individual. We are sure that this is best achieved within a clear framework of rules that are applied firmly and fairly (Home Office 1984b, para. 13).

The CRC's foundation stone is not to be laid on bare ground. It is to be placed *inside* a security system which will *determine* the nature of control in long-term prisons, and thus the nature of staff–prisoner relationships. Far from being the foundation stone, staff–prisoner relations will be the *object* of the whole edifice the CRC wants to erect — in the long term through 'new generation designs'. For it is these designs — very much in vogue in the United States — which provide the possibility to realise the good of 'concentration', without the dangers that led Radzinowicz and May to advise against such a policy. The CRC's interest in new generation architecture is not dissimilar to that of Bentham quoted earlier. It is the same *utilitarianism* of design which makes it attractive to the Committee for the same sorts of reason.

New generation architecture is the long-term strategy. In the short term, 15 years (a long term of imprisonment!), the options open to the CRC were more limited.

Planning for control: the theory of management

The consequences and limitations of the Committee's definition of the conceptual problem became even clearer in looking at the short-term proposals. These depend in large measure on a theory of management which the Committee both explicitly and implicitly threads throughout the report.

I am not arguing that the problem with the CRC report is that it provides 'managerialist' definitions of the problems, and proposes 'managerialist' solutions. Such a view is oversimplistic and one-dimensional. Rather it is the theory of management expressed in the report, and to be found in other recent policy documents of the Prison Department, with which I want to take issue.

It is not management *per se* which concerns me, but rather the Committee's oversimplified, and even naive understanding of what management is, and how it is practised which worries me. (It caused major headaches for the May Inquiry, too.)

Essentially, the theory of management one finds in the report is that managers determine policy from above, and hand it down — through detailed management systems spreading out from Prison Department headquarters to every penal institution in the country — for the managed to implement in strict accordance with management's intentions and instructions. But such a theory is wholly unrealistic. Whatever the organisation and 'chains of command' established, and however frequently management systems are overhauled, effective management depends upon relationships with the managed. Management is a co-operative venture, with the flow of communication being multi- rather than unidimensional. Simply because people in management positions propose particular policies, and establish particular systems, that does not mean that policies will be implemented. The assertion of the 'right to manage' no more ensures the legitimacy and authority of management, than the assertion by the managed of their right to be managed properly ensures that they will be.

As recent reports from within the prison service have made clear, the service is no longer able to operate in the highly rigid, hierarchical ways in which it might have done in the past. It is interesting, for example, to note that references to 'industrial relations' are now regularly found in the annual reports of a service whose traditions and history owe more to the military than to the commercial. The prison service, like the police and armed forces themselves, is having to adapt to, and adopt different forms of managerial organisation, based on different assumptions, procedures, practices *and* styles. 'Chains of command' have to be replaced by 'lines of acountability', 'compliance' and 'obedience' by 'negotiation', and 'co-operation'.

Consent can no longer be assumed. It has to be worked for, and maintained.

The industrial action by staff referred to above is an illustration of the difficulties the prison authorities face in their managerial task. The increasing outspokenness of staff about the limitations of management in the prison service should be a major concern to the Prison Department. It is interesting to note that in their description of the disturbance at Gartree in 1978, the CRC omits any reference to the reaction to management of prison staff who produced their own account of the disorder.

> It has now become obvious, even to the general public, that these misguided people in the Home Office responsible for the administration of the Prison Service have failed dismally. The Home Office Prison Department can now be seen for what it really is — a rambling, inefficient, bureaucratic machine that seems unable to correct itself despite being constantly reminded of its inadequacy (quoted in Fitzgerald and Sim 1982, p. 15).

Most recently, the reactions of different categories of staff to the report of the Review Team on the *Management Structure in Prison Department Establishments* (Home Office 1984a) indicate how much needs to be done if staff are to have confidence in management, and its strategies for managing (see, for example, the *Prison Service Journal*, January 1985, pp. 12–16). Without such confidence, there will be major problems in the implementation of short-term proposals for change.

Developing an alternative proposal
Having examined the 'general orientation' of the CRC, I want briefly to sketch out some of the elements for an alternative basis for looking at problems of long-term imprisonment. I do not claim that this scenario is complete or fully worked out. But what matters is the principles on which it is based.

The prison population
As the CRC recognises, any proposals for the dispersal system cannot be made without reference to the rest of the prison system. The first priority, then, of any alternative proposal should be to demonstrate why the overall prison population should be dramatically reduced. Sentencing policies must be changed to take significantly more people out of the prison system altogether, and to reduce the lengths of sentences of many of those who will continue to be sent there. This is not, I hasten to add, a radical or idealist proposal. It is one which has been recommended by official enquiries, and which has actually been implemented with some success in the last

few years. None the less, it still remains the case that the majority of people sent to prison are sent for periods of one year or less. Overcrowding continues to be rife in the prison system. The consequences of overcrowding have been well documented, for example in the work of Her Majesty's Chief Inspector of Prisons. Overcrowding is a major problem for the prison service which threatens the CRC proposals for the dispersal system. Overcrowding, for example, poses a direct threat to classification procedures, to which the report attaches much importance and which it seeks to enhance. Classification is often put forward as a key to successful prison management. The CRC report (Home Office 1984b, para. 25) itself expresses concern that 'the decision to allocate a prisoner to one establishment rather than another is a disturbingly arbitrary one', and the Chief Inspector of Prisons has been less than complimentary about existing categorisation procedures and practices (Home Office 1984c).

There are a whole set of issues around classification and its possibilities which has produced a huge amount of research-based literature, particularly in the United States. I do not want to rehearse the arguments about classification here, save to say that it is apparent that classification procedures owe more to largely administratively-based convenience and unsupported assumptions about human behaviour than they do to anything else. Rather, I simply want to draw attention to the consequences of overcrowding for classification systems of whatever type. Penal practices and research have demonstrated conclusively how 'efforts to match offenders reasonably with facilities and programmes — a major goal of classification — is directly undermined by sheer weight of numbers' (Clements 1982, p. 73). Clements (1982, p. 75) shows how the tendency to overclassify implicit in any system of classification is compounded under conditions of overcrowding:

> The most flagrant abuse of classification procedures is the initial assignment of inmates to correctional facilities solely according to where space is available. Most space is made available so to speak, in the maximum security institutions . . . One consequence of the 'space available' approach is initial overclassification of offenders.

Without substantial reductions in prison numbers throughout the prison system, then, overcrowding will continue to constrain and undermine proposals for shifts in penal policies and practices.

Staff–prisoner relationships

Any alternative strategy for dealing with the problems of long-term imprisonment must use as a *foundation* staff–prisoner relationships. I have already commented on the contradictions in the CRC's position on this. An alternative strategy for long-term imprisonment necessarily involves a different conceptualisation of the problem, a different analysis of 'the problem on the ground', and a different theory of prison management.

Conceptualisation of the problem　The starting point should be the explicit recognition that the major problem facing those sentenced to long-term imprisonment is the *fact* that they have been so sentenced, rather than the regimes and conditions in which they serve that sentence. As Flanagan (1982, p. 85) has observed:

> The principal punishment inflicted on the majority of offenders receiving the sanction of incarceration is deprivation of liberty, autonomy and relationships with persons in the larger society. In several recent studies data derived from interviews with long-term prisoners have shown that these types of deprivation, which are inherent in the sanction of removal and confinement, are perceived by the inmates as its most serious consequences. Secondary punishments inflicted on the offender — including denial of certain political rights, lack of meaningful work opportunities, restricted personal space, loss of privacy, substandard medical care, economic dependency, regimentation, verbal and physical harassment by fellow inmates and guards, a milieu of tension and violence — pale in comparison with the primary sanction of removal from society.

Recognition of the overriding importance of the sentence itself provides a very different starting point to that in the CRC report. Most importantly, it suggests that policy should be oriented towards *minimising* rather than *compounding* the fact of long-term imprisonment by secondary deprivations and punishments within the prison itself. In making this argument, I am following Flanagan (1982, p. 86) who defines such a proposal as less radical than conservative!

> Proposals to minimise the potentially deleterious consequences of confinement are advanced not because of an assumption that humanising prisons will make them any more effective in rehabilitating or reintegrating offenders; rather prisons need not be onerous places in which to live and work in order to accomplish the tasks assigned them by society — protecting the public and punishing offenders.

The problem on the ground　If the intention is to minimise rather than compound the fact of imprisonment by secondary punishments or deprivations, the prison authorities must be prepared to *take seriously* prisoners' definitions of problems and anxieties about penal policies and practices. Let me be quite clear: I am not suggesting that this involves 'equal partnership'. Far from it. The fact of incarceration and the over-determination of the prison system on the individual prisoner establishes beyond any doubt the one-sidedness of power relationships inherent in any system for long-term imprisonment. Indeed it is clear from Jimmy Boyle's (1984) accounts of the Special Unit that taking seriously staff–prisoner relationships as the foundation on which to build long-term prison regimes may actually *increase* rather than lessen the 'pains of imprisonment'.

But if prisoner–staff relationships are to be used as the basis of prison regimes, serious consideration must be given to staff and prisoner accounts of prison life. Staff–prisoner relationships involve negotiations, and for negotiations to take place each side must be able to speak, and to have its accounts heard and granted meaning by the other.

The CRC recognised this early on in its report when it acknowledged that grievance procedures and disciplinary systems have 'an important bearing on prisoners' perceptions of the fairness with which they are treated, and we are naturally aware that unanswered grievances and a sense of unfairness have often been found at the root of disorders in many countries and at many periods' (Home Office 1984b, para. 17).

Unfortunately the CRC largely ignored this crucial paragraph in its own proposals. If staff–prisoner relationships are to be the basis of any regime, both formal and informal rules, regulations and practices must be acknowledged, and put into the arena of negotiation. Long-term prisoner accounts of prison life reveal the levels of discretion and negotiations available on a day-to-day basis on the ground. Under present arrangements, these can create major problems for prison managers, as Philip Wheatley (1981), for example, has documented.

It is in the routines of day-to-day life that relations between staff and prisoners have their greatest impact. It was precisely this level which the regime developed at the Special Unit began by addressing.

And when outbreaks of disorder occur — either individual or collective — the meanings attached to such outbreaks by all sides must also be considered as the basis on which to propose changes to regimes. This requires a major shift in Home Office thinking, as the accounts of serious disorders in Annex D of the CRC report make clear. No recognition of any sort is given to competing definitions of these disturbances, even, for example, when prisoners' accounts of events were subsequently upheld in external courts of law.

If staff–prisoner relationships are to be the basis for regimes, trust and confidence must be built on all sides. This will not be easy. To build such trust and confidence, it is essential that secondary punishments are minimised. Existing formal and informal methods for controlling individual prisoners or staff need to be reconsidered.

Transfers, for example, should not be used as a disciplinary device for either staff or prisoners. Basic provisions for education, work, communications with the outside world, accommodation, health, recreation and association should be established, and not subject to the one-sided discretion of individual staff or institutions. Such provisions should not be privileges to be won and withdrawn at the behest of the prison authorities. Rather, they should be 'rights', a constituent part of any prison regime.

Both staff and prisoners must also have clear channels for ensuring those rights. Where appropriate, these should be legally based to guard against the arbitrariness and abuses of power so much in evidence in existing informal and formal systems of control.

Planning a career The CRC has much to say about planning 'careers' for long-term prisoners. Rather than go through their proposals point by point, I want to offer an alternative view of planning a career, based firmly on the preceding sections of this paper. This involves accepting that such plans are an integral feature of long-term prison regimes, rather than the ultimate expression of security and related control strategies.

In planning a career, the consequence of a long-term sentence must be explicitly recognised. Prisoners sentenced to 15 years, for example, are going to spend a significant proportion of their adult life inside the prison system. If planning a career is to mean anything, it must involve a recognition of the long-term nature of long-term imprisonment. Programmes of education and training, for example, cannot be based on programmes that run for a couple of years at most, and seek to provide specific skills which long-term prisoners taking such a course are often unable to utilise. Educational training programmes must be geared towards equipping individual long-term prisoners with skills and qualifications which they can make use of during later stages of their imprisonment.

A career approach to long-term imprisonment, then, involves goals which are themselves long-term, and which make sense for prisoners in the context in which they are serving their sentences. It necessarily involves removing the discretion to disrupt individuals' agreed plans by sudden transfers, or withdrawal of 'privileges' or facilities, avoiding sudden shifts in policy imposed from on high, and protecting agreed regimes from becoming the site on which different categories of staff take action against each other.

New generation prison management In sketching out an alternative starting point for long-term prison regimes, I am also arguing for a 'new generation' of management in the prison system. Security and control strategies would not determine staff–prisoner relations, rather, staff–prisoner relations would provide the basis for 'good order and discipline' through the development of control strategies which are built up, rather than handed down. Security provisions would be assured separately without being overdetermining, as the example of the Special Unit illustrates.

Such a model has profound implications for prison management. Management must plan resources (human and physical) to facilitate the development of the overall strategy. Career planning, for example, requires that resource planning takes account of and responds to regimes built on staff–prisoner relations rather than seeking to determine what those regimes should be. As I have already indicated, a recognition that the key deprivation is the deprivation of liberty requires that management seek to minimise secondary deprivations.

New generation prison management should work on the principle of 'bottom-up' rather than 'top-down' patterns of building this alternative long-term prison strategy. Management systems need to be developed to meet the needs of a prison system based on multilevel decision-making and multidirectional communication.

The major shift in new generation prison management would be in the area of *accountability*. Management could no longer simply assert 'the right to manage' as the basis for seeking co-operation. The Prison Department will need to open itself up to both internal and external scrutiny. Internally, managers would play a full role in the determination of institutional regimes and priorities, and be accountable to the staff and inmates of that institution. This is not a simple-minded recipe for 'prisoner power': it is the logical consequence of establishing a prison system which will recognise the centrality of staff–prisoner relations. It represents not restrictions on management, but a means by which management can develop trust, confidence and co-operation in its decision-making processes, characteristics which official and unofficial enquiries have shown are currently notable largely by their absence in contemporary British prisons.

New generation prison management should also be accountable externally. This might present as many difficulties as internal accountability for a Prison Department characterised historically by its obsession with secrecy. Visibility and accountability should be provided, for example, through the guarantee of legal rights for prisoners previously proposed. Independent public enquiries into outbreaks of serious disorder, or proposals for major shifts in penal policy should ensure that all interests are able to take part in debates about penal affairs.

It is in the interests of the prison service to open itself up in these ways, for ultimately the problems of long-term imprisonment are not of the making of the keepers and kept but are part of a set of wider issues in crime and society. Undoubtedly the implications of a new strategy for long-term imprisonment are daunting, but the prospects of simply sitting waiting for the telephone to ring are arguably even more so.[1]

Note

1 I am solely responsible for the content of this paper, but as always I am deeply indebted to Joe Sim.

References

Advisory Council on the Penal System (1968), *The Regime for Long-Term Prisoners in Conditions of Maximum Security* (Radzinowicz Report), London: HMSO.

Boyle, J. (1984), *The Pain of Confinement*, London: Cannongate.

Clements, C. (1982), 'The Relationship of Offender Classification to Problems of Prison Overcrowding', *Crime and Delinquency*, vol. 28, pp. 72–81.

Cohen, S. and Taylor, L. (1981), *Psychological Survival*, 2nd edn, Harmondsworth: Penguin.

Fitzgerald, M. and Sim, J. (1980), 'Legitimating the Prison Crisis: a Critical Review of the May Report', *Howard Journal*, vol 19, pp. 73–84.

Fitzgerald, M. and Sim, J. (1982), *British Prisons*, 2nd edn, Oxford: Basil Blackwell.

Flanagan, T.J. (1982), 'Correctional Policy and the Long-term Prisoner', *Crime and Delinquency*, vol. 28, pp. 82–95.

Home Office (1966), *Report of the Inquiry into Prison Escapes and Security*, (Mountbatten Report), Cmnd. 3175. London: HMSO.

Home Office (1979), *Report of the Committee of Inquiry into the United Kingdom Prison Services* (May Report), Cmnd. 7673, London: HMSO.

Home Office (1984a), *Management Structure in Prison Department Establishments: Report of the Review Team*, London: Home Office.

Home Office (1984b), *Managing the Long-Term Prison System: The Report of the Control Review Committee*, London: HMSO.

Home Office (1984c), *Prison Categorisation Procedures: Report by H.M. Chief Inspector of Prisons*, London: Home Office.

Home Office (1985), *New Directions in Prison Design: Report of a Home Office Working Party on American New Generation Prisons*, (Platt Report), London: HMSO.

King, R. and Elliott, K.W. (1977), *Albany: The Birth of a Prison, End of an Era?*, London: Routledge and Kegan Paul.

Langdon, A.J. (1985), 'Control Review Committee', *Prison Service Journal* no. 57, pp. 8–12.

MacDonald, D. and Sim, J. (1977), *Scottish Prisons and the Special Unit*, Edinburgh: Scottish Council for Civil Liberties.

Wheatley, P. (1981), 'Riots and Mass Disorder', *Prison Service Journal*, no. 44, pp. 1–4.

7 Civil liberties, the law and the long-term prisoner
Rod Morgan and Genevra Richardson

In one sense the 'civil liberty' implications of imprisonment remain constant whatever the duration of the sentence. All adult sentenced prisoners are subject to the same statutory provisions governing custodial conditions and the duration of a sentence has no legal significance except in relation to release, parole and remission. Only where their legal status differs (the untried, the convicted but unsentenced and the sentenced), or where different sentences apply (detention centre, youth custody or imprisonment), are prisoners subject to different statutory rules, and even then the differences are few and are subject to the same procedures for inspection, grievance ventilation and judicial oversight. Yet there are important administrative and cultural distinctions which affect the degree to which long-term prisoners are vulnerable to particular prison conditions and procedures.

First, ever since the introduction by the Prison Commission in the 1940s of the distinction between 'trainable' and 'non-trainable' prisoners, long-termers have been subject to some degree of sentence planning involving classification and allocation to more or less specialised institutions. Secondly, long-term prisoners are by definition those prisoners guilty of more serious crimes, the possible repetition of which invariably leads them initially to be classified in Categories A or B. For both reasons, whereas short- and medium-term prisoners generally serve their sentences in one or two institutions located near the area where they live and were convicted, long-termers tend to be housed in specialist institutions organised regionally and nationally.

This arrangement produces an irony. There is a cultural affinity between long-term prisoners and the prison authorities. They have genuinely to live *with* each other and tend, in consequence, to live *for* each other. Historically, the training prison sector has been the fulcrum of the service's objectives and planning and the major beneficiary of resources. Long-term prisoners generally are allocated the best facilities; short-term unsentenced and untried prisoners the worst. Short-term prisoners have little interest in and capacity for collective action; and being exploitable in a system under pressure of scarce resources, they are exploited. Yet, though long-termers as a *group* are generally bought off with the best conditions, the collective threat they pose renders them liable *individually* to close surveillance and special control provision.

Some provisions are routine, for example the rules restricting visitors, ordering frequent cell changes, limiting cell furnishings and laying down close escort arrangements for Category A prisoners (Circular Instruction 10/1976 as amended), or planning for lifers (Circular Instruction 2/1986). Other provisions, which can be either formal or informal, are employed intermittently when individual prisoners are deemed troublesome. However, we shall argue that the apparatus with which prison staff negotiate the control of long-term prisoners in England and Wales is for the most part secretive, coercive and discretionary, and that it is the long-term population, despite their relatively superior physical conditions, whose 'civil liberties' are most vulnerable. They bear the impact of those aspects of prisons administration which are most covert in application and damaging in consequence. In this paper we shall consider three aspects of imprisonment with profound consequences for the quality of life and careers of individual long-term prisoners — physical and regime standards (including their inspection); the formal disciplinary system and other control measures; and parole and licence decisions.

Before doing so we need to say something about two general themes: the concept of 'prisoners' rights' and the manner in which the Prison Department accounts for its work. The 'civil liberties' of any class of persons are safeguarded both by their capacity to seek remedies individually, and by provisions whereby the public authorities whose policies affect their quality of life can be monitored.

Prisoners' rights

The term 'civil liberties' is being used here in a loose prescriptive sense to convey the combination of rights and freedoms which any acceptable prison regime must respect. It is necessary, however, to be more specific. Claims are being made increasingly to prisoners' rights. We shall argue that while many such claims are merely rhetorical, the concept of prisoners' rights has validity and relevance. Strictly, an individual asserts a right only when he or she makes a claim to performance by another. The right is legal when the correlative duty is owed at law and moral when the duty is morally enforceable. The two are not coterminous but arguably the latter should inform the former. The claim to a right in this strict sense must be distinguished from the assertion of a mere 'liberty', which implies no correlative duty to act or forbear (Hohfeld 1919; Hart 1955).

The argument here will proceed on the assumption that basic (or moral) rights exist (Gewirth 1984), that they provide an essential safeguard for the individual against any state, whatever its ideological hue (Campbell 1983), and that they should be reflected in the law. Further, it will be assumed that punishment inevitably involves some loss of those rights, although the precise extent of that loss will vary.

In the UK imprisonment formally constitutes the law's most severe penalty. As a consequence of breaking the criminal law individuals are segregated from the rest of society and subjected to a variety of constraints, frequently resulting in the alteration of their legally recognised rights and liberties. Certain of these restrictions flow inevitably from the fact of imprisonment, while others are less directly related. It will be argued that precisely because all prisoners automatically suffer the loss of certain legal rights, they become particularly vulnerable to further loss and special care is thus required to safeguard and even to supplement their remaining basic rights. What is true of all prisoners, we shall argue, is particularly true of long-termers.

In principle any alteration in the legal rights of a prisoner must be justified by reference to the justification of punishment in general and imprisonment in particular. It follows, therefore, that the extent of the 'acceptable' alteration will vary depending on the nature of the justification. Of course, in a situation where no specific aim or justification commands general support, such a prescription does little to clarify the position. However, it can be argued that, although the extent of the residue will vary widely, the prisoner must always retain some rights under any view of imprisonment (Richardson 1985a), if only to distinguish the sanction of imprisonment from yet more intrusive forms of punishment (for example, slavery).

Thus the recognition of rights in prisoners is essential whatever view of imprisonment prevails. Here a minimalist approach will be adopted. It will be assumed that, for whatever reason, segregation from the community is the primary function of imprisonment and that once segregation is achieved conditions within prison should approximate as closely as possible to those outside. Under such a regime the prisoner would retain all legal rights and duties which do not conflict with the fact of segregation. Such an approach has been widely advocated (King and Morgan 1980) and has received some support from official bodies (HM Chief Inspector of Prisons 1983; Home Office 1984a, para. 108).

However, the scope of the prisoner's rights cannot be limited to the retention of the rights generally held outside prison: precisely because he is a prisoner he should possess additional special rights (Hart 1955) deriving from his imprisonment. Imprisonment increases an individual's dependence through deprivation of certain basic rights. This dependence imposes additional duties of provision and protection on the state, with correlative rights in the imprisoned. While this is true of all prisoners, it can be argued that the longer the term of imprisonment served the greater the dependence and so the more extensive the resulting obligations. Again, the nature of the additional special rights will reflect the preferred view of imprisonment. Where normalisation is the aim the authorities would, in an ideal world, be under a duty to provide an adequate range of all the facilities available in the community, not merely those to which a free individual might claim a legal right.

According to the above argument a prisoner should retain all those general rights which are not forfeited by the fact of segregation. In addition, a special duty should be imposed on the authorities to provide a certain range of facilities with correlative rights in the prisoner. The application of this ideal to long-term imprisonment immediately raises the question of variation throughout the sentence. Strictly, any variation in a prisoner's rights can be justified only by reference to a change in the demands of segregation (security and control), or by reference to a change in the consequences of a prisoner's dependency. A prisoner who, for example, poses a demonstrably exceptional high security or control risk might properly suffer a further reduction in his freedom of movement, while a life-sentence prisoner nearing release might require special facilities to enable him to counteract the effects of prolonged dependency. This need to justify any alteration in a prisoner's rights itself implies additional 'due process' rights in the prisoner in order to enable the adequacy of any justification to be tested.

The ideal combination of rights advocated here will be compared below with the current legal status of long-term prisoners. But it is necessary first to place the question of *legal* rights in context. The rights urged above would be legal and enforceable in court. Despite the problems attaching to court enforcement on both a practical (Aronson 1982; Morgan and Bronstein 1985) and a fundamental level (Unger 1976; Prosser 1982), its advantages arguably outweigh its disadvantages. Legal recognition implies the ultimate stamp of formal authority and carries the political significance essential in a world of limited resources. However, we are certainly not advocating constant resort to legal adjudication. The courts should be used as a last resort, to supplement rather than to supplant less formal control mechanisms.

Prisons' accountability

Were the above approach to prisoners' rights to be adopted in law, it would provide the core feature of what we would regard as a fully accountable prison system by providing a means for individual redress. Unlike the current statutory framework, the law would set out unambiguously and in detail what rights prisoners do forfeit and to what they are specifically entitled (JUSTICE 1983; Plotnikoff 1986). But in addition the law would need also to provide for, and to be underpinned by, a network of administrative mechanisms to facilitate the effective monitoring of prison conditions and authority decisions. Proper accountability requires a precise statement of who is accountable to whom and for what. And, where one (inferior) body is made accountable to an external body (as the Director-General and Prisons Board are to the Secretary of State and the latter to Parliament), accountability demands not only a clear statement of the inferior body's purposes, powers, duties and responsibilities, but also corresponding statements outlining management accountability systems *within* the inferior body.

We have suggested that ideally the precise nature of the general rights retained and the special rights acquired by long-term prisoners should relate to the demands of segregation and the degree of dependency, and that they might vary according to the duration or stage in the sentence. The factors relating to either segregation or dependency which might themselves vary and thus justify a corresponding variation in rights would include: discipline, security, control, personal needs and welfare, all of which are open to broad interpretation by the administration. Thus, in order that all variations *are* justified, full accountability is required concerning the allocation of prisoners to classes, the entitlements of prisoner classes, and measures of the delivery of services to classes. This would suggest that, in so far as allocation and entitlement criteria are not stated in the relevant statutes or statutory instruments, the administrative directives (standing orders and circular instructions) dealing with them must be detailed, comprehensive, unambiguous and publicly available.

Most prisons currently provide most prisoners with more 'privileges' than they need be given most of the time. Despite the pessimistic predictions of persons resisting the introduction of legally enforceable prisoners' rights (Home Office 1979, para. 4.28) there is no reason to believe it would result in a 'moral vacuum' with prisoners being given their minimum entitlements and no more. We take the minimalist approach to segregation to mean that prisoners' quality of life should rise above the entitled minimum whenever pressures on public expenditure ease and resources permit. That being so, the question arises as to whether individual prisoners should ever be given fewer facilities than are the organisational norm (but not legal minimum) for a particular class of prisoners or prison if staff, for whatever reason, so decide. Such selective treatment can never be avoided absolutely and arguably should not be. Social order in any organisation is achieved through such negotiations. The regime in a single ostensibly undifferentiated prison is never the same for all prisoners: it varies by job, cell location, staff grouping, and so on. But we would argue that the regime should not differ with regard to basic facilities and opportunities likely to be the subject of special prisoner rights — such matters as letters and visits, personal possessions, association with fellow prisoners, and so on. To prevent unjustifiable discrimination against individual prisoners we need regularly to know what the basic regime comprises, what the 'hotel service' outputs are.

The Director-General has annually to produced a written report including certain information (accommodation, population, nature of prisoners' work and punishments) specified in section 5 of the Prison Act 1952. However, the Department is not statutorily obliged to report on most aspects of its work, and chooses to remain silent about many of its decisions and services, including those relating to long-term prisoners. Even the increased flow and publication of data, financial and administrative, stemming from the application of the governments' Financial Management Initiative omits all reference to several crucial decision-making and service areas (see Home Office 1985b). We cite examples of these deficiencies below. For the moment we need assert simply that most administrative directives covering decisions and services are secret, and there are few regime output measures either collected or published. For the most part we know neither how individuals are allocated to classes generally, nor what facilities they receive once allocated (Morgan, R. 1983).

To support the framework of rights we have outlined, there is need for more openness of *transparent stewardship* (Morgan 1985a). In the same way as the Director-General accounts for his budget, so also must he account for the manner in which he exercises his delegated powers with regard to prisoners. Administrative directives should be published, the evidentiary basis on which allocation decisions are made should be more open, and physical standards and regime performance indicators devised and published (Casale 1984).

Further, more effective inspection is required, particularly with regard to long-term prisoners, in order to bolster a more transparent stewardship. It is precisely in the area of long-term prisoner careers that existing inspection mechanisms are weakest. Though he is now undertaking 'thematic' inspections, the Chief Inspector of Prisons devotes most of his attention to the inspection of individual institutions and their day-to-day delivery of services (Morgan 1985b). Further, the local watchdogs, the Boards of Visitors, have a specifically local mandate. Once prisoners in whose career characteristics they may begin to take an interest are transferred (as is not infrequently the pattern), their scrutiny is effectively nullified. Boards are told they are appointed to individual institutions and not to the prison system, and they have yet to develop an effective collective framework for national monitoring or action.

In addition to the general absence of prisoner career data, neither the Chief Inspector nor the Boards of Visitors publish systematic information on prisoner facilities or regime characteristics for individual establishments. Indeed the Boards of Visitors are not even required constitutionally to make public any report on their duties and virtually none do so (Maguire and Vagg 1984). These shortcomings in the 'independent' yet 'internal' inspection mechanisms are all the more important because prisons are subject to Crown immunity. We can see no justification for the perpetuation of this arrangement. The reports of the Chief Inspector repeatedly attest to the inadequacy of inspection by prison medical officers (as opposed to environmental health officers) of prison kitchens for the purposes of the Food and Drugs Act 1955 and the Food Hygiene (General) Regulations 1970 (see, for example, the Chief Inspector's reports on Pucklechurch, Albany, Hollesley Bay and Dartmoor, all 1985).

Given the natural invisibility of most decisions and services in prisons, it follows that external observers cannot easily monitor the degree to which the Department is safeguarding the civil liberties of any category of prisoners nor how the delivery of services to prisoners is changing over time (Morgan, R. 1983). The transparent stewardship for which we have argued needs to be reinforced by detailed reports from the Inspectorate as to the gap between standards sought and found, and some similar public sign of life is required from the local watchdogs. The provision of these fuller accounts would then enable the courts, when considering individual wrongs and remedies, to judge more accurately the weight to be attached to security and other administrative considerations.

Prison standards
Outside the prison context statutorily imposed duties can give rise to special rights in the affected individual. He or she can bring an action for breach of statutory duty and claim damages arising from any failure to meet that duty. It might be assumed, therefore,

that the duties imposed on the prison authorities by the Prison Rules, a piece of delegated legislation, would provide a source of special rights in prisoners. However, the courts have persistently denied that the Prison Rules can give rise to an action for breach of statutory duty (*Arbon* v *Anderson* [1943] KB 252). In any context the availability of such an action will depend on the court's view of the intentions of the legislature and, with regard to the Prison Rules, it is clear that policy considerations have played a significant part: 'it would be fatal to all discipline in prisons if governors and warders had to perform their duties always with the fear of an action before their eyes if they in any way deviated from the rules' (*Arbon* v *Anderson*, at p. 255).

Thus, despite the occasional show of strength by the courts (*Raymond* v *Honey* [1982] 1 All ER 756), it would seem that, for the moment at least, prisoners have no direct private legal means of enforcing compliance with the Prison Rules (*O'Reilly* v *Mackman* [1982] 3 All ER 1124). However, a possible means of collateral enforcement is illustrated by a remand prisoner's attempt to challenge his transfer to a distant prison (*R* v *Secretary of State ex p. McAvoy* [1984] 3 All ER 417). McAvoy claimed that his transfer was illegal since the Secretary of State had failed to give due weight to his 'rights', reflected in the Prison Rules, concerning lay and legal visits (Rules 34(1) and 37(1)). The judge agreed that the obligations contained in the Prison Rules must be taken into account by the Secretary of State when making transfer decisions under the Act (Prison Act 1952, s. 12(2)), but declared that if 'operational and security reasons' are claimed for the transfer, then the court should not look behind those reasons which will almost invariably outweigh the prisoner's 'right' to visits.

Thus, ostensibly at least, the court was providing a means for the indirect enforcement of the Prison Rules by expressing itself willing to ensure that the powers in the Act are exercised with regard to the obligations in the Rules. However, the case also provides a revealing comment on the nature of the obligations contained in the Rules. *McAvoy* established a right to have the authority's obligations taken into account. But the prisoner concerned never claimed a justiciable right to receive visits, and in the event the court retreated before the Home Secretary's evocation of 'operational and security reasons'. It can be argued, however, that even were a right to visits recognised under the Prison Rules, such a right could never be absolute since the wording of the Rules (as is so often the case) vests the authorities with extensive unstructured discretion (Zellick 1981; JUSTICE 1983). Indeed, under the present law the right to have visits considered is perhaps all the prisoner could expect, though the degree to which the court was prepared to monitor that exercise in 'consideration' fell far short of the level of inquiry envisaged by the due process rights advocated earlier.

The failure to establish special rights under the Prison Rules has led prisoners aggrieved by an alleged breach of the Rules to seek to establish an additional legal wrong. Thus, a prisoner who believed the control unit in which he had been detained had been set up and operated in breach of the Rules, being unable to claim directly for breach of statutory duty, had instead to allege false imprisonment (*Williams* v *Home Office (No 2)* [1981] 1 All ER 1211). This approach required the court to decide whether imprisonment which was lawful at its inception could later become unlawful due either to a deterioration in the physical conditions or to a subsequent misapplication of the Rules. In *Williams* the court held that it could not. This approach was endorsed in *R* v *Board of Visitors of Gartree Prison ex p. Sears, The Times,* 20 March 1985. On the other hand, there has been a suggestion (*R* v *Commissioner of Police for the Metropolis ex p. Nahar, The Times,* 28 May 1983), recently supported by the Court of Appeal in *Middleweek* v *Chief Constable of Merseyside, The Times,* 1 August 1985, that the physical conditions of detention can be such as to render that detention unlawful. The standard, however, is undemanding: Ackner LJ talks in terms of 'serious flooding' and leaking gas pipes.

In addition to their various attempts to ensure the enforcement of the Prison Rules and/or the maintenance of basic standards, prisoners have sought in other ways to persuade the courts to oversee the provision of facilities within prisons. In one context they have met with some success. Judicial activity in the area of prisoners' correspondence and access to lawyers has had a significant impact. Admittedly the initiative has come mainly from Strasbourg (*Golder* v *UK* ECHR 1975 and *Silver* v *UK* ECHR 1983), but the British courts have played a part. *R* v *Secretary of State ex p. Anderson* [1984] 1 All ER 920 challenged the 'simultaneous ventilation' rule prohibiting visits from and letters to lawyers containing complaints about prison treatment which the prisoner had not ventilated internally. In upholding the challenge the court held that the rule constituted an impediment to the right of access to the courts. Uncharacteristically, Anderson's general right was found to prevail over the claims of administrative convenience.

However, it would be unwise to assume that such enthusiasm for the rights of prisoners would necessarily be displayed in other contexts (Richardson 1984). *Anderson* effectively presented the courts with a direct threat to their independence and thus might be expected to attract a judicial response (see also *Raymond* v *Honey*). By contrast, in areas concerning routine prison management the courts have typically maintained their distance (see *McAvoy*). In a case involving the alleged administration of drugs against a prisoner's will, the Court of Appeal attached little formal significance to the difficulties surrounding the notion of 'consent' to treatment within the prison setting (*Freeman* v *Home Office* [1984] 1 All ER 1036). Further, the courts have held that a prisoner need not be given the opportunity to argue his case prior to categorisation (*Payne* v *Home Office*, 2 May 1977, unreported) and have refused directly to interfere with 'administrative' decisions in such areas as parole and governors' hearings (see below).

From the above it is evident that the courts generally have been reluctant to act as overseers of prison conditions. To date they have failed to recognise any special rights in prisoners under the Prison Rules, and the minimum requirements of legality to which the judges have recently referred cannot be intended to represent the minimum acceptable standard. We would argue, however, that even if the Prison Rules were held to create special rights in prisoners, the extent of the discretion typically permitted to the authorities by the Rules is such as to render those rights too conditional to have any practical impact.

It is, of course, essential that the authorities retain a degree of discretion when ordering transfers, permitting visits, and so on: we are not arguing for absolute rights. Rather, the prisoner should possess the right, for example, to a given number and type of visits. The authorities would then be expected to justify any reduction in that provision by reference to pre-ordained criteria designed to meet the demands of security and control. Such a scheme would reflect the ideal described earlier where any reduction in rights must be justified by reference to the requirements of segregation. (In practice it might be argued that no system could, for operational reasons, function without the acceptance of variation in regimes or facilities, in which case it would again be incumbent on the authorities to specify criteria in advance.)

The requirement that the authority 'justify' decisions by reference to stated criteria must imply more than the mere recitation of these criteria as in *McAvoy*. A form of due process is required which would enable the prisoner both to question the evidence on which the authority proposed to act and to present his own arguments. Inevitably the precise nature of the required 'hearing' would depend on the gravity of the proposed interference with the prisoner's rights and, in extreme cases, the demands of security. In any event it is encouraging that the court has recently recognised a mother's right to a 'hearing' prior to separation from her baby (*R* v *Secretary of State ex p. Hickling, The Times,* 7 November 1985). The case may be extreme but, nevertheless, it illustrates a welcome departure from the dismissive attitude previously displayed in response to prisoners' requests for due process (*Payne* 1977; and *Payne* v *Lord Harris of Greenwich* [1981] 2 All ER 842).

In addition to the question of procedural requirements, however, *Hickling* provides a clear illustration of the hidden nature of the criteria on which such 'administrative' decisions are made. In *Hickling* the relevant Circular Instruction (51/1983) was not known to Ms Hickling's lawyers until the proceedings had begun. Similarly in *McAvoy* the majority of the relevant administrative directives setting out the basis on which the Secretary of State expects prison staff to exercise their discretion were not known, and even the one relevant order that had been published was extremely unrevealing. Standing Order 5 on 'Communications' was published following the decision of the European Commission on Human Rights in *Silver* v *UK*. But it is silent with regard to the manner in which prison governors should exercise their discretion to restrict visits in the interests of 'good order and discipline' granted under Prison Rule 33(1). The phrase from the Rule is simply repeated, with an additional reference to 'security'. Nor, in the case of *McAvoy*, would the publication of the relevant Standing Orders concerned with 'Transfer' (SO 1h) or 'Unconvicted Prisoners' (SO 8a) have advanced the matter. In neither directive are there stated criteria or procedures (other than to inform or seek permission from headquarters) for transferring prisoners on security or control grounds.

In terms of volume the administrative directives called Standing Orders are exceeded annually by Circular Instructions (some of which amend Standing Orders as in *Hickling*) none of which are available to prisoners. Circular Instructions deal with transitory administrative issues, for example, rates of prisoners' pay. But they also fill the gaps in and interpret Standing Orders. For example, and of particular relevance to long-term prisoners, all the directives concerning the security classification of prisoners, or the planning of life-sentence prisoners' careers, are found in Circular Instructions, not Standing Orders. But while the publication of Circular Instructions would reveal substantially more about how decisions are made and what facilities the Prison Department headquarters considers should be available, they would still provide no objectively defined procedures, criteria and standards governing many of the aspects of imprisonment which we suggest should be the subject of special rights.

Two examples will serve to illustrate our argument. The first concerns the fundamental issue of overcrowding. It is now well established and officially admitted that no objective basis exists for the calculation of the Certified Normal Accommodation figures under section 14 of the Prison Act 1952 from which 'overcrowding' data are derived (King and Morgan 1980, pp. 114–21; Home Office 1979, vol. 1, paper IIC(2), para. 32). Thus no prisoner claiming that the cell in which he is accommodated is inadequate for the aims endorsed by the Prison Rules can point to officially recognised objective criteria with respect to 'size, lighting, heating, ventilation and fittings' for the purposes of s. 14.

The regulations governing prisoners' clothing, a fundamental aspect of personal dignity, provide a second example. Prison Rule 20 (2) states that 'a convicted prisoner shall be provided with clothing adequate for warmth and health in accordance with a scale approved by the Secretary of State.' The relevant Standing Order (2c) is not published, but in any case it includes no scale. It simply asserts that 'governors are responsible for ensuring that a high standard is maintained in the cleanliness and condition of the clothing provided, and for seeing that all prisoners are adequately clad at all times' (SO 2c(3)). We do not know whether a Circular Instruction has ever been issued setting out a clothing scale or defining what 'adequately' should mean.

These examples of the absence of standards, or the inadequacy of criteria for making decisions could be duplicated almost endlessly. The implications are as serious for prison inspectors as for managers. Chief Inspectors of Prisons have repeatedly made reference to their regret that there are no binding regime standards (see Morgan 1985b, p. 123). Although the reports of the Inspectorate make reference to the Prison Rules and the Council of Europe's Standard Minimum Rules, neither document provides a coherent set of benchmarks for inspection purposes (see Casale 1984; and Plotnikoff 1986). In judging the adequacy of provision the Chief Inspector has until now had to rely, somewhat limply, on his 'subjective ... experience of life and of the Prison Service' (HM Chief Inspector of Prisons 1982, para. 1.7). For good operational reasons this plainly will not do. Prison governors, confronted with inspection reports employing terms like 'inadequate', 'insufficient', 'unacceptable', and so on, quite rightly demand to know what is meant. And the Inspectorate, unable to refer to standards of either the Prison Department's or its own devising, is unable to provide a coherent answer. In the wake of the Home Secretary's decision not to publish regime standards within the Prison Department, the Chief Inspector had little alternative but to announce that he would set about the task of devising standards of his own (HM Chief Inspector of Prisons 1985, para. 3.01). This will be a valuable step. However, since the Inspectorate's function is simply to advise, it can do little directly to advance the cause of prisoners' rights.

The absence of standards is no less a handicap for the credibility of local Boards of Visitors. Their first general duty is to 'satisfy themselves as to the state of the prison premises . . . and the treatment of the prisoners' (Prison Rule 94(1)). Prisoners are guaranteed access to boards in order to make requests or complaints (Prison Rule 95(1)). Yet the evidence suggests that board members, however well intentioned, generally fulfil their inspectoral and grievance-ventilation roles most inadequately and that their credibility in the eyes of prisoners suffers as a consequence (see Maguire and Vagg 1984). This is not surprising. How can individual board members respond decisively to prisoner complaints about overcrowding, the absence of association or the infrequency of clothing changes (all commonplace 'applications'), when prisoners have no entitlements? Like the courts, board members tend to accept governors' assertions that facilities are dictated by the limited staff or resources available, or by security or control considerations, and communicate the same to prisoners. Seldom can a wrong be righted because, from the standpoint of administrative regulation, there is no demonstrable wrong.

Further, board members can seldom satisfy themselves that the prisoners in their local establishment are not disadvantaged compared to similarly categorised prisoners held elsewhere, nor can they be assured that an individual prisoner making a complaint is not being unfairly discriminated against. The problem, again, concerns the absence of accounts. Thus, to take the example of visits, it is not possible to conclude from data published by the Prison Department, or the reports of the Inspectorate, or anything the Boards of Visitors do, whether prisoners in one prison get better visiting facilities than those in another, or whether the frequency or duration of visits generally has improved or deteriorated. Since all visits are recorded, these data could be made available and it would be possible to check on visits received by an individual prisoner. But the same is not true of most activities. For example, there is seldom any record as to who is allowed association or for how long.

Which brings us back to the fundamental issues of overcrowding, and the position of long-term prisoners. Most attempts systematically to provide objective measures of crowding seek to interrelate physical plant and regime characteristics (Casale 1984; see also Morgan and Bronstein 1985 on court rulings in the United States). Cells which prisoners use only for sleeping might reasonably be smaller, afford less privacy and contain fewer facilities than cells in which prisoners spend most of their time. Similarly, on grounds of dependency, long-term prisoners, particularly those who are ostracised or subject to high security and whose freedom of movement within the prison is strictly curtailed, arguably have a need for better cell facilities than short-term prisoners. What special rights a prisoner should have is indissolubly tied up with the establishment of regime standards and system accountability generally.

Discipline and control

Both the long-term prison population and those responsible for their custody are directly affected by the nature of the methods available for the maintenance of discipline within prisons. In an essentially coercive system some sanctions must be available to the authorities to enable them to maintain control. In England and Wales the formal disciplinary system is provided by section 47 of the Prison Act 1952, which, in combination with Prison Rules 47–56, creates both a catalogue of disciplinary offences and a system for the imposition of formal sanctions.

While we recognise that the demands of segregation can justify a specific reduction in the general and special rights (ideally) possessed by a prisoner, we would argue that such a reduction must be justified and that due process rights are required to ensure the adequacy of that justification. We would argue further that all behaviour amounting to a criminal offence should be dealt with as such unless the requirements of segregation (security and control) can be demonstrated to demand otherwise.

The attitude of the courts towards disciplinary hearings before Boards of Visitors is therefore to be welcomed. Boards are now bound by the rules of natural justice (*R v Board of Visitors of Hull ex p. St Germain (No 1)* [1979] 1 All ER 701 and *(No 2)* [1979] 3 All ER 545) and have been empowered, and in certain circumstances, required, to allow legal representation (*R v Secretary of State ex p. Tarrant* [1985] 1 QB 251; and see Fitzgerald 1985). Thus prisoners possess special rights to certain procedures before Boards of Visitors, and disciplinary awards reached in non-compliance with these rights will be invalidated. Further, prisoners have successfully claimed the right not to be penalised save in accordance with the strict interpretation of the Prison Rules (*R v Board of Visitors of Highpoint Prison ex p. McConkey, The Times,* 23 September 1982 and *R v Board of Visitors of Swansea Prison ex p. McGrath, The Times,* 20 November 1984).

This judicial enthusiasm for intervention in the case of Boards of Visitors is in marked contrast to the current attitude to governors' hearings where the Court of Appeal has refused to intervene directly (*R v Deputy Governor of Camp Hill Prison ex p. King* [1984] 3

All ER 897). Elsewhere it has been argued that no true legal distinction exists between governors' hearings and those before Boards of Visitors. Instead the reason behind the current approach lies in the courts' attitude to the different roles of the two bodies, one 'administrative' and the other 'quasi-judicial' (Richardson 1985b). Indeed the speciousness of any legal distinction has recently been recognised by the Court of Appeal in Northern Ireland (*R* v *Governor of Maze Prison ex p. McKiernan*, 10 November 1984, unreported).

The judicial imposition of some due process requirements on Boards of Visitors' hearings has done much to improve the formal disciplinary system, and the implementation of the Prior Committee's recommendations (Home Office 1985a), with all their limitations (Morgan 1986), would improve the system still further. Of course, under present conditions, where the prisoner possesses few 'privileges' (special rights in an ideal world), and where loss of remission is consequently the most common disciplinary award (Home Office 1985b), it is inevitable that resort will be made to disproportionate sanctions, awards which are greater than the minimum required by the demands of segregation. Whatever the problems attaching to the formal disciplinary system, however, it is the 'informal' system which gives most cause for concern.

By 'informal' system we mean those methods of control the occasional use of which undeniably substitutes for formal disciplinary proceedings, methods which the Home Office has correctly though disingenuously described as 'entirely administrative in character' (Home Office 1984b, para. 10), but the Prison Officers' Association (1984) has more honestly termed the 'alternative' disciplinary system. In practice these methods can range from truly informal sanctions, like an adverse work allocation, to procedures authorised by the Prison Rules, such as segregation for 'good order and discipline' under Rule 43.

In theory we would argue that the use of any informal sanction which affects a prisoner's rights must be justified by reference to a change in the demands of either segregation or dependency. Further, the existence of an informal system suggests that the formal system on its own is inadequate to ensure the proper achievement of segregation (security and control). It is necessary, therefore, to examine the reasons for this perceived inadequacy since it is at least arguable that the validity of the informal system depends on the adequacy of the formal system.

In the first place, staff may regard the formal disciplinary system as insufficiently severe. Provided the formal system is in fact imposing sanctions appropriate to the demands of segregation (however defined), such an argument is clearly unjustifiable. Alternatively, security and control might be thought to require swifter intervention than the disciplinary process permits; or to be prejudiced by behaviour which could not be classified as a disciplinary offence; or even to be compromised by threatened events of too speculative a nature to support a disciplinary charge. Whatever the reason, we would argue that the reduction of a prisoner's (ideal) rights by means of an informal sanction should be justified by reference to segregation, and due process rights should attach to the prisoner to ensure the adequacy of that justification.

At present, apart from those relating to release, the informal sanctions which most significantly affect a prisoner's (ideal) rights are: removal from association under Rule 43; physical restraint under Rule 46; transfer, especially under Circular Instruction 10/1974; security categorisation and recategorisation; and the alleged coercive use of drugs (*The Times*, 14 February 1986). Resort to some of these devices is subject to certain safeguards imposed by the Prison Rules (for example, Rule 43(2) and Rule 46(2)). However, and although due process is extremely flexible, such statutory safeguards do not begin to meet even the most basic requirements. There is, for example, no express requirement that a prisoner be informed of the reasons why he is to be restrained, nor that the persons overseeing the use of the restraint or the removal from association hear the prisoner prior to their decision to authorise. Further, a purported exercise of the powers under these Rules will not be invalidated by failure to comply with the limited procedures required (*Williams*).

Most informal sanctions, however, are untrammelled by even these inadequate safeguards and, apart from petitions to the Secretary of State, the courts provide the only recognised means of challenge open to the prisoner. With regard to such 'administrative' decisions, however, the prisoner's chances of success are minimal. For example, the courts have refused to recognise any right to a 'hearing' in relation to categorisation (*Payne* 1977). Admittedly, they have held transfer decisions to be reviewable but in light of their retreat before 'operational and security reasons' it seems highly unlikely that they would be prepared effectively to review any CI 10/1974 transfers. Further, the difficulties involved in obtaining evidence within the prison setting are amply illustrated by *Freeman* concerning allegations of coerced medical treatment. On the other hand, one possible ground for challenge was raised in *Williams* (at p. 1235), where it was suggested that the use of Rule 43 as a punishment would be improper. However, Tudor Evans J refused to commit himself as to the legal consequences of such impropriety, even if it could be established.

In sum, while use of the informal sanctions listed above could in certain circumstances be justified, we would argue that existing procedures do not adequately provide those justifications. This failure to meet the test of due process in individual cases is matched by the absence of a general account from the authority about resort to the battery of informal sanctions at its disposal.

While section 5(2)(c) of the Prison Act 1952 requires that an annual statement be made of punishments and the offences for which they were inflicted, the Department chooses to provide no more information than the minimum required. No data are routinely available as to the proportion of prisoners segregated under Rule 48 prior to adjudication, pleading not guilty and found guilty, and since *Tarrant*, requesting legal or other assistance and granted it.

As to the 'informal' system, virtually no data are published about even those controls provided for in the Prison Rules let alone those others (like 'strip cells') which have been introduced administratively without reference to Parliament. Those few data that have been made available are presented in so obfuscatory a form that all reasonable efforts at interpretation are confounded. Thus, no routine information, cross-sectional or longitudinal, is available about security categorisation and recategorisation; segregation under Rules 43 and 45; and CI 10/1974 transfers. Further, whereas data are published annually about the almost outmoded and little used physical restraints (to which safeguards are attached under Prison Rule 46), no details are made available about the involuntary use of drugs, nor do the Prison Rules lay down procedures for their administration. Annual Reports from the Prison Department now include data for selected establishments (the basis of or need for selection is unclear) about drug doses given to prisoners, but since the size of the doses is undefined, all meaningful comparisons between establishments or over time are made impossible (see Home Office 1985b, Table 10).

Thus, insofar as there is a symbiotic relationship between the formal and informal disciplinary systems, the nature and extent of that relationship cannot be assessed, nor changes monitored. There is some evidence that resort to Boards of Visitors' hearings has declined since *Tarrant* (Home Office 1985b, Table 9(a)). If the Prison Officers' Association (1984, paras. 11–12) has lost confidence in the formal system to the extent claimed, and if the problems officers encounter in controlling prisoners have grown to the extent maintained, then it seems possible that the informal system may have been displacing formal controls over a longer period. Certainly, it is generally accepted that a growing number of prisoners are subject to Rule 43 and the Prior Committee was informed that the number of CI 10/1974 transfers is rising (Home Office 1985a, para. 2.38).

Displacement of formal by informal disciplinary controls clearly constitutes a backward step for prisoners' rights and, by implication, subverts the process of judicial review. It means that hard-fought-for special rights and due process procedures are effectively evaded. The informal system is for the most part covert and lacking in safeguards. Applied repeatedly to long-term prisoners, the informal controls can involve extremes of segregation and dependency.

The remedies we advocate are similar to those described above for prison standards. All administrative directives concerning decisions substantially to increase the degree to which a prisoner is segregated (by security recategorisation, transfer, physical separation or reduced privileges) should specify clearly the basis on which such decisions are to be made, should provide for due process and should be published. Further, the degree to which discretionary powers are resorted to should be publicly accounted for annually. Three categories of data are required. First, we need to know how often all the measures we have cited are used. Secondly, we need to know how many prisoners are subject to each measure at any one time. There is no reason, for example, why the number of prisoners segregated under Rule 43, or subject to CI 10/1974 transfer, should not be provided for 30 June each year as is done currently for prisoners' work allocation. Thirdly, and of particular relevance to long-term prisoners' careers, we need to know for how long prisoners are subject to each measure.

Finally, if the Prior Committee's proposals are implemented and Boards of Visitors' hearings are replaced by disciplinary tribunals, there is need to consider how the boards' residual inspectoral and grievance-ventilation functions can best be performed. We assume that Boards of Visitors, or some similarly constituted body, will be retained for these purposes. However, we suggest that even were boards in receipt of the fuller administrative directives and the more transparent decision-making accounts for which we have argued, the careers of individual long-term prisoners would remain relatively difficult to monitor. We discern the need for some regional or national watchdog body (mirroring the national arrangements within the Department for managing lifers and Category A prisoners) whose task it should be to oversee the custodial careers of long-term prisoners. Such bodies might be appointed for the purpose, or could comprise representatives of local boards.

Release and parole
The parole system established by the Criminal Justice Act 1967 ensures that every long-term prisoner experiences some degree of indeterminacy. The arguments concerning the merits and demerits of the executive discretion to release (Hood 1975; Walker 1975;

Morgan, N. 1983), the effects of indeterminacy and the alleged procedural shortcomings of the present system (Hawkins 1973), are too familiar to require repetition here. Suffice it to say that the adverse effects of the parole system are merely exacerbated in the case of long-term prisoners who, by definition, suffer both longer periods of indeterminacy and more frequent procedural frustration. Further, there is the control potential of parole. The refusal of parole is an obvious and valuable informal control device which may be employed on its own or in concert with the formal disciplinary system. The relationship between disciplinary awards of loss of remission, or cellular confinement in the case of lifers, and adverse parole decisions, has given rise to the suspicion that prisoners may be punished twice for the same disciplinary offence (Home Office 1985a, paras. 8.26–8.40). Such control potential is presumably greatest where long periods of time are at stake.

Executive discretion to release either in the form of two-thirds parole for fixed-term prisoners or release on licence in the case of lifers is hard to reconcile with the ideals we have advocated. In the first place, the presence of release discretion colours the issue of coercion throughout the whole system: voluntariness cannot be guaranteed where early release must be earned. Secondly, a minimalist approach to imprisonment demands the imposition of the *minimum* custody necessary to reflect the gravity of the offence. The discretionary granting of early release on the basis of subsequent behaviour, as opposed to the formal postponement of release as a consequence of specific instances of indiscipline, cannot meet the requirements of such a system. To these fundamental objections must be added the procedural inadequacies of the present scheme. The virtual absence of due process and the effectively unchallengeable nature of both the individual decisions and the policies and criteria underlying the scheme as a whole, serve further to condemn the already unacceptable.

On the question of procedural safeguards, the statutory scheme itself provides for few and the courts have refused to supplement the statute with the common law requirements of natural justice (*Payne* v *Lord Harris of Greenwich* [1981] 2 All ER 842 and *R* v *Secretary of State ex p. Gunnell, The Times,* 7 November 1984). Potential parolees have effectively been denied special rights to the procedural requirements before the relevant decision-makers which would enable them to question the validity of the ultimate decision. The judicial attitude here is in marked contrast to the courts' approach to Boards of Visitors' hearings although, arguably, there is no significant analytical distinction between the two (Richardson 1984). Instead it resembles the attitude to governors' hearings and has been manifestly influenced by the authority's claims to administrative convenience (see Denning MR in *Payne*).

While the procedural inadequacies of the scheme have long been recognised, the substantive problems have been given prominence recently by the changes in policy announced by Leon Brittan in 1983 (HC Deb. Vol. 49, col. 505, 30 November) and the subsequent court action (*Findlay v Secretary of State for the Home Department* [1984] 3 All ER 801). According to the House of Lords, the Home Secretary, in exercising his discretion under the 1967 Act, is entitled effectively to deny parole to certain categories of offender if he feels that deterrence, retribution and public confidence so demand *and* provided each case is examined for the presence of 'exceptional circumstances'. Whatever the precise legal implications of this decision (Richardson 1985c), it has served to emphasise the executive element within the scheme and consequently to reduce the significance of the Parole Board. Further, the House of Lords' acceptance of Brittan's policy itself as proper (see, by way of contrast, Browne-Wilkinson LJ in the Court of Appeal (*Findlay v Secretary of State for the Home Department*, at p. 819)) and their refusal to find 'exceptional' the cases of the two lifers returned to closed conditions, illustrates the effectively unchallengeable nature of that executive element. Certainly, the significant postponement in reasonably anticipated release suffered by the two lifers would be quite unacceptable under the system of rights we have advocated, particularly since no attempt was made to justify the postponement by reference to the prisoners' own behaviour, nor were the most basic due process requirements met.

To an extent the *Findlay* saga merely highlights the unacceptable nature of executive release in general and life sentences in particular. The European Commission of Human Rights has reservations about the existing release and recall procedures affecting life sentence prisoners in the UK. The Commission has concluded that a recalled life-sentence prisoner 'was unable to have the lawfulness of his re-detention determined by a court or to have a periodic review of the lawfulness of his continued detention at reasonable intervals throughout his imprisonment' (*Weeks v UK* ECHR 1984). In the Commission's view such procedural inadequacies constitute a breach of Article 5(4) of the European Convention on Human Rights.

Given the almost inevitable survival of both life sentences and parole, we can do no more than argue that the general policies underlying the executive discretion be made more explicit and susceptible to challenge and urge that sufficient due process protection be introduced to ensure that individual decisions are justified in terms of stated criteria. At the very least prisoners should be entitled to periodic reviews, they should know the criteria on which decisions are based, they should be told the evidence in their own cases and be given reasons for the eventual decision.

Conclusions

We have argued that prisoners are entitled to retain all legal rights not inevitably curtailed by the demands of segregation and, further, by virtue of their increased dependence, are entitled to additional special rights *vis-à-vis* the authorities. The precise nature of these rights will depend on prevailing attitudes to imprisonment, but any variation from the agreed norm must be justified by reference to a variation in the demands of segregation or in the consequences of dependency. Such justifiable variations may frequently occur in the case of long-term prisoners: we have argued that the very need to justify them demands increased due process provision and more transparent stewardship in order to facilitate both individual challenge and general accountability.

The current regime falls far short of such an ideal. In the first place, the rights in practice retained by prisoners in England and Wales are poorly protected at law and vulnerable to the claims of administrative convenience, while the effective recognition of additional rights is extremely rare. Further, individual prisoners are given few opportunities to challenge decisions affecting their 'rights'. Finally, the prison system is in practice subjected to only the most superficial degree of general accountability. Most administrative directives remain secret, and few data are collected or published setting out how often and with what precise consequences decisions affecting segregation and dependency are made. There is no comprehensive code of standards covering physical conditions and regimes and, as a consequence, those whose task it is to inspect prisons and investigate prisoner grievances are rudderless.

Long-term prisoners are particularly vulnerable to unjustified interference, especially with regard to informal disciplinary processes. Only a clear statement of their rights in combination with the provision of effective mechanisms for both individual challenge and general accountability can ensure that their prolonged detention is acceptable.

References

Aronson, D.H. (1982), 'Prisoners' Rights', *Annual Survey of American Law*, pp. 79–106.
Campbell, T.D. (1983), *The Left and Rights*, London: Routledge and Kegan Paul.
Casale, S. (1984), *Minimum Standards for Prison Establishments*, London: NACRO.
Casale, S. (1985), 'A Practical Design for Standards' in M. Maguire, J. Vagg and R. Morgan (eds), *Accountability and Prisons*, London: Tavistock.

Fitzgerald, E. (1985), 'Prison Discipline and the Courts' in M. Maguire, J. Vagg and R. Morgan (eds), *Accountability and Prisons*, London: Tavistock.

Fox, L.W. (1952), *The English Prison and Borstal Systems*, London: Routledge and Kegan Paul.

Gewirth, A. (1984), 'The Epistemology of Human Rights', *Social Philosophy and Policy*, vol. 1, no. 2, pp. 1–24.

Hart, H.L.A. (1955), 'Are There Any Natural Rights?' *Philosophical Review*, vol. 64, pp. 175–91.

Hawkins, K.O. (1973), 'Parole Procedure: an Alternative Approach', *British Journal of Criminology*, vol 13, pp. 6–25.

HM Chief Inspector of Prisons (1982), *Chief Inspector of Prisons, Annual Report 1981*, Cmnd. 8532, London: HMSO.

HM Chief Inspector of Prisons (1983), *Chief Inspector of Prisons, Annual Report 1982*, HC 260, London: HMSO.

HM Chief Inspector of Prisons (1984), *Chief Inspector of Prisons, Annual Report 1983*, HC 618, London: HMSO.

HM Chief Inspector of Prisons (1985), *Chief Inspector of Prisons, Annual Report 1984*, HC 589, London: HMSO.

Hohfeld, W.N. (1919), *Fundamental Legal Conceptions*, New Haven, CT: Yale University Press.

Home Office (1979), *Inquiry into the United Kingdom Prison Services: Evidence by the Home Office, the Scottish Home and Health Department and the Northern Ireland Office* (3 vols), London: HMSO.

Home Office (1984a), *Managing the Long-Term Prison System: The Report of the Control Review Committee*, London: HMSO.

Home Office (1984b), 'The Prison Disciplinary System: a Descriptive Memorandum, Evidence to the Committee on the Prison Disciplinary System', London: Home Office (unpublished).

Home Office (1985a), *Report of the Committee on the Prison Disciplinary System* (Prior Report), Cmnd. 9641, London: HMSO.

Home Office (1985b), *Report on the Work of the Prison Department 1984/85*, Cmnd. 9699, London: HMSO.

Hood, R. (1975), 'The Case Against Executive Control over Time in Custody', *Criminal Law Review*, pp. 545–52.

JUSTICE (1983), *Justice in Prison*, London: JUSTICE.

King, R.D. and Morgan, R. (1980), *The Future of the Prison System*, Farnborough: Gower.

Maguire, M. and Vagg, J. (1984), *The 'Watchdog' Role of Boards of Visitors*, London: Home Office.

Maguire, M., Vagg, J. and Morgan, R. (eds) (1985), *Accountability and Prisons*, London: Tavistock.

Morgan, N. (1983), 'The Shaping of Parole in England and Wales', *Criminal Law Review*, pp. 137–51.

Morgan, R. (1983), 'The Use of Resources in the Prison System' in *A Prison System for the 80's and Beyond*, London: NACRO.

Morgan, R. (1985a), 'Police Accountability: Current Developments and Future Prospects', paper presented to the Police Foundation Conference, Harrogate, December.

Morgan, R. (1985b), 'Her Majesty's Inspectorate of Prisons' in M. Maguire, J. Vagg and R. Morgan (eds), *Accountability and Prisons:* London, Tavistock.

Morgan, R. (1986), 'The Prior Proposals for Prison Discipline', *British Journal of Criminology*, vol. 26, pp. 79–87.

Morgan, R. and Bronstein, A.J. (1985), 'Prisoners and the Courts: the US Experience', in: M. Maguire, J. Vagg and R. Morgan (eds), *Accountability and Prisons*, London: Tavistock.

Plotnikoff, J. (1986), *Prison Rules: A Working Guide*, London: Prison Reform Trust.

Prison Officers' Association (1984), *The Prison Disciplinary System: Submission to the Home Office Departmental Committee on the Prison Disciplinary System*, London: Prison Officers' Association.

Prosser, T. (1982), 'Towards a Critical Public Law', *Journal of Law and Society*, vol. 9, pp. 1–19.

Richardson, G. (1984), 'Time to Take Prisoners' Rights Seriously', *Journal of Law and Society*, vol. 11, pp.1–32.

Richardson, G (1985a), 'The Case for Prisoners' Rights' in M. Maguire, J. Vagg and R. Morgan (eds), *Accountability and Prisons*, London: Tavistock.

Richardson, G. (1985b), 'Judicial Intervention in Prison Life' in M. Maguire, J. Vagg and R. Morgan (eds), *Accountability and Prisons*, London: Tavistock.

Richardson, G (1985c), 'Judicial Review of Parole Policy', *Public Law*, pp. 34–9.

Unger, R.M. (1976), *Law in Modern Society*, New York: Free Press.

Walker, N. (1975), 'Release by Executive Discretion: a Defence', *Criminal Law Review*, pp. 540–4.

Zellick, G. (1981), 'The Prison Rules and the Courts', *Criminal Law Review*, p. 602.

PART II
SPECIAL ISSUES

8 The unwanted effects of long-term imprisonment
Nigel Walker

There was a time when the worst thing that was said about imprisonment was that it did no good to the offender or his victims. Like most sweeping statements this was subject to quite a few exceptions; but it made a good slogan for penal reformers. Nowadays they have a better one: prison does more harm than good.

But this paper is not about the art of slogan-making. It is an attempt to distinguish the various kinds of harm which imprisonment is sometimes said to inflict on prisoners, and to see what the evidence — if any — is like. I have added 'if any' because now and again what has been taken for evidence turns out to be nothing of the sort.

The focus of this paper is on long- or medium-term incarceration under ordinary conditions: not, that is, under the extreme conditions of 'death rows', gulags, concentration camps or solitary cells. Nor does it try to deal with the harm done to prisoners' dependants. In passing, however, it is worth noting how little research into this topic has been published since Pauline Morris (1965). She was concerned mainly with the difficulties faced by wives, and did not study their children, an omission which needs to be remedied.[1] As for women prisoners, it is hard to find any systematic study of the ways in which they are affected by substantial periods of incarceration; and no such study seems to have been reported in Britain.

Physical health
A subject about which we have remarkably little that can be called evidence is the effects which British penal establishments have on their inmates' physical health. There have been occasional *causes célèbres* in which prisoners have claimed that their illnesses or injuries have been left untreated, or treated incompetently, during their detention. At intervals of roughly a decade there have been campaigns against the Prison Medical Service: one is proceeding at the moment. Noticeably lacking, however, has been any attempt to answer with scientific comparisons the most relevant question. This is not how

many of the claims of inadequate medical treatment are true but whether such claims are likely to be true with greater frequency than under the National Health Service. Not that it would be easy to make such comparisons. Properly matched samples of prisoners and controls from general practice would be difficult both to design and to collect.

A slightly easier question to answer is whether prisoners are more likely, while inside, to suffer from physical illness or injury than while outside. Yet I know of only one researcher who has addressed this question; and he did his work in Tennessee. Nevertheless, Jones (1976) is worth studying as an example of research design. Essentially, it was a comparison of the medical records of: adult males in Tennessee State Penitentiary; adult males on parole in Tennessee; and adult males on probation in Tennessee. He wisely excluded: chronic conditions, since these might have been present before the men were imprisoned, paroled or put on probation; prisoners who had served less than six months, in order to eliminate most, if not all, the illnesses which might have originated before admission; and non-acute disorders, since these were less likely to be reported by men who were at liberty. Research based on medical records is open to at least one serious criticism. It is unlikely, in Tennessee or elsewhere, that medical attention is equally accessible to prisoners and to their free controls, or, if accessible, of the same standard. In some, probably all, prisons it is easier to 'report sick' than it is to attend one's general practitioner's surgery. Sick-bays are more comfortable than cells, and a visit to them 'makes a break'. The ways of life of parolees and probationers may make resort to medical practitioners less easy or attractive than it is for prisoners. Costs may also enter into the matter. Even if Jones's findings are accepted as likely to be sound, it cannot be assumed that the same differences would be observable between the medical histories of British prisoners, parolees and probationers, under a different prison system and a different health service.

Yet with all these reservations both the method and the findings are of interest. Jones's penitentiary inmates were apparently subject to four types of disorder much more often than his parolees or probationers: 'acute respiratory' disorders; 'acute or chronic digestive' disorders; 'acute infectious or parasitic' disorders; and 'acute injuries'. The English Prison Medical Service makes considerable efforts to keep such disorders at a minimum. In the 1970s, mass miniature radiography detected the occasional case of pulmonary tuberculosis, but there was seldom if ever any indication that it had been contracted from infection within prison (see Home Office Prison Department 1977, p. 58; 1978, p. 49; 1979, p. 42). No outbreaks of legionnaire's disease in prisons have been reported, perhaps because their ventilation and plumbing systems are not hospitable to the organism. As for digestive disorders, a great deal of attention is paid to prisoners' diets. Conditions in some prison kitchens are good, in some much less good. One small outbreak of food poisoning by Salmonella was reported in 1980 (Home Office PD 1980, p. 52); but if newspapers can be relied upon such incidents seem commoner in NHS hospitals. Diets have been blamed not for malnutrition but for producing excess fat. In 1986 the Harvey (1986) Working Party recommended a reduction in the fat content of prison food, and the addition of more sources of vitamin D, as well as more attention to diets for religious and other minorities. But prisoners' preferences for foods, which are not always healthy, mean that care and tact is needed when diets are being improved.

Immunisation against poliomyelitis is offered to prisoners who have not already had it, as are other kinds of immunisation when it seems necessary. Parasitic infestations (which are said to be less common than in the United States) are likely to be detected at or soon after reception, and do not seem to be a problem in training or dispersal prisons.

AIDS

Since auto-immune deficiency syndrome (AIDS) has been the focus of recent concern, especially in North American prisons, some facts about the English experience are relevant. So far, only one inmate of an English prison has been found to be suffering from the full-blown condition: an intravenous drug-abuser. Although there is no compulsory screening of high-risk groups (for ethical reasons) between 30 and 40 inmates have been detected as HTLV III positive, but it is unlikely that any acquired the virus while in prison. However that may be, they are carefully segregated. What the future may bring, of course, is another question. Perhaps, to quote the President of the United States out of context, 'we ain't seen nothing yet'.

Illicit use of drugs

Another dangerous infection, however, is hepatitis B. In 1984 (Home Office 1985, p. 70) sporadic outbreaks of this in English prisons were reported, and some 200 chronic hepatitis carriers were detected. (Vaccination was offered to staff who seemed to be particularly at risk). As in the case of AIDS, one of the likely modes of transmission is the sharing of unsterilised needles among drug users (others are anal intercourse and — much less likely in prisons — blood transfusions). This, and other risks to health, are among the strongest reasons for trying to prevent intravenous or parenteric drug abuse.

Discoveries of illicit drugs (chiefly cannabis but occasionally heroin, cocaine and other substances) are required to be reported to the Prison Department; but illicit drug use is not mentioned as a problem in the Department's annual reports even in connection with outbreaks of hepatitis B. I have so far found no publication, official or unofficial, which deals specifically with illicit drug use in British prisons; but two unpublished documents, prepared by the Prison Officers' Association (POA) and the Prison Medical Association (PMA) in 1985, testify to the extent of the problem. The POA (1985) memorandum is based on a questionnaire completed by 75 branches (that is, about 55 per cent of all branches). Only 12 said that illicit drug use was *not* a problem in their establishments, and seven of those 12 said that there was evidence of *some* illicit use. The memorandum claims that many discoveries of drugs had not been officially reported to the Prison Department's headquarters as instructions require (for example, that only one such discovery was reported by Liverpool Prison in 1954 whereas in reality there were 54). But the highest numbers of notified discoveries were at Albany, Long Lartin and Ford: the problem is clearly not confined to prisons for short-termers. The PMA (1985) memorandum (which was submitted to the Social Services Committee of the House of Commons) does not refer to the POA report, but paints an equally startling picture. In Brixton, for example, heroin abusers refuse to be transferred to the hospital wing because in the other parts of the prison they can get heroin, syringes and needles. The memorandum emphasises 'the permissive attitude to alcohol and drug consumption by prisoners' in 'the more liberal regimes of the dispersal prisons'.

The POA's report also reflects permissiveness when it says that some officers believe that 'drugs can have a calming effect on the establishment'. In general, however, it emphasises the overconfidence which results from drug abuse, making some users hard to control. The main smuggling routes seem to be permitted visits, home leaves and food supplied to remand prisoners; and the memorandum stresses both the inadequacies and the difficulties of search procedures. The Swedish prison system now employs search squads with special training and equipment and powers (Edholm and Bishop 1983). The impression given, however, by the two English memoranda is that governors are reluctant to allow strict searches because they are likely to antagonise both inmates and visitors. In Long Lartin, for example, sniffer dogs are used only in the workshops.

Whatever degree of tolerance seems best in this or that establishment, there is a strong case, in the interests of physical health, for thorough screening of self-injectors — not to mention practising homosexuals — for the hepatitis B virus — not to mention the AIDS virus — and segregating carriers in special units. Such procedures are admittedly open to the objection that they not only alarm identified carriers but also label them, with social consequences which can be serious. Yet such objections must be weighed against the risks to which other prisoners are exposed, without their consent, by close association with unidentified carriers.

Physical injuries

Injuries need more thorough study than David Jones in Tennessee was able to devote to them. They may be: deliberately self-inflicted; the result of assaults, usually by other prisoners, but occasionally by staff; accidental, although some 'accidental' injuries are really the results of assaults about which the victims prefer to remain silent, or are not believed. Comparison with the injuries of 'outsiders' is made almost impossible by the substantial proportion of assaults not reported to the police; and there are similar difficulties in comparing frequencies of accidental injuries at work, inside and outside penal establishments. We do not know whether prisoners in general are more likely to be the victims of assaults, or accidental injuries, while imprisoned than while at liberty: only a victim survey would tell us this.

Actuarial information of so general a kind, however, would be of less practical value than some of the things we already know about prison assaults. For example, it is generally agreed that certain categories of inmate are at most risk: informers, child-victimisers, defaulters on 'inside' debts, and, probably, ex-policemen and ex-prison officers. These categories are recognised as prima facie cases for protection, either under Rule 43 or otherwise. Secondly, we can be fairly sure, on the evidence of disciplinary proceedings, that the incidence of assaults is higher than average in establishments for young adults, and consistently higher than average in some of the closed prisons for long- or medium-sentence men, such as Albany, Camp Hill, Gartree and Parkhurst. On the other hand, it does not seem to be true, at least on similar evidence, that assaults are more frequent, per head of prison population, in the larger establishments or the more overcrowded ones (Farrington and Nuttall 1980).

Mental disorder

There is no sound evidence that periods of incarceration — long or short — under ordinary conditions of the kind experienced in British prisons result in mental disorders. A prison sentence is sometimes the first occasion on which an offender becomes the subject of a positive psychiatric diagnosis; but much more often it is found that he or she has a history of in-patient or out-patient treatment.

There are debatable exceptions. A disorder, for example, which used to be mentioned by psychiatric writers in connection with long-term incarceration was the Ganser Syndrome: a transient state of clouded consciousness in which only approximate answers are given to questions, and which is sometimes accompanied by somatic conversion features and subsequent amnesia for the episode. McKay *et al.* (1979) are probably justified in dismissing the evidence for its connection with incarceration as 'scanty', and the definition of it as controversial. The same is probably true of other so-called prison psychoses.[2] Of more interest is depression. When this occurs soon after reception it is usually no more than an understandable reactive state — a response to the prospect of separation from family and liberty. Sometimes, however, it is a chronic mood which the offender has hitherto kept at bay by means of alcohol or other drugs, and which reasserts itself when he is deprived of the drug. In Canadian penitentiaries, Porporino and Zamble (1984, p. 413) found, amongst inmates who had served about six months, that depression was significantly (p < 0.001) associated with poor education. Interestingly, it was not associated with the length of the sentence to be faced. (The same seemed true of anxiety.) In English prisons acute cases are treated with anti-depressants, but most have to cope on their own (see below).

Suicide and self-inflicted injury

Although it is a minority of the depressed who commit or attempt suicide, and not all who do are noticeably depressed beforehand, depression seems to be the only predictor of suicide worth consideration (apart from threats of, and previous attempts at, suicide). Certainly researchers' attempts to find other predictors of prison suicides have yielded nothing worth the name. Suicides are more likely to take place at an early stage of incarceration, and there is no real evidence to support the theory that there is a minor peak towards the ends of long sentences (Burtch and Ericson 1979, p. 40; Jenkins 1982; Home Office 1985). On the other hand, Burtch and Ericson (1979, pp. 35–40) found that suicide was somewhat more likely amongst lifers (in Canadian penitentiaries) than among fixed-termers (lifers accounted for only 6 per cent of the inmate population, but 16 per cent of the suicides). Whether the same can be said about self-inflicted non-suicidal injuries is unclear from the very little that has been published about them. The prevention of suicide is certainly a responsibility which is taken very seriously by prison staff, and prisoners who are regarded as suicide risks are put under special surveillance. The most effective form of surveillance is the sharing of cells or dormitories with other prisoners: but there are always short periods when the prisoner is left alone. In any case, enforced cell-sharing with a suicidal prisoner is an imposition which is hard to justify. The 1985 report of the Chief Inspector of Prisons made a number of recommendations on this subject which are being considered by the Prison Department (Home Office 1985).

Vulnerability

Yet even when imprisonment cannot be blamed for the mental disorder, those who suffer from it present the staff with special problems and responsibilities. However mild the illness or the personality disorder it is unsafe to rule out the possibility that it will worsen as a result of incarceration. That apart, some disorders, particularly those involving low intelligence, make those who suffer from them liable to exploitation by the cunning. Other disorders, and especially aggressive personality disorders, represent dangers for fellow prisoners, and a focus of anxiety for staff. Repeated surveys have shown that the percentage of the English prison population with some degree of mental disorder is very substantial (see Gunn 1977; Gunn *et al.* 1978). Only a fraction of this group is accommodated in units with specially adapted regimes; and there seems to be no prospect of dealing with the whole problem in this way, or at least in the foreseeable future, whether within the prison system or under the National Health Service. The Prison Rules provide that:

(1) the medical officer shall report to the governor on the case of any prisoner whose health is likely to be injuriously affected by imprisonment or any conditions of imprisonment . . .
(2) the medical officer shall pay special attention to any prisoner whose mental condition appears to require it, and make any special arrangements which appear necessary for his supervision or care (Rule 18).

It seems unlikely that this Rule is wholly effective in the overcrowded conditions of most local prisons. Whether it is effective in closed training or dispersal prisons is a question which only the medical officers there can answer.

Psychological effects

It is the psychological rather than the psychiatric effects of long detention which have been the subject of most concern, but also the most exaggeration. It was Goffman's (1961) influential book *Asylums* which drew much-needed attention to the nature of 'total institutions' and the ways in which inmates adapted to them. Unfortunately he was guilty of sleight of hand, juggling with the literature of mental hospitals, penal establishments, concentration camps, barracks and even public schools and nunneries in order to attribute 'mortifying' practices to every kind of total institution, and so argue that 'the processes by which a person's self is mortified are fairly standard in total institutions' (Goffman 1961, p. 14). Another conjuring trick was achieved in Cohen and Taylor's (1972) *Psychological Survival*. This had the merit of being based on close acquaintance with prisoners in the high-security wing of Durham Prison. It has been widely read as evidence of the inmates' psychological deterioration, although in fact all that it documents is their *fears* of deterioration: fears, moreover, which were probably encouraged by the discussions and reading material with which Cohen and Taylor's 'classes' provided them.

Nevertheless, the concept of 'institutionalisation', or the special variety sometimes called 'prisonisation', must be taken seriously, and especially where long-term prisoners are concerned. It raises two problems: how to tell when it is happening, and what to do about it. Telling when it is happening is a task for psychologists rather than sociologists or psychiatrists; and it is psychologists who have developed ideas for measuring it. Since institutionalisation is a protean notion, which takes quite different shapes in different hands, psychologists have wisely dissected it into aspects of personality which seem capable of being measured, or at least assessed, without being confused with each other.

Mental skills

Thus the Durham University team, whose work on this subject has received deserved attention abroad as well as in Britain, subjected adult male prisoners to batteries of intellectual and attitudinal tests at an early stage of their sentences, and after they had served, on average, about 19 months. The testers found 'no evidence of psychological deterioration. On the contrary, verbal intelligence showed a significant increase between first and second testing, and there were significant reductions in hostility, which were associated with increasing emotional maturity' (Bolton, *et al.* 1976, p. 47). A critic could point out that even by the time of their second testing the subjects had served less than two years of their current sentences; and that this did not guarantee that there would be no deterioration after, say, five or ten years, although it lays the onus of proof upon anyone who argues that there would. Providing proof, or disproof, would be a lengthy as well as a difficult business. As the Durham team realised, it is not sufficient to test 'cross-sectional' samples; that is, samples of prisoners who have spent different fractions of long sentences inside. It cannot be assumed that their personalities or experiences inside have been well matched. It is necessary to achieve a 'longitudinal' study, in which the same prisoners are tested, and with the same tests, after serving short, medium and long periods inside. Even then, many will have been moved around the prison system. Some will have been transferred to hospitals. Some will have been paroled. Some may have died. That is why so few, if any, longitudinal follow-ups are really long.

Prisoners' interests and problems

A natural consequence of the Durham psychologists' findings, the earliest of which were published in 1973, was that prison psychologists turned their attention to other possible manifestations of institutionalisation. In 1978 Sapsford and Richards published separate and quite different studies of long-sentence men in English prisons. Richards's (1978) work was done in an establishment with the reputation of being 'an easy nick'. His subjects were eight lifers and three fixed-termers who were in the first 18 months of their sentences; these were compared with seven lifers and four fixed-termers who had served at least eight years. He asked them to rank a list of 20 problems in order of severity. His findings 'ran counter to the assumption (easily drawn, for example, from the work of Goffman, 1961) that it is the internal conditions of an institution which dominate inmates' experience of an institution' (Richards 1978, p. 168). It is worth noting, by the way, that 'being afraid of going mad' and 'feeling suicidal' were 'problems' which both groups ranked lowest of all.

Sapsford's (1978) subjects were all homicidal lifers in a larger maximum-security prison; and he deliberately excluded fixed-termers. They consisted of three matching groups: 20 very recently received under sentence, 20 in their sixth year who had not yet been interviewed for parole review by the Local Review Committee, and a 'hard core' of ten who had passed the average date for release (at that time eleven years) and therefore faced the possibility of serving a very long time. Youths aged under 17 and men aged over 49 were deliberately excluded. Like those of Richards, Sapsford's samples were cross-sectional: but they were larger and better chosen. He used not only well-tried tests but also information from the lifers' files. He found, among those who had served longer periods: a greater tendency to talk and think about the past rather than the future; greater introversion — less interest in social activities and 'out-going behaviour' (an ironic choice of words); more dependence on routine even in petty matters, and less ability to take trivial decisions; no significant decrease in interest in the outside world, but less actual involvement in relations with outsiders (the two long-serving groups had nearly all lost contact with their wives or girlfriends, for example); amongst the hard-core men a greater tendency to see themselves as aligned with the staff (Sapsford did not imply that this was undesirable); but this tendency was not reflected in the staff's view of the hard-core men.

'Coping'

As Sapsford (1983, Chapter 4) later acknowledged, some of these changes should perhaps be regarded not as involuntary processes but as men's ways of coping with the psychological strains of long detention.[3] Prison sociologists recognised long ago that inmates consciously or unconsciously find ways of adapting to their situations, and that these ways differ according to their personalities and histories. If these adaptations lessen the stress they can be called 'coping strategies'. There are more ways than one of classifying them. While studying the inmates of Albany, King and Elliott (1977) found one method of classification which seemed to them to 'capture the fundamental aspects of criminal identity and prisoner response'. This was Irwin's (1970) typology, and it must be said in its favour that, unlike most sociologists, Irwin himself had 'done time' in an American penitentiary. Like Irwin, King and Elliott (1977, p. 238) make the point that adaptations to prison are 'fluid': 'Though there is an element of strategic choice about these adaptations, the choices are not mutually exclusive. Most prisoners probably adapt in different ways at different times and many follow elements of several adaptations at one and the same time'. Because there is this degree of choice — conscious or unconscious — on the prisoner's part, it seems likely that coping strategies are something that can be influenced by staff. If so, it seems that this should be an objective of policy, and that ways of achieving it should be studied more thoroughly than they have been in British prisons.

For the moment, it is probably sufficient to outline the main strategies which King and Elliott found among Albany inmates. Although everyone with an interest in this subject should read the whole of Chapter 8 of King and Elliott (1977), it is convenient here to cite Mott's (1985, p. 30) summary:

> (i)   *uncertain negative retreat* — difficulties in coping both with the staff and the other inmates;
> (ii) *secondary comfort indulgence* — simply enjoying the comforts of the prison;
> (iii) *jailing* — considerable involvement in the inmate social system with access to, and marketing of, contraband items;
> (iv) *gleaning* — frequent contacts with specialist treatment staff, attending many educational courses in the hope of acquiring useful qualifications;

(v) *opportunism* — exploiting both the inmate social system and the specialist staff and educational resources;

(vi) *'doing your bird'* — never attracting staff or inmate attention, but respected by both, while enjoying the comforts of the regime.

Obviously some of these strategies are more desirable than others from the point of view of management as well as mental health. Two points, however, should be kept in mind. However desirable this or that strategy — for example, 'gleaning' — may be from the staff's point of view, and however much it may seem to be in the prisoner's own interest — gleaning is again the best example — some strategies are ruled out by the capacities or personalities of individual prisoners, and attempts to force them in an apparently desirable direction may misfire.

Coping with depression in the early stages of a long prison sentence is another matter. Acute depressions can be alleviated by anti-depressant drugs; but these are not usually prescribed for what can be called 'realistic gloom'. It is left to non-medical staff to offer what help they can. Whether any special training would improve the quality of their help is doubtful. Claims[4] have been made for the technique called 'cognitive therapy', which deals with pathological depression by attacking the patient's distorted perception of his situation; but it is not easy to apply this to a prisoner whose appraisal of his situation is only too realistic.

Reversibility

The other point of prime importance was also made by Sapsford (1978, p. 143). Undesirable changes in a prisoner should be considered as deterioration only if they prove irreversible after his release. In 1983 Coker, who had followed up 239 released lifers, most of them from 'the lowest socio-economic group and poorly educated' (the sort whom one would expect to be most vulnerable to permanent deterioration) wrote:

> These men showed no evidence of deterioration as a result of their long years in prison, in so far as this can be measured. In general, after a short period of resettlement, sometimes accompanied by restlessness, they obtained and kept work and accommodation — satisfactory by their own standards as well as those of the Probation Service and the Home Office — and many married or remarried and made new homes. In some cases men improved upon their previous levels of employment. Additionally, these lifers revealed, generally, a fierce desire for independence and a capacity to manage their own lives competently, though some valued an opportunity to discuss matters with the probation officer (Letter in *British Journal of Criminology*, 1983, pp. 307–8, but see also Coker and Martin (1985)).

In other words, even if these men had experienced the changes found by Sapsford amongst his lifers, most of the changes seem to have been reversed. That is not to say that they are unimportant, or that no effort need be made to counter them: some of the changes which have been described have an undesirable effect on the 'quality of life' of long-term prisoners. What is quite unjustifiable, however, is the prevalent assumption that they persist for long periods after release, or are permanent.

Indiscipline

Individual breaches of discipline are only a little commoner in closed training prisons than in locals, if we can judge by the punishments recorded in Tables 9.2–9.8 of the annual prison statistics, although no doubt there are differences between degrees of enforcement in different prisons. It is remand centres, detention centres and youth custody centres — all for the young — which stand out. Concerted indiscipline, on the other hand, does seem commoner in establishments for long-termers: few, if any, of the reported riots of recent years have happened in other kinds of establishments. Research workers have tried to identify signs and symptoms which could be used to alert staff to the likelihood of a riot: their efforts were reviewed in the CRC report (Home Office 1984, pp. 96ff). They have focused either on the measurable attitudes of inmates immediately before rioting began, or on the personalities of troublesome or subversive inmates. Neither line of research seems to have yielded very useful findings. Smith (1980) suggests that when the 'degree of antagonism' and 'support for disruptive action' increase *rapidly* to high levels a major breakdown in control is likeliest; but he added that an experienced governor might well be a better predictor.

Recidivism

Imprisonment, however, has some intended aims, and the most important of these is obviously the reduction of the volume of crime. The efficacy of long sentences in deterring potential offenders is outside the scope of this paper, which is concerned with what imprisonment does to the imprisoned. As for incapacitation, there is no doubt that substantial periods of detention achieve some reductions in crime rates, although estimates of their importance vary. Critics of long sentences cannot deny their effectiveness as a means of postponing an offender's next crime — at least against a member of the free public. What such critics do condemn is the detention of offenders for longer than their proven offences deserve (whatever 'deserve' means), if the sole object of the extra period of detention is the prevention of an offence which the individual is not certain to commit. I have argued elsewhere (Walker 1982) that even this criticism has been carried to fallacious lengths: but this is not the place to pursue the point, which is of more relevance for sentencing and parole.

More germane to our present concern is the question whether long, or fairly long, sentences are particularly effective in deterring or otherwise discouraging prisoners from reoffending after release. More precisely, are such sentences followed by lower reconviction rates than are shorter sentences, and if so can this be attributed to the extra length? At first sight the reconviction tables in the annual prison statistics for England and Wales seem to show that the answer is 'yes', at least so far as adult men are concerned. The longer the nominal length of the sentence from which they are released, the lower the percentage reconvicted over the next two years. Unfortunately these tables make no allowances for differences in age (reconviction rates decline with age), types of offence (sexual offenders, for example, have rather low reconviction rates) and previous records (the shorter these are the better the reconviction rate). Nor do they distinguish ex-prisoners who were on licence for some of the follow-up period from those who were not; and being under licence seems to have a beneficial effect on reconviction rates. It is not easy to justify the crude and misleading form in which these tables are published.

In fact it is by no means certain that longer sentences are followed by lower reconviction rates, when allowance is made for the important variables. It did not seem to be so in the case of Californian burglars (see Jaman *et al.* 1972). But the best of the North American evidence still seems to be the inadvertent experiment which resulted from the decision of the US Supreme Court in the *Gideon* case. Large numbers of inmates had to be released from penitentiaries before their normal dates. In Florida, Eichman (1966) matched 110 of them with another 110 who had served their normal time, and followed up both groups for about two years. Neither group was under supervision during the follow-up. Sixty per cent of the 'Gideon group' had served less than 18 months, compared with 47 per cent of the others. Yet the reconviction rate of the Gideon group was lower than that of the 'controls' (14 per cent compared with 25 per cent).

I know of no British study which has tried to relate time actually spent 'inside' to subsequent reconvictions. Yet data must be available which could be used to improve on the American studies which have been cited. The Florida 'experiment' used, perforce, a rather early 'cut-off point': 18 months. The Californian research chose 45 months as its cut-off stage, simply because it was the point at which its sample split into equal halves. It would be better to choose at least two cut-off points, in case there is a curvilinear association between time inside and reconviction.

'Schools for crime'?

All we have at the moment, so far as British prisoners are concerned, is the finding by Nuttall *et al.* (1977, p. 69), in their study of parole, that there were differences in 'failure-rates' according to the parolees' previous criminal records and their previous experiences of imprisonment. This can be read as support for Sidney Smith's often repeated claim that penal establishments are 'schools for crime'. Most of the support for this rests on the impressions of those in charge of prisoners or ex-prisoners, and on autobiographical writings by ex-prisoners. What is said is that inmates form friendships with persistent offenders, and learn techniques of offending from them; and that independently or together these friendships and techniques lead them into the commission of further offences.

An alternative possibility, however, is that these merely make it easier to trace their offences to them, and to lay hands on them. An important fact — especially when the known facts are so few — is that the persistent offenders whom prisoners encounter inside are offenders who have not been competent enough to avoid conviction. High post-release conviction rates may be the result of learning incompetent techniques or of committing offences in concert with incompetent accomplices. Given the low clear-up rates for most of the types of offence for which men are imprisoned, this is by no means an implausible hypothesis.

What all this amounts to is that we have, as yet, no sound evidence for claiming either that longer periods of detention result in lower reconviction rates or that association with recidivists results in a higher rate of offending, as distinct from a higher rate of detection and conviction; and the distinction is all-important.

Grievances

Imprisonment not only exposes prisoners to the influence of other inmates. It also places them to some extent at the mercy of staff. The rules and standing orders which prohibit or restrict activities that would be unhindered in the world outside can be applied generously or with bureaucratic strictness. They may even be used punitively against an inmate who has made himself unpopular with staff. It is very hard for officers to steer a middle course between laxity and strictness, although many succeed in learning to do this successfully. What has an effect that must be undesirable is rule-enforcement which prisoners see as unnecessary or vindictive. 'Unlawful or unnecessary exercise of authority' by an officer is a disciplinary offence, which is spelt out as 'deliberately acting in a manner calculated to provoke a prisoner' or as the use of unnecessary or undue force. How often it occurs is hard to tell: it is only exceptionally that it receives publicity, for example in the aftermath of the Hull riots. Without denying the importance of major incidents, it should be recognised that it is the trivial but repeated instances which have more effects on the attitudes of larger numbers of prisoners, and which fertilise the antagonism of prisoners towards 'screws'. A similar antagonism can easily be observed in other authoritarian settings, such as a conscript army, where the non-commissioned officers who enforce rules — as distinct from decisions — are more unpopular than their superiors who make the rules. In prison an individual occasionally — whether through mishandling or because of his personality — becomes more or less unmanageable; and it is these cases which attract proper concern. What we do not yet know is the extent to which antagonism to prison officers, in its extreme or its endemic form, lingers on after release, and colours ex-prisoners' attitudes to other agents of the law. Nobody seems to have compared ex-prisoners with other convicted offenders in this respect.

Bathwater and babies

Research in British prisons — chiefly by psychologists — has done much to deflate the sweeping exaggerations — chiefly by sociologists — about the ill-effects of normal incarceration. Yet every exaggeration has, by definition, a small hard core of truth, which can be overlooked in the process of deflation. There *are* live babies in the bathwater. I have tried to locate them before they are thrown away. Some of them are unanswered questions which call out for more and better research. Some are questions that have not yet been clearly and precisely posed. But a few are questions that have been answered, at least with enough clarity to enable us to discuss what needs to be done about the answers.[5]

Bibliographical note

The literature on the unwanted effects of incarceration has been reviewed with differing degrees of thoroughness by several authors. Mott (1985) devotes two chapters to the main findings of British research, but lets some researchers off more lightly than others. McKay *et al.* (1979) provide an extensive bibliography, together with critical chapters which discuss policy implications from the Canadian point of view (Wormith's (1984) article in the *Canadian Journal of Criminology* seems largely based on the unpublished and more extensive work by McKay *et al.*) So far as psychological research is concerned, by far the best review is Bukstel and Kilmann (1980), which sorts out the wheat from the chaff, and summarises the research that seems to stand up to methodological criticism. The best review of research into prison suicides is Burtch and Ericson (1979).

Notes

1 Monger (1970) was a small-scale study, and has never been published. Monger *et al.* (1981) was largely based on reports in files, and not on a project designed to assess effects on children. Roger Shaw, however, has completed a study of prisoners' children, carried out whilst he was a Teaching and Research Fellow at the Institute of Criminology, University of Cambridge (Shaw 1987).

2 As Professor Gunn confirms (in a personal communication) the cases which used to be described as 'prison psychoses' are debatable. Sometimes they occur in extreme situations, such as prisoner-of-war camps. Even when this is not so 'no proper scientific data have been adduced to demonstrate whether the psychiatric problems are in fact directly attributable to the imprisonment or would have happened anyway'. And, of course, as is said later in this paper, some people are psychiatrically 'vulnerable'. I have seen reactive depressions in academics on sabbatical in very foreign countries.

3 This chapter has an excellent discussion of the psychodynamics of coping; but does not offer as clear a classification of coping 'styles' as do King and Elliott (1977). Sapsford's (1978) empirical study of lifers had not been designed with this in mind.

4 See, for example, Beck *et al.* (1977), reporting a controlled trial in which out-patients who underwent Beck's type of cognitive therapy showed greater improvement than those treated pharmacologically, although both groups showed improvement. Like all forms of psychotherapy, however, cognitive therapy seems to make considerable demands on time: in this experiment each patient underwent 20 weekly sessions, each of 50 minutes duration.

5 I am very much indebted to Professor Anthony Bottoms, Professor David Canter, Professor Richard Ericson, Professor John Gunn, to the Director of Prison Medical Services, to the Prison Medical Association and the Prison Officers' Association for helpful comments and references; but they are not responsible for the use I have made of them.

References

Beck, A.T. *et al.* (1977), 'Comparative Efficiency of Cognitive Therapy and Pharmacotherapy in the Treatment of Depressed Out Patients', *Cognitive Therapy and Research*, vol. 1, no. 1, pp. 17–37.

Bolton, N. *et al.* (1976), 'Psychological Correlates of Long-term Imprisonment', *British Journal of Criminology*, vol. 16, pp. 38–47.

Bukstel, L.H. and Kilmann, P.R. (1980), 'Psychological Effects of Imprisonment on Confined Individuals', *Psychological Bulletin*, vol. 88, pp. 469–93.

Burtch, B.E. and Ericson, R.V. (1979), *The Silent System: An Inquiry into Prisoners who Suicide and an Annotated Bibliography*, Toronto: Centre of Criminology, University of Toronto.

Cohen, S. and Taylor, L. (1972), *Psychological Survival*, Harmondsworth: Penguin.

Coker, J. and Martin, J.P. (1985), *Licensed to Live*, Oxford: Basil Blackwell.

Edholm, L. and Bishop, N. (1983), 'Serious Drug Misusers in the Swedish Prison and Probation System', *Prison Service Journal*, no. 55, pp. 14–16.

Eichman, C. (1966), *The Impact of the Gideon Decision upon Crime and Sentencing in Florida* (Monograph no. 2), Tallahassee: Florida Division of Corrections

Farrington, D.P. and Nuttall, C. (1980), 'Prison Size, Overcrowding, Prison Violence and Recidivism', *Journal of Criminal Justice*, vol. 8, pp. 221–31.

Goffman, E. (1961), *Asylums*, New York: Anchor Books.

Gunn, J. (1977), 'Mental Disorder and Criminality', *British Journal of Psychiatry*, vol. 130, 317–29.

Gunn, J. *et al.* (1978), *Psychiatric Aspects of Imprisonment*, London: Academic Press.

Harvey, J.B. (1986), 'Review of the Dietary Scale in Penal Establishments in England and Wales' (unpublished, obtainable from the Home Office Prison Department).

Home Office (1984), *Managing the Long-Term Prison System: The Report Control Review Committee,* London: HMSO.

Home Office (1985) *Report on Suicides in Prison,* London: Home Office.

Home Office Prison Department (annually), *Report of the Prison Department,* HMSO.

Irwin, J. (1970), *The Felon,* Englewood Cliffs, NJ: Prentice-Hall.

Jaman, D. *et al.* (1972), 'Parole Outcome as a Function of Time Served', *British Journal of Criminology,* vol. 12, pp. 5–34.

Jenkins, J.S. (1982), 'Suicide in Prisoners: an Overview', *Prison Medical Journal,* vol. 23, pp. 33–41.

Jones, D. (1976), *The Health Risks of Imprisonment,* Lexington, MA: Lexington Books.

King, R. and Elliott, K.W. (1977), *Albany: The Birth of a Prison — End of an Era?,* London: Routledge and Kegan Paul.

McKay, H.B. *et al.* (1979) *The Effects of Long-Term Incarceration: and a Proposed Strategy for Future Research,* Ottawa: Ministry of the Solicitor-General for Canada.

Monger, J. (1970), 'Prisoners' Children: a Descriptive Study of Some of the Effects on Children of their Fathers' Imprisonment', (unpublished, lodged in Barnett House Library, University of Oxford).

Monger, M., *et al.* (1981), *Through-Care With Prisoners' Families* (Social Work Study no. 3), Nottingham: University of Nottingham.

Morris, P. (1965), *Prisoners and Their Families,* London: Allen and Unwin.

Mott, J. (1985), *Adult Prisons and Prisoners in England and Wales 1970–1982: A Review of the Findings of Social Research,* London: HMSO.

Nuttall, C., *et al.* (1977), *Parole in England and Wales* (Home Office Research Study no. 38), London: HMSO.

Porporino, F.J. and Zamble, E. (1984), 'Coping with Imprisonment', *Canadian Journal of Criminology,* vol. 26, no. 2, pp. 403–21.

Prison Medical Association (1985), 'The Misuse of Drugs, with Special Reference to Treatment and Rehabilitation of Misusers of hard drugs', submission to the Social Services Committee of the House of Commons (unpublished).

Prison Officers' Association (1985), 'Report into Drug Abuse in Penal Establishments in England and Wales' (unpublished).

Richards, E. (1978), 'The Experience of Long-term Imprisonment', *British Journal of Criminology,* vol. 18, pp. 162–8.

Sapsford, R.J. (1978), 'Life-sentence Prisoners: Psychological Changes During Sentence', *British Journal of Criminology,* vol. 18, pp. 128–45.

Sapsford, R.J.(1983), *Life Sentence Prisoners: Reaction, Response and Change,* Milton Keynes: Open University Press.

Shaw, R. (1987), *Children of Imprisoned Fathers,* London: Hodder and Stoughton.

Smith, J.Q. (1980), 'The Prediction of Prison Riots', *British Journal of Mathematical and Statistical Psychology',* vol. 33, pp. 151–60.

Walker, N. (1982), 'Unscientific, Unwise, Unprofitable or Unjust?', *British Journal of Criminology,* vol. 22, pp. 276–84.

Wormith, J. (1984), 'The Controversy over the Effects of Long-term Incarceration', *Canadian Journal of Criminology,* vol. 36, pp. 423–37.

9 The American Federal system: control and classification
Gilbert Ingram

The process of classification as used in American corrections refers to the process by which inmate populations are systematically divided into smaller groups. The factors used to subdivide the population and the uses to which classification is put distinguish correctional systems, but every progressive American correctional agency acknowledges its dependence on a classification process. The vast majority of American inmates are housed in state and local facilities, but this paper is focused on control and classification issues in the American Federal prison system.

The primary purpose of classification in the United States Federal Bureau of Prisons is to assist staff in controlling the offender population. The 38,000 inmate population ranges in age from 17 to 88, with an average age of 36.5 years. Eighty-seven per cent of the population is sentenced, and the rest are immigration detainees and other unsentenced inmates awaiting trial or sentencing in United States Federal courts.

Average sentence length of the sentenced population is over ten years. This population includes 34 per cent who are drug-law violators; 27 per cent, who are convicted of violent crimes of assault, homicide, kidnapping, rape, or robbery; 8 per cent who are sentenced for larceny or theft; and 7 per cent who represent the white-collar crimes of income-tax violations, embezzlement and fraud. The population also includes 950 state or territorial commitments, 60 military prisoners, 1,900 Cubans, and 2,300 District of Columbia offenders.

Managing this heterogeneous population requires appropriate security measures, including the monitoring of inmate movements, restricting contact with others at times, and maintaining a realistic disciplinary process. These security goals are effectively advanced by a meaningful classification system. The underlying philosophy of the American Federal classification system is to place prisoners in the lowest custody classification consistent with their behaviour, and with both institution and community safety. Further, this classification system concentrates the most difficult and dangerous inmates at the highest security level, which is served by one institution. This function was performed by Alcatraz for many years, and except for a few years immediately after the closing of Alcatraz, has since been fulfilled by Marion. This classification policy has resulted in very positive gains for the American Federal prison system. By separating out the more predacious or escape-prone inmates from others within a given environment, by using the minimum security necessary for all inmates, and by placing inmates requiring the same general security requirements within the same institution, staff do not have to waste time or resources in protecting large numbers of inmates from a few; imposing unnecessary security restrictions on a whole population because a small number require them; or keeping lower-security inmates in more expensive higher-security beds. Identifying inmates for proper placement from the time of first entry into the prison system is essential in achieving these goals. Therefore, valid and reliable classification is a necessary management tool in maintaining control and preserving scarce resources. Because of these significant benefits, an emphasis on proper classification is found throughout the Federal Bureau of Prisons.

Institution classification
Classification activities in the Federal Bureau of Prisons are found at every step of the inmate's interaction with the agency, from initial commitment by the courts, to assignment to an institution, to his eventual return into the community. Initially, inmate information is gathered to allow designation to an appropriate institution, which has been classified by the level of security provided. Institutional security procedures have to be capable of controlling the most dangerous, escape-prone, or otherwise troublesome inmates in the population. Therefore, placing inmates into institutions with security appropriate to their needs allows a more economical use of institutions. Otherwise, every institution would have to be run as if it were a maximum-security institution.

The 46 Federal institutions are grouped into six security levels and one administrative category. Security levels range from a level 1, minimum-security (camp-like) facility, to a level 6, maximum-security institution. The administrative category, which includes institutions housing populations for medical, mental health, and other special reasons, must be able to handle all security levels. The six security levels are determined by seven factors: type of perimeter security; presence of towers; external patrols; detection devices; security of housing areas; type of living quarters; and level of staffing per population size.

The initial designation process aims to keep the inmate population in balance, decrease the number of moves between institutions, and minimise the number of cases that need protection from other inmates. Placing inmates who require the same degree of security into an institution consistent with their supervision needs accomplishes these goals. Additionally, the philosophy of using the minimum level of security necessary to contain the inmate safely forces staff continually to monitor the inmate's progress by re-evaluating his security level classification at specific times. Most inmates move towards lower-security institutions as they approach their release dates. This movement serves as a cost-effective way to house the population. However, a small group of recalcitrant offenders move up in security level based on their continued negative behaviour. In both cases the inmates are kept in environments consistent with their current security requirements.

Initial inmate designation/classification process

Inmate information used in the initial designation to an institution includes six items chosen through research to be relevant to security designation: history of escapes or attempts; history of violence; type of detainers lodged by other agencies; severity of current offence; expected length of incarceration; and type of prior commitments. The management variables are release residence; judicial recommendations; degree of overcrowding; sentence limitation; and racial balance at alternative institutions of the same security level. However, variables such as race or factors related to poverty are not used in this system in determining security level.

The designation system is based on observable and clearly defined variables that appear reasonable to staff and inmates. It is important that a classification system which has significant impact during an inmate's period of incarceration should appear just in its application. For that reason, even if non-criminal, non-offence-based variables were found to be predictive of acts of violence or escape attempts, they would not be used in designation to higher-level security facilities because of the inherent unfairness. Further, the present classification system functions very well without using such variables. The system takes advantage of a simple, yet useful basic fact; namely, the best predictor of future behaviour continues to be past behaviour.

Designation through this kind of process also makes operational sense to staff because it uses factors that appear logically relevant and that have been used traditionally in making correctional classification decisions. However, the current process applies the factors more consistently than could be done without a system, thus allowing all six items to make a statistically significant contribution to the security-level determination. Also, from the time of initial designation and throughout the inmate's incarceration, all information involved in general classification is entered into an automated data system. It remains immediately available to all staff as the inmate transfers to different institutions.

Inmates are aware that factors leading to their institution placement are based on past behaviour because they are clearly identified as such. The factors are easily understood because they are related to inmates' life experiences, thus allowing for easier communication between staff and inmates.

Custody classification

The second phase of the classification effort, closely related to the initial designation, occurs after the inmate arrives at the institution. This results in assigning the inmate to a custody level within the institution which provides the proper amount of staff supervision. Four levels of custody are used in the American Federal prison system:

Maximum

This classification requires continuous supervision and maximum control for such inmates. This level of custody can be applied only in a penitentiary (maximum-security institution) and is appropriate for individuals who are assaultive, violent, or prone to escape. These offenders have demonstrated their inability to function in the open population of an institution without endangering others, or endangering the orderly running of the prison.

Control of these inmates requires designation to a level 5 or 6 (penitentiary) institution, assignment of *maximum* custody and communication of this fact to all staff. The basic consequence of this custody assignment for the inmate is that, when out of his cell, he is restricted to specified, more secure areas of the institution and kept under constant staff monitoring. The inmate is not allowed outside the institution to participate in programmes but may take part in any inside activities that meet the above criteria.

In

This classification requires the routine staff supervision which can occur within any institution with a secure perimeter. Therefore, this level of custody can be applied in any level 2 to 6 institution. The inmate is assigned to a regular housing unit, single-cell preferably, but any type of cell used for inmates in that level of institution is acceptable. He is allowed to participate in any appropriate activities inside the institution with normal supervision, but never outside the institution perimeter.

Out

This classification allows the inmate to live in less-secure housing within any institution, including open dormitories. Only intermittent staff supervision is required and the inmate may participate in assigned activities inside or outside the institution's perimeter.

Community

This is the lowest custody level given to inmates in the Federal system. It allows living in the least secure housing units, including those outside the normal institution's perimeter. Inmates may participate in activities, inside and outside the institution's perimeter, and in community-based programmes. Minimal staff supervision is required to control such inmates.

Inmate custody/classification process

After inmates arrive at their designated institution, they are ordinarily assigned to *in* custody in all facilities except security level 1 where they are assigned to *out* custody. After six months in most cases, the inmate will be reviewed for possible custody change. This process recurs at regularly specified intervals of between three and 12 months as determined by the custody status.

Custody changes are determined by comparing the inmate's current status with that at the time of initial designation. A custody/classification form provides a consistent method of determining whether the inmate has moved in a positive (lower custody) or negative (higher custody) direction since his last review. Either type of custody change may also mandate a redesignation transfer to a different institution which can provide for the appropriate custody level. Inmates are aware that they may move down the security system, as well as up.

In addition to reviewing the six variables used in the initial designation process for possible change, the items affecting the custody change decision are: percentage of projected incarceration (time already served); historical or current involvement with drugs or alcohol (use or trafficking); current mental/psychological stability; severity and number of disciplinary reports received during the past year; responsibility demonstrated by inmate behaviour on reports from work and programme assignments; and nature of inmate's established and continuing family and community involvement.

The magnitude and direction of the inmate's change in these factors relative to his earlier status results in a numerical score and a resultant prescribed recommendation to consider increasing, decreasing, or not changing the custody. However, staff make the final decision and simply indicate in writing why no change was made only if they did not follow the recommendation. The key feature of this classification system is the intent for staff to use professional judgment within the specific guidelines. Consistent decision-making across all institutions results from this process while preserving staff flexibility.

Practical results of the classification system
In terms of management and control, this classification system is definitely an improvement over earlier classification efforts. The system is monitored to ensure that it is doing what is intended. For example, all six items used in the security classification/ designation process have been found to be significantly related to relevant post-admission behaviours such as disciplinary transfers, violence and misconduct. Also, inmates designated to the different security-level institutions have been found to be distinguishable from each other in terms of their subsequent behaviour. Inmates in higher security-level institutions have more disciplinary problems than inmates in lower-level institutions, and the differences increase as one goes up in level. One study also demonstrated that a disciplinary transfer was likely to occur when an inmate was placed in a security level, either above or below the appropriate level. Additionally, the greater the designation error, the more likely such a transfer would occur.

One obvious consequence of the security classification system has been a shift downwards in the overall security level of the inmate population. By properly identifying inmates who can handle placement in less secure facilities, a greater proportion of the Bureau of Prisons population can be housed in level 1 security institutions. This reduces population pressures and concomitant problems for higher-level institutions while saving a great deal of money. The budgetary implications of this downshifting of the inmate population are substantial. There is $42 per day difference between the per capita cost of a minimum-security bed in a camp and a maximum-security cell at USP Marion. More importantly to institutional staff, the escape rate of inmates has also declined since the adoption of this classification system. Staff at all levels appreciate the positive effect that the classification process has had on controlling the inmate population.

Unit management and facility design as tools for control
The custody and security classification system fits nicely with the unit management concept which the American Federal prison system adopted in 1973 after a successful pilot scheme. A unit is one of a number of small, self-contained housing areas with a permanently

assigned team of staff members who work with a relatively small number of offenders. The offices of the team members are located in the unit with the team having decision-making authority in all intra-institution aspects of classification. The assignment of offenders to units is accomplished in a number of ways according to the institution. For example, some assign inmates based upon services required (that is, drug-abuse programmes or pre-release activities), some according to work assignments, and some according to their need for specific types of supervision.

A key feature of unit management is the decentralisation of the institution's authority structure resulting in a flattening out ot the typical hierarchical chain of command. This places unit team members, who have the authority to make inmate case-management decisions, into direct contact with inmates and top-level management. Thus a smaller gap exists between inmates and the warden/associate warden than in a typical organisational link, contributing to communication in both directions. Unit staff as decision-makers are also able to spell out the institution's rules and regulations clearly and immediately upon the inmate's assignment to the unit.

Because unit management allows staff to maintain daily contact with the inmate population, they may deal with problems before they become major issues. Unit management also breaks the population into smaller, more manageable segments for staff and allows an inmate to relate to the same group of people during his incarceration. The result of this approach is to facilitate staff control of the institution, particularly when unit management is combined with a facility design that allows for decentralised, yet secure institutions.

The design of most modern American facilities is aimed at allowing some feeling of normality inside a secure perimeter. A safer and more humane institutional environment is the ultimate goal of both the unit management approach and this modern facility design. Staff are encouraged through the design to interact with inmates directly, because architectural barriers are omitted whenever possible. A balance is sought between a feeling of openness inside the perimeter, and necessary internal security. Decentralised, campus-like institutions, without the traditional bars, grilles, and towers in all security levels below 5 and 6, foster some sense of normality and enhance staff interactions with inmates. Direct supervision of inmates is consistent with this architectural design and with the unit management system. Better control of the population results from this combination. Another advantage of the new facility design is its operational flexibility which allows for adapting to security needs as population changes occur over time. Different units may be run with more or less control as circumstances evolve.

Housing units are usually designed for no more than 150 inmates, subdivided into small modules with office space for unit staff. The building exterior is constructed of secure materials but the interior walls, including inmates's rooms, are generally built with standard construction materials. This saves money and allows more options for building a pleasing, natural environment inside the unit. Colourful designs and murals are used throughout the unit to provide stimulation and normality. Many exterior walls, including the inmate rooms, have secure windows rather than solid walls, providing an outside view and a feeling of openness.

Inmate rooms are designed for single occupancy which gives some degree of privacy within the institution. Single cells also serve as one of the best control techniques available to reduce inmate tension, and to use as a temporary isolation area for disruptive inmates when necessary. Although overcrowding often precludes the use of single bunking, the built-in flexibility of the inmate rooms easily allows for double occupancy. Each of the unit designs also provides for common areas and small multi-use spaces which add to a sense of community and give inmates a choice of activities and alternate living space.

In the new facility design, the control-room officer operates the external gates and serves as the central communications link within the institution from a centrally located position. The officer is either in a building with a direct, unobstructed view of the compound or he has electronic surveillance of all key areas. If inmates requiring more security are housed in one particular unit within an institution, that area can be monitored more closely and frequently by the control-room officer. The location of the popular activity buildings, in clusters connected by walkways, forces inmate movement into natural patterns that can be easily monitored by staff while they are also engaged in other duties.

The importance of the location of these activity buildings, including industrial, vocational, and educational operations, underscores one other aspect of control that should be mentioned. Staff, working closely with inmates in their units, are better able to place them in activities that meet their interests and keep them as productively occupied as possible. Naturally, inmate security needs become more critical in decision-making for unit staff than inmate interests as one moves up the security level. However, reducing inmate idleness is one of the most essential factors in maintaining control at all levels, and a well-informed unit team can better accomplish this task. Therefore, providing meaningful activities, especially well-run industrial opportunities, is a necessary ingredient in the success of these decentralised institutional environments.

Regardless of the design of institutions, or the presence of sophisticated surveillance devices, technology cannot replace staff supervision. Inmates have demonstrated repeatedly that they cannot be controlled successfully if staff do not remain involved, vigilant and visible. Unit management and decentralised facility design encourage this type of staff behaviour. Useful classification procedures mesh naturally with these concepts and make the control objective easier for staff to achieve.

Special classification/control techniques

The current classification system in conjunction with unit management and decentralised facility design allows trained staff to control the majority of Federal inmates. However, there are always present a small group of recalcitrant or extraordinary inmates who must be handled with special techniques. That is the rationale for the traditional segregation units found in every correctional institution, including the United States Bureau of Prisons. Discussion of that type of control technique is unnecessary because everyone is familiar with it. However, two special features of the American classification system that aid in managing the population should be described: the central inmate monitoring system and several aspects of the only level 6 institution, the penitentiary at Marion, Illinois.

Central inmate monitoring system

This part of the classification system elevates, to a higher level, the decision-making process for those extraordinary inmates who require special management attention or whose circumstances warrant special consideration prior to a final decision about their assignments. For example, decisions concerning routine transfers to other institutions, temporary release to other jurisdictions or agencies, or participation in community-based activities for these inmates require higher-level review. Inmates monitored under this system are not necessarily assaultive or escape-prone, but their placement in institutions without special precautions could easily cause serious problems.

Special management considerations for these individuals are aimed at co-ordinating procedures to ensure the safety and security of individuals or groups and the orderly operation of institutions. Also, many of these are sensitive cases that need to be handled consistently so that undue public attention is not focused on them. Finally, this classification effort attempts to assure that staff judgment errors do not result in a depreciation of the seriousness of criminal behaviour.

Eight categories require classification under the central inmate monitoring system: government witnesses in cases involving organised crime; individuals involved in sophisticated criminal activity, usually in a leadership or key role and involving a significant amount of money; inmates who have threatened government officials and who require special surveillance; individuals who have received widespread publicity because of their criminal activity; members of disruptive groups (prison gangs) and those who must be separated from them; prisoners housed by the Federal system for service of state sentence (including co-operating state witnesses); individuals who must be separated from other individuals for their own safety; and special supervision cases, such as former law-enforcement officers, who require protection while confined because of previous occupations or affiliations with organisations.

The level of review necessary before final decisions on their cases depends on the monitoring category and the recommended action. For example, all clearances for United States government witnesses involved in testifying against organised crime are handled at the central office level. Clearances for routine community trips for separation cases, on the other hand, are dealt with by the five regional offices in the Federal system.

The use of special monitoring procedures for cases in the central inmate monitoring system has been successful in reducing violence against these individuals, and others, and is an extremely important part of the classification/control process.

Marion

USP Marion serves the Federal prison system as a specialised, closely controlled, high-security institution. Marion usually receives inmates by way of disciplinary transfer from other institutions because of changes in individual security needs, but it also receives a small number of high-security inmates committed directly from the courts. The typical inmate in the population of 350 is serving a very long sentence (41 year average) for a serious offence such as armed bank robbery, and has committed serious rule violations such as murder, assault or escape in other prisons. Additionally, approximately 100 state inmates are housed at Marion because they are unmanageable in the states' institutions. Most Marion inmates also face additional sentences with other jurisdictions when their Federal time expires.

Removal of the most violent, escape-prone inmates to Marion has served to reduce disruptive behaviour at other Federal facilities, and allows them to be operated as decentralised, relatively open environments. Placement of these inmates into one location at Marion provides invaluable assistance to the entire Federal prison system. Recognition by the inmate population that there is an end-of-the-road institution also provides a deterrent effect on negative behaviour by inmates in other institutions. According to both staff observations and inmate statements, inmates do try to avoid problems that may lead to transfer to Marion. Statistics on assault data support these conclusions.

Inmates housed at Marion cause problems wherever they are located, but concentration of them in one location allows for a tighter and more focused security programme which reduces the havoc they can cause. With this type of inmate, an open population concept is not feasible. Therefore, the general population of Marion is subject to tighter controls than those maintained in any other American Federal institution. The evolution of the current operation was not without difficulty. The tightly controlled, unitised regimen was introduced only after a series of assaults and homicides against both staff and other inmates. Unfortunately, the classification system was more effective in identifying the inmates for Marion than was anticipated, and preceded by several years the development of appropriate control techniques for this special group of offenders.

Historical analysis reveals that the more violent population assigned to Marion was augmented by the growing presence of organised prison gangs. This combination intensified disruptions at that institution and attempts at controlling this population with more traditional forms of operation (programming which allowed for varying degrees of open movement and inmate freedom) met with failure. Subsequently, a high-security operation was developed which places great emphasis on inmate control with attendant limitation on certain inmate freedoms. Many programmes and services formerly provided on a group basis are delivered on an individual basis, frequently in the cell. Physical contact between staff and inmates is limited except for two units that serve pre-release purposes. No direct physical contact is allowed between inmates and non-staff from outside the institution, including family and volunteers. This restriction has led to a significant reduction in dangerous contraband and assaults with weapons.

Present operations at Marion are successful because the predictable structure allows staff and inmates to live and work safely. Constant monitoring and modification are necessary to maintain control. However, even in this maximum-security environment, controls remain restrictive only to the degree necessary, as determined by inmate behaviour.

Likewise, for most inmates Marion is viewed as a temporary assignment. Demonstration of responsible conduct over a period of time ordinarily enables an inmate to transfer back to a more open institutional setting. Providing this avenue of hope constitutes an essential element in Marion's successful management of this volatile population.

Marion staff The work environment at Marion poses significant challenges for all staff. The institution is among the most difficult and demanding assignments in the entire prison system. Daily contact with sophisticated, dangerous prisoners and the need for constant vigilance place great pressure on staff. Therefore, considerable attention is given to recruiting only the best-qualified individuals for both line and supervisory positions. Emphasis is placed on providing staff with training to prepare them physically and mentally for their arduous tasks, to develop the interpersonal skills necessary to deal with an antagonistic inmate population, and to promote staff cohesion. These efforts have been successful in maintaining staff morale at a high level.

Outside criticism of Marion Marion serves as a natural target for a small group of outside critics who disagree with the necessity for tight controls of any kind, and in some cases, with the total idea of imprisonment. One group in particular has, as its stated objective, the complete closing of Marion. Close scrutiny and criticism from this type of group, and of course from Marion inmates, places an additional burden on staff in responding to this criterion. Staff are required at all times to maintain a high level of professionalism in every institution, but the attention focused on Marion highlights this concern. Legal attacks also occur regularly. Documentation is necessary even for routine occurrences to counter false accusations against staff. For example, whenever possible, videotapes are taken of situations involving force. They are reviewed by administrative staff to ensure that proper procedures were followed. Staff are reassured by such measures and charges by outside critics are effectively answered. This does not silence them as it is unlikely their philosphical viewpoint can be changed in any case. Whether their motivations are humanitarian, anti-establishment, or something else, they appear to represent either misinformed or isolated groups. The vast majority of people in the United States realise that there are some individuals who pose extreme danger to ordinary citizens, including other inmates, and who need extraordinary security measures.

Marion Control Unit In addition to the special security procedures developed recently for the general population at Marion, the Federal Bureau of Prisons has concentrated disruptive inmates there in a special control unit since 1973. These inmates, who are afforded due process hearings before placement into Marion Control Unit, have proved by their behaviour in other institutions that they need to be separated from other inmates. Serious acts at another secure institution such as assault on a staff member, murder of another inmate, or involvement in a sophisticated escape attempt have led to their Control Unit placement. They are sentenced to serve a specific number of months in this unit, are kept in very secure cells, are not allowed to engage in group activities, and are otherwise tightly controlled. Their cases are reviewed every 60–90 days by a high-level team from outside the institution. Credit for time in the unit and eventual release depends upon their adjustment to rules and regulations, and their co-operation with staff. Although a few of these inmates have managed to continue their assaultive behaviour, most of them have been effectively managed in this special control unit.

K Unit   Marion also has a small, seven-cell area beneath the hospital, which is structured to house those very few inmates who cannot be safely held in Marion's general population or the Control Unit. These inmates require a combination of very high security and protection that cannot be provided elsewhere in the Federal system. They have to be kept totally isolated from the other Marion inmates and from each other. Most either have verified threats on their lives from prison gangs or are subject to extortion because of widespread publicity, and require a higher degree of security than can be provided in lower-security facilities.

   Admission to this unit is accomplished only after extensive classification work and with the specific authorisation of the Director of the Federal Bureau of Prisons. Access to this unit is limited to approved personnel and no other inmates are ever allowed entry. Movement of these inmates outside K Unit is infrequent and extraordinary precautions are taken to provide security. All services, including food, religious activities, medical attention, and attorney visits occur in the unit. Inmates participate in unit activities individually and under staff supervision. Otherwise, they live in their cells which are considerably larger than normal Marion cells. Each has a self-contained shower, a television, and provides for additional personal property and inmate movement. A self-contained recreation area is located in the unit and a small, restricted outside recreation area is used strictly for K Unit inmates. This unit, while small in size, typifies the extreme importance of proper classification in safely housing certain special inmates.

Summary

From management's perspective, proper inmate classification and the presence of trained staff are as important to effective control of inmates as are the physical security devices found in American Federal correctional institutions. Effective classification allows for the collection and immediate use of relevant background information on inmates, leading to designation of inmates to environments consistent with their security requirements. A good classification system also identifies those inmates who cannot be housed in the open population of institutions because of the danger they present to others, and to the orderly running of the institution.

A pecking-order phenomenon is present in any prison environment with the strongest or meanest rising to the top, but some inmates are so dangerous to the rest of the population that their removal is absolutely necessary for the orderly operation of the institution. Otherwise, their presence in that environment preoccupies staff and inmates to the degree that continued disruptions occur, or at least it requires an inordinate amount of staff attention. The United States Bureau of Prisons has found that the removal of these inmates to a more secure environment is a positive management step with our heterogeneous population.

Providing different environments for inmates with different security needs is a key to control, and this cannot be accomplished without a valid classification system. After this is in place, other factors necessary for control can be effective, including the presence of trained staff directly observing and talking with inmates, and the availability of meaningful opportunities for work and other activities for reducing idleness. Using the current classification system, over 95 per cent of the American Federal population is controlled in open institution environments. This does not mean that crises of one type or another do not occur because there are no simple answers in running correctional institutions and in holding dangerous people against their will. However, the American Federal experience indicates that at least with this heterogeneous population a realistic classification system can minimise the number of problems for both staff and inmates.[1]

Note

1   Some of the opinions expressed in this paper reflect the viewpoint of the author and may not necessarily represent the official policy of the Federal Bureau of Prisons or the United States Department of Justice.

10 Implications for 'new generation' prisons of existing psychological research into prison design and use
David Canter

New mistakes for old?

The whole system of events associated with imprisonment contains a network of human activities inextricably linked to places in which those activities occur. The prison building is the instrument of incarceration. This is quite unlike educational institutions, for example, where children can be taken to a park and education continue there without blackboard, classroom or school. Or, taking another contrast, the manager can take his office home in his briefcase and manage from his living room. When the term 'imprisonment' is used to refer to experiences outside of prison it is clearly a metaphorical rather than an actual imprisonment.

Given this inevitable link between the architecture and the action of prisons it is surprising that there have been so few systematic studies of the behavioural and experiential implications of prison design. For although there is now a substantial literature on the psychology of school design, office design, housing and even national parks, there are only a handful of scientific studies looking at prison design and use. Perhaps even more remarkable is the way, in Britain at least, designers have been ignorant of even the little research that has been done. There is even a proposal to produce new design guides without any published evaluations of why the original guides are now of such little value.

It is therefore a cause of some concern to discover that so many new prisons are being planned and yet so little scientific research is being carried out to guide these designs. This view is not unique to people who make their living by conducting such research. In the introduction to the Platt Report (Home Office 1985, p. 3) commissioned by one Secretary of State and with a very supportive foreword by a subsequent one, it is stated quite directly:

> It was discovered that very little in the way of published research information was available in the UK on recent developments in prison design in the USA, or indeed elsewhere. There appears to be a lack of published

analytical evaluation in this field, and there is clearly scope for further research on prison design, in particular on the psychological effect of design on inmates and staff, and on the relationship between physical environment and regime philosophies.

The Working Party which produced this statement lists the published work examined. This list does not include the study by Farbstein and Wener (1982) that won an award for applied architectural research from the well-known architectural magazine *Progressive Architecture*. It does not include the study by Wener and Olsen (1980) that involved detailed observations and interviews with staff and inmates in the New York and Chicago Metropolitan Correctional Centers, even though the New York MCC was visited by the Working Party. It does not include any reference to the major study by Canter and Ambrose (1980) drawn on in some detail by Roy King in Chapter 5 of the present volume, even though this was commissioned by the Home Office with commendable foresight to be available for consideration in the design of future prisons. Even the reference section of that report was not raided to provide a more complete list of the previous research the Working Party so urgently needed.

Yet despite this lack of systematic, scientific information, the Platt Committee felt able to put forward strong, clear proposals on what are the appropriate design solutions to take Britain's prison building programme into the twenty-first century. These proposals are based, as far as can be ascertained, on brief visits made by experienced architects, prison administrators and senior Home Office civil servants to a variety of new United States Prisons. What likelihood is there that these new designs will be any more successful than older ones? In particular, do they offer a basis for a third option between concentration and dispersal for long-term imprisonment as the Control Review Committee (Home Office 1984) and Roy King (Chapter 5) have suggested?

Before answering these questions directly it is necessary to take the opportunity, briefly, to review the main themes that have emerged from the environmental psychology literature and to indicate how this approach, illustrated by Roy King, may provide a much needed input to the debates on current and future prison design.

An environmental psychology of prisons

The game of Monopoly's distinction between being in jail and 'just visiting' is one that it seems easy to forget. The members of the Platt Committee, in various combinations, visited 15 establishments specifically to produce their report. Doubtless the 14 members of the Committee all had considerable experience of a variety of other establishments on which they could draw, but it is a notable aspect of their report that in the third of a page devoted to their 'method of work' nothing is actually said of how their visits were conducted, what information was made available to them or how they validated their conclusions (Home Office 1985, p. 3). Their report is quite clearly not intended to be a technical one, but precisely because it is so accessible and lavishly illustrated any reader needs to be able to assess how securely based are its conclusions.

It is well known that visits to any institution allow the favourable face to be presented. Given that it is essential to know how and why new designs work in one context in order to extrapolate them to other contexts, the need to get beyond the visitor's view is essential.

As it happens some simple examples of the differences between the Home Office visitors' accounts and those from psychological research can be obtained because of the published study of the New York MCC. Take the instance of the facts as stated in the Platt Report: 'Average sentence: pre-trial 60 days, sentenced 120 days'. Also consider the seemingly positive statement next to a bright photograph: 'Outdoor recreation takes place on the roof deck on the basis of 5 hours per week per inmate. But in practice 7 hours is currently being achieved' (Home Office 1985, pp. 8, 14).

Compare this with the results of systematic research by Wener and Olsen (1980, p. 492):

> Architects were told that inmates would remain in the MCC for no more than three months, during which time they would be engaged in educational or work activities. In reality, inmates may be confined in the MCCs for a year or more, and as the behavioural mapping indicates, most of the day is spent in isolated, passive activity. Resources and outdoor access might have been distributed differently had designers understood the actual nature and length of confinement.

In general from their study, carried out a few years before the Home Office visit, Wener and Olsen conclude that the MCCs are successful environments, perceived as superior to other institutions. But they add the important caveat that significant design-related problems do exist. These they trace to inadequate design information.

The British situation is today not much better than the situation described by Wener and Olsen in 1980. This is well illustrated by the *Twenty-Fifth Report From The Committee of Public Accounts* published in May 1986 dealing with the prison building programme. In its main conclusions the Committee of Public Accounts (House of Commons Committee of Public Accounts 1986, p. xviii, para. vi) states: 'There have been design and building defects on which the Departments were slow to take action because of poor appraisal and feedback arrangements. Some past faults are giving rise to excessive

staff costs or buildings that cannot be used. We condemn these failures.'
In their response to the Committee, Home Office and Property Service
Agency officials insisted that they had now improved their strategic
planning and feedback procedures, but the lack of clear evidence of
the basis for the conclusions of the report on new generation American
prisons does not indicate that anything more than one set of opinions
have replaced another set. There was much general debate and
enthusiasm about the designs of prisons built ten and 20 years ago.
Experienced architects, prison governors and senior administrators were
involved in preparing those designs. No one has suggested they were
malicious or even incompetent. Yet in their report the Committee of
Public Accounts (House of Commons Committee of Public Accounts,
PSA 1986, p. xvii, para. 47) have this to say:

> We are encouraged that the Home Office are now seeking to eliminate
> from the programme those designs which are costly in terms of manpower
> to run. We approve of their looking again at prison design, but must
> emphasise the importance of seeking experience of proven systems so
> as to avoid the sort of mistakes made in the 1960's and 1970's with
> the novel 'hotel-corridor' prisons.

Of course, in the way of politicians the Committee does not identify
what types of 'experience' would be most effective to seek, nor does
it indicate how a system such as the design of a prison might be
'proven'. From other comments in the report it would seem that
their central and very proper concern is to reduce overcrowding
within limited budgets. This means effective use of the places available without an additional burden of staff time. So their attention
has been drawn to the way in which certain designs are seen as
placing demands on the staffing levels.

A simple example of how design relates to staffing levels can
be readily given. In essence a closed corridor, the end of which
is not in view from some central location, is seen by prison officers
as a potential threat and so more staff will be required in that location
than would be the case for an open, galleried, radial design. Or
to take another example, facilities that are at some distance from
the cells may pose particular problems by requiring staff to escort
prisoners to those facilities. In very high-security situations these
and related matters may be of such great concern that cells will
be left empty and densities deliberately kept low so that existing
staffing levels can cope. Roy King (Chapter 5) discusses the way
in which these procedures leave a large number of cells in the prison
system empty.

These examples serve to highlight three aspects of any consideration of prison design and use. First, there is the seemingly inevitable
prospect of prison accommodation being overcrowded and inade-

quate through into the next century. So, whatever is done about long-stay prison facilities, there will always be an implicit pressure, and often an explicit one, for places to deal with the prison populations as a whole. Secondly, the provision of appropriate accommodation is inextricably interlinked with management procedures and agreed staffing levels. The design cannot be 'experienced' or 'proven' without a clear understanding of how it will be managed and used. Thirdly, there is a difficult balance to be achieved between providing respect and dignity for the prisoner and the maintenance of effective control of the prison population. These three aspects operate together within the present English prison system, no matter how they may be separated out for discussion or alleviating action. Therefore, before turning to some of the psychological implications of new prison designs it is fruitful to consider, briefly, each of these aspects and their interconnections.

Crowding

The problem of overcrowding in prisons is not restricted to Britain. It seems to be almost inevitable in many countries. The United States is no exception. However, because under the American Constitution it is possible for prisoners to bring lawsuits against the authorities to claim that overcrowded conditions are unconstitutional, there has been much more open debate in the United States about the consequences of crowding. As part of these discussions McCain *et al.* (1980) carried out a major study for the US Bureau of Prisons. Their report is salutory reading. They obtained information from over 1,400 prisoners, including prisoner's records, physiological measures and questionnaire responses. Their two principal conclusions are worth quoting in full (McCain *et al.* 1980, p. 1):

> 1. High degrees of sustained crowding have a wide variety of negative psychological and physiological effects including increased illness complaint rates, higher death and suicide rates, and higher disciplinary infraction rates.
> 2. Large institutions produce much more severe negative psychological and physiological effects than small institutions, as expressed in higher death, suicide, and psychiatric commitment rates.

The importance of these results can be traced to the fact that the biggest influence of crowding came from what the authors called 'social density' rather than 'spatial density'. In other words it was the number of people who shared a space that was the critical contribution to the effects they found, not the amount of space per person overall. Larger cells did not help if they still required two people to be in them. Dormitories yielded much higher illness rates, for example, than single cells although the spatial density was not greatly increased in the dormitories.

This finding fits rather well with studies from a quite different context. Canter *et al.* (1975) found that a house price was more readily predicted from the number of rooms in the house than from the total floor area. As human beings it is the identification of particular spaces for particular people and activities that is the essence of the utilisation of space. Once the possibilities of particular spaces, identifiably associated with a person's own activities, are withdrawn from residential spaces then stress is a likely consequence. This stress can reveal itself in many forms, including aggression and suicide.

Crowding, then, is not just an administrative nuisance. It is not just an inconvenience and mild discomfort for prisoners. It can be a totally unjust and really debilitating component of the prison experience. It can certainly be a major contributor to making prison more of a destructive experience than is necessary. It is therefore essential that any new designs are able to provide the possibility of increased numbers without a drastic reduction in the social space available, that is, the number of identifiable rooms available for each prisoner.

Regime influences design effects
In those United States prisons where the regime did not allow access out of the cells or dormitories for much of the day the relative effects of social crowding were found to be much stronger. It would seem not surprising to find that if prisoners are forced to experience the prison mainly through their cells then the number of people in those cells is more likely to become a source of problems.

These findings on the impact of the regime in relation to the design accord well with results of the detailed study, mentioned earlier, of six prisons in Britain carried out by Canter and Ambrose (1980). They asked inmates their views on a number of aspects of prison design and compared their satisfaction scores across six very different institutions, selected so that none of them was severely overcrowded at the time of the study.

Three of the institutions housed Category C and D prisoners, being of campus, block or satellite design. These were consequently relatively low-security establishments that had considerable possibilities for work and other activities away from the cell and the wing. The other three establishments were a dispersal, a local, and a training prison with nuclear or radial designs, having much higher security levels and less ready access for prisoners to various facilities.

The average satisfaction scores compared across the six institutions

Table 10.1   Mean dissatisfaction scores given by inmates in six prisons showing effects of regime.

Questionnaire topic	Medium-security establishments			High-security establishments		
Talking to inmates in the association area	2.3	2.7	1.9	3.2	3.3	4.2
Meeting inmates from other association areas	2.9	3.5	1.8	3.4	4.9	5.5
Personal safety	3.1	3.5	2.9	3.5	3.6	4.2
Religious atmosphere of chapel	3.0	3.6	2.6	3.0	4.2	4.2
Talking in bathroom	3.0	3.0	3.2	3.8	3.5	4.8
Spaciousness of wing design	2.9	3.9	3.2	4.4	4.7	5.7
Being alone in association area	4.5	4.7	3.9	5.2	4.6	5.4
Satisfaction of cell design for association	4.4	4.7	3.7	5.1	4.6	5.8
Certified normal accommodation	320	376	484	296	200	709
Actual population	260	313	476	270	120	996
Occupation (%)	81	83	92	91	60	140

Note: Scores are from the highest satisfaction of 1.0 to the highest dissatisfaction of 7.0
Source: Canter and Ambrose (1980, p. 234, Table 17)

revealed some interesting patterns, especially when attention is drawn to those questions that clearly discriminate between the two sets of institutions. The results for the seven questions showing clear discrimination are given in Table 10.1. The scoring system was such that the most satisfactory score possible was 1 and the least was 7. As can be seen, in all cases, the discrimination is on questions that show lower satisfaction for all three highly secure establishments when compared with the three other less-secure establishments. But what is also apparent is that the questions identified by this process are all to do with areas for association.

This consistently higher dissatisfaction with the space and possibilities for association are not a function of the degree of crowding of the establishments overall. The higher-security establishments include rates of occupation that are lower as well as higher than the medium-security establishments studied. Very different types of design are also included amongst the higher-security establishments studied. Clearly it is the regime that makes the various spatial possibilities available to the inmates. In a higher-security establishment, with the control over movement and the restrictions to wings, there is much more pressure on those association spaces closest to the cell.

What Table 10.1 is not able to show is that the judgments about the cells in the different establishments have different correlations with other items, depending on the security level of the establishment. In the two highest-security establishments the judgments made on the cells had the highest average correlations with all the other items. In other words, it was satisfaction with the cell that determined reactions to the prison as a whole. This was not the case for the other establishments. Of particular importance in this regard was the fact that the questions on personal safety were highly correlated in the high-security establishments with the questions about the cells. It was the lack of ready access to the cells by staff and the pressure on the area around the cells used for association that gave rise to the fears for personal safety. In the less-secure establishments these fears were linked to association and other areas away from the cell blocks.

These findings do have special relevance to central principles in 'new generation' concepts. This is especially because these concepts are built around an enhancement of the dominance of the wing and the cell as a focal part of prison planning. Yet there seems to be little consideration of the way access to the rest of the prison influences the experience of the individual unit. We will return to this shortly.

Who is in control?
The emphasis on the view from within an establishment is important because environmental psychologists have found, in many situations, that the perspective a person has on a place is a product of the reasons that person has for being in that place. Designers, users and managers will all experience any given building in their own particular way, their daily routines and their job-related motivations will draw their attention to aspects particular to their own circumstances.

In prison this special perspective is critically important. All governors will agree that a prison runs smoothly in so far as prisoners will allow it to. They may have to be coerced into allowing routines to happen, but under any foreseeable manning levels the broad co-operation of even the most sullen prisoners is important. Indeed Canter and Ambrose (1980) report a study from three establishments that showed the great extent to which prison officers and prisoners do share a common view of the nature of each of the establishments. It is important that design features facilitate the evolution of such a consensus.

Both the British and the United States evaluation research show something that might be regarded as rather paradoxical. Critical to all prisoners in their evaluation of the acceptability of an institution is the extent to which they have control over aspects of their lives. To an outsider or visitor these aspects may seem to be of little significance, but to the prisoner they can be very significant.

It is worth quoting again from the Wener and Olsen (1980, p. 492) study of the New York and Chicago MCCs. Their examples, whilst directly pertinent to the concerns here, illustrate results also found in other studies in Britain, in prisons and other institutions:

> Many of the best features of the MCCs are those which provided inmates with some degree of control over their environment — such as the ability to isolate themselves in their rooms when so desired. Environmental problems, on the other hand, frequently indicate areas where control is lacking. For example, inmates unable to regulate airflow and temperature stuffed paper or cloth in air vents in an attempt to exercise control over that function.

The idea of 'doing your own time' is about just such controls over small aspects of day-to-day existence in prison. Design details, like ventilation, and layout that demands certain types of administrative control, all contribute to these aspects of the prison experience. In terms of layout, for example, Farbstein and Wener (1982) point out that a multiple-bed cell can be less stressful than a single cell if the former has access to many spaces while the latter is confined to one or two small areas. As has been mentioned, the same principle was illustrated in Canter and Ambrose's (1980) study by the fact that the cell was less significant to satisfaction in open establishments than in high-security ones.

A cognitive ecology

The problem of control by staff and access by prisoners may be modified in prisons by a process that can be found in all institutions. This is the mechanism whereby certain areas become designated for use by, or under the control of, particular groups or individuals. This is not wholly bad because the demarcation of distinct areas may help to reduce tensions by keeping potentially conflicting groups out of each other's way. But as Drinkwater (1982) reported for psychiatric hospitals, areas can also become associated with unwanted activities such as violence.

This seems to be less of an issue in British prisons than in those in the United States for two possible reasons. One is that the three-way racial divide, with all its antagonisms, is not so apparent here. The other is that the United States tradition, especially in high-security establishments, of in effect leaving the prisoners to their own devices providing they keep within understood limits, is less apparent here.

This is an important difference because the idea of observation gantries and their later development into observation cubicles or offices, so popular in United States prisons, derives directly from the view that there are places for staff and other places for inmates. Many environmental psychology studies show that if staff are given a space of their own from which they can see their charges they will be more likely to spend time in that 'staff room'. Some aspects of United States designs could, therefore, counteract the objective of ensuring that staff are part of the same community as prisoners through spending as much time as possible with inmates.

The structuring of who does what where is aggravated by the endemic problem of crowding in prisons. One important point that has emerged from studies of crowding is that its significance lies in the extent to which it limits the prisoner's freedom of choice and access to resources within the prison. If he can no longer escape to the library, his cell, or the playing field because of multiple use, magnified by populations way above those for which the prison was designed, and constrained by regimes, then trouble is predictable. Wener and Olsen (1980, p. 491) quote one officer as saying: 'When I leave on a Friday with a census of 70 or more, I know there will be several fights over the weekend.'

New generation prisons must somehow allow for the possibility of overcrowding, if not by design then by administration.

The human factor

Throughout the above summary transactions between people and places they inhabit have been emphasised. National cultural variations will count for a lot, and regime variations will account for more. The Platt Committee were aware of the latter, although they did not emphasise the former as much as they might have done. It is therefore important that any planning of new prisons does integrate men, management and the architectural machinery.

In Canter and Ambrose's (1980) study it was possible to monitor the commissioning of Featherstone Prison. This showed that a large number of modifications to the fabric of the building were necessary in order to make it operable by the staff, and many more modifications were necessary to the usage of parts of the prison from those originally intended. At the very least such modifications are a valuable source of information about the mismatch between design and management. It is a pity that the Committee gave no information of such changes in their pictorial account of the places they visited in the United States.

Is there a third option?

In considering the relevance of 'new generation' designs to the provision for long-term imprisonment the suggestion has been made by the CRC and by Roy King that they may provide a third option somewhere between dispersal and concentration. This idea is based on the possibility provided by separate 'pods' of having different regimes in each pod and the ready ability to separate or join pods at the whim of management. Ideas that develop in the United States always benefit from an inventive use of the English language. The central idea that wings of prisons should stand alone takes on more elegant nuances with the botanic analogy of a 'pod'.

These units certainly respond to two important requirements noted earlier from the research literature. One is that the cell is given a great deal of significance, being as spacious as possible with integral sanitation and the possibility of pleasant views out. The second is that the layout of the cells around some common association area does mean that visibility and surveillance are more feasible.

The essentially triangular design of cells around an open space can be seen as the broadening out of the old galleried, typically radial design. From one position the entrance to all cells can be seen. The advantage of this is that staffing levels could be considerably reduced when compared with the designs of the 1960s. The United States proposals lead readily also to the provision of an officer's bubble within the open 'association' area. The United States practice of having officers in surveillance positions whilst others move amongst the prisoners grows out of a particular ethos that is not central to many British prisons. But, as already noted, once staff in most institutions (hospitals, schools or whatever) are given a location distinctively theirs (separate from their charges, but where they can see them without communicating with them), there is a strong likelihood that organisational processes will follow the design possibilities.

The focus on the pod-specific association area, onto which cells open, certainly allows for more control over these areas and for prisoners to develop a particular commitment to them. But, as has been noted earlier, this could all too readily become a very severe limitation in high-security regimes. The cell and association area could become the whole of the prison experience for inmates. If the cells became crowded above their design levels this could actually become a much greater problem than in an old radial design because of the greater limits on ready access to other parts of the prison.

There are really two interrelated questions here that the debate so far has not tackled directly. One is the best size for a 'pod', that is, the appropriate number of cells. The other is the most effective way of interconnecting the various separate podular wings and of managing those interconnections.

The number of cells in a unit will have management and staffing implications, but it will also determine the scale of resources available to the prisoners in that unit. It must not be forgotten that the essence of the argument in favour of 'new generation' designs as a third option is that they allow distinct, separate administrative entities with their own regimes. This means that it must be possible for these entities to be virtually self-contained. One could become over-crowded with Category C prisoners and another under-utilised with a Category A regime within it. But, as is clear from the research reviewed, the prisoner's experience will be a function of the regime and the various parts of the prison that the regime gives him access to. Can our architects design 'pods' that will function equally well under such different conditions? If not, then the flexibility urged as part of the overall philosophy will not be achievable. In the situation of such flexibility, how many people should be housed in each 'pod'?

The key to the possible uses of these units lies in the interconnections between them. The most elegant American solution to controlled yet flexible connection between separate sets of cells opening onto their own association areas is Oak Park Heights. By the use of two separate secure corridors around a large, almost circular track it is possible to have a design that achieves many possibilities in an elegant way. But it has two related disadvantages. One is that it uses the sort of very large greenfield site that is both rare in Britain and discouraged because it leads to such distance for visitors. The second is that the size and dispersion of buildings over the site can mean a considerable requirement for staffing to control movement around that site. As was noted with the evaluation of New York MCC in use, this type of administrative requirement can lead to the distant facilities simply not being made available. The use of secure internal, indoor corridors in prisons such as Featherstone was a deliberate attempt to give prisoners the possibility of access to many parts of the prison without the need for high staffing levels, much escorting and the unlocking and locking of many doors. It would seem worthwhile to consider more closely the value of such an approach to design — which in its own way was just as innovative as the podular approach — before dismissing it entirely.

The prisoner's control over access to parts of the prison other than his cell and immediate association area combines with the ready access that staff have to cells to create an atmosphere and facilities within which prison life will be tolerated by prisoners not constantly challenged.

The Platt Committee proposal of multi-purpose facilities and central dining raises the question of how prevailing tendencies for these to become 'designated' as under control of one or other part of the formal (or informal) organisation can be counterbalanced. Similarly once a house unit has been identified as having its own character (or characters) there will be great opposition to any attempts to change that. This could have advantages or not depending on how sensitive the administration was to these issues.

Beyond custody

As mentioned initially, the notion of a prison is a curious and intriguing one. It is difficult to identify any other physical or architectural solution that is seen as being, of itself, an answer to a social problem. Sending people 'to prison' is widely seen as the answer to crime. When sending children to school as the answer to ignorance or to hospital as an answer to illness, these buildings are seen as mere receptacles for education or for the provision of medical treatment. But what a prison provides is imprisonment. Indeed, with the acceptance that therapeutic objectives are no longer to be part even of the rhetoric of prison management, it is especially apparent now that absolutely central to the concept of a prison is the notion of secure, physical separation in time and space.

The problem is that this separation generates a range of other problems that are not part of the requirements of imprisonment. At last this appears to be a major issue to be faced in the design of the new generation of prisons. The way in which new designs, internally at least, try to counteract the concomitants of custody is laudable. The attempts to use as many symbols and images as can carry through the messages of these objectives, using bright colours, avoiding bars and so on are all an important step forward. The evidence is accumulating that they contribute directly to safer and less destructive environments, but a lot more needs to be known of what lies behind this surface.

Needs for the future

The major need, now, is for post-occupancy evaluation of existing, especially recently built establishments. It is indefensible that new public money is poured after old without a systematic, scientific evaluation of the successes and failures of previous designs, particularly given that the British taxpayer has already paid for the development of psychological evaluation procedures specifically for use in prisons. These procedures will help to make sure that the noble aspirations enshrined in the Platt Committee report can be effectively achieved.

The development of British and United States prisons has often been guided by noble aspirations but, as Robert Sommer (1976) argues, the objectives of incarceration and their associated designs have often been confused. In this regard the Quaker origins of the modern prison are worth recalling. As Sommer (1976, p. 4) puts it: 'The Quaker advocacy of imprisonment was motivated by moral outrage at the sight of public humiliations, whippings, and executions. The idea was that the inmate, confined in a solitary cell with only the Bible to keep him company, would have time to reflect on his misdeeds.' There has been progress in that it is no longer considered necessary for prisoners to be brought face to face daily with their misdeeds. It is to be hoped that in the future the same will not be said of those who design the prisons of today.

References

Canter, D. and Ambrose, I. (1980), 'Prison Design and Use Study: Final Report', Guildford: Department of Psychology, University of Surrey (mimeo).

Canter, D., Brown, J., Bycroft, P. and Richardson, H. (1975), 'The Psychology of House Buying: Final Report to the Leverhulme Trust Fund', Guildford: University of Surrey (mimeo).

Drinkwater, J. (1982), 'Violence in Psychiatric Hospital', in P. Feldman (ed.), *Developments in the Study of Criminal Behaviour: Volume 2, Violence*, Chichester: Wiley.

Farbstein, J. and Wener, R.E. (1982), 'Evaluation of Correctional Environments', *Environment and Behavior*, vol. 14, pp. 671–94.

Home Office (1984), *Managing the Long-Term Prison System: The Report of the Control Review Committee*, London: HMSO.

Home Office (1985), *New Directions in Prison Design: Report of a Home Office Working Party on American New Generation Prisons* (Platt Report), London: HMSO.

House of Commons Committee of Public Accounts (1986) *Twenty-fifth Report from the Committee of Public Accounts: Prison Building Programme: Home Office and Property Service Agency*, HC 248, London: HMSO.

McCain, G., Cox, V. C. and Paulus, P. B. (1980), 'The Effect of Prison Crowding on Inmate Behaviour', Arlington: Psychology Department, University of Texas (mimeo).

Sommer, R. (1976), *The End of Imprisonment*, New York: Oxford University Press.

Wener, R. and Olsen, R. (1980), 'Innovative Correctional Environments: a User Assessment,' *Environment and Behavior*, vol. 12, pp. 478–93.

11 The Scottish experience with small units
Andrew G. Coyle

The passing of the Act of Union of the parliaments of Scotland and England left Scotland with several of its national institutions intact. The most important of these were the legal system and judiciary, the church and the education system. The continued independence of these three fundamental elements of Scottish society has contributed in no small way to the maintenance of a Scottish national identity over the last 250 years. One feature of the development of the Scottish criminal justice process has been the close relationship which has been fostered and maintained between the court system and the prison system. In Scotland, a small country with a population of something in excess of 5 million, the tightly knit legal establishment, based in Edinburgh, has always exerted a strong influence on the country's affairs. The close link between the court and the prison, however, came about not by chance but because the prison was seen to be primarily the servant of the court with the prison system placed firmly within the wider criminal justice system.

The centralisation of administration of Scottish prisons, which began in 1835 and was completed in 1877, confirmed the close involvement of the Scottish legal establishment in the Scottish prison system. The Scottish Prison Commission, which held office between 1877 and 1929, had the Crown Agent, one of the senior government law officers, and the Sheriff Principal of Perthshire as influential and active members.

Scotland has a liberal penal tradition. It was not uncommon in the eighteenth and nineteenth centuries for several years to pass without an execution taking place. In 1826 the House of Commons Select Committee on Scottish Prisons was informed that 'the long periods of imprisonment that take place in England are unknown in Scotland, where the period very rarely exceeds a year' (House of Commons 1826, p. 46). Per head of population, the Scottish rate of transportation was one-quarter that of England.

The two distinctive features of the Scottish prison system have always been the separation of prisoners and the importance given to the role and influence of staff. With respect to the first of these features, I have described elsewhere (Coyle 1982) how the first government inspectors of prisons appointed in 1835 discovered that, although the development of the Separate System of imprisonment is credited to the Eastern Penitentiary of Philadelphia, it had in fact been in operation in Glasgow at least five years before the American prison was built. There were several distinctive features of the Scottish version of the Separate System, all of which were based on a desire to provide individual prisoners with opportunities to better themselves during the course of their sentence. In 1844, for example, the Scottish General Board of Directors had to reply to criticisms made to the Home Secretary by two visiting English convict prison commissioners, Crawford and Jebb, who were shocked to discover that prison employment had 'nothing which partakes of the character of hard labour'; that prisoners were allowed to retain a portion of their earnings, either for release or to be sent to relatives; that they were allowed to write to friends, to receive visits every three months and to receive letters 'at all times' (letter dated 19 September 1844 from Crawford and Jebb to the General Board of Directors of Prisons in Scotland, SRO, HH, 6/5). The response of the Directors was that the deprivation of liberty was in itself punishment enough.

As regards staff, the early reports of the General Board of Directors note that no matter what is done in planning a prison, in providing funds and in drawing up regulations the crucial factor is the appointment of suitable staff. The basic grade staff were required not merely to be a physical presence but to exert influence on their charges: 'In some prisons an unusual degree of good conduct is induced, and the number of punishments kept low, by the personal influence of the officers, and by their care in reasoning with prisoners before resorting to punishment' (Inspector of Prisons for Scotland 1844, p. iv).

These are the historical foundations on which the Scottish prison system has been built. Today it includes 20 establishments which held an average of approximately 5,300 inmates in 1985. Parliamentary responsibility for the Scottish prison system lies with the Secretary of State for Scotland. Administrative control is in the hands of the Prisons Group of the Scottish Home and Health Department, headed by the Director of the Scottish Prison Service. The Scottish prison system has its own Act of Parliament, Rules, administrative Standing Orders and Instructions.

This paper is concerned only with the management of convicted adult male prisoners, of whom there are some 3,000 in custody at any one time.[1] Of these, 1,350 are serving sentences of over 18 months and it is generally within this group that the prisoners who are most dangerous and difficult to control are to be found. Scotland adopted the recommendation on security categorisation of prisoners which the Mountbatten Report (Home Office 1966) made for England

and Wales. At the moment there are ten prisoners who have been classed as Category A. These are the most dangerous prisoners in terms of the threat which they present to society. They are not necessarily the most difficult prisoners to control. Some prisoners who fall into the latter category, while they present a major threat to the good order of prisons, do not present a maximum degree of threat to society. According to our present system of classification there are three main prisons for the detention of long-term adult male prisoners in closed conditions: they are Edinburgh, Perth and Peterhead. (Two more will open in the course of the next 18 months.) The majority of long-term prisoners in Edinburgh have first-offender status. That means that those of the most difficult and dangerous prisoners who are in the main stream are contained in only two establishments, the majority being in Peterhead which at present holds some 180 prisoners.

Let me finish setting the scene with a few general comments. The ultimate responsibility for prisons in Scotland, as for those in England and Wales, lies with the government of the United Kingdom. Within that context the Scottish system, retaining as it does close links with other parts of the Scottish criminal justice process, is autonomous and self-contained. It is subject to the judgments of domestic courts and takes account of decisions reached in English courts. It has an obligation to regard rulings made by the European Commission on Human Rights, to which its prisoners have access. The Scottish Prison Service is almost parochial in that many long-term and recidivist prisoners, particularly the ones with whom I am concerned in this paper, are known personally at least to senior members of staff such as governors. Many careers, for example, will run in parallel. Borstal assistant governors may well have graduated to being deputies in young offender institutions and subsequently governors of adult prisons at the same time as individual prisoners have graduated through the same steps on the 'client' side. There is little room for anonymity in the Scottish Prison Service.

The problem in context

On the other hand, a lot of people question the ethics of labelling a specified individual as dangerous in order to justify special measures of control. Their arguments vary. Some hold that labelling a man as dangerous can make him more so, even make a dangerous man out of a non-dangerous one. The way in which he is treated by police and prison staff can make him respond aggressively to any attempts to control him, or indeed other forms of frustration when he is at liberty again. This is not, however, an argument against labelling anyone as dangerous, but against careless labelling and certain techniques of inmate management (Walker 1980, p. 90).

Much of the discussion concerning offenders who can be described as dangerous or who exhibit that tendency to violence which Floud and Young (1981, p. 7) assert is 'almost universally regarded as the hall-mark of dangerousness' concentrates, understandably, on the danger to society at large and deals either with methods of assessment before sentence is passed or with the length of time for which the public should be protected from such dangerous prisoners. This development has led to what Bottoms (1977) has called the 'bifurcation' in penal policy, by which he means the tendency to separate the 'mad' and the 'bad', against whom serious action must be taken, from the run-of-the-mill prisoner, against whom a more lenient line can be taken.

The best Scottish example of this concern for public safety is to be found in the recommendation of the Scottish Council on Crime (SCC 1975) that a new court disposal entitled a public protection order should be introduced which would allow the detention for indeterminate periods of dangerous offenders. The Council defined the dangerousness of a convicted person as 'the probability that he will inflict serious and irremediable personal injury in the future' (SCC 1975, para. 122).

As far as the period of imprisonment is concerned, the literature on this subject concentrates on the degree of security under which this type of prisoner requires to be held. The provision of an adequate degree of security for all prisoners is the primary task of the prison service; the difference as regards the type of prisoner with which we are concerned here is one of degree. However, prison administrators are faced with another concern which is not explicitly addressed by other agencies. 'If custody is elevated to the first rank in the list of tasks to be accomplished by the prison, the objective of maintaining internal order is a close second' (Sykes 1958, p. 21). My concern in this paper is with this further task, which is the particular reponsibility of the prison system, that of control of the long-term prisoner who presents, in any of several ways which I shall shortly discuss, a threat to the smooth running of a prison. I should like to describe specifically the system of alternative regimes which has been developed in the Scottish prison service for dealing with particular groups of prisoners who present severe management problems.

In general terms the Scottish prison system has developed in parallel with the main stream of penal practices in the Western world. However, when necessary it has not been slow to develop its models based on particularly Scottish traditions. The method of handling difficult prisoners is one instance. We have, of course, taken account of developments in other systems and have paid particular attention to those which have taken place in Canada, the United States and England. Following the recommendation of a Study Group on Dissociation in 1975 the Correctional Service of Canada developed two units, known as Special Handling Units, to contain particularly dangerous prisoners. The methodology used was exhaustive. A clear definition of what management considered to be a 'particularly dangerous prisoner' was provided; the function of the Special Handling Units was stated as was the method of transfer into and out of the units as well as the regimes to be operated. Despite this a series of serious incidents occurred in one of the units during the 15 months from 1 January 1983. In Scotland we took note of the ten recommendations subsequently made in the Vantour Report (1984) on these events.

As regards the United States Federal Bureau of Prisons the two principal models are arguably at either end of the penological spectrum. The Control Unit at Marion Penitentiary in Illinois appears to the outside observer to have developed in a purely pragmatic manner without any firm theoretical base. It was set up as an ad hoc response to a pressing and very real problem. For a variety of reasons, not least the continuing violence of the prisoners located there, the unit has developed a regime which approximates to simple warehousing. This now presents the administration with the prospect that this regime of very tight containment is in danger of becoming self-perpetuating, a danger underlined in the consultants' report to the Committee on the Judiciary of the United States House of Representatives made in December 1984:

> One of the greatest challenges to penal policy makers is the need to control the most violent prisoners in the country while at the same time exercising creativity in trying to devise and then try, on an experimental basis, activities that will not contribute to further deterioration of these inmates — deterioration which can lead in turn to greater risks of serious injury to staff, other prisoners, and often to the community upon the inmate's eventual release (Ward and Breed 1985, p. 21).

An attempt to meet this challenge has been made at the Federal Correctional Institution in Butner, North Carolina, which has been described as 'the jewel in the Federal Prison system' (Smith 1984). The regime is modelled directly on that proposed by Morris (1974) which called for a humane, secure environment in which a prisoner, aware of a release date and a graduated release plan, could focus attention on acquiring self-knowledge and self-control. The institution is an expression of the positive elements of the justice model. The system does not appear to have more effect on future recidivism than any other; a feature which is consonant with the principles of the justice model. From a management point of view, it does have an effect on how individuals cope with their sentences and how willing they are to take part in programmes which are available. The institution began and continues as a form of applied research.

Morris contrasted his model with that of the small maximum-security prison for the most troublesome offenders, a 'maxi-maxi' institution, whose plan read 'like the design of the inner circles of hell'. The latter model, though surely not the plan, was that recommended by Lord Mountbatten in 1966 for our sister service in England and Wales (Home Office 1966). This model was not accepted by the Home Office which preferred that of dispersal proposed in the Radzinowicz Report (Advisory Council on the Penal System 1968). Since then the Home Office has experimented with a series of models designed to cope with the prisoner who presents severe management problems. The latest initiative springs from the excellent report submitted by the Control Review Committee (Home Office 1984). I should like to sound one warning note about the manner in which that report has been perceived by several sections of the press which have appeared to suggest that the main answer to this problem lies in a proper development of prison architecture as epitomised in the 'new generation' prisons in the United States. That, of course, was not what the Control Review Committee suggested. What it did observe was that this form of architecture permitted the development of what it considered to be the two central elements in the control of difficult long-term prisoners (Home Office 1984, paras. 16, 20):

> At the end of the day, nothing else we can say will be as important as the general proposition that relations between staff and prisoners are at the heart of the whole prison system and that control and security flow from getting that relationship right. Prisons cannot be run by coercion: they depend on staff having a firm, confident and humane approach that enables them to make close contact with inmates without abrasive confrontation . . .
>
> Prisons that are made up of self-contained units in the 'new generation' style obviously have an inbuilt capacity to separate groups of prisoners. They also offer great flexibility since the units need not all run in the same way and may be operated in as separate or concerted [a] manner as the operational situation requires.

These two elements are the bedrock on which the Scottish system of small units has developed over the last 20 years.

The Scottish experience
Because of the relatively small number of prisoners involved, and also because of the absence of the pressures which led to the setting

up of the Mountbatten Inquiry in England, the Scottish prison service has never had to choose between the two models of containment for prisoners who require to be held in conditions of maximum security, concentration and dispersal. We have continued as a general principle to locate these prisoners in our one maximum-security prison which is at Peterhead on the north-east coast of Scotland. This restriction of choice has obliged us to concentrate our attention on the two factors which are fundamental when it comes to managing the small number of prisoners in this group who are particularly difficult or violent. Given that we had no other prison to which they could be transferred, we appreciated at an early stage that the dual key to good management and proper control was the relationship between staff and prisoners and the separation of the prisoners concerned into small groups.

From the earliest days of the Scottish prison system there has been recognition of the pivotal role which is played by the prison officer in the management of all prisoners. Since the early 1960s the most frequent expression of this has been through some form of group officer system. This has normally involved one or two officers being given specific responsibility for a group of up to ten prisoners. The officers will often meet regularly with 'their prisoners' to discuss affairs within the establishment as well as other common matters of concern. Prisoners will use the nominated officer as their first avenue of approach when they have a particular difficulty or complaint (Coyle and Kelso 1981). There has been increasing appreciation that there are particular benefits to be obtained from developing this type of staff–prisoner relationship for prisoners who pose special problems. The Chiswick Report (1985) of the Review of Suicide Precautions at HM Detention Centre and HM Young Offenders' Institution Glenochil, for example, recommended that this system should be developed in both the Young Offenders' Institution and the Detention Centre. We shall see shortly that this feature underpins the Scottish experience with small units.

One consequence of a system which allows prisoners to congregate at work, at exercise and at recreation is that from time to time there will be a small number of prisoners who will seriously disrupt the smooth running of establishments and who will require to be segregated. In the majority of cases it is possible to segregate prisoners within the parent establishment. This is normally done under the terms of Prison (Scotland) Rule 36, which states:

> If at any time it appears to the Visiting Committee or the Secretary of State that it is desirable for the maintenance of good order or discipline, or in the interests of a prisoner, that he should not be employed in association with others, the Visiting Committee or the Secretary of State

may authorise the Governor to arrange for him to work in a cell, and not in association for a period not exceeding one month from the date of each authorisation.

Such segregation is not imposed as a punishment, although it normally involves deprivation of some privileges and may well be regarded by the prisoner concerned as a punishment. It is a measure of management aimed essentially at the isolation of the prisoner at the centre of subversive or disruptive activity and providing a 'cooling off' period to allow prisoners to settle down.

Experience suggested that occasionally segregation in the facilities available in the prison of allocation or simple transfer to another prison were not adequate solutions to the problem created by some prisoners. In the 1950s special segregation facilities were established at Peterhead but these did not prove entirely satisfactory. The influence of some prisoners in their prison of allocation continues to be exerted even from segregation, particularly since local segregation leaves the clear expectation of return to circulation in the main prison in due course. Simple removal to another prison, whether or not to initial segregation there, is sometimes practicable and effective, but the circumstances calling for a prisoner's removal may affect more than one establishment and in the mid-1960s it was decided that there was a need for segregation facilities away from the main potential centres of prison trouble as a means of coping with the increasing incidence of violent assaults committed against both staff and prisoners. Staff were particularly concerned at this trend with the prospect of the impending abolition of the death penalty.

The Inverness Unit

Coincidentally with the introduction of the Murder (Abolition of the Death Penalty) Act 1965 a departmental working party on inmate classification recommended that a unit be set up at Inverness Prison to which particularly difficult prisoners could be sent. It was suggested that the proposed unit might serve to reduce the likelihood of assaults on prison officers. The report recommended that the type of prisoner who required to be segregated in the unit would be one with a record of serious, subversive behaviour, usually accompanied by violence against other prisoners and/or staff. Not uncommonly he would have been involved in factional feuds among prisoners in his prison of allocation, where he would probably have spent a number of periods in segregation.

Inverness is a small local prison serving courts in the north of Scotland. In October 1966 the main hall of the prison was opened as a segregation unit and seven prisoners from other establishments were admitted.

The basic principle underlying the unit was that any prisoner who was deemed to be violent, subversive or recalcitrant could be held there until such time as he was considered to have demonstrated fitness to return to his prison of classification. Governors could recommend prisoners for transfer to the unit although these had to be approved by headquarters. Subsequent response was reviewed by an internal board. The unit was regarded as a resource for the whole service although in practice the majority of prisoners who were sent there had previously been in Peterhead Prison. The regime within the unit was deliberately spartan. Prisoners worked in association but recreation and other privileges were severely curtailed.

In the course of 1969 several incidents took place in the unit. At the annual conference of the Scottish Prison Officers' Association that year, complaints were voiced at the privileges which were being granted to the prisoners in the unit. The staff at Inverness informed the Inspector of Prisons, who carried out an internal investigation into the incidents, that they strongly resented the fact that, in their estimation, prisoners were detained in the unit beyond the point at which, according to their behaviour and conduct, they could have been returned to their prison of classification.

Following the subsequent report by the Inspector, work was put in hand to improve the security of what had been previously the punishment block for the prison and of adjacent ancillary accommodation. The alterations provided a larger cell area together with improved heating and lighting. The Inspector's recommendation that the door in the main corridor should lead to a grilled corridor within the cell area which would serve to separate staff from the area occupied by the prisoners was incorporated in the alterations. The upgraded unit contained places for five prisoners and was first occupied in April 1971.

On 28 December 1972 there was a serious incident of violence in the unit when four prisoners, all of whom were regarded as very dangerous, launched an organised attack on staff during an evening period of recreation in association. A fifth prisoner was indisposed and in his cell at the time. They were subdued only after a battle in which one officer lost an eye, others sustained stab wounds and two of the prisoners were injured. The four prisoners were later convicted of assault to severe injury and attempting to escape and each was sentenced to six years' imprisonment. A decision to set up the Special Unit at Barlinnie Prison had already been taken and, when it opened early in 1973, three of the prisoners from Inverness were transferred to it. The two others were returned to their prison of classification. Between February and June 1973 ten out of 43 staff in post at Inverness Prison at the time of the incident left the Service.

Although no prisoners were sent to the unit after the incident of December 1972, the official view was that the unit had never closed and was available for use. This position was confirmed by the Under-Secretary of State for Scotland in October 1973. In June of that year representatives of the Scottish Prison Officers' Association (SPOA) had met the Minister and asked among other things that in future all inmates held in the unit should be under Rule 36 conditions. A review of staffing and procedures in the unit began in consultation with the SPOA. Although the unit was technically available for use governors were aware that this review was taking place and felt discouraged from identifying and putting forward prisoners for transfer.

In 1976 the review was completed and amended regulations for the unit were drawn up. The purpose of the unit was defined as follows:

> The Unit will be used for the secure custody, for a limited period, of prisoners who, despite repeated employment of appropriate correctional methods within their establishment of classification, continue to exert by their behaviour and attitude a marked subversive influence and flagrant refusal to co-operate in the course of the normal daily routine in the work of the establishment.
>
> Save in exceptional circumstances the maximum period will not exceed three months. (Scottish Home and Health Department, internal memorandum.)

There was to be no association at work, recreation or exercise.

Throughout the 1970s a public campaign was mounted, largely supported by the press, in opposition to any further use of the unit. This campaign was energetically countered by the SPOA. The Secretary of State for Scotland announced that no prisoner would be transferred to the unit without his personal authority and that 'this will only be given if and when I consider that it is necessary'.[2] The Secretary of State first gave that authority in December 1978 and since that date the unit has been used on a regular although not continuous basis. The response of prisoners in the unit is overseen by the Standing Committee on Difficult Prisoners, to which I shall refer later.

The Inverness Unit remains in 1986 an integral part of the Scottish prison system. It is at one end of the spectrum of available facilities but it provides a necessary alternative. Its existence is required for those prisoners who have to be taken from the main prison, which is normally Peterhead, to allow a breathing space for themselves, for the staff and for the other inmates at Peterhead.

In July 1984 the European Commission on Human Rights rejected a complaint by a prisoner that his period of detention in the Inverness Unit constituted a breach of Article 3 of the European Convention on Human Rights which states that 'No one shall be subjected to torture or to inhuman or degrading treatment or punishment'.

In the course of the last ten years we have learned several lessons from our experience with the Inverness Unit. As far as the staff are concerned, we were wrong to assume initially that the existing staff at Inverness Prison, a small establishment which normally holds short-term local inmates, could operate the unit without special training. Before the unit admitted its first prisoner after a break of some years in 1978 all staff at Inverness Prison were given training in what to expect and how to respond. All staff at Inverness are expected to work in rotation in the unit. This arrangement is in preference to having specially selected unit staff. As far as prisoners are concerned, we have learned that the unit is not suitable for all 'violent, subversive and recalcitrant prisoners'. Some prisoners do not respond to the spartan conditions in the unit and in the early days this resulted in some being held there for periods considerably in excess of the originally estimated length of four months. As regards the regime of the unit, we established the need for a clearly defined frame of reference which was understood by all those involved in the unit. The smooth operation of the unit since 1978 has also been considerably assisted by the existence of a central monitoring body under an independent chairman. That is not to say that the detailed running of the unit is under total central control. This would be neither practicable nor desirable. What has happened is that an informal and unwritten contract exists between staff and prisoners. Those of the latter who prefer to be left severely alone have their wish granted, receiving only the necessary supervision and physical care from staff. Other prisoners, however, sometimes over the course of several periods in the unit, have built up what almost amounts to a rapport with the staff which allows them to discuss the difficulties which they have in coping with their sentences. While some prisoners continue to present management problems in the unit, the majority would appear to regard their stay there as an opportunity for 'time out' from the pressure of normal prison life.

The Barlinnie Special Unit

In May 1970 representatives of the SPOA met with the Parliamentary Under-Secretary of State for Scotland to discuss the safety of prison staff. At this meeting the Minister agreed to set up a working party 'to consider what arrangements should be made for the treatment of certain inmates likely to be detained in custody for very long periods or with propensities to violence towards staff'. The working party, consisting of prison administrators, governors, officers and a psychiatrist, was duly constituted and required to report on the treatment of certain male long-term prisoners and potentially violent prisoners. In February 1971 the working party submitted its report, which contained 16 recommendations (Scottish Home and Health Department 1971). The first of these was that 'A special unit should be provided within the Scottish Penal System for the treatment of known violent inmates, those considered potentially violent and selected long-term inmates' (SHHD 1971, para. 59). It was recommended that the unit should be purpose-built, should have accommodation for 20 prisoners, should include adequate working and recreational facilities and 'must not be made so attractive as to encourage inmates to misbehave in order to be transferred there'. The staff, who were to be volunteers, were to be a mixture of discipline and nursing officers and, it was recommended, would require special training. The unit was to have its own governor, who was to be closely supported by a psychiatrist. Finally, 'the traditional officer/inmate relationship should be modified to approximate more closely to a therapist/patient basis while retaining a firm but fair discipline system' (SHHD 1971, para. 65). Subsequent investigation showed that it was not structurally possible to build a new unit within the grounds of Perth Prison as the working party had recommended. The former female block at Barlinnie Prison in Glasgow was vacant at that time and it was decided that the new Special Unit should be located there. In November 1972 the initial staff volunteers and the appointed governor began an 11-week training course consisting of five weeks at Polmont Officers' Training School and six weeks at Grendon Underwood, Broadmoor and Carstairs. On 5 February 1973 the unit opened and within a short period five prisoners had been admitted, including three transferred from the Inverness Unit in the aftermath of the riot.

Following the Scottish tradition of pragmatic regime development the unit was largely allowed to develop it own ethos. What evolved, particularly in the early years, was a strong sense of community which encompassed both staff and prisoners. The unit quickly attracted considerable external attention. One Sunday newspaper complained of the 'expensive kid glove treatment' being accorded to prisoners in the unit, a charge which was rebutted by the General Secretary of the SPOA. The virtual absence of restriction on visits led to a steady stream of interested individuals to the unit, several of whom attended on a regular basis. Within the secure perimeter, prisoners had relative freedom of movement for most of the day. In the absence of organised work some of them took to painting, sculpting and writing which in turn generated further outside interest in the unit.

The unit as presently operated holds a maximum of eight prisoners. All are serving long sentences and are typically potentially violent, volatile and intelligent. Prisoners with serious psychiatric problems or drug dependency are not admitted. Potential candidates are initially recommended by the governor of the prison of classification. The assessment of suitability is carried out by a group of staff from the unit and the implications of transfer are discussed with the prisoner. If the latter is assessed as being suitable for transfer the case is referred to the Scottish Home and Health Department for final approval. One of the early difficulties was that some prisoners elsewhere in the system regarded the unit as a soft option and took the view that if they created maximum unrest, often by assaulting staff, they were more likely to be transferred to the unit. The method of assessment and selection has attempted to exclude such motives for transfer and has been generally successful in doing so. With the exception of the Governor, all staff in the unit are volunteers. They go through an assessment period and a screening process before being recommended for work in the unit.

The main community activities centre on a series of regular meetings. The most important of these is the formal weekly community meeting. Those present elect a chairman and a record is kept of the discussion. Security and staffing issues cannot be raised but other matters are open to full debate. Domestic matters are decided at the meeting. Other issues are referred to the Governor or to headquarters as necessary. There is no formalised system of punishment within the unit. A serious breach of rules may result in a prisoner being transferred from the unit. When internally agreed procedures are broken the prisoner concerned has to explain his actions to other members of the community. There is no structured programme of work. Prisoners are encouraged to develop individual interests in art, sculpting, education, woodwork, physical training or hobbies. The standard rate of earnings is paid. Correspondence is censored only during an early supervised period. There is no restriction on the number of visits. Visitors must be approved by the community. After the initial supervised periods visits may be taken in cells. Visitors are permitted to bring in small amounts of food, tobacco and money.

Not surprisingly for a unit of this nature there have been difficult periods. In the mid-1970s some individuals, in their enthusiasm for the unit, appeared to lose sight of the reason for its existence and of the part which it had to play within the prison service. At the beginning of 1976 new guidelines were drawn up which underlined the fact that the Governor was expected to govern, that departmental representatives would not automatically attend community meetings and that independent meetings of staff would be held as necessary. In March 1976 a serious incident occurred when one prisoner stabbed another 13 times. The assailant was subsequently sentenced to a further six years' imprisonment. In September 1977 a prisoner was found dead in the unit after having consumed a quantity of drugs which had been brought into the unit surreptitiously. The Secretary of State set up an internal review into the procedures operating at the unit. This was completed in December 1977 and certain changes of procedure were subsequently introduced.

Over the years a series of unwritten and formally unapproved norms have evolved which affect the operation of the unit The precise content of these norms is open to debate but arguably the main ones are:

(i) The unit selects its own prisoners.

(ii) All staff are volunteers with the exception of the Governor who is appointed since he is the only member of staff who is externally accountable for the unit.

(iii) 'Once out, never back'.

(iv) No violence, drug abuse or gross offence against discipline.

(v) Prisoners must be able to submit disputes and disagreements to argument within the community and to accept community decisions.

(vi) The open visit principle applies not only to a prisoner's personal visitors but also to official and semi-official individuals and groups.

(vii) The price which the system demands is that prisoners must come to terms with the fact of being in custody.

Any attempt to establish a self-governing regime within a prison system creates its own pressure. There is continuing tension between attempts at self-government and the necessary limitations which exist because of the high degree of perimeter security. In the early years errors of judgment were arguably made in the operational development of the unit, not least by allowing external interests, including the media, to turn too fierce a spotlight on it during its formative period. A formal assessment and continuing evaluation of the achievements of the unit would have been of considerable assistance to the rest of the prison service. Steps are now being taken to set this in motion. At the same time, it is hard to deny the relative success of the unit. Successive governments have confirmed their view that the unit forms an integral part of the Scottish prison system. It has the whole-hearted support of the SPOA. It has arguably contributed to a reduction of tension in other prisons by isolating some of the system's worst troublemakers; it has allowed many of these difficult prisoners to cope with their long sentences in a positive manner and in several instances has facilitated an earlier return to the outside community than otherwise might have been expected. In a word, it has provided an alternative means of managing difficult prisoners.

Additional small units in Peterhead Prison

One might describe the Barlinnie Special Unit and Inverness Unit as being at the extreme ends of a spectrum of small units. All prisoners held in such units in Scotland require to be kept in conditions of maximum security. Both units, therefore, have a high level of perimeter security, much of it provided by the fact that the units are located within a larger prison. They also have high staffing ratios. Within these contexts, however, different regimes have been developed. The internal operation of the Barlinnie Special Unit is unstructured and relatively unsupervised while that of the Inverness Unit is tightly controlled and supervised. Not all prisoners who present severe management problems are suitable for location in one of these two units. Most prisoners in this category are initially classified for or subsequently are transferred to Peterhead Prison. The latter prison has a punishment unit with 16 places where prisoners who have been found guilty of breaches of prison discipline can be held. In addition we have developed several small alternative units in this prison.

Protection Unit

All prisoners who need to be kept out of normal circulation for any length of time for their own safety are held in Peterhead Prison. The policy of the Scottish Home and Health Department is to try to keep to a minimum the number of prisoners held out of general association and it believes that the location of this unit at Peterhead Prison discourages trivial and unjustified requests for long-term protection. These prisoners are located in a separate section of the prison containing some 20 cells and a small workshed area. Within the unit prisoners lead a life not dissimilar to that of the general population in Peterhead.

Individual Unit

In 1976 two patients who were detained in the State Hospital,

Carstairs, carried out an escape from the hospital in the course of which they committed three murders. At their subsequent trial they were found to be sane and were both sentenced to life imprisonment. It was decided that one of them, although requiring conditions of stringent supervision, could be located in one of the halls in Perth Prison. The second one, however, was considered to be so dangerous that he needed to be located in a specially converted unit in Peterhead Prison. The unit, which has housed this prisoner since that time, includes a cell, work room and ablutions. The prisoner is allowed to circulate within this area during the day. Throughout that period he is supervised by three members of staff.

Ten-Cell unit

In 1982 the Secretary of State for Scotland agreed that there was a need for a purpose-built 'Rule 36' unit in Peterhead Prison and building work commenced to provide a unit with ten places. There was to be no communal activity or significant communal facility. By the time the building had been completed it was decided that the use of the unit should not be restricted to those prisoners held under 'Rule 36' conditions and that, while the unit would be available only for Peterhead prisoners and only the Governor of Peterhead could recommend prisoners for transfer to it, for a trial period of 12 months from the date of entry of the first prisoner the procedures for transfer to the unit would be the same as for transfer to the Inverness Unit; that is, the unit would be brought within the terms of reference of the Standing Committee on Difficult Prisoners.

On 1 November 1984 the Secretary of State announced the conditions under which prisoners would be held in the unit:

> In general candidates for the Unit will be those who ... indulge in subversive activities but who do not usually act violently themselves.
>
> Inmates housed in the Unit will not initially enjoy the privileges of normal association with other prisoners. The hope is, however, that away from the main prison and its influences, and their ability to influence it, prisoners in the Unit will respond in a more positive way to the staff who will make special efforts to find out — and will be better able to do so in the 10 cell unit conditions — why the inmates behave as they do and to counsel them appropriately. Where a measure of what is positive response is forthcoming the aim will be to allow a measure of association within the Unit; the primary objective being to get inmates back into normal circulation in the main prison at the earliest date.
>
> Prisoners held in the unit will not, as has been made clear on a number of occasions, be there as a punishment.[3]

The first prisoner was transferred to the unit in December 1984 and it has been in regular use since that date. The regime of the unit was due up for review in December 1985. That review has not been completed at the time of writing.

B Hall unit

Following a serious riot in Peterhead in January 1984, the Governor presented a case to the Scottish Home and Health Department arguing the need for a further unit and regime which would provide him with another option in the management of prisoners regularly given to offering violence to staff or to damaging the fabric of the prison. After discussion and investigation it was decided that such a unit should be located within B Hall, the smallest of the four main accommodation blocks in the prison. The alterations which were subsequently carried out involved blocking off all but the ground floor of the hall, strengthening the security within each cell and providing an exercise yard.

On 1 November 1984 the Secretary of State wrote to advise the local Member of Parliament that the new unit was ready for use by:

> prisoners who are ready to use violence against staff or property.
>
> The regime will, of necessity, be strict. It will not, however, be punitive. The main feature will be that at no time will the number of prisoners in association be allowed to exceed the number of staff in attendance. Work (where it can be found), exercise and recreation will normally be in association but will be in groups of no more than three prisoners. It is recognised, however that for some prisoners full association will not always be appropriate, in which case permission will be sought in the normal way, in terms of Rule 36 of the Prison (Scotland) Rules to restrict association.[3]

The unit has been used intermittently since the end of 1984.

Standing Committee on Difficult Prisoners

On 28 March 1979 the Secretary of State announced the establishment of a Standing Committee to consider the allocation and treatment of unruly, violent and/or subversive prisoners. The functions of this Committee were to be:

> (i) to advise the Department on the allocation and management of prisoners referred to it by the Department because of difficulties created by their unruly, violent and/or subversive behaviour;
>
> (ii) in the case of prisoners detained in the Inverness Unit, to advise on the basis of periodic reports from the Inverness Prison Assessment Team on the management and, in particular, their transfer from the Unit in accordance with the Rules governing the Unit.
>
> The Committee may, if their experience suggests that alternative regimes or units are desirable for the management of violent, unruly and subversive prisoners, make recommendations on the subject to the

Department. (Scottish Home and Health Department, internal memorandum).

The seven members of the new committee were to be two representatives of the governors, two representatives of the SPOA, a departmental representative, a psychiatrist and a lay member. At the first meeting of the committee, held in June 1979, the lay member was elected chairman. The committee presents annual reports. In 1984 it expressed the view 'that what is required is a Unit which would be able to deal with inmates who exhibited irresponsible aggressive psychopathic behaviour who are not considered suitable for a transfer to the State Hospital' (Scottish Home and Health Department, internal memorandum).

Conclusion

> Nor did we examine the many practical penological problems raised by the detention of dangerous offenders: to decide the requirements of a regime of such offenders that would be humane and constructive as well as secure is an urgent and important task, but one for another working party of different composition and character (Floud and Young 1981, p. x).

In 1983 the Scottish Prison Service Management Group established a working party to consider and make recommendations on: the need for specific forms of regimes for particular groups of inmates who present severe management problems; the conditions and circumstances in which regimes, if needed, might be provided; the form that any special units that might be needed should take, and their location; the type of building, the staffing and the staff training that would be required for any such purposes; and the estimated cost of any recommendations that might be made. The working party has not yet reported but there have been some indications as to how its thinking has been developing. It has examined elements of the existing penal system which might contribute to the behaviour of such inmates and it has apparently identified the need for proper classification, continuing assessment and a coherent system of privileges which would encourage responsive behaviour. It remains to be seen what the group will recommend with regard to the existing units which I have described, or whether there is any need for additional alternative units.

In considering how the system of managing long-term prisoners within the Scottish prison system has developed we now appreciate that in some cases it would have been helpful to have had a more precise statement of objectives before units were set up, together with a system of evaluation and assessment of whether they were achieving the purpose for which they had been set up or indeed whether that purpose had altered in any way. In the case of the Inverness Unit it does appear that the statement of objectives and system of assessment of prisoners involved which were developed in the late 1970s have been successful. Indications now are that the unit is achieving more than the objectives require of it, particularly in terms of staff–prisoner relationships. One might well argue that the ethos of the Barlinnie Special Unit prohibited any prior definition of objective or regime. In the absence of a proper evaluation of the unit it is difficult to conclude whether that is an a posteriori judgment. The Prisons Group in the Scottish Home and Health Department is now considering proposals for continuous monitoring and evaluation of the objectives and regimes both of these two units and of the ones recently established in Peterhead. One option for achieving this might be through a re-definition of the role of the Standing Committee on Difficult Prisoners.

Such a definition of objective and of ongoing evaluation will be of considerable assistance to the staff who are asked to run these units. It will also be a useful means of measuring the success of what we regard as the two essential components in the management of difficult inmates. The first is that they should be identified and separated into small groups apart from the main body of prisoners. It appears that we are achieving success with regard to this element of management. This system ensures that, while necessary relief is provided to the mainstream system, the prisoners concerned are not placed in total isolation and do have the opportunity to continue and to develop a relationship both with a small group of other prisoners and also with staff. This latter feature is the second essential component in the Scottish style of management of these prisoners: intensive staff involvement. 'Intensive' is not at all the same as 'saturation'; the former refers to the quality of staff involvement, the latter to the quantity. The Platt Report (Home Office 1985) noted a tendency, in American new generation prisons, to relatively low levels of staffing with a view to ensuring that staff spent as much time as possible with prisoners. In most of our units we have a high staff–prisoner ratio. If this presence is to be translated into involvement a great deal of effort is required of staff. Many prisoners are unlikely to welcome initially any attempt by staff to work with them. Management expects a great deal of the staff who are required to work in such units; the latter in turn are entitled to expect clear leadership and support from the former.

The management of difficult long-term prisoners continues to be one of the major problems facing the Scottish prison system, and one which is likely to consume a great deal of time, effort and resource for some considerable time to come. We are aware that, even allowing for our relatively successful experience with small units, we are still left with the problem of subsequently managing in the mainstream prisoners who have been through the experience of one or more units; and also of managing prisoners who cannot cope with life in any of the units that we have so far developed. Without being at all complacent we are convinced, both from our own experience and from the conclusions which others are now reaching, that in pursuing a double objective of separation into small groups and fostering intensive staff involvement with these prisoners we are pursuing a policy which will prove both efficient and effective.[4]

Notes

1 The Scottish female prisoner population consists of some 170 inmates who are held in Cornton Vale Institution near Stirling. This institution is also managed on a system of small units. This style of prisoner management is worthy of further discussion in a more general context than the specific one being addressed in this paper (cf. Carlen 1983).

2 Press statement issued by the Secretary of State for Scotland on 2 February 1978.

3 Public letter dated 1 November 1984 from the Secretary of State for Scotland to Albert McQuarrie, MP in a press release.

4 I should like to thank Tom Kelly, Deputy Director (Administration) of the Scottish Prison Service for his helpful observations on the first draft of this paper.

References

Advisory Council on the Penal System (1968), *The Regime for Long-Term Prisoners in Conditions of Maximum Security* (Radzinowicz Report), London: HMSO.

Bottoms, A.E. (1977), 'Reflections on the Renaissance of Dangerousness,' *Howard Journal*, vol. 16, pp. 70–96.

Carlen, P. (1983), *Women's Imprisonment*, London: Routledge and Kegan Paul.

Chiswick Report (1985), *Report of the Review of Suicide Precautions at HM Detention Centre and HM Young Offenders' Institution, Glenochil*, Edinburgh: HMSO.

Coyle, A.G. (1982), 'The Founding Father of the Scottish Prison Service', *Journal of the Association of Scottish Prison Governors*, vol. 1, pp. 7–14.

Coyle, A.G. and Kelso, B.C.F. (1981), 'The Truncated Monster', *Prison Service Journal*, no. 41, pp. 13–24.

Floud, J. and Young, W. (1981), *Dangerousness and Criminal Justice*, London: Heinemann.

Home Office (1966), *Report of the Inquiry into Prison Escapes and Security* (Mountbatten Report), Cmnd. 3175, London: HMSO.

Home Office (1984), *Managing the Long-Term Prison System: The Report of the Control Review Committee*, London: HMSO.

Home Office (1985), *New Directions in Prison Design: Report of a Home Office Working Party on American New Generation Prisons* (Platt Report), London: HMSO.

House of Commons (1826), *House of Commons Select Committee on Scottish Prisons: Report*, London: HMSO.

Inspector of Prisons for Scotland (1844), *Annual Report*, London: HMSO.

Morris, N. (1974), *The Future of Imprisonment*, Chicago: University of Chicago Press.

Scottish Council on Crime (1975), *Crime and the Prevention of Crime*, Edinburgh: HMSO.

Scottish Home and Health Department (1971), *Report of a Departmental Working Party on the Treatment of Certain Male Long-Term Prisoners and Potentially Violent Prisoners*, Edinburgh: SHHD.

Smith, R (1984), *Prison Health Care*, London: British Medical Association.

Sykes, G.M. (1958), *The Society of Captives*, Princeton, NJ: Princeton University Press.

Vantour Report (1984), *Report of the Study Group on Murders and Assaults in the Ontario Region*, Ottawa: Correctional Service of Canada.

Walker, N. (1980), *Punishment, Danger and Stigma*, Oxford: Basil Blackwell.

Ward, D.A. and Breed, A.F. (1985), *The United States Penitentiary, Marion, Illinois: Consultants' Report Submitted to Committee on the Judiciary, U.S. House of Representatives* (ser. no. 21), Washington, D.C: US Government Printing Office.

12 Barlinnie Special Unit: an insider's view
Peter B. Whatmore

In 1970, the Scottish Prison Officers' Association (SPOA) expressed concern about the vulnerability of its members, particularly in relation to prisoners serving life sentences. In that year capital punishment for murder was finally abolished, after a five-year experimental period. During the three years 1968–70, there were 14 attacks on prison officers involving a weapon or sharp instrument. Over the same period, 34 prisoners were assaulted by fellow prisoners and 16 of these involved a weapon or sharp instrument. However, when viewed in the context of the increasing size of the prison population during the previous 20 years and the increase in crimes of violence in the community, the degree of violence in Scottish prisons is relatively small.

Violence in prisons is a complex affair, but amongst some of the factors involved are:

(i) Frustration at the beginning of a long sentence. The violence involved is usually of a minor nature and settles down within a year or so.

(ii) The personality-disordered prisoner who does not come within the terms of the Mental Health (Scotland) Act 1984.

(iii) The well-known violent criminal who, when admitted to prison, will feel pressure from the jail culture to demonstrate his leadership by violence, sometimes against other prisoners but particularly against staff. These jail-culture pressures will reinforce his need to demonstrate his leadership by repeated violence. Such a personality will attract staff surveillance, and he may feel victimised.

The well-known sanctions against acts of violence within the prison are loss of remission, forfeiture of privileges and deprivation of association. In the majority of cases, these conventional methods, which may include a change of prison, are adequate to deal with the situation.

However, with the abolition of capital punishment, there was clearly going to be an increasing number of people sentenced to indeterminate periods of detention, perhaps in excess of 15–20 years. It was in this setting that a Working Party was set up within the Scottish Home and Health Department in 1970 to consider the treatment of certain male long-term and potentially violent prisoners. It consisted of senior prison governors, representatives from the SPOA, departmental representation and a consultant psychiatrist.

The Working Party visited a number of prisons including Parkhurst and Grendon Underwood. They also visited Broadmoor and the State Hospital, Carstairs, and studied the practice in other countries, particularly Denmark where capital punishment had been obsolete for many years.

The purpose of visiting Special Hospitals was that they represented maximum-security institutions containing people who were considered dangerous because of mental disorder. A large proportion of these disturbed patients were on restriction orders of unlimited time and their management, if they were violent to nursing staff, had to be contained within the Special Hospitals without the intervention of the courts. In addition, for historical reasons, the Special Hospital nursing staff were members of the SPOA.

In February 1971, the Working Party (Scottish Home and Health Department 1971) made a large number of recommendations amongst which were:

(i) A Special Unit be provided within the Scottish prison system for the treatment of known violent inmates, those considered potentially violent, and selected long-term prisoners.

(ii) The original recommendation was that an independent unit with its own governor be set up, providing accommodation for 20 places. Unfortunately, for various economic and administrative reasons, the eventual unit had to be placed in an adapted but segregated part of Barlinnie Prison, Glasgow, with accommodation for ten places only.

(iii) The staff were to be selected from volunteers and were to be a mixture of discipline and nursing officers whose duties, apart from purely nursing, were interchangeable. There would never be less than four officers on duty at any time.

(iv) The traditional officer–inmate relationship would be modified to resemble a therapist–patient basis. The governor and staff were to be supported by a psychiatrist.

In November 1972 the selected volunteer staff and appointed governor started an 11-week training course. This consisted of a basic introductory course, followed by a six-week period of being resident for two weeks in each of Grendon Underwood, Broadmoor

Hospital and the State Hospital. The object of these institutional visits was to allow staff to work on-site with staff in Special Hospitals and Grendon Prison. They were able to observe and take part in patient/inmate management as a member of a team. They were given a variety of written tasks to perform so that they would be encouraged to examine in depth their experiences. Finally, they returned to the Polmont Officers' Training School for debriefing on their experiences, and were set the task of producing a practical regime for the proposed Unit. This early training exercise of the selected volunteers, and their active participation in developing the proposed regime are essential factors in the successful early development of the Unit.

The basic concept of the Unit was to develop a social community and involve the prisoner in his own management as well as that of his fellows. Members of the community, both staff and prisoners, were encouraged to develop a sense of responsibility towards decision-making in the community and to be answerable to a weekly community meeting. This involved a radical change in the basic attitude of prison officers and prisoners towards each other. It required a breakdown of the usual prison culture pressures and the staff–prisoner barrier. A key element in achieving this change of attitude between staff and prisoners was to be the weekly community meeting in which all Unit members participated. The object of this meeting was to allow free interchange of ideas, information, fears and complaints. It was also a decision-making body for the *internal* management of the Unit. Security and staff issues were specifically excluded.

Before the Unit was opened, a week was considered too long a period for problems to ferment, so as a defusing mechanism the rule was made that anyone in the community could call an immediate meeting to discuss a potential or real crisis. In addition, it was evident that the staff would require a lot of mutual support and a weekly staff meeting was arranged.

The essence of the experiment was to find out if such radical changes in attitude and behaviour could be achieved within a secure perimeter.

On the basis of their own professional experiences and discussions, the staff concluded that the only way to overcome mutual distrust was for staff and inmates to try and work together for a common community purpose within a secure perimeter. This would involve both groups accepting responsibility for the daily maintenance of the Unit and working together for the future development of the community.

Initially, there was no way of being certain that the inmates were willing or able to take part in such a social experiment. The staff, who had formulated the idea, were willing to put this into operation, but the inmates' co-operation was required if the venture was to succeed. The ideas behind the Unit had to be explained to inmates so that after consideration they were in a position to 'give it a try'. Thus, the inmate had to be willing to be transferred to the Unit. Those who had got into serious difficulties due to violence and additional sentences might view the Unit as the only way out of their difficulties.

The Barlinnie Special Unit opened on 5 February 1973 and three inmates were admitted. Two had completed over nine years' and one four-and-a-half years' imprisonment.

The decisions that were taken by the community during the first year were the most crucial because they formed the basis of the future development of the Unit.

Initially, there was marked suspicion between both staff and inmates, some of whom had a history of repeated violence in prison, and all of them had experienced difficulty in accepting conventional prison routine. At the same time, most of the staff did not know the inmates personally and were having to work out their new prison officer role. Clearly, many factors were involved before one could say at the end of the first year that the Unit had progressed from a containment unit to a social community. A number of matters proved to be relevant. First, emphasis was placed on staff–inmate meetings and their importance to the smooth running of the Unit. Everyone was entitled to express his viewpoint, and although at the beginning opinions tended to be mainly critical and acted as a safety valve for frustration, as the months passed the meetings became more constructive and would deal in depth with a variety of problems. From the early days a chairman, who could be a member of staff or a prisoner, would be elected to run each meeting and minutes were kept of the discussions that took place and the democratically decided group decisions that were taken. At the following meetings, these minutes were carefully reviewed and have since provided a valuable social record of the Unit's development.

The usual difficulties inherent in any group involving staff and inmates were found in the community meeting. Initially, there was a clear 'them and us' barrier which inhibited free comment and tended to make both factions protective about their own groups and apprehensive about the reactions of others. Slowly the two groups began to work together towards mutually accepted goals, such as organising work facilities and dealing with outside criticism of the Unit. Under the stimulus of two or three active participants, the community's confidence grew in verbalising opinions and expressing disagreement. When staff and inmates could openly disagree with their colleagues and debate the various issues involved, it became evident that many of the old prison culture attitudes of how staff and inmates should respond to each other were being reappraised and reformed. This was made possible by the small size of the community, and the willingness of staff and inmates to develop a new form of relationship based upon mutual respect and tolerance.

In addition to the weekly community meetings, it was accepted that anyone, staff or inmate, could request a group meeting at any time to deal with what he considered was an issue that required to be dealt with at once. These emergency meetings have been used on many occasions, and in the opinion of staff and inmates, have been invaluable in coping with the many tense situations or misunderstandings that arose. It is to the credit of the community members that slowly and progressively they were able to verbalise their mutual suspicions and apprehension of each other, and by means of open discussions about the day-to-day management of the Special Unit, develop a sense of corporate identity and individual responsibility. These meetings were not intended to be psychotherapeutic, and psychological jargon has always been avoided.

As a form of social control, community meetings have a number of advantages. Antisocial behaviour can quickly be brought to the notice of the group, and the individual concerned called to account for his actions. During its development, the community response has evolved along the lines of establishing the facts and then deciding on what action to take. Adverse comment on unacceptable conduct tends to be forthright, but it is an encouraging aspect of the group's functioning that a sense of fairness has always been evident, and in the end a reasoned decision appears.

As the group members progressively learned the techniques of group involvement, so the barrier between staff and inmates became less evident. As those who have attended any of the group meetings will confirm, group interaction can be vigorous and opinions expressed in no uncertain terms. This has had great value in releasing verbally much of the aggression and frustration inherent in such a community. Sometimes staff members of the community and inmates experienced personal difficulty in coming to terms with group criticism or comments. As the community matured and became aware of its own destructive power against individuals, it was interesting to note how a more balanced and objective approach became evident when dealing with individual or community problems.

When the Unit opened, the staff considered that they should hold a weekly meeting from which inmates were excluded. The purpose of this meeting was to discuss matters considered exclusively relating to staff, including a review of inmates' progress. After several months, during discussion at the community meeting about the value of staff meetings, the view was expressed that any matters that caused staff concern would affect the inmates either directly or indirectly, and that inmates would usually be aware of the matter anyway. At the same time, it became accepted that inmates' progress could be discussed more effectively in a community meeting since in such a small group everyone's behaviour pattern was common knowledge. Antisocial behaviour or poor progress could be examined at community level and the person under discussion could defend himself or accept the criticism. The progressive development of confidence in the relationship between staff and inmates made it possible for most staff to feel able to criticise an inmate's behaviour or poor progress in front of other inmates without fear of reprisal, and for inmates to be critical of staff behaviour. As a result of these developments, it was decided to stop separate staff meetings with the exception of discussion about security matters. They remained in abeyance until 1975 when they were reintroduced to discuss items such as rosters and other staffing matters that were of no direct interest to inmates. From these meetings developed a regular weekly meeting with a visiting clinical psychologist to discuss current problems in the Unit. After a short time, it was decided to include inmates in these discussions for the same reasons as exclusive staff groups were phased out in the past.

From the beginning, inmates and staff participated in a variety of activities. During the first few months cleaning and decorating involved most of the personnel in the Unit. The value of staff participating in activities, rather than just adopting a supervisory role, allowed the staff to get to know the inmates on a more personal basis than would otherwise have been possible. During the first year people were encouraged to become involved in a programme of their own choice. The type of activities that developed were toy-making for a mental deficiency hospital, string craft, candle-making, chess modelling, making chessboards and sculpturing. In the education field, studies developed in psychology, sociology, arithmetic, German and guitar playing. At weekends, the inmates cooked their own meals from the raw materials provided from the parent prison kitchen. At a later date, they were all to do their own cooking. The Unit produced a magazine that ran for several editions and to which staff and inmates contributed.

Also, from the beginning, there has been a steady flow of visitors to the Unit. Their selection and regulation played an important part in maintaining contact with the outside world in such a Unit that tended to be inward-looking and to have a nucleus of inmates who would rarely go outside the perimeter wall.

To avoid the risk of visitors coming 'just to look', it has been the rule that the community are notified beforehand about a proposed visit and told the purpose of it and something about the visitors. The community then decides who shall come in and what number at any one time. In this way, the 'goldfish bowl' effect has been avoided and the Unit has been fortunate in attracting a wide range of visitors from the universities, the health service, politicians, trade unionists, sports figures and entertainers. Many of the visitors have returned and taken part in community debates upon their chosen field of interest or a general discussion on the Unit and what it was trying to do.

These debates have had considerable value — they made community members think about the Unit and what they were trying to do; they placed the community in a position of defending or criticising the concept of the Unit to people outside the penal system; and they helped to ensure that members of the public were informed of the management methods and behaviour of the community members. This reduced some of the rumours and innuendoes that frequently surround security units — though naturally quite a lot spread abroad.

During the first year, visitors had an interesting side effect on both staff and inmates. Both groups looked upon the visitors as an insurance policy against feared excesses by each other. This aspect was very important during the first year in helping both groups to develop an increasing degree of trust in each other. As many will know, it eventually led to the position when the press were allowed into the Unit — and television films made by *World in Action* and the BBC.

The question of women visitors had been discussed with staff before the Unit opened and, understandably, anxiety was expressed by some members of staff. However, it was thought that to avoid many of the problems inherent in a monastic security institution, female visitors should be allowed in. Initially, a female art therapist and occupational therapist began visiting the Unit on a regular basis and this has continued with various additions. Everyone concerned with the Unit has been appreciative of the success of this venture — the degree of responsibility shown by all concerned and the improvement in the general day-to-day atmosphere of the Unit.

Personal visitors are allowed to come in at times convenient to the daily running of the Unit. In the early days, visits were supervised, but progressively non-supervised visits were allowed. It has always been understood that any abuse of these visits would lead to an immediate investigation and probable curtailment. New inmates automatically have supervised visits and their mail is censored until it is considered by the community that abuse is unlikely to occur. The emphasis has always been on the individual taking personal responsibility for his own behaviour, but also a responsibility to the community for the conduct of others.

The value of personal visitors is difficult to evaluate in general terms. Staff have no doubt that frequent contact with specific personal visitors has had both a stabilising and maturing effect upon a number of inmates. The fact that concern about an inmate's behaviour or attitude might be discussed by staff with appropriate visitors has had the positive effect of bringing the incomer's personal influence to bear on specific personal problems. The freedom granted to regular visitors within the Unit allowed them to become aware of the institution's regime and avoid the many misconceptions that can develop about closed communities.

The problem of the maintenance of discipline, and its reinforcement by sanctions, alway arises in any institution. In a small community like the Special Unit, it has been found that confrontation in the community meeting with a request for an explanation of incidents of commission or omission has usually been all that is required. Group pressures, particularly from amongst one's peers in front of the community, appears to be the most effective way of maintaining the degree of order necessary for the smooth running of the Unit. On rare occasions the community has not been satisfied with the response obtained and has imposed some restrictions of privilege for a short period.

The question of the community's response to physical violence was clearly a crucial issue. To date there has been no incident of physical violence towards staff, and only one serious incident of violence by one inmate upon another.

It is tempting to suggest that the Unit should contain and deal with incidents of physical violence. Apart from wishing to deal with such problems internally, the community wanted to avoid the possible criticism that when difficulties arose the people concerned were transferred. However, after prolonged discussion within the Unit, it was decided that if anyone used extreme violence or continued to use physical violence as a means of influence, then he would be recommended for transfer. The reason for this decision was that if facilities were provided to deal with physically violent individuals — and it would be easy enough to provide them — the relaxed atmosphere of the Unit would be radically altered, and the type of community that appeared to be developing would not be possible. In this context, inmates were encouraged to develop both a community sense of responsibility, and to be aware that their own future progress was dependent upon the behaviour of other inmates in the Unit. The idea of being constructively involved in each other's behaviour progressively developed when it was realised that the whole community, or an individual's progress, can be adversely influenced by irresponsible conduct. The willingness of inmates to criticise one another's behaviour has fluctuated over the years. Some influencing factors appear to be close relationships before admission to the Unit; and the degree to which criticism was viewed as 'grassing'. Some inmates took a long time to cope with this problem. On occasions, some inmates would say they could not inform on colleagues, and this provided an opportunity to discuss the problem. At other times, people would prefer to pretend not to be aware of what was going on. Such group mechanisms would be discussed when undesirable behaviour was discovered.

The procedure for admission to the Unit has continued to be carefully controlled. The initiative is made by local prison governors who recommend various people for transfer to the Unit. Those recommended at the start of the Special Unit project were all interviewed by three members of staff. Recommendations of acceptance were discussed with the remainder of the staff before final acceptance. After a few months, it was decided to incorporate the inmates into the decision-making process for several very positive reasons. Although the staff had a wide personal knowledge of many of the inmates suggested for admission, it was clearly undesirable and dangerous to accept some, who for a variety of reasons, would not be acceptable to some of the resident inmates. Factors such as type of offence (that is, sex offences against children), and possible old gang or personal feuds immediately spring to mind. People who might be unable to benefit from the group approach — due to intellectual limitation — or who resented being transferred to the Unit, were other points to consider. In this way, the assessment team and the community were fully briefed as to the areas they should explore before going to see those recommended for admission.

During recent years, the procedure before admission to the Unit has developed in the following way. First, a report is received from the recommending prison outlining the inmate's background and a detailed account of why his recent behaviour and long-term management indicate that he should be considered for the regime available in the Special Unit. Second, after these reports have been discussed by staff, the community review what is known about the proposed admission. Third, the interviewing team visit the referring prison. The group usually consists of the Governor, the Chief Officer and/or a principal officer. The consultant psychiatrist has always been a member of the admissions team, and during the past two years a principal clinical psychologist, who regularly visits the Unit, has also accompanied the group. Fourth, on arrival at the referring prison, the reason for the admissions request is discussed with the Governor and senior staff. Then some members of both shifts of prison staff who work with the proposed admission are interviewed to obtain their views on the inmate's day-to-day management. Other relevant personnel may be the medical officer, visiting psychiatrist, psychologist, nursing staff and social worker. The discipline staff together interview the inmate. The psychiatrist and psychologist together have a separate interview. The purpose of the latter interview is to allow a detailed clinical assessment to be made of the inmate's personality difficulties, the possibility of underlying mental disorder, and his potential ability to respond constructively to the Unit regime. Fifth, the assessment team, before leaving the prison, review their findings, outline the specific needs of the inmate and decide if the specific problems presented by the proposed admission can be effectively dealt with by coming to the Special Unit. Sixth, the members of the assessment team submit written reports to the Special Unit Governor. If the recommendation is not to accept the inmate, reasons are given and alternative means of management will be suggested. Seventh, the recommendations of the assessment team are presented to the community. On occasions, the discussion has been very searching. Lastly, the group recommendation is sent to the Scottish Home and Health Department for final approval.

The procedures for arranging individual training programmes, reviews of progress and consideration for transfer back to the ordinary prison all take place at a community level. The value of this is that inmates are encouraged to take a responsible attitude towards other people's careers and to take part in the decision-making process before a recommendation is sent to the Department.

An extension of group activity was the development of 'four groups' during the fourth year. New inmates and staff had commented on their personal difficulties during their first few weeks in the Unit. To help them during the first few weeks, it was arranged for small groups to meet daily to discuss with the new person — whether staff or inmate — any difficulties they experienced either in their personal activities or those of others. The 'four groups' would be made up of two staff and two inmates and they would continue to meet until their function was considered unnecessary. The value of these small groups was that new personnel were slowly indoctrinated into the historical development and functions of the Unit and were enabled to express their difficulties at an early stage.

In addition to the community group interaction, much individual work goes on at a one-to-one level with various members of staff.

During the past five years, two groups of inmates can be identified who seem appropriately placed in the Unit. The first are those, very long-term people who have lost hope of ever getting out of prison. They have considerable difficulty in coping with the conventional prison life and feel they have nothing to lose by anti-authority behaviour. In relative terms additional sanctions have very little practical meaning. This group is given the opportunity to work out a way of life for themselves which gives them some degree of day-to-day satisfaction and at the same time help them to adopt a positive approach towards working for their ultimate release. The second are people who may be in the latter part of a long sentence and need detailed assessment and intensive support to prepare them for eventual release.

To date 24 inmates have been admitted to the Unit. At present there are seven prisoners, all serving life sentences. Amongst 24 admissions, 16 were serving life sentences and two had sentences in excess of 17 years. The remaining six had sentences ranging from four years to nine years.

Five inmates have been removed from the Unit. Two, who had been in the Unit for under two years, were guilty of drug abuse. One inmate assaulted another with a knife and was removed after four months. Another had to be removed as he was unable to cope with the community pressures. He became progressively agitated, depressed and socially isolated, despite active group and individual attempts to help him. The fifth inmate was removed following a gross breach of parole licence.

Two inmates have requested to leave. As one was on a fixed sentence he was allowed to do so. Following release, he expressed regret about his request to leave to a member of the Unit staff. The other, serving a life sentence imposed seven years earlier, requested to leave after two years and four months. He considered that his parole prospects would be improved by the transfer, and the community agreed with him. Following release from prison, he was later convicted of rape.

One inmate died from a drug overdosage. The drugs were smuggled in to him by another inmate.

Excluding the inmate removed for assaulting another prisoner after four months, the length of stay has ranged from 11 months to seven-and-a-half years. Amongst the present inmates, one has been in the Unit for over six years.

Excluding the Governor, all Unit staff members are volunteers who undergo a selection procedure. During recent years, the procedure is that the volunteer spends a week in the Special Unit on

detailed duty. At the end of the week, he can decide if he wishes
to proceed with his application. At the same time, members of the
Unit staff will submit a report indicating their views on the volun-
teer's suitability. The next stage is a Selection Board chaired by
the Governor, and including the Chief Officer or his deputy, the
Unit psychiatrist and psychologist. The purpose of the Selection
Board is to decide if a volunteer is considered suitable for the Special
Unit staff. The total number of prison staff is 18, excluding the
Governor.

During the period the Special Unit has been in operation, there
have been eight governors, the longest serving one being in post
three years and seven months.

A programme for ongoing monitoring and evaluation of the regime
in the Special Unit is at present being evolved by the visiting clinical
psychologist. At this stage in the Unit's development, such an assessment is urgently required if the Special Unit is going to progress.

Conclusions

(i) For the purpose that it was created, the Special Unit has
proved itself to be a viable institution.

(ii) To date, no staff have been assaulted — the reasons for this
would appear to be, first, the prison officer–inmate relationship
that has been allowed to develop; and second, the defusing
mechanisms via the community meetings and emergency meetings.

(iii) Other prisons have noted a decrease in violence against staff
since the Unit opened.

(iv) In the longer term, it is hoped that the attitudes of institutional
management that have developed will slowly spread over to other
institutions and be modified for their specific needs.

(v) For highly selected difficult management problems, there
would seem to be a case for the development of other types of
self-contained unit that should be allowed to develop their own
different management techniques.

Reference

Scottish Home and Health Department (1971), *Report of a Departmental Working Party on the Treatment of Certain Male Long-Term Prisoners and Potentially Violent Prisoners*, Edinburgh: SHHD

13 Control problems in dispersals
Michael Jenkins

Long Lartin put forward one candidate for Parkhurst 'C' wing, a Category A lifer who had previously been in a mental hospital. He had come to us from another dispersal where he did not settle: during two years at Long Lartin he had been tried on just about every wing but remained friendless, unlovable, laconic, isolated and destructive. Staff were wary of his moods: his parents had great difficulty visiting whichever dispersal he was in. He spent long periods in the Segregation Unit where we exchanged just more than formal greetings daily. He has been accepted and transferred. You might say by deduction and comparison that the other 390 are not control problems!

There are other control problems, but I can only talk of one establishment (which, thankfully, has had no riot) and three years' experience. But during this period Mr Brittan announced his restrictions on parole for those serving over five years for offences involving violence, drugs and children and on the careers of lifers (Home Office 1985b, para. 135); this issue unified just about everyone! The lid just stayed on, partly because prisoners decided to take the Home Secretary to court (*R* v *Secretary of State for the Home Department ex p. Findlay and others, The Times,* 16 November 1984); [1984] 3 All ER 801) and partly through staff investing much time and energy in absorbing flak and supporting men through a period of great frustration. Staff too felt bereft because they lost the positive leverage of early release. Now that the policy has settled down, but with a serious rise in both serious crime and the prison population (*Guardian,* 14 January 1986), we can look more generally at control problems in dispersal prisons.

I am not going to write about individuals as control problems; Mark Williams (Chapter 14) treats this subject, and I wonder how many exist. Rather, institutions have a tendency to create problems (or occasionally dissipate them). They create them either by operating such a lax regime that some exploiters get out of control, or by overcontrolling. The Radzinowicz Committee (Advisory Council on the Penal System 1968, para. 42) recognised that: 'There will, however, be a certain number of prisoners who need to be removed from the general population of a long-term prison if its regime is not going to be disrupted.' But I am also very much aware of a wise observation of one of my successful predecessors at Long Lartin (Perrie 1981, p. 11): 'What is more frustrating to those wishing to develop a more effective prison system is the knowledge that the more control authority imposes, the more control it will need to maintain its grip. Imposed control for its own, exclusive purpose is self-defeating.' I remember some astute observations by a French psychiatrist many years ago, that the most appropriate response to an institution is to resist it; ideally the energy of resistance is converted into positive action. Individually, 'if he opposes his situation and if this opposition is not utilised therapeutically, it will be expressed by his refusal of treatment or even by escape or violence' (Sivadon 1957, p. 209). And, generally, 'It is to the extent that this real metabolism of energy is perpetuated — in opposition, aggressiveness, activity and creation — that the hospital community remains alive and maintains its active therapeutic character' (Sivadon 1957, p. 209). Such a resolution of the dilemma of control implies a degree of trust and reciprocity between jailers and inmates which neither side is usually keen to acknowledge; it relies on involvement rather than distance and has a distinct effect upon the prison culture. At a less ideal level the natural energy of resistance is channelled into the subculture to institutionalise the resistance and to 'make out', easing the miseries of institutional life. My starting point therefore is that the prison system has a tendency to create more problems than it receives and has an equal tendency to fail inmates because, out of its survival fear, it tends to respond to corporate threats, real or imaginary, rather than the real problems of inmates. However we do have a dispersal system and it has a history which is on the point of change; that history includes serious riots but also a number of positives, especially as reported by Margaret Shaw (1974). We shall need to consider the formal and informal controls and the formal and informal rewards; this will point us in the direction of regimes and perhaps further innovation.

Formal controls
The dispersal system is itself a control mechanism — seven[1] prisons with high perimeter security and high staffing levels and behind them two special security wings.[2] P2 and P3 divisions of the Prison Department headquarters work closely with regional offices to distribute the population, nearly all long-termers and lifers. Long Lartin currently has no one serving less than five years and 135 of its population of just under 400 are serving life imprisonment (including 'detention during Her Majesty's pleasure'). Up to 20 of the popu-

lation would be counted as 'terrorists' — IRA, Libyan, and so on; Long Lartin has no specially favoured population compared with other dispersals, though it seldom has any first-stage lifers. The prisoners do not overtly challenge this system in the courts, though they pursue individual grievances there. While in theory the national Category A population of 300 is distributed within a dispersal population of just under 3,000 as a means of dilution, in practice the whole population of dispersals is controlled in dispersal, high-cost, security. While 'dispersal' began as a neutral word it now has its negative aura of trouble, disaffection and difficulty. 'Long-term training prison' is less evocative, less macho and more descriptive of our role.

Within that system, categorisation and allocation have security and control functions. Some regions send long-termers to a special allocation unit, others perform the function within the normal classification unit of the local prison. If very high security is indicated, reference is made to headquarters; if Category A is confirmed, headquarters also decides allocation. Otherwise classification units refer their categorisation and allocation recommendations to their regional offices (South-East, South-West, North and Midland). Allocations within regions require adding a new name at the bottom of an old list; allocations across regional boundaries are subject to negotiation first. Regions help one another but are wary of suffering an unequal contract, and know that an inmate once received may be impossible to return, for good or ill reason. There still seems to be some tacit approval of the Roman Empire principle, namely that troops will not cause trouble if sent to the opposite end of the earth; it is a principle I shall attack later.

Transfer follows and induction — with varying degrees of formality and emphasis. Receptions usually come in very small groups, so individual attention is normal. Long Lartin has no separate induction unit and receptions are lodged on one of the six wings; placement depends on vacancies, staff preparation (especially in respect of lifers) and inmate choice. Residents usually know when their relatives and friends are coming and will suggest helping to receive them; enemies, too, communicate and we hear about combinations that are better avoided. We are now beginning to talk about 'accommodation' rather than formal control. Induction is an introduction to the facilities and people and style of the pl   it is also inmate induction with its ingredients of trust, distrust and intrigue. Workshop allocations are arranged and withi to ten days the new inmate is fed into the system.

I hope I need spend little time on the mechanism set out in the Prison Rules: segregation under Rul charge) for either own protection or good order — subject to approval by the Board of Visitors; special segregation under Rule 45 for the 'refractory' (who else is refractory but Eliot's camels?); 'punishment' under Rule 47; and remand in segregation under Rule 48. Most 'local difficulties' are dealt with under these rules and usually only for brief periods. My own view of governors' reports is that they are a means of determining what did happen, what should have happened and what is sufficient to restore a status quo which is stable for staff and inmates. I do see the function therefore as regulatory or managing rather than a simple pursuit of justice.[3] In passing I would add a note of sadness that the Prior Committee (Home Office 1985d) did not say remission had had its day — losses of remission sound brave and positive but only take effect at the back end of a sentence, a time better uncomplicated by any extra feelings of resentment. Shorter sentences *with* parole possibilities and *without* remission would be much simpler, more directly understandable and the lost power of stopping remission could, I am sure, be accommodated. Lost privileges, lost earnings and simple segregation are normally enough. Serious crime is after all referred to the police for investigation and prosecution and Boards of Visitors still hold the middle ground between, though we await the Home Office's response to the recommendations of the Prior Committee that a separate legal system should operate in place of the Board of Visitors. For completeness I should draw attention to the current discretion of Boards of Visitors to grant inmates legal representation in accordance with the principles set out in the *Tarrant* case (*R* v *Secretary of State for the Home Department and Board of Visitors of Albany Prison ex p. Tarrant and others* [1985] 1 QB 251).

These regulatory levers are backed up by facilities for temporary transfer; Long Lartin does transfer men to local prisons under Circular Instruction 10/1974. Such men spend 28 days on Rule 43 while there to enable the prison to regain stability. Twelve men were so transferred during 1985, and most other dispersals have a similar average. Some regions allow longer periods away (but not on Rule 43, a 'regional lie-down') and others allow the return of difficult prisoners to their allocation centre for reallocation when their behaviour becomes intolerable. This can be an ambivalent message because misbehaviour leads to transfer and there is a fair chance that this will be no worse a place and probably nearer home.

I believe parole is more a formal reward than a formal control; others might disagree.

Informal controls

There is always an abundance of informal controls in institutional systems. The most powerful in this context is the trans, the present dispersal to another, probably less convenient an certainly with fewer privileges. It is not often used but is a c gesture noted by staff and inmates, often with approval l if the man concerned is indeed behaving like an outlaw and upsetting everyone. There are lesser negative controls — such as not being selected for 'cleaners' or some other desirable work party and on down the scale to the proverbial 'cold shoulder'. However, long-termers can watch closely how we as staff behave, and are quick to pursue any complaint of capricious behaviour. Given the regular proximity of the same staff with the same prisoners, any capriciousness is noted and reduces staff credibility for 'fairness'. In an open regime 'fairness' has much more meaning than power and its reciprocal quality is a better contributor to control.

Formal rewards
Formal rewards comprise a wide range of privileges, pay, recreation, education, and, for some, parole, transfer and home leave. By Prison Rule 4 the Home Secretary is empowered to devise a system of privileges and has done so recently by publishing a new Standing Order 4; for dispersal prisons this has been developed as a Dispersal Privilege List. It seems to embrace as many pursuits as the Home Secretary covers — including caged birds but not au pairs. Prisoners can pursue a variety of hobbies, cook, have sports equipment, read, listen to tapes or records or radio, and so on. All are termed 'privileges' which may seem patronising or an unfair exercise of power. Inmates may not watch televisions in their cells — and why such a restriction? It is not on the privilege list! But Wilberforce LJ said: 'Under English law, a convicted prisoner, in spite of his imprisonment, retains all civil rights which are not taken away expressly or by necessary implication' (*Raymond* v *Honey* [1982] 1 All ER 756 at 759). Do I have a *right* to watch television, use electricity, and so on as long as I pay the fee or cost? I don't think we know! While some privileges have moved to a higher status following our acceptance of the European Convention on Human Rights, others remain as privileges and inmates have not challenged.

Inmates work about 25 hours per week at Long Lartin and are paid in cash; some are on a higher-incentive earnings scheme and receive more than £4; others are on a lower education rate (because they engage in vocational training or full-time education) and others again are on 'basic' because they decline to produce anything. Earnings are spent in the canteen — on tobacco, food, toiletries, sweets, cards, stamps, and so on. Private cash can be spent on larger privilege items, newspapers, and so on — but is via an account rather than cash in hand.

There is a good gymnasium in use throughout every day and on four evenings a week. Various sports wax and wane in popularity, though weights are always popular. The sports field is available each weekend afternoon and in the evenings midweek during (approximately) British summertime. The availability of 'fresh air and fun' reassures inmates that they are not becoming cabbages and works as a very effective reward.

Education reassures those similarly concerned about their minds as well as (or instead of) their bodies. There is a wide range of classes, some formal, some informal, with a healthy emphasis on Open University, full-time education for those who can use it; and hobbies. Many of Long Lartin's charitable enterprises have developed from activities on the 'Thursday Group' — the poetry book and handicraft sales have been exciting projects raising considerable sums for charity. There are many other components of the regime — chaplains, probation staff, discipline staff and a multiplicity of outsiders, especially prison visitors and voluntary associates. Why are they provided? In line with a principle of 'normalisation'? As a means of treatment? As a way of occupying prisoners?

Despite this variety imprisonment can be very dull; but for many it provides a new outlet and the vigour of those who provide the service can inspire those who take part. Those who tune in to their potential *for their sake* give us, the authorities, a benefit, too. Such inputs into the regime draw inmates out from the delinquent subculture either for a period or for good, they weaken its power by reducing the number of adherents, they change the stereotypes of 'them and us'. Such rewards are an antidote to delinquent and destructive behaviour and reduce the need for overt control — while we still watch for those who pilfer hobbies materials, escape equipment and other 'currency items'.

Release on licence has been much curtailed since the Home Secretary's policy statement to the Conservative Party Conference in 1983; numbers released from Long Lartin on licence have fallen as have periods on parole. In 1983 68 prisoners were released, for an average of 14½ months; in 1984 31 were released, for an average of 10 months; while in 1985 22 were released, for an average of only six months. The possibility is more remote and it is less to the forefront of exchanges between staff and inmates.

Transfer is sometimes seen as a reward but not often — except for lifers. For a lifer, transfer to Long Lartin after three or four years in a 'main centre' means that he is on a slower route towards discharge; for him the next transfer should at least be out of the

Table 13.1   Movement for lifers from Long Lartin

	Type of prison to which moved				
	Dispersal prison	Cat B prison	Cat C prison	Cat D prison	Other*	Total
1983	10	20	8	1	1	40
1984	7	13	3	–	1	24
1985	7	14	7	–	2	30

*Grendon or psychiatric hospital

dispersal system either to Category B (such as Nottingham, Lewes or Blundeston) or to Category C (such as The Verne, Preston or Featherstone). He may get less freedom of movement and fewer privileges but it is a marked step of progress towards release and is usually welcome. Movement for lifers has diminished over the past three years, as Table 13.1 shows. For the fixed-term man the move is of little significance to release or to parole; at present, unless he is transferring nearer home, he can see only disadvantages. Long Lartin is anticipating (after about five years!) the recommendations of the Categorisation Working Party (Home Office 1981) that a man's category should be reduced by a grade half way through sentence (rather like a presumption in favour of bail) unless there are positive reasons for seeing him as a security risk in Category C. So far this only gives an illusion of progress — either because his 'home' region will make no provision for him or because more frequent home leave is only available to Category Ds in open establishments. I look forward to the extension of extra home leave to Category C establishments, too, as proposed by the Categorisation Working Party and the CRC report (Home Office 1984b). I frequently turn down appeals against recategorisation and the only men who actively seek it are those who languish in Category A.

Transfer to hospital or to Grendon seems now to be regarded neutrally rather than described pejoratively as 'being nutted off'. As men cross the boundary to hospital and back again, familiarity gives confidence that hospitalisation is neither too dangerous nor too much of a cissy 'cop-out'; it is neither a reward nor a control. There is no anxiety among prisoners at Long Lartin that they are being controlled by drugs against their will; reporting sick or special sick is a frequent occurrence but medicines are only prescribed against a request or agreed need.

Home leave, pre-parole leave and employment parole are certainly desirable and again we make a presumption in favour — except for Category As. The processes weed out the biggest risks but most men — if they are still in Long Lartin at the back end of a sentence — can expect either short or terminal home leave or both. It may be special pleading but we believe a man who goes on home leave must in effect be seen as Category D at least.

Restoration of lost remission carries no such presumption in favour, but I cannot say that our expectations are as high as those of our legislators; we look for a significant improvement in behaviour but see transformation into a new being as too high a criterion to be useful. Reinforcement of improved behaviour is regarded as fair by both staff and inmates and encourages hope as men look towards discharge. The arrangement of accumulated visits in a prison near home and the organisation of inter-prison visits are important contributors to the good order of the prison; it is sad that the latter are under some threat through shortage of staff and funds to cover enough overtime. There is a danger that this selection of examples of rewards will go all the way down to sharing mince pies with visitors (not family) after the annual carol service, but I would like to mention as rewards both pre-release courses and social skills courses. Both have short- and long-term pay-offs for inmates — easier relationships, some (fun and) games and a lifting of the eyes towards release. To these we plan to add summer schools to open up potentialities and satisfactions. Leaving work for a week or more for such special ventures increases everyone's morale — even in times of gloom and despondency. There is something of a reward in food, too, even in the everyday service of three institutional meals. Choices of meals and a chance to participate in a catering committee are plusses that we strive to maintain and develop.

Questions are asked from time to time about use of force by staff. Restraint is authorised and new methods are now taught to staff under 'control and restraint' to minimise the risk of injury to both staff and prisoners. Training has also been given for dealing with more serious unrest (minimum use of force, tactical intervention (MUFTI) but thankfully we have not had to employ the technique.

Informal rewards
I do not mean to countenance any form of trafficking under 'informal rewards'. It happens from time to time and we have always to be on watch for it. Rumours are probably a great exaggeration on fact, but does all dried yeast, money and cannabis enter the prison anally? Informal rewards rather cover the willingness to take time to explain or to find alternative paths out of problems and difficulties, to route

an old lifer to his next establishment by a devious route because some older officer may remember him from another prison as the one who deservedly got corporal punishment there, to substitute a carrot for a tomato when a man is at the end of his rational tether. Men know that they can almost certainly and usually quickly get a peaceful hearing in the back office of the wing manager, that a cup replay being screened to 9.15pm will not normally be turned off at the proper finishing time of 9pm.

How it really works

But again the discussion of informal rewards points towards the levels of accommodation, the unwritten contract by which any organisation works or has life. The unwritten contract involves inmates, staff and management and is connected with both security and control. It is in one sense healthy to distinguish these features and the Inspectorate did in its latest report (Home Office 1985a, para. 3.02):

> Security and control are central core functions of all prison establishments, and their separate demands inevitably affect all regimes. This being so it is vitally important in our view that the two functions are carefully distinguished. Security concerns the prevention of escape and as such it depends ultimately for its success on meticulous attention to security checks, the gathering and analysis of intelligence material and good perimeter defences. Control on the other hand has to do with the maintenance of order within an establishment, and may or may not have an immediate bearing on security. This simple distinction is in our experience often blurred. Thus we have found in the course of our inspections that security considerations are sometimes advanced as a reason for restricting regimes, for example, by closing workshops and stopping association — measures which are not in our view necessary on security grounds, although they may be justified on control grounds. Clear thinking is obviously needed if the risk of undue restriction on already impoverished regimes is to be avoided.

The Radzinowicz Report (Advisory Council on the Penal System 1968) also relied upon perimeter security and a considerable degree of internal freedom as if we could neatly separate security and control. In fact the two concepts overlap — for example we check tool cupboards and inmates after a hobby class and before they leave the education department for their wings. Tools can aid an escape or be used to intimidate or injure. More broadly, if control is humane and relaxed inmates equally relax and escape becomes less important; and if control is excessive the reaction can be either riot or escape or both.

There is therefore an unwritten contract; even to acknowledge one is to attract an accusation of collusion — this fear haunted the Inspectorate on its last visit to Long Lartin in 1983 (Home Office 1984a). The prime function of this unwritten contract is to get people sensibly through their sentences. From the staff point of view this reduces hassle, stress and injury; for the management it avoids hostility from staff and inmates and keeps costs within bounds; for prisoners it allows men to 'do their bird'. There is a momentum towards 'balancing the boat' or 'steering into a skid' to counteract the fear on all sides of things going out of control. It allows the majority to live in peace.

It is difficult to extract the terms of this unwritten contract but I will try to identify some examples:

(i) Yeast and 'hooch' are forbidden — if a prisoner is found with 'hooch' no one is surprised but it has to be poured away. Anyone who persists will be placed on report.

(ii) If you are angry, you may go and swear at the wing manager in his office without limit of time but not in front of all your mates. You may gesticulate but not assault. An apology should precede your next onslaught.

(iii) If out of anger or distress you barricade in your cell, you will not be dragged out by staff so long as they can see and converse with you. You may leave with dignity and usually with a member of staff of your choice en route to segregation. (Staff equally must not be injured and no general melée ensue.)

(iv) Management has standards but is tolerant to staff; staff behave similarly to prisoners; prisoners behave similarly to 'nonces'.

(v) 'Grassing' is forbidden but 'notes on the box' or a quiet word in the back office are allowed if one prisoner or group is becoming unduly dominant.

(vi) Mates will not be capriciously 'shanghai-ed' but it is better that outlaws be found a place that suits them better.

(vii) Change will not be one-sided; if a staff meeting involves the loss of association at lunchtime, canteen and exercise will take priority over returning to work.

(viii) Locks, bolts and bars will be checked daily and 'spins' (special searches) are a fact of life but inmates may have a degree of privacy during association and may visit each other's cells.

(ix) All parties will recognise that each has power and no one has absolute power.

There is a danger that such an 'ethos' will either lull staff into metaphorical slumber, or allow youthful innovation to become routine middle age. Prisoners in fact continually test the system and keep us 'on our toes', and we too know that we must justify and develop our regimes if we are to retain both credibility and resources. Staff 'intelligence systems' and inmates' 'jungle telegraphs' are continually at work and the games of cat and mouse are as inexhaustible as the now proverbial Tom and Jerry. It is thus a strange momentum with many self-balancing forces — but it accepts the delinquent subculture and elevates mutual support to the first priority. It stifles spontaneity but contains within it degrees of both humanity and exploitation.

I therefore have the comfort of knowing that Long Lartin's 'ethos' has enabled it to survive through numerous crises and it is worth my while, too, to maintain the unwritten contract. But it is not without its anxieties. Is security — electronic, mechanical and staff — as absolutely reliable as history indicates? Am I being 'conditioned'? While a degree of privacy and laying back on control contribute to stability, is the balance right — are inmates supporting one another or exploiting one another? And there is a dilemma, expressed in the report on the Maze Prison (Home Office 1984c, pp. 21–2) as follows:

> One way to eliminate smuggling would be to subject visitors to a rigorous body search before they were allowed contact with prisoners. However, many visitors are, no doubt, law-abiding citizens and if they were subjected to such intensive security measures, there might well be a public outcry. Similarly, security measures which reduce the quality of a prisoner's contact with his family are likely to be resented by both prisoners and visitors. In the past such issues have quickly become a focus for discontent and have led to widespread protests and civil disorder. Experience has shown too that staff who are faced with such hostility will eventually allow security measures which are regarded as unduly onerous to lapse.
>
> For all these reasons the Northern Ireland Office has been cautious about introducing certain security measures which might have prevented weapons being smuggled into the prison by visitors. For example intimate body searching of visitors before a visit has hitherto been regarded as unacceptable. Closed visits — where the two parties are separated by a physical barrier — have never been introduced as a general measure applied to all prisoners. Instead, reliance has been placed upon normal searching of a visitor before the visit, supervision of the visit itself, and a search of the prisoner afterwards.
>
> In the light of the escape we have looked again at a number of possible preventive measures. Foremost among these was the recommendation of the Council of Europe that in prisons such as the Maze closed visits should be the general rule. We recognise the potential effectiveness of such a measure, and have noted that it is the general rule in Germany too. But the humanitarian arguments against closed visits for all prisoners in the Maze cannot be ignored. Moreover, since their introduction might well provoke serious and widespread repercussions, the measure could prove to be counter-productive. We do not believe, therefore, that it

would be sensible to adopt such a measure, except as a last resort. Other measures of this kind, for example intimate body searches, have similar disadvantages. We have concluded that there are no simple solutions. However, we believe that the present procedures could be made much more effective.

This was neatly summarised in a recent ministerial reply (in a letter to a Member of Parliament): 'In the prison situation one must clearly have regard also to the possibility that, even if other obstacles proved surmountable, intimate searching might lead to control problems out of all proportion to its intrinsic value'. We are thus talking about limiting excesses rather than controlling all institutional delinquency, a better reflection of outside life but a realism that the popular press might attack in its eager pursuit of political scapegoats. Whose decision should it be that security or control consume too much of the resources, or that over-control gives rise to its equal and opposite reaction?

But . . .

Funds are limited, even if law and order has been, like defence, relatively favoured since 1979. The government has attempted to allay public anxiety, and if the fear of crime is more disabling than crime itself, as indicated by the British Crime Survey (Hough and Mayhew 1983), that is valuable. My 'but' remains because of the expense of dispersal prisons: in 1984–5 an inmate at Long Lartin cost an average £478 per week and that is a little lower than the dispersal average (Home Office 1985b, p. 25). It remains, too, because there are too many self-regarding elements. For all the constructive new initiatives advocated in the report of the Control Review Committee (Home Office 1984b) and the Prior Committee (Home Office 1985d) we do need stronger, more active, aspirational, positive and research-justified functions and tasks than we are currently prepared to publish (Circular Instruction 55/1984 as published in Home Office 1985b, Appendix 7). Long Lartin's experience is that tuning in to prisoners is good for control; Margaret Shaw's (1974) research at Gartree indicated (but no one seems to believe it!) that it was similarly good for reducing recidivism, both in further offending and in time spent out of custody. While I welcome the initiatives of the Platt Report I cannot be content with its incarceration principles (Home Office 1985c, p. 68):

> The Federal system now aims to provide safe, human[e] institutions which offer inmates the opportunity for change and improvement through their own efforts and through the services provided. In this approach, recidivism is not seen as a failure on the part of the prison system;

the prison provides the opportunities and encouragement, but it is up to the individual whether he chooses to respond to them.

Perhaps it depends how much you mean by 'encouragement'. There are elements to be maximised — for short-term control and longer-term stability. Once again it may be that our European neighbours have as much to offer us as our American cousins!

Review

I have so far indicated that Long Lartin has thankfully survived as a dispersal prison for 12 years without a riot; it has had many confrontations, alarms and roof incidents but its good relationships, good foundations, good training and its innovation demonstrate that a dispersal prison can work. We have been assisted by prisoners' increasing access to courts and their continuing correspondence with MPs — though the Ombudsman is seldom called. The development of judicial review with use of prerogative orders and declarations (now set out by Aldous and Alder 1985) is becoming gradually a substitute for a Bill of Rights. The European Convention on Human Rights has also been instrumental in moderating our use of power, but even long-termers need a quicker response!

There are nevertheless some practical do's and don'ts which we have learned. First, it is far better to individualise relationships with inmates than to provide them with unifying issues; we can do without mass protests against uninspiring food, new mattresses, shortage of kit, limited entertainment and restricted parole. Recently we have been able to alleviate such tense matters (except parole!) and to express a willingness to consider other possible rubbing points. Second, respect of prisoners and taking one's time pays greater dividends than rushing, abusing or using force before it is absolutely necessary to limit injury or serious damage. Third, consistency and continuity of staff together make for an easier normality, a history of understanding; previous successful working through of issues gives everyone confidence that it is worth trying again. We have enjoyed a warmth and involvement that the report on the Hull riot valued (Home Office 1977) and which Gordon Fowler remembered in his recent evidence to the Parliamentary All Party Penal Affairs Group (1986, p. 21):

> He had been alarmed in most of the dispersal prisons by the withdrawal of staff from involvement in the community life of the wing because of the fear of being assaulted or taken hostage. Most of the escapes he had investigated had started with threats to the staff that hostages would be taken. Real security and control meant knowing what someone was going to do before he did it, which implied forming a relationship.

Thus security and control are distinguishable but complementary to each other; but they cannot be reasonably expected without trust, relationships, justice, respect, hope and reward. And gains can so easily be lost through lack of attention to grievances, real or imaginary, or by the creation of stumbling blocks. The Control Review Committee (Home Office 1984b) went positively in this direction; that initiative deserves to be encouraged and sustained. But there are further developments I would wish to see.

Developments

Unit size

The Control Review Committee report (Home Office 1984b, para. 55) advocates small special units for the difficult, disturbed and destructive long-term inmates without specifying any particular size; they could be part of either local or long-term prisons. The Committee also saw a need for two prisons of between 150 and 200 comprising units of 50–100 according to American 'new generation' concepts (Home Office 1984b, paras 18–20). I would prefer to think of accommodating all long-termers in small units, without aggregating them in two new generation prisons or dispersal prisons and note the recommendation in PAPPAG (1986, p. 22):

> We recommend that a number of small units, in which life-sentence prisoners are accommodated in living units of no more than 40 prisoners, should be established on an experimental basis. These units need not necessarily consist exclusively of life-sentence prisoners, but could also include other long term prisoners. The experimental units should be closely monitored and evaluated.

Location

Dispersal prisons tend to be remote; the distribution of long-termers and lifers to seven dispersals separates the majority from homes, families and neighbourhoods. This weakens the positive effects of such outside influences, allows guilt to be ignored as a common denominator and strengthens (through isolation and projection of blame) the power of the subculture. (I have only seen these aspects considered by Fiedler and Bass 1959.)

Local prisons are Category B; recent publicity highlights their overcrowding by unsentenced inmates but allocation remains the other primary task alongside court work. Locals tend to accumulate the unclassified and the men in lower security categories awaiting places. They therefore hold many people who need less security than Category B. We might pursue more small units within local prisons for those requiring higher security and speeding lower-category men to satellite training establishments. Both types of establishment could enjoy the benefits of proximity to home especially with men from Category C and Category D establishments having more frequent opportunities for home leave. Local prison units would need more resources but the disbanding of expensive dispersal prisons would release considerable staff and cash. 'Dispersal' would also be better achieved through 25–30 local prisons.

Sentences and remission

European experience (Council of Europe 1984, p. 34) suggests that England incarcerates more people and for longer periods than other countries. The progress of the 'justice model' should enable us to establish a relatively just tariff, namely one that puts crimes in a relative order of public seriousness without a continual escalation of sentence lengths. Tarling (in Brody and Tarling 1980) suggests that shorter sentences would have only a marginal effect upon the crime rate, though Ainsworth and Pease (1981) raise the issue of deterrence and public confidence. The Parliamentary All Party Penal Affairs Committee (1986) has suggested that life should be the maximum for murder rather than the automatic sentence and the setting of tariffs for life-sentence men indicates that determinate sentences for all serious cases, including homicides, are now on the broader public agenda. Dell's (1984) survey of diminished responsibility cases in hospitals (primarily) indicates that safe release can be achieved in less time and without great public anxiety. Hospital release procedures may also demonstrate that release by tribunal can be trustworthy despite its greater distance from ministerial control. As suggested earlier, remission is an unnecessary complication, a superfluity in the presence of parole, an illusory benefit to control in prisons. If sentences were genuinely shorter because remission had been abolished, there need be little public anxiety and there would be benefits to prisons and prisoners. The complexities of sentence calculation and the machinery to cope with the process can be 'rubbished'; we could divert the resources released to greater enterprise. At the same time I would wish to see the Prison Department reporting briefly to magistrates and judges the number of days spent in custody on remand, so that this time can be taken into account before length of sentence is detemined. Such a change would simplify sentence calculation but, more importantly, it would reduce the attractiveness of long (and sometimes deliberately extended) periods of remand. Staying 'local' with remand privileges and remission accrued is an incentive for some defendants to put off the day of sentence for as long as possible.

I do not believe the loss of the power to stop remission would jeopardise control in prison. Brief segregation and withdrawal of privileges (now more extensive) will normally be sufficient; more serious crime can be processed through courts, though the slowness of the process gives a poor message for control. Lifers cannot lose remission, but do not offend in prison simply for lack of such a control. The Radzinowicz Report (Advisory Council on the Penal System 1968, para. 162) expressed similar ideas:

> We would suggest to all those who operate the procedures that a short period of cellular confinement with complete withdrawal of privileges is likely to be as effective as a deterrent to the commission of further breaches of discipline as a longer drawn out award. We think that the law of diminishing returns can operate when a longer period of removal from association is used.

Shorter simpler sentences with proximity to home would contribute to better control within prisons and need contribute nothing to public or staff anxiety.

'Positive custody'

The May Committee (Home Office 1979) laboured to encapsulate a positive aspiration for realising the potential of prisons and prisoners. But at present the Prison Department formally eschews aspirational statements — though the Director-General made this contribution to the last annual report (Home Office 1985b, pp. 3–4):

> prison staff across the system are increasingly providing or seeking to provide improved regimes for prisoners, regimes which reflect the stated functions of the Prison Service and have implicit in them what must be its motivating aspirations to help, to care for and, if possible, to influence for the better the inmates who are placed in custody.

This is not the time to rework the arguments from Martinson (1974) onwards but we should reconsider the positive achievements researched by Shaw (1974). It is good news for prisoners and staff if more attractive options can be set out and be realistically recommended. Staff have shown an eagerness to be involved in social work in prison, in pre-release courses and in social skills training; this more structured involvement has an immediate reward for both parties and can be developed towards more successful outcomes. I do not believe we have capitalised upon the positive research into psychotherapy and counselling which has indicated that the following attributes in staff promote a more positive outcome: accurate empathy, or an ability to tune in correctly to what matters to the client; non-possessive warmth — which is a somewhat safer term than 'love'; personal integrity — or 'integratedness'. A fourth quality seems to emerge from the literature, namely the confidence to hold the problem situation without being overwhelmed by it. Sutton (1979) expressed this as 'persuasive power' but this is not quite apt.

The main research was done by Truax and his colleagues (see Truax and Wargo 1966). In this sense control and stopping men going out of control is a valuable exercise of authority, it limits damage and allows time and space for rethinking and developing other strategies. It is not intended to foster dependency, the arch enemy of any good institutional work. There are positives yet to be realised, preferably within small units, among known regular staff; and if such units are near home and encourage community links the culture should lose much of its toxicity. Control can become less of a major issue and itself be helpful. However, there is a thundercloud in sight. All establishments have to live within even tighter budgets next year and regimes will inevitably have to be curtailed. We cannot take on desirable improvements and will have great difficulty maintaining the present somewhat unsteady equilibrium.

Conclusion

The Radzinowicz Committee (Advisory Council on the Penal System 1968) preferred 'dispersal' and open regimes to concentration and intensive control. It took a different stance from the Mountbatten Report (Home Office 1966). Similarly, the more recent report of the Control Review Committee (Home Office 1984b) committed itself to 'active treatment' (cf. Rose 1965) rather than the maximum security advocated by the Council of Europe (1983). The Platt Report (Home Office 1985c) attempts to do for prisons what *Care and Treatment in a Planned Environment* (Home Office 1970) set out for approved schools. Both CRC ideals and 'new generation prisons' are complementary, brave but vulnerable.

Despite terrorism, drug-trafficking and a rising number of lifers, we are thankfully still looking for regimes that engender hope and optimism. Some may say that we are 'conning' ourselves and trying to 'con' our inmates; I believe we can genuinely offer prisoners more than an antidote to the deterioration they fear (Cohen and Taylor 1972). The majority would prefer not to return to prison and that can be a legitimate start to new learning. As the fourth Radzinowicz recommendation puts it: 'the regime of a prison must aim to meet the needs of human beings in custody' (ACPS 1968, p. 77).

Concentration upon control is likely to stimulate resistance; tuning in to prisoners' needs reduces the emphasis upon control and the need for it.

This paper has not directly considered 'dangerousness' but this has been extensively considered by others (for example, Walker 1978; Banks *et al.* 1978; Conrad 1982; Floud and Young 1981). One man's dangerousness is another's anxiety. Most risks seem more remote than our egocentricity leads us to believe but one can foresee some form of relatively long-term imprisonment with perhaps the possibility of extensions (ACPS 1978) or reviewable sentences (Home Office 1975) or protective sentences (Floud and Young 1981) or longer licence periods if such a price has to be paid for shorter average real sentence lengths. A determinate sentence is preferable for all serious offenders without anyone having to make guesses about future dangerousness. (I am unhappy with the conclusion of Maguire *et al.* (1984) that psychiatrists can make more accurate judgments in this regard.) We shall need external controls in the community and in prison, but there is no reason why prison should not be just, humane and constructive. Rehoboam preferred the advice of the young men and lost control of Israel; I prefer the (rejected) advice of the elders: 'If today you will be a servant to these people and serve them and give them a favourable answer, they will always be your servants' (1 Kings 12:7).[4]

Notes

1 Albany, Frankland, Gartree, Long Lartin, Parkhurst, Wakefield and Wormwood Scrubs; Full Sutton will join the list and Wormwood Scrubs will leave it.
2 Parkhurst and Leicester.
3 Though I'm not sure that I agree with Aldous and Alder (1985, p.106) when they say: 'This seems to depend upon the courts' perception that the Governor's managerial authority is a superior value to that of natural justice.'
4 This paper was a personal view of control in a dispersal prison and I take responsibility for any *faux pas*, inaccuracies and omissions. I have also suggested a number of ways in which policy after the CRC report could be extended to make the control of long-termers smoother and simpler, more optimistic and constructive. Neither the description nor the special pleading carry the Prison Department's seal of approval.

References

Advisory Council on the Penal System (1968), *The Regime for Long-Term Prisoners in Conditions of Maximum Security* (Radzinowicz Report), London: HMSO.

Advisory Council on the Penal System (1978), *Sentences of Imprisonment: A Review of Maximum Penalties*, London: HMSO.

Ainsworth, P.B. and Pease, K. (1981), 'Incapacitation Revisited', *Howard Journal*, vol. 20, pp. 160–9.

Aldous, G. and Alder, J. (1985), *Applications for Judicial Review*, London: Butterworths.

Banks, C. *et al.* (1978), 'A Survey of the South East Prison Population', *Home Office Research Bulletin*, no. 5, pp. 12–24.

Brody, S. and Tarling, R. (1980), *Taking Offenders out of Circulation*, Home Office Research Study no. 64, London: HMSO.

Cohen, S. and Taylor, L. (1972), *Psychological Survival*, Harmondsworth: Penguin.

Conrad, J.P. (1982), 'The Quandary of Dangerousness', *British Journal of Criminology*, vol. 22, pp. 255–67.

Council of Europe (1983), *Custody and Treatment of Dangerous Prisoners*, Strasbourg: Council of Europe.

Council of Europe (1984), *Prison Information Bulletin No. 4*, Strasbourg: Council of Europe.

Dell, S. (1984), *Murder into Manslaughter*, Oxford: Oxford University Press.

Fiedler, F.E. and Bass, A.R. (1959), *Delinquency, Confinement and Interpersonal Perception*, Technical Report no. 6, Urbana: Group Effectiveness Research Laboratory, University of Illinois.

Floud, J. and Young, W. (1981), *Dangerousness and Criminal Justice*, Cambridge Studies in Criminology XLVII London: Heinemann.

Home Office (1966), *Report of the Inquiry into Prison Escapes and Security* (Mountbatten Report), Cmnd. 3175, London: HMSO.

Home Office (1970), *Care and Treatment in a Planned Environment*, London: HMSO.

Home Office (1975), *Report of the Committee on Mentally Abnormal Offenders* (Butler Report), Cmnd. 6244, London: HMSO.

Home Office (1977), *Report of an Inquiry by the Chief Inspector of the Prison Service into the Cause and Circumstances of the Events at H.M. Prison Hull During the Period 31st August to 3rd September, 1976*, HC 453 (Fowler Report), London: HMSO.

Home Office (1979), *Report of the Committee of Inquiry into the United Kingdom Prison Services* (May Report), Cmnd. 7673, London: HMSO

Home Office (1981), *Working Party on Categorisation Report*, London: Home Office Prison Department.

Home Office (1984a), *H.M. Prison, Long Lartin: Report by H.M. Chief Inspector of Prisons*, London: Home Office.

Home Office (1984b), *Managing the Long-Term Prison System: The Report of the Control Review Committee*, London: HMSO.

Home Office (1984c), *Report of an Inquiry by H.M. Chief Inspector of Prisons into the Security Arrangements at H.M. Prison, Maze*, London: HMSO.

Home Office (1985a), *Report of H.M. Chief Inspector of Prisons, 1984*, London: HMSO.

Home Office (1985b), *Report on the Work of the Prison Department 1984/85*, Cmnd. 9699, London: HMSO.

Home Office (1985c), *New Directions in Prison Design: Report of a Home Office Working Party on American New Generation Prisons* (Platt Report), London: HMSO.

Home Office (1985d), *Report of the Committee on the Prison Disciplinary System* (Prior Report), Cmnd. 9641, London: HMSO.

Hough, M. and Mayhew, P. (1983), *The British Crime Survey*, Home Office Research Study no. 76, London: HMSO.

Maguire, M., Pinter, F. and Collis, C. (1984), 'Dangerousness and the Tariff', *British Journal of Criminology*, vol. 24, pp. 250–68.

Martinson, R. (1974), 'What Works? Questions and Answers about Prison Reform', *The Public Interest*, vol. 35, pp. 22–54.

Parliamentary All Party Penal Affairs Group (1986), *Life Sentence Prisoners*, London: Barry Rose.

Perrie, W. (1981), 'The Prison Dilemma', *Prison Service Journal*, October, pp. 10–12.

Rose, G. (1965), 'Administrative Consequences of Penal Objectives', *Sociological Review Monograph No. 9: Sociological Studies in the British Penal Services* (ed. P. Halmos), Keele: University of Keele, pp. 211–26.

Shaw, M.J. (1974), *Social Work in Prison*, Home Office Research Study no. 22, London: HMSO.

Sivadon, P.D. (1957), 'Techniques of Sociotherapy', *Psychiatry*, vol. 20, pp. 205–10.

Sutton, C. (1979), 'Research in Psychology: Applications to Social Casework', *Social Work Today*, vol. 5, pp. 17–19.

Temple, W. (1934), *Ethics of Penal Action*, Clarke Hall Lecture no. 1, Rochester, Kent: Stanhope Press.

Truax, C.B. and Wargo, D.G. (1966), 'Psychotherapeutic Encounters that Change

Behaviour: for Better or for Worse', *American Journal of Psychotherapy*, vol. 20, pp. 499–520.

Walker, N. (1978), 'Dangerous People', *International Journal of Law and Psychiatry*, vol. 1, pp. 37–50.

14 Identifying control-problem prisoners in dispersal prisons
Mark Williams and David Longley

An almost universal claim by the managers of high-security prisons is that conditions within them would be qualitatively very different but for the presence of a small minority of difficult prisoners. This assertion is most frequently raised in the post-mortem following a prison riot, when the events are invariably ascribed to the behaviour and/or influence of small groups of particular prisoners. An example illustrating that this is not simply a recent development may be found in the official report of the enquiry into the causes of the 1932 riot in Dartmoor prison: 'prisoners had no substantial grievances and such grievances as they had would not have led to any disorder unless a few of the dangerous prisoners, partly by their power of leadership, partly by intimidation, had played on the feelings and fears of others' (Home Office 1932, p. 33). Sometimes the assessment of cause is more equivocal: 'was the riot premeditated? I do not think anyone will ever really know, but I personally doubt it. In my view it was a planned passive demonstration that went wrong, and was exploited by a number of prime movers in the inmate population' (Home Office 1977, para. 11). But common to both of these explanations of control breakdown is the disproportionate influence (at some point) ascribed to the behaviour of a minority of prisoners. The simplest direct test of this hypothesis would be to see how far the judicious removal of 'control-problem prisoners' (however these were to be defined) would result in the decline of disorder as such.

In the context of the existing dispersal policy for dealing with maximum-security prisoners, the situation is slightly more complex. Not only does that policy specify the placement of the really dangerous prisoners, it also prescribes the conditions — a relatively open regime within a secure perimeter — that should obtain for the resulting mix. Thus to the problem of the difficult minority in general is added the particular problem of differences of reaction to the dispersal prison regimes *per se*. It is possible therefore to argue that an objective and accurate procedure for identifying the hypothetical minority of difficult and dangerous prisoners is essential on two grounds: to test the hypothesis that the smooth running of dispersal prisons is critically determined by the behaviour of a minority of difficult prisoners, and hence will be disproportionately improved by their selective removal; and to explore the extent to which persistent offenders against discipline in dispersal prisons exhibit special treatment needs that might be met in environments outside those prisons. Of course, implicit in the search for an accurate and objective procedure for identifying control-problem prisoners is a test of the validity of the concept of the 'control problem' itself.

Using identification of the putative difficult prisoners as the starting point, evidence bearing on these issues may be collected under several different but related headings:

(i) the extent to which different indices of 'difficulty' correlate, and support the notion of relatively stable individual differences in degree of 'difficulty';

(ii) the characteristics of the judgments of the governors as to who the difficult prisoners are (for example, are those judgments consistent over time and is there reliability among judges?);

(iii) the characteristics of those identified as control problems compared with those in the dispersal system not so identified;

(iv) differences within the groups of prisoners identified as difficult, related to possible differences in approach to their management; and

(v) the effects of acting on the results of these enquiries, along the lines recommended in the CRC report (Home Office 1984).

What follows is a brief description of the progress that has been made so far in various studies directed along these lines.

Agreement between different measures of control difficulty (study I)

Evidence collected for the CRC itself makes a convenient starting point. In August 1983, dispersal prison governors provided lists of the names of those they considered to be dangerously disruptive in their respective institutions at that time. These names were then compared with the names of prisoners drawn from other sources, considered indicative of a current control problem. The details of these other sources are set out below:

(i) *Disciplinary transfers.* The first list contained the names of men who were transferred from dispersal to local prisons under the terms of Circular Instruction 10/1974, from January 1980 to December 1982 inclusive. Details of the use of these transfers are normally sent to the Adult Offender Psychology Unit (AOPU), but the list of names obtained was not necessarily complete. Experience has shown that the collection and recording of information relating to the use of this measure can be erratic. Occasionally, inmates are transferred so quickly that the paperwork is not immediately completed, and it may become ambiguous as to whether or not this is in fact a CI 10/1974 transfer (the terms of which are that the transfer should be of one month's duration, and that the inmate should return to his sending prison thereafter).

(ii) *Security summaries (January 1980–December 1982)*. The second list contained the names of inmates noted as having been involved in a serious incident in the monthly reports of security and control sent to P5 Division of the Home Office Prison Department headquarters. These security summaries contain details of any incident occurring within the dispersal prisons which may have a bearing on security or control. The incidents vary greatly in their degree of severity and the extent to which they present a threat to the institution. For the purpose of the present enquiry, only inmates involved in incidents which represented a genuine threat were included. Interpretation of the security reports was complicated by their informal nature, and in order to minimise the effect of this, the final list of names included only those who: were involved in a serious assault on an inmate; or an assault on staff; or were mentioned in at least two separate reports. By selecting only the more serious incidents it was hoped to minimise the problem of variability between establishments in the reporting process itself.

(iii) *P3 list*. This consisted of eight inmates who were notified by P3 Division of Prison Department headquarters as having murdered another inmate. They obviously represent the most dangerous men in the system.

(iv) *Inmates segregated to maintain good order and discipline (GOAD) (January 1980–December 1982)*. Two further lists were derived from the AOPU monitoring of all inmates segregated to maintain good order and discipline under Rule 43 (GOAD). The first of these lists consisted of all dispersal prisoners segregated for six months or more continuously, and the second was of those who were segregated twice or more in any one year.

The numbers of inmates identified by each of these four sources, together, with those classed as 'dangerously disruptive' by governors, are set out in Table 14.1. Analysis of these date began by collating the various lists of names in order to determine how many inmates appeared on more than one occasion. The results are set out in

Table 14.1   Number of inmates identified by each source (study I)

Source	No. of mentions
'Dangerously disruptive' (governors' lists)	338
Disciplinary transfers (CI 10/1974)	115
Security summaries	207
P3 list	8
GOAD (six months continuously)	97
GOAD (twice or more in any one year)	268
Total	1033

Table 14.2   Numbers of repeated mentions (study I)

No. of times mentioned	No. of inmates	% total inmates	No. of mentions	% total mentions
1	589	77.20	589	57.02
2	103	13.50	206	19.94
3	47	6.16	141	13.65
4	23	3.01	92	8.91
5+	1	0.13	5	0.48
Total	763	100.00	1033	100.00

Table 14.2, in which it may be seen a total of 174 (22.80 per cent) inmates appeared in more than one list, and that these 174 accounted for 444 (42.98 per cent) of the incidents. Statistically, this result is not compatible with independent membership of the different lists, and supports the suggestion that a minority cause a disproportionate amount of the reported difficulties in dispersal prisons.

In order to see which lists were most likely to contain inmates included on other lists, Table 14.3 was constructed. This shows for each list the number of men who appear on that list only. The list from P3 Division and the Disciplinary Transfers (CI 10/1974s) contained the highest proportion of repeaters, with all eight of the P3 inmates appearing on other lists, and 76 per cent of the Disciplinary Transfers (CI 10/1974s) doing so. The very low proportion (24 per cent) of repeated names from the 'continuous GOAD list' perhaps needs the comment that men who are in continuous segregation would have considerably less opportunity to be involved in disruptive behaviour and are therefore less likely than men not segregated to appear on other lists.

Table 14.3   Numbers of inmates who appeared in only one list (study I)

Source	Total in list	No. who appear on that list only	%
'Dangerously disruptive' (governors' lists)	338	234	69.23
Disciplinary transfers (CI 10/1974)	115	28	24.35
Security summaries	207	114	55.07
P3 list	8	0	0.00
GOAD (six months continuously)	97	74	76.29
GOAD (twice or more in one year)	268	158	58.96

Major characteristics of the control problems (study II)

Discovering the characteristics most directly related to 'difficulty' from these results seemed to suggest a strategy of concentrating on movement between prisons, where that movement was unambiguously related to bad behaviour. This was done by taking all those who were permanently transferred from a dispersal prison, during the period 1 January 1983 to 30 June 1984 inclusive, following either at least 30 days under Rule 43 (GOAD), or temporary transfer for segregation under CI 10/1974. This produced 65 prisoners, of whom ten occurred on both lists. Using the existing database for the current dispersal system, it was possible to compare this group with a randomly-selected comparison group of similar size, who were also contemporaries of the problem group. The most salient results of the comparison are shown in Table 14.4. What these results suggest is that although there was no absolute distinction between the most difficult prisoners and the rest, there were nevertheless reasonable grounds for supposing that a significant minority of notably difficult prisoners existed, and that they could be identified (though not without some arbitrary decisions about criteria) using conventional measures. A more formal development of this line of enquiry was initiated in 1985.

Table 14.4   *Comparing control problems with other dispersal prisoners (study II)*

	Control problem group (%)	Comparison group (%)
Category A	49.0	16.1
Life sentence	46.0	33.0
20+ governors reports	83.0	18.3
Violence to staff	61.5	13.4
Violence to prisoners	44.5	15.9
Rule 43 (GOAD) this sentence	89.2	14.7
	($n = 65$)	($n = 65$)

Control problems identified in 1985 (study III)

In 1985 the names of potential candidates for special units for control problems were sought from the major potential sources of referral to such units, especially: the current governors of the eight dispersal prisons; the section in Prison Department headquarters responsible for the allocation and management of prisoners having Category A status (the Category A Section); and the section in Prison Department headquarters responsible for the allocation and management of life-sentence prisoners (which excludes Category A lifers) (the Lifer Section). In addition, the AOPU file of movement and segregation within the dispersal system was used to provide the names of those who met the criteria set out above in relation to Study II; and Regional Offices and two Category B training prisons were also trawled.

There were distinct limits to the degree to which the different sources could agree as to control problems. The Category A and Lifer Sections in Prison Department headquarters of course provided lists that were mutually exclusive (being different security categories: see above). There were, however, also apparent differences of definition of control problem as between personnel in headquarters and those in the field. And finally, the numbers nominated by the different sources were very different: dispersal prison governors nominated 108 (106 unique names); the Category A Section nominated 32; the Lifer Section nominated 41; the AOPU nominated 62; the Regional Offices nominated 34; and two Category B training prisons nominated 10. Thus there was a total of 287 nominations, with the total number of different prisoners nominated being 226.

Table 14.5 *The identification of the same Category A control problems by different referral sources (study III)*

Source	Number of prisoners
Governors only	22
Category A Section only	10
AOPU only	8
Region	1
Governors, Category A Section	9
Governors, AOPU	7
Governors, Region	3
Category A Section, AOPU	4
Governors, Category A Section, AOPU	7
Governors, Category A Section, Region	1
Governors, Category A Section, AOPU, Region	1
Total	73

Agreement between the different sources was analysed according to category of prisoner. For the 73 Category A prisoners nominated, the sources were distributed as set out in Table 14.5. For the Category B prisoners, the result may be summed up rather more succinctly; of the 151 names, only 12 were mentioned twice, and only one was mentioned three times. (The remaining two of the total sample of 226 were two Category C prisoners nominated by Lifer Section, of whom all other sources were by definition ignorant.) It is apparent, therefore, that although there is modest agreement as to who constitutes the Category A problem cases, there is very little agreement as to the remainder.

Initially, analysis of this group of control-problem prisoners was restricted to those nominated by the dispersal prison governors, the headquarters sections and the AOPU (a total of 170). This was because the lists produced by these four sources were exhaustive, whereas the regional offices and non-dispersal Category B training prisons were only partially represented. A random comparison sample of 175 prisoners was taken from the dispersal system database, after the control problems had been excluded. Seventeen characteristics were considered, and the basic comparisons are presented in Table 14.6. The major distinctions are obvious: the control problems are more violent (items 4, 7, 11, 12), have been deemed more dangerous (item 14), have had more trouble inside prison (items 10, 11, 13) and are more disturbed (items 16 and 17).

Table 14.6 Comparing control problems with other dispersal prisoners (study III)

Characteristic	Control problem group (%)	Comparison group (%)
1. Date of birth pre-1952	45.9	45.1
2. Serving a life sentence	51.8	27.4
3. Sentence date post-1979	56.5	84.6
4. Offence of murder/attempted murder	50.6	30.9
5. Offence of robbery	24.1	32.0
6. Previous offence of robbery	25.9	25.7
7. Previous offence of violence	60.0	49.1
8. Previous convictions >3	77.6	71.4
9. Previous custodial sentences >1	68.2	58.3
10. Governor's reports >19	51.8	7.4
11. Staff assaults >1	34.1	4.6
12. Inmate assaults >1	21.8	5.1
13. Previous prisons this sentence >2	70.6	20.6
14. Category A	40.0	8.6
15. Rule 43 (GOAD) >2 occasions	16.5	1.7
16. Any incident of self-injury	25.3	13.7
17. Previous psychiatric history	21.8	9.1
	(n = 170)	(n = 175)

The various sources were compared with respect to these same characteristics, and for the central qualities were found to be very similar. Of course, by definition some characteristics were strongly represented by one source in particular: Category A by the Category A Section; Lifers (murderers) by the Lifer Section, and GOAD by the AOPU list.

Subgroups within the control problems (study III)
In order to provide some characterisation of the different types represented within the control problems as a whole, an internal analysis was made of 127 cases from the full sample of 226 (that is, all those for whom at the time there were complete data, including the additions mentioned below). This took the form of a cluster analysis: an empirical procedure that simply sorts a heterogeneous group of individuals into a smaller number of more homogeneous subsets. The same 17 characteristics listed in Table 14.6 were used

Table 14.7 Brief descriptions of the eight clusters of control problems (study III)

1	2
Robbers	Older, long-stay murderers
Extensive criminal history	Extensive criminal history
Assaults on staff only	Assaultive
Extensive movement/segregation	Extensive segregation
High governor's reports	High psychiatric history
Category Bs	

3
Older, long-stay mixed offenders
Extensive criminal history
Assaultive
Extensive movements/segregation
Category As

4	5
Long-stay murderers	Young, recent arrivals
Medium assaultive	Mixed offences
Low criminal history	Low criminal history
High segregation/movement	High governor's reports
Medium psychiatric history	Assaultive
	High movement
	Category As

6
Recent arrivals
Mixed offences
Extensive criminal history
High psychiatric history
Category As

7	8
Young, recent arrivals	Murderers
Robbers	High movement
Extensive criminal history	Medium psychiatric history
Category Bs	Category Bs

with two alterations: life-sentence was deleted; and transfer under CI 10/1974 was added. The cluster analysis produced eight subsets of control-problem types (labelled clusters 1 to 8), which are briefly described in Table 14.7. More detailed characteristics of these clusters (on which the brief descriptions are based) are set out in Table 14.8. To understand the substantive nature of these clusters is not unproblematic. But what the procedure guarantees is that the details set out in Table 14.7 and 14.8 represent an objective set of distinctions within the total. What the analysis does seem

Table 14.8 Percentage within each cluster having particular characteristics (study III)

Characteristic	Cluster							
	1	2	3	4	5	6	7	8
Born before 1952	73	100	72	50	11	60	11	37
Sentence date post-1979	55	14	28	13	78	100	94	42
Offence of murder/ attempt	0	86	56	83	67	50	11	100
Offence of robbery	73	0	6	8	0	0	50	0
Previous offence of robbery	45	43	33	4	11	50	11	5
Previous offence of violence	77	100	89	13	56	70	67	32
Previous convictions >3	100	100	94	29	11	100	94	79
Previous custodial sentences >1	100	86	83	21	0	100	83	53
Staff assaults >1	41	57	67	38	100	20	0	0
Inmate assaults >1	0	57	50	21	11	20	0	5
Governor's reports >19	82	71	94	96	78	0	17	0
Previous prisons this sentence >2	91	57	78	58	89	10	72	79
Transferred under CI 10/1974	45	14	94	67	56	0	44	0
Rule 43 (GOAD) >2 occasions	68	86	72	83	11	10	5	11
Category A	23	43	61	67	56	70	0	16
Any incident of self-injury	9	86	6	38	22	10	5	42
Previous psychiatric history	0	86	11	21	11	60	11	32
Absolute numbers in each cluster	22	7	18	24	9	10	18	19

(*n* = 127)

to highlight is the central importance of assaultiveness, psychiatric history and security category as the elements in distinguishing different kinds of control-problem prisoners.

The July 1985 list (study IV)
The dispersal prison governors were asked to provide a second list of their control problems in July 1985, six months after the previous request. This revealed many of the practical or organisational problems of such an exercise that exist in addition to the conceptual problems. Only 54 of the original 106 nominees (from study III)

were still in the prisons which had nominated them: 12 had either been released or their release was imminent; there was ambiguity as to whether or not those accepted for transfer to a Special Hospital should still be included; and some were no longer in the dispersal system. Details of the status of the initial nominees are presented in Table 14.9.

Table 14.9 Nomination status in July 1985 of inmates nominated by governors in January 1985 (studies III and IV)

Renominated	
In original dispersal	32 (1)* [2] †
Nominated by a different dispersal	10
Nominated by original dispersal after transfer	8
Not renominated	
In original dispersal	22 (6)*
Special Hospital transfers	4
Transferred outside dispersals	15 (5)*
Transferred within dispersals	15
Total	106

Note: *Figures in parentheses represent those of the specified number subsequently released on licence or discharged.
† Figure in square brackets indicates inmates who were renominated, but scheduled for transfer to Special Hospitals.

In addition to the dispersal system governors, other sources (where appropriate) were also trawled a second time. Taken altogether, the comparatively low proportion of those renominated echoes the results of earlier (though more artificial) exercises by governors. But although the proportion is low, there is ample evidence that this reflects the organisational complexity of the phenomenon. On objective evidence the nominees of every status differ from their peers in the dispersal system. Thus the set of control problems thrown up by the two separate trawls scores significantly higher on the National Institute of Corrections (1982) control index (see Table 14.10) than does a non-problem comparison sample matched for date and length of sentence which was also held in the dispersal system (see Table 14.11). Considering the nature of the comparison group, the NIC scores discriminate very well between the various

Table 14.10 Slightly modified NIC (1982) custody (reclassification) rating scale

---

1 HISTORY OF INSTITUTIONAL VIOLENCE:
(most serious offence within last five years to be coded)

None	0
Assault not involving use of a weapon or resulting in serious injury	3
Assault involving a weapon and/or resulting in serious injury	7

Did above assault occur within last six months?

Yes	3
No	0

2 SEVERITY OF CURRENT OFFENCE:
(score the most severe of current offences)

Non-violent offences	0
Assaults (police, common)	1
GBH, AOBH	2
Robbery, wounding, rape, terrorism.	3
Murder, homicide.	4

3 PRIOR ASSAULTIVE CONVICTION HISTORY:
(score the most severe in inmate's history)

None	0
Assaults (police, common)	1
GBH, AOBH	2
Robbery, wounding, rape, terrorism.	3
Murder, homicide.	4

4 ESCAPE HISTORY:
(rate last three years of incarceration)

No escapes or attempts	−3

Escape or attempt from minimum custody, no actual or threatened violence

Over a year ago	−1
Within the last year	1

Escape or attempt from secure conditions or an escape with actual or threatened violence:

Over a year ago	5
Within the last year	7

5 NUMBER OF DISCIPLINARY REPORTS:

None in last 13–18 months	−5
None in last 7–12 months	−3
None in last 6 months	−1
One in last 6 months	0
Two or more in last 6 months	4

6 MOST SEVERE DISCIPLINARY REPORT RECEIVED (last 18 months):

None	0
Insubordination, GOAD, other non-violent reports	1
Cell-smashing, barricading, fighting, possession of weapon	2
Assaults on staff or inmates	5
Mutiny, riot, gross personal violence	7

7 PRIOR CONVICTIONS:

None	0
One	2
Two or more.	4

sets of prisoners, all of whom were currently in the dispersal system. This is particularly so for the basic contrast between the control problems (defined as anyone mentioned on either occasion) and the matched sample of dispersal prisoners who were not a control problem. The actual distribution of NIC scores for these two groups are presented in Figure 14.1 and the numbers are quite large; 203 control problems and 208 non-problem prisoners (although matched, some NIC scores are still unavailable so the numbers are not exactly equal).

Table 14.11   NIC custody (reclassification) scores for control-problem prisoners and comparison (non-problem) sample (studies III and IV)

Group	All sources			Governors only		
	No.	NIC Score Mean	S.E.	No.	NIC Score Mean	S.E.
Either occasion	203	12.5	0.60	135	13.5	0.73
Both occasions	63	14.8	1.07	41	14.2	1.40
Only first time	93	11.2	0.86	47	13.1	1.25
Only second time	47	11.9	1.22	47	13.2	1.18
Non-problem sample	208	5.4	0.46	208	5.4	0.46

(Numbers accurate to time of going to press)

Conclusion

This paper has been very much a description of work in progress, and the work is obviously continuing. We now have a well-defined sample of difficult prisoners, and a matched group of long-term inmates of the dispersal system. The information about these groups, when complete, will provide the basis for a systematic analysis of the differences between and within them. Without this information, the results of the work so far are often difficult to interpret, but some things seem to be clear: some prisoners are reliably identified as causing problems in the dispersal system, and exhibit distinctive characteristics when compared to their peers; considerable difficulties remain in their identification, and in our understanding of the nature of those difficulties; nevertheless, there is considerable evidence that it will be possible to define some objective procedure for at least the initiation of the process of identifying and dealing with the members of this difficult minority.

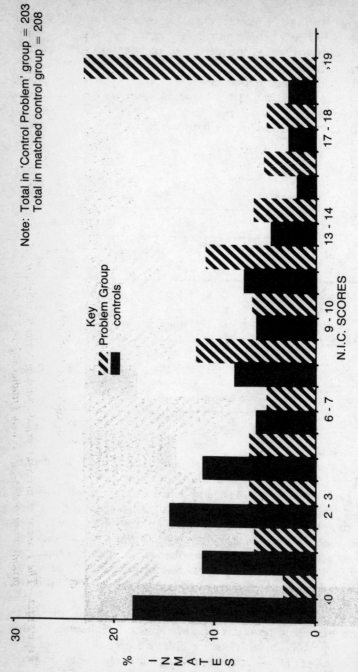

Note: Total in 'Control Problem' group = 203
Total in matched control group = 208

Key
Problem Group
controls

N.I.C. SCORES

Figure 14.1 Scores on the National Institute of Corrections (NIC) rating scale for a group of control problems and a set of matched prisoners in the dispersal system (studies III and IV).

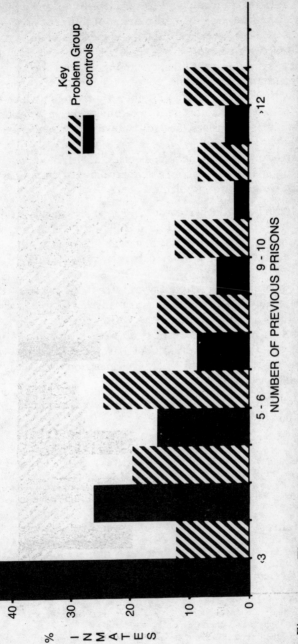

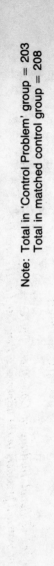

Note: Total in 'Control Problem' group = 203
Total in matched control group = 208

Key
Problem Group
controls

NUMBER OF PREVIOUS PRISONS

% I N M A T E S

50
40
30
20
10
0

‹3   5 - 6   9 - 10   ›12

Figure 14.2   The number of previous prisons this sentence for a group of control problems and a set of matched prisoners in the dispersal system (studies III and IV).

However the control problems are ultimately to be identified, it is possible to argue that a central element to any objective part of the procedure should be the number of different prisons in which the sentence has been served (taking some kind of account of length of sentence, of course). There is ample evidence that this index is a key 'symptom' of difficulty; in Figure 14.2 the same problem group and matched control group as in Figure 14.1 are compared, but this time on the basis of number of prisons in which they have been located during this sentence (obviously an inferior measure to disciplinary transfers, but still showing differences between the groups).

Apart from these empirical considerations, however, there are other arguments in favour of the importance of disciplinary transfer in identifying control problems:

(i) It can be routinely recorded and as a measure it is unambiguous;
(ii) as an index of control-difficulty, disciplinary transfer represents a central element of that difficulty in that it reflects the interaction between the particular prisoner and the particular prison;
(iii) as a process, disciplinary transfer is the natural 'emergency' treatment of control problems, arguably preferable to segregation;
(iv) as a record, the number of disciplinary transfers not only alerts us to the really difficult inmate, it also allows inspection that all the alternative locations have been tried (or what alternative locations remain before consideration for special treatment should be considered).

The collation and analysis of disciplinary transfer data is currently being pursued.[1]

Note

1   The authors wish to thank Danny Clark, Kay Nooney, Lorraine Eastwood, Ian Ray, Clare Wiggins and Alison Taylor for their invaluable contributions to this work. Special thanks are also extended to all field psychologists and psychological assistants who collected the bulk of the data summarised in this paper.

References

Home Office (1932), *Report on the Circumstances connected with the Recent Disorder at Dartmoor Convict Prison,* (Du Parcq Report), Cmd. 4010, London: HMSO.

Home Office (1977), *Report of an Inquiry by the Chief Inspector of the Prison Service into the Cause and Circumstances of the Events at H.M. Prison Hull During the Period 31st August to 3rd September, 1976,* HC 453 (Fowler Report), London: HMSO.

Home Office (1984), *Managing the Long-Term Prison System, The Report of the Control Review Committee,* London: HMSO.

National Institute of Corrections (1982), *Prison Classification: A Model Systems Approach,* Washington, DC : National Institute of Corrections.

15 Special Unit, 'C' wing, HMP Parkhurst
Susan Evershed

On the afternoon of 30 December 1985 the first inmate was received into the new Special Unit in 'C' wing, HMP Parkhurst. By 8 o'clock that evening the unit staff ended their first day of operation with a roll of three, and looking foward to more prisoners arriving. This paper sets out to examine the new Unit in terms of its role within the system, the staff involved, the inmate population, and the Unit regime. It will describe the Unit as it is currently, it will look at the problems already arising, and it will briefly describe some proposals for developing the Unit further.

Background
The reopening of the new Unit came about as a direct result of the Control Review Committee's report (Home Office 1984). In their report the Committee noted that there was in the system a group of prisoners who represented serious control problems for prison management, and that the facilities for dealing with such persistently disruptive prisoners were inadequate. The report outlined a variety of recommendations, but one of the most far-reaching was to establish a number of special small units, operating a variety of regimes, to house such prisoners and so provide relief for the long-term prisons (Home Office 1984, paras 51–6).

A second recommendation advocated the reopening of the old 'C' wing at Parkhurst Prison, as the first of these small units. The old 'C' wing regime had been discontinued in 1979 (in order to accommodate prisoners from the main prison following a disturbance), and the CRC report recommended that the new unit should operate along similar lines to the original (Home Office 1984, paras. 60–2).

Another facility for certain kinds of highly disturbed prisoners was provided in the therapeutic unit in C wing at Parkhurst Prison... This unit provided a kind of halfway house, between normal prison location and the prison hospital... The basic aim of the unit was to devise a constructive way of managing these prisoners so that they could achieve an optimum level of behaviour consistent with their make-up ... We therefore recommend that every effort should be made to re-establish such a facility as soon as possible.

At Head Office a Control Review Committee Implementation Team was set up within P3 Division of the Prison Department to take forward a number of CRC recommendations, including the opening of the new special units. In November 1984 a Governor IV was posted to Parkhurst Prison and given the task of opening the new unit by the end of 1985. In the style of the old 'C' wing, he was to work with a multidisciplinary management team consisting of a medical officer, a senior psychologist, and a hospital chief officer. The development of the unit was to be overseen by the Principal Medical Officer at Parkhurst Prison Hospital, who had also been involved in the previous 'C' wing.

Aims and objectives

One of the first tasks to be undertaken by these two groups was to agree upon a set of aims for the unit and to outline its objectives. One of the aims clearly had to reflect the recommendation of the Control Review Committee that the unit should help relieve the long-term prison system of prisoners who presented a problem of control. At the same time the new unit was to be based upon the old 'C' wing, and thus the aims had to indicate the unit's specialist function. After much debate, four main aims were identified: to provide a national resource for the management of certain types of disruptive and disturbed prisoners who are at present contained largely in the dispersal system; to achieve a constructive way of managing such prisoners within a discrete unit by individualising the management of inmates, and by encouraging a high degree of staff involvement; to facilitate observation of inmate behaviour in order that early signs of impending crisis could be identified, and preventive or remedial action taken; and to encourage attitude changes and improvements in the mental state, behaviour and social skills of the inmates. These four aims were expanded to form 13 statements about the unit, loosely termed 'objectives', which set out to describe in more detail the role, management and regime of the unit:

1 Referrals to 'C' wing will be considered from all dispersal and Category B establishments, giving priority to dispersal prisons.
2 The inmate population will comprise prisoners who are currently

presenting and have persistently presented at more than one establishment one or more of the following behaviours in an uncon-
trolled fashion:

2.1 Violence towards staff and/or prisoners;

2.2 Repeated offences against discipline;

2.3 Damage to property within institutions;

2.4 Behaviour that generally and persistently gives cause for
concern including behaviour that is dangerous to self and others;
and who have a history or who present symptoms of mental
abnormality.

3 The balance of behavioural problems exhibited by the inmates
in the unit will be monitored and maintained with a view to
reducing the possibility of disturbances, that is, the emphasis
to be on behaviour in the group situation as well as individual
behaviour within the unit.

4 Immediate responsibility for the management, monitoring and
treatment of each inmate will be undertaken by his designated
supervising uniformed officer.

5 Hospital, discipline and specialist staff will be integrated in
the day-to-day management of the Unit.

6 Emphasis will be placed on the training and support of staff
in whatever skills are considered necessary and appropriate.

7 Weekly case conferences and Unit meetings will be established
and held to provide stimulus and support, and to allow for
adequate communication amongst staff. Every prisoner will be
reviewed intially at least once every six months — this time-scale
to be reviewed if required.

8 The regime will be designed to reduce tension within the unit
to the lowest possible level.

9 Staff will observe and record the behaviour and attitude, and
changes in behaviour and attitude, of prisoners and the possible
consequences of such behaviour or changes.

10 When warning signals are identified staff will react in a manner
appropriate to the individual prisoner and his situation with the
aim of reducing possible crises.

11 Staff will attempt to reduce the level of unacceptable behaviour
in prisoners by employing their skills as prison officers.

12 All resources — medical, psychiatric, educational, social,
behavioural, and so on — to form part of the overall treatment
programme available for the inmates in the Unit.

13 Prisoners will be regularly reviewed with a view to assessment
of their progress and needs, and consideration will be given to
whether it is more appropriate for them to stay where they are
or to be transferred elsewhere.

Each of the 13 objectives deals with particular aspects of the Unit, the details of which will be enlarged upon in the remainder of this paper. The first two identify the types of prisoner for which the Unit has been designed.

Inmate population

The Unit was set up to take prisoners who persistently cause disruption within the long-term prison system, and who have shown signs of mental abnormality at some time. They should have displayed similarly violent or disruptive behaviour at a number of establishments, so that the likelihood of their settling in a normal prison regime is limited. (The specific types of behaviour concerned are outlined in the objectives.) The Unit is therapeutically orientated and as such is intended to help inmates whose behaviour appears not to have rational motivation. Such men are referred to the Unit by their governors, giving details of the specific problem behaviours, and the results of any efforts to control them. A variety of reports from wing officers, managers and specialists are also required including a description of any medical treatment administered. Thus, whilst the process of referring an inmate is time-consuming for the holding establishment, it does allow a great deal of information to be made available to the Selection Committee, and subsequently to the staff on the Unit, should the referral be successful. All inmates held in dispersal prisons and Category B establishments, including training prisons and local prisons, may be referred.

The Selection Committee consists of representatives of the CRC Implementation Team, the Unit Management Team and the Directorate of Prison Medical Services, the Directorate of Psychological Services and those at headquarters who have responsibility for the allocation and career management of life-sentence and Category A prisoners. The Committee selects those inmates most appropriate for the Unit, giving priority to those held in the dispersal prisons, and those serving more than a five-year sentence. At the same time the population of inmates already held on the Unit is taken into account in order that control within the Unit will not be completely upset by selecting a very disturbed or disruptive prisoner at a difficult time.

From initial enquiries during the planning stages of the Unit there seemed to be a sufficient number of inmates to require two such units. Eighteen inmates have so far been referred to the Committee for consideration, and of these 12 were selected, three have since been transferred to Special Hospitals, one was withdrawn for a longer trial at the referring prison, and two were considered not to meet the admission criteria.

The unit was designed to hold a maximum of 35 prisoners but a temporary maximum roll of 18 has been determined until June 1986, when the staff–inmate ratio will be reviewed in the light of the experiences of the first six months of opening. It was decided that the number of inmates on the unit should be allowed to build up gradually so that the regime and routines might become well established. At the present time in the third month of operation, there are 11 prisoners in the Unit, all from either the Hospital or Segregation Units of dispersal prisons or Category B establishments. Seven of them are Category A prisoners; a different seven are serving life sentences, and of the remaining four, three are serving sentences of over ten years. They have already spent between three and 16 years in prison on their current sentences, and as a group they have committed over 350 offences against discipline this sentence; eight of them have more than one report for violence on staff; eight have repeated offences for violence to inmates and for damaging prison property. Two men have mutilated themselves repeatedly, and seven of them have spent time in Special Hospitals. Thus far there have been no serious incidents at all in the Unit.

Unit regime

In general the Unit aims to provide a relaxed and safe environment where prisoners who have probably spent a great deal of time segregated from other prisoners can associate more freely with their peers. At the same time it is hoped that their attitudes to prison, prison staff and other inmates might change, and as a result, their institutional behaviour improve. Given the nature of the inmate population, it was felt that, in order to maintain a safe environment in a way that maximised the inmates' freedom to associate, the very strict monitoring of prisoners was essential. The officers need to know the inmates very well; the problems they were likely to cause; the situations in which they were likely to become difficult and how best to prevent or cope with the problem behaviour to maintain calm. For this reason a 'personal officer' scheme was introduced, overseen by the Unit's probation officer. Every inmate arriving in the new Unit is assigned to a personal officer (and a deputy officer working opposite shifts to the personal officer). It is the responsibility of the personal officer to develop a close knowledge of his inmate, to monitor and record his misbehaviour and his progress, and to build up a relationship with him. The personal officer is the inmate's representative and his first point of contact with the Unit; nothing should happen to him without the officer's knowledge (unless in an emergency). Thus none of the specialist staff should see the inmate without alerting the officer, and the content of all interviews should be fed back to him.

In fact the Unit operates its own documentation system, the mainstay of which are the Unit case files. These are separate from the inmate's prison record and contain a precise and detailed account of the inmate's life on the Unit. All Unit staff have access to the case files, and all may contribute to them. Again, the personal officer is responsible for the case file of his inmate, ensuring that adequate reports are made, and that any information of significance is properly communicated to the relevant Unit staff.

The inmate's first ten weeks on the Unit are treated as an 'assessment' period. During this time his personal officer and all of the specialists will assess his needs, his interests, his strengths and his weaknesses. At the end of the period a meeting is held of all concerned (including where possible the inmate himself) to draw up an individual 'training plan' for the prisoner. This document will set out his activities and provide him with a set of targets (based upon the results of the assessment) for the following 15 weeks. The activities and targets may relate to a variety of areas — educational, behavioural, social — depending upon his needs. Every 15 weeks thereafter his progress will be reviewed, and amendments made to the training programme as appropriate. The ultimate aim of this process is to help the inmate to change sufficiently to be able to cope in normal location in another establishment. The end result of this system is that every inmate has his own individual plan co-ordinated and supervised by his personal officer.

Four of the stated Unit objectives relate to the Unit policy for dealing with inmates' disruptive behaviour. The general ethos within the Unit is one of non-confrontation. Staff are encouraged to use their interpersonal skills in dealing with such antagonistic behaviour as verbal abuse; to use the discipline system as a last resort; and to employ their skills to prevent difficult situations arising. The detailed monitoring of inmate behaviour is crucial to this policy, as is the quality of the relationship between the inmates and their personal officers. Thus far on the Unit there have been two clear incidents which under normal circumstances would probably have escalated into violence, but which were defused by staff ignorinig the incident and later calming the inmate in question. At the same time the inmates are encouraged to talk through with staff issues that concern them, and they may ask, if they feel the need, to be locked in their cells. The Unit also has four 'quiet cells' on its ground floor where inmates may be located temporarily if they so request. The cells may also be used to remove inmates from the other prisoners if their behaviour is so disruptive that it threatens the stability of the Unit (for example, if an inmate is causing a disturbance by smashing the furniture). Both of these uses for the quiet cells are foreseen as short-term measures only. As soon as the inmate appears to have calmed down he will be encouraged to return to his normal routine. For longer-term measures the Unit is able to make use of Parkhurst's Segregation Unit, and in cases where the disruptive behaviour is seen to be the result of a psychiatric condition, the inmates can be placed in Parkhurst's hospital wing.

Facilities

The Unit itself is very spacious; although it was designed to hold only 36 inmates there are almost twice as many cells on the living areas, the first and second landings. At the present time, with only six inmates, the second landing is unused and will probably remain so as long as the maximum inmate population remains at 18. The extra space in the Unit was felt to be important to counteract he effects of containment within such a small unit with a small and fairly static population (in terms of both inmates and staff). Access to other parts of Parkhurst Prison is extremely limited for the inmates, since the Unit is for the most part self-contained. Figure 15.1 shows a plan of the ground floor of the Unit and illustrates the fact that the Unit has workshop and gymnasium facilities of its own. Both education and religious activities are conducted in the Unit itself, and there is an exercise yard just outside the Unit used by 'C' wing alone. The inmates are able to make use of some Parkhurst facilities, however — they have access to the main gymnasium for three one-hour periods a week; they can use the main prison library and canteen facilities at specific times, and their visits from family and friends take place in Parkhurst's visits room. The aim remains, however, to keep the Unit separate from the main prison as far as possible — a discrete prison within a prison, where it is possible to encourage the breakdown of hostile attitudes towards prison staff.

The inmates are encouraged to spend as much time as possible out of their cells, mixing with both staff and other inmates. It was felt that the majority of inmates referred to the Unit would have offences for violence against staff and inmates, and they would have problems in mixing with others. If any improvements were to be made the inmates must be encouraged to associate with both groups; to be allowed to develop more social behaviour.

At the same time it is seen as important from a control aspect to encourage the inmates out of their cells. The more time an inmate spends in his cell, alone, the less opportunity is afforded to the

Figure 15.1. Ground floor plan: Special Unit, 'C' wing, Parkhurst.

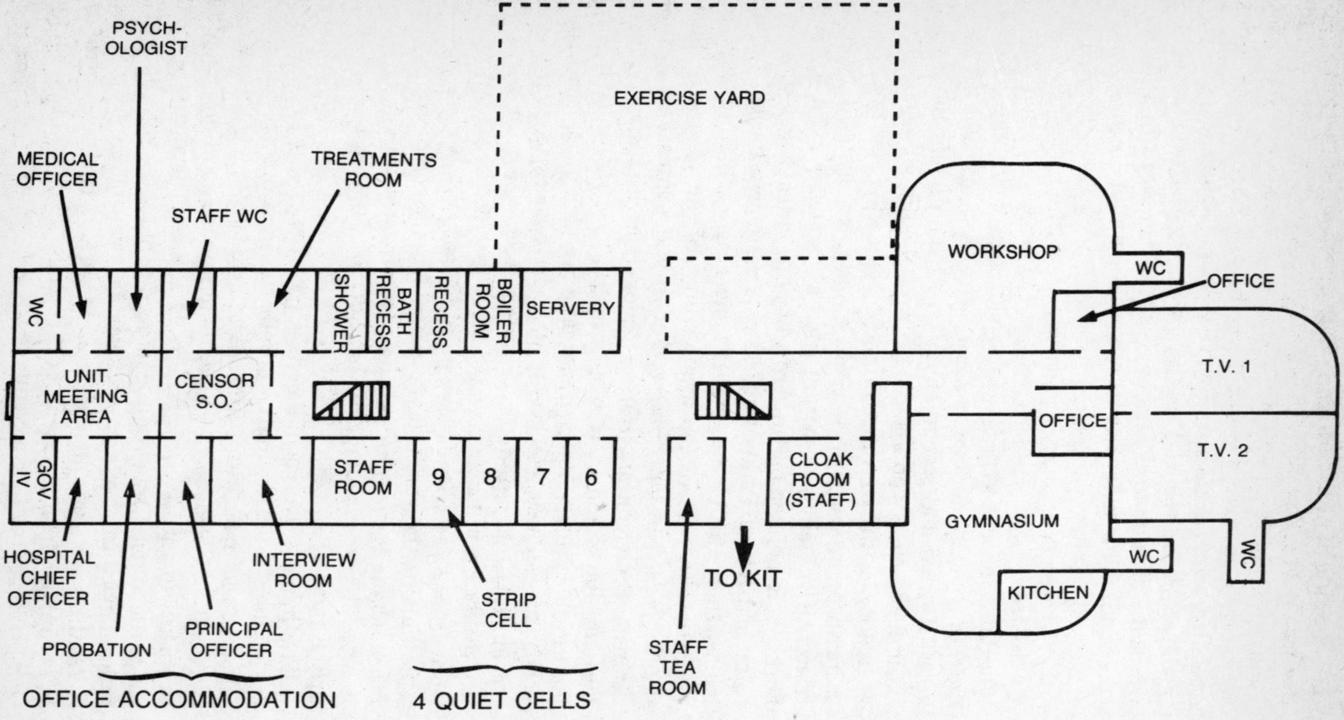

staff to get to know him and to learn how he reacts to specific situations.

The workshop currently provides only one activity — the manufacture of wooden toys and furniture for a local charity organisation concerned with mentally and physically handicapped children. So far the work has proved popular with the six inmates, but it is hoped in the near future to extend the range of activities beyond woodwork. The emphasis is on the inmates making up items individually or in small groups according to their level of skill rather than employing a 'conveyor belt' style of working.

The educational facilities of the Unit are wide-ranging. Currently one of the inmates is working for an O level in German, one is studying Greek mythology, and a third is doing a course in remedial English. Physical education has proved particularly popular with two of the inmates, who are developing an interest in weight-training. The Unit gymnasium is currently equipped with a table tennis table, a punchbag and some mats, with a 'multigym' arriving in the near future. Apart from the skills of the specialist PE instructor the inmates are encouraged to make use of the enthusiasm of the staff who regularly take part in physical education activities with prisoners, having completed a one-week 'sports and games' course.

In line with the relaxed atmosphere in the Unit, the prisoners are able to decline all Unit activities, including work. In normal circumstances an inmate would incur a disciplinary report if he refused to work but on 'C' wing this does not happen. However, if he declines all of the activities on offer he must be locked in his cell. The regime in the Unit does not allow the inmates to associate in their cells at any time, nor to move unsupervised around the Unit. In the old 'C' wing there were a large number of incidents involving inmates taking hostages, and it was felt that limiting the ability to congregate in cells might reduce this danger. As a consequence of this, an inmate can either take part in whatever activities are in process, or he must be locked up. For most of the time there is more than one activity going on since education, physical education and interviews with staff all take place during workshop hours. However, the amount of time spent on education, PE and interviews for each inmate is limited, so that in reality if a man chooses not to work it is likely that his only alternative is to be locked up in his cell. The exercise period in particular is problematic in this respect, being so staff-intensive an activity. For the present, during the statutory hour's exercise period, all other activities must cease, and those inmates who decline exercise must be locked up. The Unit management is currently looking for a solution to this situation.

Staffing

The Unit's staff consists of a team of 18 basic-grade officers, two senior officers and two principal officers, the management team and a number of specialists including a probation officer and a teacher. Other specialists (the chaplain, a PE instructor and a second teacher) from the main prison provide additional help. All of the basic-grade staff had previously worked in Parkhurst Prison, and applied to work in the new Unit. The role of these staff in the Unit's regime was seen to be central to its success, both in terms of inmate welfare and inmate control. Thus great care was taken in their selection from over 50 applicants. The selection process took account of their skills and previous experiences, their attitudes to the proposed personal officer scheme, their motivation for wishing to work in the Unit and their ability to communicate effectively during the interview. Twenty-four officers were subsequently successful, six of whom will continue to work in the main prison until vacancies arise in the Unit. The SOs and POs in the Unit were detailed into 'C' wing on a two-year fixed post by the Chief Officer in the main prison in consultation with the Governor IV in charge of the Unit.

success of the Unit, especially with respect to the personal officer scheme. The regime was intended to differ significantly from the regime in a normal prison, and it would be almost impossible for an officer to work effectively in the Unit unless he was accustomed to it. Thus it was proposed that, except in the case of an emergency or at night, no members of staff other than designated 'C' wing staff would work in the Unit. Unfortunately, problems have already arisen in this area. It has recently been suggested, for example, the Unit staff should be available for the less-popular duty of staffing the main prison's control room, which would entail them leaving the Unit for a full year. It has also been suggested that main prison SOs and POs should substitute when both of the two 'C' wing SOs and POs are off duty on the same shift.

Future developments

There are many ideas to develop the Unit but there are two main areas under consideration. The first of these is to do with a proposed scheme for paying inmates. In a normal prison wing, they would be expected to work full-time in order to achieve a maximum rate; they would lose money for non-attendance, and they would be punished for actual refusal to work. On this Unit the inmates may choose to exempt themselves from the daily activities, including work, and still receive a basic level of pay. Thus the Unit offers less financial incentive to work. One way of dealing with this problem in the longer term might be to restructure the system of inmate wages. For example, one might allow every inmate to earn a standard minimum rate of pay regardless of his behaviour, but with the opportunity of earning bonuses for every half-day he participates in Unit activities. The amount of bonus offered to each inmate for each half-day session could be contingent upon his level of effort and the quality and quantity of his work. A possible feature of such a scheme would be to link pay to the inmate's participation in Unit activities (in accordance with his individual training plan) rather than to work alone. Thus, if a particular inmate requires (and is happy to undertake) remedial PE or work with another of the specialists, then his attendance at these sessions could be rewarded.

Along similar lines the Unit might in the longer term consider how privileges could be linked more explicitly to appropriate Unit behaviour (and this might entail extending the privileges currently available).

For the most part, however, the immediate aims of the Unit must be to consolidate its regime and daily routines, and to build up its inmate population. At the time of writing the new 'C' wing is approaching the end of its eleventh week of operation, and so it is too early to make any evaluation of its success. However, the initial signs are hopeful in that it does appear to be taking prisoners who fit the criteria, and is managing them effectively.

Reference

Home Office (1984), *Managing the Long-Term Prison System: The Report of the Control Review Committee*, London: HMSO.

The probation officer and long-term
prisoners
John Coker

The probation officer is part of the theatre of prison operations,
therefore we must first consider those features which determine the
probation officer's contribution. The prison is a powerful organisation, efficient, stable, with an intricate criss-cross structure and
a simple set of custodial aims. It is managed centrally by the Home
Office. The probation service is comprised of 56 different county
areas and nearly 6,000 officers, about one-fifth of the personnel
of the prison service. The probation service has a reputation for
helping criminals, but its aims are diverse and based only on a
generalised liberal 'treatment' stance. It has little universally agreed
knowledge and, perforce, fits into the prison system.

Prison, as is well known from the popularisation of Goffman's
(1961) deliverance, *Asylums*, is, for its inmates, an almost totally
encasing system that deprives and constrains individuality and
personal freedom. Its manifestations are faithfully represented in
the grey, harsh dominance of its high, unyielding stone boundary
walls which denote it as 'a life such as is lived nowhere else'. Prison,
it seems, is an environment in which the common humanity of staff
and inmates struggles to survive. Benevolence needs to do more
than shout to be heard above the metallic overtones of the machinery
of security. Prison officers are misrepresented by the term 'screws',
just as nurses are by the term 'angels'. Prison officers find their
finer qualities suppressed by the demands of their image, their jobs,
their environment and a popularly held, 'somewhat exaggerated view
of convicts which suggests that they are uneasily expecting to be
attacked by any one of them ... without warning' (Dostoevsky 1983,
p. 61). Nurses, on the other hand, may be equally institutionalised
but their standing and a general fear of death develop images and
attitudes that are as essentially crustaceous as those of the prison
officer. For the prison officer, opportunities to show compassion
are circumscribed, not least by the separation of the welfare task
and the appointment to it of probation officers who often have degrees. This is a pernicious and unnatural, though administratively

convenient, division of duties and opportunities which denies the custodian of his just recognition as a whole person. The Control Review Committee (Home Office 1984) emphasises that prisons depend on good staff–prisoner relationships, understanding and generosity of spirit; but prison is essentially punitive, it restricts individual freedom and deprives most prisoners of their dignity and the comforts to which they have become accustomed, not least — for the heterosexual — female company and companionship.

These burdens are experienced individually rather than collectively, and with varying degrees of acceptance, resentment or anger both by prisoners and staff. Experiences and responses are personalised even if it is convenient to classify them for the sake of comprehension. Dostoevsky (1983, p. 59) himself a lifer, pointed to 'the inequality consequent in punishment' by imprisonment, for one man it is ' . . . a gay life, . . . a happy collection of bold spirits . . .' for another 'the pain in his own heart is alone enough to kill him with its agonies before any punishment begins', For prisoners, though, there is an inescapable permanence and omnipresence of the institution of punishment; the staff cross the frontier and go home daily to the outside world, the prisoner is captive.

However, in spite of this generally repressive, depressing milieu, there is a constant reforming humanitarian zeal at all levels in the prison service that slowly moves the balance towards improving the prisoner's life and chances on release. This is particularly noticeable with prisoners serving long-term and life sentences; the pressing need to consider the management of long-term 'disruptive' and 'dangerous' prisoners gives a fillip both to reform and repression alike.

The prison officer's part is determined by the essentially punishing and vengeful nature of imprisonment, but he can mitigate or exacerbate consequences for the individual prisoner. The seconded probation officer finds himself in a similar strait-jacket with the additional constraint that the prison officers' trade union believes that the welfare task should be undertaken by prison officers.

Probation officers, by their calling and 'treatment' approach, support the liberal improving cause as they see it, though it has little if any reference to the prisoners' views. Generally — for there are notable exceptions — the probation officers' contribution and ability to influence the prison organisation is limited by their position as 'outsiders', their lack of power and forcefulness, their deferential attitudes to the prison officer, and their uneasy acceptance of their prison role.

These constraints are now examined further in the light of recent developments in ideas about crime and punishment, or as Dostoevsky (1983, p. 59) puts it, 'attempts to square the circle'.

Recent influences

This is more a glance over the shoulder at some of the main features of the past 25 years than a careful, critical historical review of the probation service's involvement in the prison system and with long-term prisoners on licence from prison.

Until some 20 years ago, the main work of the probation service was as officers of the court, providing reports in selected 'deserving' cases and supervising on probation those people — mostly first offenders — chosen by the courts. There was some acquaintance with prisons and borstals through the supervision of such categories as preventive detainees, young prisoners and borstal licensees. However, it was not a significant part of the caseload, and it was dealt with in the same way as probation supervision, though it was generally given a lesser status and priority. Then, attention was given to some of the effects of imprisonment and the problems of release, particularly for homeless men and women leaving prison. Many kindly beliefs arose, after-care hostels were opened. NACRO was formed and the probation service, as a well-organised, experienced and skilled group of personnel, was given the duty of providing appropriate numbers of welfare staff in each prison, on secondment.

People who have become probation officers have chosen a non-institutional organisation where they can work with considerable personal freedom and autonomy and unaccountability — in a treatment-dominated style with individual people in a 'one-to-one' relationship. Not many probation officers, therefore, wanted to work in prisons in spite of the inducements of more regular hours, travelling allowances and the opportunity to do social work with the most deprived category of criminals. Prison work has attracted many skilled and dedicated officers, but equally it is regarded as a 'siding' into which officers may be shunted for one purpose or another; the management of the probation service has failed to accord parity of status to prison work.

The prison service has responded to, or reflected more readily and quickly, the relegation of the 'treatment' model than has the probation service. Indeed, it is hardly surprising that the therapeutic notion is around in a service that grew out of a desire to help the individual, nor that it makes a place for itself, somewhat incongruously, in the probation officer's work in prisons.

The stroke of the pen that wrote the probation service into prisons also assigned it responsibilities for voluntary after-care and supervision of parole licensees. In the prison the service was to take part in a range of administrative procedures and to be the focal point of social work and after-care; it was to link, naturally, the inside, rehabilitative control task with outside assistance and oversight. All these functions were to be carried out according to guidelines issued by the Home Office, which always recognises the political sensitivity of serious crimes committed by those in its custody; witness the consequences of the escapes of Blake and, to a lesser extent, Mitchell and Biggs. A further important development during the period was the abolition of the dealth penalty; both services had to cope with growing numbers of long-term prisoners.

Furthermore, the probation service's traditional, individually based, sometimes idiosyncratic practices have been affected by two powerful coincidental forces. Firstly, in the 1970s, the probation service increased its manpower by approximately 90 per cent, but its workload grew by roughly only 8 per cent. Simultaneously, the use of the probation order as a disposal had been declining in all courts. Secondly, the probation service has become embroiled in attempts to reduce the prison population by providing alternative sentences for the courts to use instead of sentencing people to immediate imprisonment.

Additionally, disillusionment with the explanation of crime as personal pathology requiring individual treatment braced other arguments for change. So the probation service offered the 'beefed-up' probation order. This stronger order, with its 'package', rather than personal, basis had been intimated by Chief Probation Officers' Conference but opposed by the probation officers' union. This approach to, or some would say revitalisation of, the probation order was given an official governmental fillip in the Criminal Justice Act, 1982, schedule 11, which empowered courts to make restriction or activity conditions in probation orders. National statistics on these new conditions are not available, but both probation and immediate imprisonment have enjoyed an increased usage in the last five years.

Concurrently, with all these pressures and changes, the probation service itself is divided on whether it should be working in prisons at all. Chief probation officers believe it should continue to second officers (471 were seconded to prisons in 1983), but the National Association of Probation Officers takes the opposite view. At the same time as the prison service is promoting greater involvement of prison officers in the welfare task, the probation service is coming to grips with more central Home Office control of its work. The probation officer is no longer solely an officer of the court, about a third of his caseload now derives from prisons. Furthermore, there is a continuing, but subtle emphasis away from individually determined help to processes which emphasise social control.

The probation service cannot isolate itself from the labile society of which it forms a part, especially since that society pays its wages, but it is not surprising if some critics have said the service has a crisis of confidence. On the other hand, the probation service has the deep-rooted hallmarks of stability and justice, assistance to and supervision of individuals, internal soul-searching and professional humility that have always characterised it. The service's view of the prisoner is shaped to some extent by the influences we have just considered; we now explore it further.

Probation officers and prisoners

If the probation officer's duty is partly to help the prisoner, then the prisoner's opinions must be incorporated for any personal process to succeed, but the prisoner's views are generally excluded. The importance of including the prisoner's ideas is highlighted by several recent 'consumer' investigations, including my own study of released lifers (Coker and Martin 1985). In short, 'client' studies reveal divergence and not congruence between probation officer and licensee, social worker and client, in matters central to the purposes of oversight and assistance. This fundamental problem is set aside for the moment, but it is considered more fully later.

The intangible, complex structures of the prison culture are as important as the visible features; what we think of prisoners affects the way we treat them and how they respond to us. Systems depend on categorisation, they cannot integrate completely the view that 'every different personality means a different crime ... it is impossible to reconcile or smooth over these differences, that it is by its very nature an insoluble problem, like squaring the circle' (Dostoevsky 1983, p. 59). Institutions subsume individual differences into categories. However, administrative utility is not to be underrated for it promotes an accommodation of staff and prisoners in a roughly balanced, tolerable, but tense, configuration of forces. Prisons need their prisoner-classifications for they are both administratively useful and reassuring to staff even though they try to square the circle of human nature and personal distinctiveness. Many overlapping sometimes conflicting, common classifications impinge on the probation officer's views of the prisoners he is trying to help; we may consider some before turning to the perceptions of the probation officer.

Firstly, there is Mountbatten's (Home Office 1966) predominant assignment of prisoners into security categories ranging from Category A to Category D. This comprehensive classification is a device for sorting prisoners into different prisons and regimes. It is based essentially on security needs and the criminality and past record of the prisoner. It is a simple, popular classification device, but not without the disadvantages of labelling. Security is paramount even though it may impede the welfare task. Cutting across the security classifications are, *inter alia,* descriptions of prisoners according to common characteristics such as age, intelligence, social class, employment and marital status. These indicate that the 'average prisoner' (a misleading term) is probably a young adult male, unemployed or in labouring or unskilled work, single and with a tenuous marital or family link and a fifty-fifty chance of having drunk too much around the time of the offence; he (for women prisoners have always been in the minority) is generally also a petty recidivist: 'poor material', as he was described, wrongly, in the reports of prison officials in the earlier part of this century. His prospects generally are depressing, but little different from other groups of poor people. Some observers have offered further groupings. Psychiatrists, for example, have found that minor psychiatric conditions are common; yet others think — mistakenly, I believe — that prisoners have only a limited capacity for personal relationships and a general inadequacy. Additionally, many prisoners may be classified as having unhelpful or fragile social systems. Furthermore there are also vague moral condemnatory designations expressed by all and sundry, but especially 'spokesmen'.

In yet other typologies, prisoners may be divided according to length of sentence, that is, more or less than five years; they may also be typified as psychopathic, dangerous or disruptive or both, and these conditions may be defined additionally as permanent, intermittent, transitory or occasional responses to particular stimuli, or condemned as pathological conditions. If there could be certainty about the predictive value of these identifications and we could be sure that they were mainly pathological, or mainly responses to institutional processes, it would be of some value in managing and providing for long-term prisoners. We cannot do this, for experience tells us that no such certainty can ever exist. Indeed it cannot be demonstrated that there is a reasonable probability that people will behave in all situations in the way suggested by these stigmas. However, because of the nature of imprisonment and the political pressures on the system, doubt about future conduct must be resolved in favour of institutional stability and individual safety. The prison must, on behalf of society, contain and provide for those who are usually unwelcome in other institutions and who range from fanatical terrorists to itinerants seeking refuge. Prison's position as a universal Aunt Sally eclipses the dexterity with which its staff (and prisoners) resolve these competing demands.

The serviceability of such classifications to institutional stability is apparent in their ubiquity; but they deny the untidiness, integrity, variety and sacredness of individuality. They do not square the circle, they may depress it.

The generalised assorting of prisoners into formal but changing categories is used, too, in their education and reformation. Programmes are provided for their edification and they are based on assumptions which, in the main, can be fulfilled in a collective, mass way (Open University qualifications and private study are promising exceptions). Currently, social skills training — possibly to be displaced by 'offending behaviour' training — may have considerable appeal for staff who want to help (but who feel an inner bewilderment and impotence). However, there is no evidence that I know to show that these programmes do much more than relieve some of the monotony of prisoners' lives. On the other hand, group provision imposed according to the 'treatment' ideal seriously diverts efforts from the sensitive appreciation and alleviation of individual discomforts which the probation officer, by calling, training and experience, might offer.

Finally, but possibly most importantly, classifications have failed to note the prisoner's capacity for survival. Coping with imprisonment requires adaptability, social competence, cunning and self-control. These personal qualities are largely ignored because of popular professional images of the criminal. He is regarded as inadequate and in need of treatment rather than practical assistance and the restoration of personal dignity.

We may seem to have taken a circuitous route to the probation officer's perceptions and potential, but the navigator cannot just draw a straight line across the chart to his destination; to arrive safely in the right place he must consider many things — crew, equipment, weather, other people and so on, and so it is with our subject.

Generally probation officers want to work in a non-institutional environment where they have freedom to work individually with people whom they wish to advise, assist and befriend, as well as oversee and urge in the general direction of society's mores. However, probation officers are people and they have personal likes and dislikes which colour their attitudes and behaviour towards other people (called offenders) for and to whom they have a responsibility. Some people they like and want to help; others they do not like and therefore officers have to resolve this dilemma to accommodate the broad ideal that 'the probation officer is there to help you' if he can. However, in case this analysis of the reality of the situation seems cynically depreciative of the probation officer, let me add that most people join the service with a desire to be helpful to people who have been convicted of a crime, who need assistance and who appear to be able to appreciate it. These common desires — which sit with all the other requirements of the job — have been cultivated in the probation service milieu. They are not easily transplanted into the prison environment. The seconded probation officer himself has to adjust to unfamiliar and different ways of working in a regulated, disciplined environment. This is not easy because his perceptions, attitudes and nescience derive from his personality, training and work outside the prison with people in a relatively unstructured way. As he makes his adjustments and concessions to the prison's regime, the probation officer will try to integrate his understanding of people, derived from the patronising medical model, his own common sense, personality, training, experience and work outside prison with relatively free people. It is as likely as not that the seconded probation officer will expect the average prisoner to be inadequate, mixed-up, disadvantaged and more or less disenfranchised in a class-based and inequitable society.

These generalisations are similar to sociological taxonomies, but the probation officer will assert his particular professonalism by trying to see and treat the prisoner as a caged person to be liberated. Many do this by using common titles when addressing prisoners; 'Good morning Mr (Ms, Miss, Mrs) Smith' may symbolise respect for the individual, but it sounds discordant in prison.

The seconded probation officer's attempts to recognise the prisoners' distinctive needs, family links and social systems cut across other classifications. Furthermore, probation officers do not recognise, fully, the prisoner's capacity to adapt to the prison culture, the necessity to do so, nor their own collusion with the prisoners' deprivation of rights. Probation officers do sense strains. They will have anxieties, in an almost exclusively male environment, about being thought a soft representative of 'the Burglars Aid Society'. Self-preservation, for the probation officer, is on a par with good service to the prisoner. However, above all, it must be recognised that the prisoner is amongst the most deprived of all people in the Western world.

We have observed above that there is a divergence of perceptions about the nature and effects of the social work relationship between probation officer and client or prisoner. This finding is well-documented and there is little methodologically sound evidence to the contrary. 'Social work has placed too little reliance on the clients' perceptions of the services it offers' (Mayer and Timms 1970, p. 14). 'I expected to learn something about myself, but what I learned was that they (the prison staff) had no insight at all' (McVicar 1974, p. 48). 'More significant is the fact that the perception of parolees and probation officers as to the nature of the help given differed markedly' (Morris and Beverly 1975, p. 133). Disparities continue, and were noted in Home Office (1985). Unfortunately, despite a minor outbreak in the probation service of client-need questionnaires in the early 1980s, little consequent change of direction or emphasis has been apparent in the practice of probation officers. Indeed, on the contrary, practice may become less 'client-centred'. Government concern over 'law and order' has, if anything, relegated the criminal's views and needs. In my own research study, released lifers (who probably get more individual attention than ordinary parolees) who had experienced supervision by probation officers on the whole thought them likeable and friendly. However, they regarded their officers as comparatively uninfluential and unable to provide practical help when it was sought. On the other hand, there was a strong desire in most lifers for an acknowledgement of their personal responsibility and dignity. They also thought, in the main, that, apart from his supervisory duties, the probation officer could help by being respectful, trusting and understanding (Coker and Martin 1985). In practice, therefore, the officer should listen creatively and objectively without giving unsolicited advice or trying to organise the lifer's conduct or affairs. The probation officer should be a sounding board.

In general, those who come into contact compulsorily or voluntarily with probation officers resent being 'caseworked or treated'; they must be accorded their dignity; they do not perceive their lives in the same light as probation officers; both, however, are responding to systems.

Essentially, the probation officer sees an individual in need, the prison officer sees an individual to be managed systematically and the prisoner sees himself as relatively impotent, but desirous of maintaining a sense of distinctiveness. Where these perceptions naturally coincide may be the only point at which the probation officer can offer service to the prison, the prisoner and his own professional ideals.

The welfare role

Probation officers working in prison never liked the title 'welfare officer' and, after some 20 years, it has now gone, the probation officer keeping his outside designation when he goes into prison to the probation office, no longer the welfare office. This is a small concession in recognition of the functions expected from the prison probation officer. Those duties were described in guidelines issued in 1966 by the Probation Department of the Home Office: essentially they defined the probation officer as the focal point of prison social work, that is as someone whose job it would be to help the prisoner according to social work theory and method against the background of social work ethics. As recently as 1984 the Association of Chief

Officers of Probation reiterated the probation officer's social work role. They also declared that prisons have difficulty in changing their ethos and probation officers arriving from outside might facilitate this process. Put another way, it has been said that the probation service can help to humanise the prisons. There is, however, some difference between these somewhat arrogant good intentions and achievements. For example, the probation service acquiesced in the use of dogs to guard and frighten prisoners, and the peremptory closing of the family unit at Pentonville. Furthermore, the prison probation officer does not influence the 'ghosting' of prisoners for security purposes with arguments about social or personal needs. Helping the individual in need was, therefore, the probation officer's expectation rather than seeing to him if he were likely to disturb the institution's balance, though the two aims are not necessarily incompatible.

However, the guidelines also listed ways in which the probation officer would be involved in prison routines, such as the preparation of reports. This process no doubt makes for equilibrium. Responsibility for the probation officer was divided between the governor, on the one hand, and the chief probation officer, on the other, with the governor having final authority on all prison matters. Probation officers soon found that they were unable to use all their skills. Many of the prisoners' or the prison's requests for help were essentially simple, for example, tracing lost luggage, or helping to claim back income tax. They also found that their skills were undervalued and that colleagues on the outside did not respond to requests as instantaneously as the system often required. Furthermore, voluntary after-care — which afforded so much potential for both prisoner and probation officer — remained an unfulfilled opportunity. Prison probation work still has not acheived parity of status with fieldwork and it is not much sought after by probation officers. Nevertheless progress has been made. Probation officers are more familiar figures in the prison and sit more frequently at its council tables. On the other hand, prison officers continue to press to take over the welfare role and the probation officer, like the chaplain and the education officer, remains largely peripheral to the system. This limits the seconded probation officers' input and confines them to an institutional role that leaves insufficient time for individual attention to the prisoner. The welfare role is also limited by the size of the potential market of 46,000 prisoners. If the time available for personal consultation is expressed as a function of the total number of prisoners and probation officers in prison, it amounts to approximately 20 minutes per prisoner per week, gross. However, allowance has to be made for probation officers' holidays, meetings, training courses and routine duties, which leaves barely ten minutes per prisoner per week. Fortunately, this equation is not so simple; many men do not want to see a probation officer except to facilitate their release on licence, others do not want to see one at all. Similarly, the probation officer is also selective. Aside from the processing of files and reports, the probation officer can choose a small number of prisoners and see them either singly or in groups. This select band may be those in whom the probation officer is personally interested, perhaps because of their notoriety. These prisoners may be sex offenders, murderers or other special categories. Seldom will they be small-time petty recidivists. Chosen cases will usually be articulate men and women who seem susceptible to casework or a 'treatment' approach and willing to acknowledge 'insight' (Tomasic and Dobinson 1979). They will probably not be selected on the basis of need and potential as indicated perhaps by the type of check list suggested in Home Office (1985). A further category of eligibility will be prisoners who themselves ask to see the probation officers, almost invariably to seek assistance in dealing with a practical problem (for example a phone call home to ask about a sick friend or relative). Prisoners themselves cannot deal with most of these practical problems because of the restrictions of imprisonment. It is, of course, demeaning to have to ask for help in this way, and games may have to be played to get the phone call made by the probation officer who is probably also aware of the undignifying necessity to make such childish requests. Few prisoners come seeking insight into their difficulties or the improvement of their skills to overcome life's 'slings and arrows', though there are those who are oppressed by inner troubles that could be relieved by probation officers in the right circumstances. Indeed prison literature indicates that the welfare officer — like the chaplain, education officer and medical officer, are seen as unimportant figures compared with the prison officer with whom there is continuous day-to-day contact. This daily jowl-by-jowl proximity often leads the prisoner to talk about his worries to the prison officer. There are some indications that prisoners prefer this to going to 'the Welfare', particularly prisoners who work with trade instructors.

These general observations apply to all prisoners, but those serving long sentences are likely to get more attention. This is partly because they are there for longer, because more reports have to be prepared and because special attention is given to preparation for their release on licence. They form an elite group — some 4,000 — many of whom resist the system and attempts to invade their mental privacy. Others are interesting and interested in the probation officer's services.

However, since the system is paramount, the probation officers can make only a minor contribution to the management of long-term prisoners whether or not they are considered dangerous or disruptive. A sympathetic, timely response by a probation officer may well pacify a riotous prisoner. There is little the service can do to prevent wholesale riotous behaviour, for that is an expression of discontent with the deprivation of rights and the humiliations of imprisonment.

The probation officer in prison symbolises a desire to help as well as punish the imprisoned criminal, but at the same time he may also be facilitating the smooth running of the system; the two aims are not essentially antithetical. The utilitarian qualities of beneficence cannot be demonstrated as cost-effective, but kindness stands on its own as being worthwhile.

In practice it means, in short, that a percipient probation officer writes reports that are useful to the system and possibly the prisoner; assists some men prepare for their release; offers individual help in selected 'interesting' cases, facilitates some contact with families and friends outside and speaks with a probation voice at prison councils. In these councils and elsewhere the probation service should promote changes in regimes so that prison officers can undertake a greater part in an integrated welfare role. Perhaps the probation officer's most important contribution is to encourage the prisoner to do things for himself and to promote the conditions in which this becomes more possible than it is at the moment.

The supervision on licence of long-term prisoners

Early release on licence of prisoners who pose little risk to the public serves several purposes. It rewards good behaviour in prison, provides oversight and assistance to the prisoner who is serving the balance of his sentence in the community (a Category E prisoner as he has been called), and is hailed as an economic measure because it reduces the prison population (Home Office 1981). (There are, however, those who argue that parole should be abolished.)

Prisoners themselves find anxiety in not knowing if they are to be released on parole, but nevertheless are glad of the chance to get out of prison early. Officers have misgivings about parole's fairness and the recall of men on licence without trial, but otherwise regard it favourably because it releases people sooner than otherwise would be the case; this assumes that courts do not take into account the possibility of parole when fixing the length of imprisonment.

The prison probation officer is involved in preparation for early release by the provision of reports on the prisoner and his home circumstances. If the prisoner is homeless then the probation officer is expected to find accommodation. Sometimes this is in a hostel, in spite of indications that parolees do not prosper in hostels. The outside probation officer will generally be involved to some extent in pre-release plans and always in the supervision and assistance of the long-term prisoner on licence.

Preparation for licence is well secured through the pre-release employment scheme (PRES) for those prisoners fortunate enough to be selected. It represents all interests but it also gives prison officers an opportunity to demonstrate that they are capable of being as helpful as anyone else. Indeed the PRES is one of the many unsung achievements of the prison service.

Although prisoners do not feel much involved in preparations for their release there is a confluence of interests; prison, prisoner, probation officer and the Home Office want there to be appropriate accommodation and, if possible, 'good' employment. To fulfil these requirements is both felicitous and functional; everyone is pleased if the long-term prisoner can step through the gate with a light heart and good prospects.

Long-term prisoners may be serving either determinate sentences of five years or more, or alternatively life imprisonment. The former category are likely to be released only as they near the end of their sentences, with certain exclusions defined by the Home Secretary in October 1983 at the Conservative Party Conference. Lifers may be licensed at any time after starting their sentences but usually only after many years in prison. Determinate prisoners will generally be on licence for less than 12 months; lifers may expect to serve at least three to four years under supervision but will remain on licence, with the possibility of recall, until they eventually die. Predictions are that reoffending is most likely to occur soon after release but that the possibility of recidivism remains almost perennial. Probation officers, therefore, must be alert throughout the period of supervision for danger signals; often, however, these are not apparent. Whilst probation officers' techniques are the same for parole as for other forms of supervision, there is no doubt that, in the main, they are more assiduous in dealing with lifers and long-termers. Currently the probation service is moving towards the practice of more frequent, regular and rigidly defined contacts with people under supervision — so called 'strict supervision'. Whilst this may have the advantage of appearing to be politically reassuring, the notion of 'strict' supervision is of doubtful validity and likely to result in a 'cat and mouse' relationship between the probation officer and licensee. Most parolees resent supervision but prefer it to remaining in prison. On the other hand, lifers generally liked their probation officers (Coker and Martin 1985) and, where mutual trust existed, were prepared to confide in a limited way in their officers. Probation officers should be open, firm and, in Irwin's (1970) term, a 'right' man or woman. This is likely to be the more effective way to supervise and forestall or foretell danger to the public. We must remember, though, that in predicting future violence we are more likely to be wrong than right (Walker 1980, p. 97). Furthermore, the probation officer should define clearly, after consultation with the licensee, the framework of reporting and try to dignify the licence by reassuring the licensee that he can and should run his life in his own way. Nevertheless, the simple statistics of reoffending whilst on licence indicate that most men and women complete this period satisfactorily (Home Office 1981). Of course, success always depends on the yardstick used; intricate methodological and statistical considerations are often too abstruse for ordinary understanding, but if a further homicide is the ultimate measure then the release and supervision of those who have committed grave crimes is over 99 per cent successful.

Supervising men and women who have served long terms of imprisonment is a comparatively rare experience, but probation officers are tending to specialise their duties and so fewer may gain such experience. Guidelines for the supervision of lifers (and by implication other grave offenders) have been agreed and the probation service is continuously acquiring more expertise.

Probation officers may have only a routine contribution to make in prison, but as supervising officers they are central. Currently the ratio of lifers on licence to probation officers is very low, approximately 1:41. The ratio for other long-term prisoners is not available but there is no reason to suppose that it is in a different range. Without either additional stress on the probation service or appreciable risk to the public, and if politics allowed, more long-term prisoners could be released sooner in their sentences than is currently the case.

To return to the broad canvas, the probation officer is an agent of society and a part of the criminal justice system. The criminal justice system itself — an agglomeration, for all its parts operate independently of each other — is in a mess. Its aims are confused and convoluted and 'it' has been constantly subjected to the tamperings of one government after another, often as the consequence of bureaucratic pressure to improve the system. Furthermore, although much is achieved by both the prison and probation services, the juxtaposition of retribution or revenge and reformation is comprehensively expensive and ultimately unsuccessful.

However great the current political pressure to impose social order by, *inter alia*, the use of stern penalties for crimes, 'order breeds not peace of mind but greater anxiety and recurring demands for more order. It is a need that knows no satisfaction, at least not in this type of society' (Ignatieff 1978, p. 218). We compound our problems by overcomplicating our penal machinery. Instead of refining both 'thumbscrews' and remedies we should work for fewer prison sentences, shorter prison sentences, better prison conditions — the loss of freedom is sufficient punishment — and for a simpler system of penalties. All that is needed are fines related to income, community service orders, probation and straightforward imprisonment as a last resort. This may seem idealistic but nowhere are ideals more necessary than in dealing with criminals.

In the meantime, prison staff and probation officers must do what they can, perhaps in a multidisciplinary team, to humanise the prison for those within its walls.

References

Coker, J.B. and Martin, J.P. (1985), *Licensed to Live*, Oxford: Basil Blackwell.

Dostoevsky, F. (1983), *Memories from the House of the Dead*, Oxford: Oxford University Press.

Goffman, E. (1961), *Asylums*, New York: Anchor Books.

Home Office (1966), *Report of the Inquiry into Prison Escapes and Security* (Mountbatten Report), Cmnd. 3175, London: HMSO.

Home Office (1981), *Review of Parole in England and Wales*, London: HMSO.

Home Office (1984), *Managing the Long-Term Prison System: The Report of the Control Review Committee*, London: HMSO.

Home Office (1985), *The Review of the Role of the Probation Service in Adult Establishments: Report of the Working Group*, London: Home Office Prison Department.

Ignatieff, M. (1978), *A Just Measure of Pain*, London: Macmillan.

Irwin, J. (1970), *The Felon*, Englewood Cliffs, NJ: Prentice-Hall.

Mayer, J.E. and Timms, N. (1970), *The Client Speaks: Working Class Impressions of Casework*, London: Routledge and Kegan Paul.

McVicar, J. (1974), *McVicar by Himself*, London: Hutchinson.

Morris, P. and Beverly, F. (1975), *On Licence: A Study Of Parole*, London: Wiley.

Tomasic, R. and Dobinson, I.D. (1979), *The Failure of Imprisonment: An Australian Perspective*, London: Allen and Unwin, for the Law Foundation of New South Wales.

Walker, N. (1980), *Punishment, Danger and Stigma: The Morality of Criminal Justice*, Oxford: Basil Blackwell.

Notes on contributors

Bottoms, Anthony. Wolfson Professor of Criminology and Director of the Institute of Criminology, University of Cambridge. Member of the Home Office Research and Advisory Group on the Long-Term Prison System.

Canter, David. Professor of Applied Psychology, University of Surrey. Author of *The Psychology of Place* (Architectural Press, 1977). Has conducted various studies on the evaluation of the design of institutional buildings, including prisons.

Coker, John. Deputy Chief Probation Officer, Hampshire, and member of the Parole Board for England and Wales. Co-author (with J.P. Martin) of *Licensed to Live* (Basil Blackwell, 1985).

Coyle, Andrew G. Governor of Greenock Prison, Scotland. Undertook a comparative study of prison systems in North America during 1984 on a Winston Churchill Fellowship. Author of several papers, particularly relating to the management of difficult and dangerous prisoners. Chairman of Prison Governors' Committee; Vice-Chairman of the Scottish Association for the Study of Delinquency; and member of the Scottish Home and Health Department Working Party on Alternative Regimes.

Evershed, Susan. Senior Psychologist, 'C' wing Special Unit, HMP Parkhurst. Formerly Psychologist at HMP Long Lartin.

Fitzgerald, Mike. Deputy Director, Coventry (Lanchester) Polytechnic. Author of *Prisoners in Revolt* (Penguin, 1978) and co-author (with Joe Sim) of *British Prisons* (Basil Blackwell, 1982, 2nd edn) and (with J. Muncie) of *System of Justice* (Basil Blackwell, 1983).

Ingram, Gilbert. Assistant Director for Correctional Programs, Federal Bureau of Prisons, USA. Author of numerous articles and chapters in the professional literature on corrections and criminology. Formerly Warden at two federal prisons.

Jenkins, Michael. Deputy Director, Prison Department Midland Regional Office, Birmingham, and Editor of the *Prison Service Journal*. Formerly Governor of Long Lartin Prison, 1983–6.

King, Roy D. Professor of Social Theory and Institutions, University College of North Wales, Bangor. Co-author (with Rod Morgan) of *A Taste of Prison* (Routledge, 1976) and *The Future of the Prison System* (Gower, 1980); and (with K.W. Elliott) of *Albany: Birth of a Prison — End of an Era?* (Routledge, 1977). Member of the Home Office Research and Advisory Group on the Long-Term Prison System, 1984–6.

Light, Roy. Senior Lecturer, Department of Law, Bristol Polytechnic. Author of a number of articles on criminology, penology and criminal justice.

Longley, David. Senior Psychologist, Adult Offender Pscyhology Unit, Home Office Prison Department.

Morgan, Rod. Senior Lecturer in Criminology, University of Bath. Co-author (with Roy King) of *A Taste of Prison* (Routledge, 1976) and *The Future of the Prison System* (Gower, 1980); and (with M. Maguire and J. Vagg) of *Accountability and Prisons* (Tavistock, 1985). Member of the Board of Visitors of Pucklechurch Remand Centre, 1972–84. Currently undertaking research on accountability mechanisms in policing.

Norris, S.G. Director of Operational Policy, Home Office Prison Department, and Chairman of the Home Office Research and Advisory Group on the Long-Term Prison System.

Pearson, A.J. HM Deputy Chief Inspector of Prisons, Home Office. Formerly Governor of Gartree Prison, 1977–81 and Brixton Prison, 1981–5. Member of the Prison Department Control Review Committee, 1983–4.

Platt, Terence C. Director of Regimes and Services, Home Office Prison Department, 1982–6. Chairman of the Home Office Working Party on New Directions in Prison Design, 1984–5. Member of the Home Office Research Group on the Long-Term Prison System, 1984–86.

Richardson, Genevra. Lecturer in Law, University of East Anglia. Contributor to *Accountability and Prisons,* (Tavistock, 1985) and author of articles on prisoners and the law. Formerly a research officer at the Centre for Socio-legal Studies, University of Oxford.

Rutherford, Andrew. Senior Lecturer in the Faculty of Law, University of Southampton. Author of *Prisons and the Process of Justice* (Oxford University Press, 1986) and *Growing Out of Crime* (Penguin, 1986). Chairman of the Howard League for Penal Reform.

Walker, Nigel. Emeritus Wolfson Professor of Criminology and former Director of the Institute of Criminology, University of Cambridge. Has worked in several prisons, and is currently a member of the Parole Board for England and Wales. Author of *Sentencing: Theory, Law and Practice* (Butterworth, 1986), *Punishment, Danger and Stigma* (Basil Blackwell, 1980), *Behaviour and Misbehaviour* (Basil Blackwell, 1977), *Crime and Insanity in England* (Edinburgh University Press, 1968 and 1973) and other books.

Ward, David A. Professor of Sociology and Chairman of the Department of Sociology, University of Minnesota, USA. Consultant on Marion Penitentiary, Committee on the Judiciary, US House of Representatives. Director of research project on the effects of long-term confinement under conditions of maximum security at Alcatraz Penitentiary (National Institute of Justice). Co-author (with Gene Kassebaum and Daniel Wilner) of *Prison Treatment and Parole Survival* (Wiley, 1971) and co-editor (with Kenneth F. Schoen) of *Confinement in Maximum Custody* (D.C. Heath, 1981)

Whatmore, Peter B. Consultant Forensic Psychiatrist, Douglas Inch Centre, Glasgow and the Scottish Home and Health Department (Prisons Division). Formerly Deputy Physician Superintendent, the State Hospital, Carstairs. Member of the Scottish Home and Health Department Working Party on the Treatment of Certain Male Long-Term Prisoners and Potentially Violent Prisoners, 1971.

Williams, Mark. Principal Psychologist in charge of the Adult Offender Psychology Unit, Home Office Prison Department. Member of the Home Office Working Party on New Directions in Prison Design, 1984–5, and member of the Home Office Research and Advisory Group on the Long-Term Prison System.

Young, Peter. Lecturer in Criminology, Centre for Criminology and the Social and Philosophical Study of Law, University of Edinburgh. Co-editor (with D. Garland) of *The Power to Punish* (Heinemann, 1983).

Conference participants

Rt Revd Mgr R. Atherton, Prison Service Chaplaincy.

Mr D.R. Birleson, Directorate of Regimes and Services Management Unit, HM Prison Service.

Professor A.E. Bottoms, Institute of Criminology, University of Cambridge.

Mr D. Brooke, Governor, HM Prison Service.

Mr D. Brown, Governor, HM Prison Service.

Mr A. Butler, Home Office Prison Department.

Professor David Canter, Department of Psychology, University of Surrey.

Dr John Coker, Hampshire Probation Service.

Mr Andrew Coyle, Governor, Scottish Prison Service.

Ms Frances Crook, Howard League.

Mr J.A. Ditchfield, Home Office Research and Planning Unit.

Mr I. Dunbar, Home Office Prison Department.

Ms Susan Evershed, Prison Service Psychology Department.

Dr M.R. Fitzgerald, Department of Social Sciences, Open University.

Miss Kay Foad, Institute of Criminology, University of Cambridge and Essex Probation Service.

Professor J. Gunn, Institute of Psychiatry, University of London.

Dr Gilbert L. Ingram, Federal Bureau of Prisons, US Department of Justice.

Mr Michael Jenkins, Governor, HM Prison Service.

Professor Norman Jepson, University of Leeds.

Ms Helen Jones, NACRO

His Honour Judge E. Jowitt.

Professor J.M.N. Kakooza, Makerere University, Uganda.

Mr T.J. Kelly, Scottish Home and Health Department.

Mr A.O. Kennedy, Chief Officer, HM Prison Service.

Dr J. Kilgour, Prison Medical Service.

Professor Roy D. King, University College of North Wales.

Mr Roy Light, Department of Law, Bristol Polytechnic and Institute of Criminology, University of Cambridge.

Mr B.D. Palmer, Prison Department, Northern Ireland Office.

Mr Anthony J. Pearson, Inspectorate of Prisons, Home Office.

Mr J.F. Perriss, Home Office Prison Department.

Mr T.C. Platt, Home Office Prison Department.

Professor J.P. Martin, Department of Sociology and Social Administration, University of Southampton.

Mr D. McMullan, Governor, Northern Ireland Prison Service.

Dr W. McWilliams, Institute of Criminology, University of Cambridge.

Mr W. McVey, Governor, Scottish Prison Service.

Ms E. Moody, Home Office Prison Department.

Mr R. Morgan, Department of Social Administration, University of Bath.

Mr S.G. Norris, Home Office Prison Department.

Mr J. Ramwell, Chief Officer, HM Prison Service.

Mr A. Rawson, Governor, HM Prison Service.

Ms Genevra Richardson, Department of Law, University of East Anglia.

Mr Andrew Rutherford, Department of Law, University of Southampton.

Mr J.R. Sandy, Home Office Prison Department.

Mr D.F. Scagell, Home Office Prison Department.

Mr J. Sim, Department of Combined Studies, Liverpool Polytechnic.

Mr P.H. Shapland, Home Office Prison Department.

Mr B.V. Smith, Governor, HM Prison Service.

Miss P. Teare, Home Office Prison Department.

Professor J.E. Thomas, Department of Adult Education, University of Nottingham.

Mr A.H. Turney, Home Office Prison Department.

Professor N.D. Walker, Institute of Criminology, University of Cambridge.

Mr R. Walmsley, Home Office Research and Planning Unit.

Professor David A. Ward, Department of Sociology, University of Minnesota, USA.

Dr Peter Whatmore, Consultant Psychiatrist, Glasgow.

Mr J. Whitty, Governor, HM Prison Service.

Mr Mark Williams, Principal Psychologist, Home Office Prison Department.

Mr D. Wilson, Governor, HM Prison Service.

Mr Peter Young, Centre for Criminology, University of Edinburgh.

Papers on previous Cropwood Conferences

The papers in this book are the product of the eighteenth Cropwood Conference held at the Institute of Criminology, University of Cambridge, with financial assistance from the Cropwood Trust (see Preface). All previous Cropwood Conference proceedings, save one, have been published by the Institute of Criminology, and those which are still in print may be purchased from the Administrative Secretary, Institute of Criminology, 7 West Road, Cambridge CB3 9DT, United Kingdom.

The full list of previous conference proceedings is as follows:

1 *Psychopathic Offenders*, edited by D.J. West, 1968. Out of print.
2 *The Residential Treatment of Disturbed and Delinquent Boys*, edited by R.F. Sparks and R.G. Hood, 1968. Out of print.
3 *Community Homes and the Approved School System*, edited by R.G. Hood and R.F. Sparks, 1969. Out of print.
4 *Criminological Implications of Chromosome Abnormalities*, edited by D.J. West, 1969. Out of print.
5 *The Security Industry in the United Kingdom*, edited by Paul Wiles and F.H. McClintock, 1972. Out of print.
6 *Parole: Its Implications for the Criminal Justice and Penal Systems*, edited by D.A. Thomas, 1974. Out of print.
7 *The British Jury System*, edited by Nigel Walker with the assistance of Annette Pearson, 1975. Out of print.
8 *Control Without Custody?* edited by J.F.S. King with the assistance of Warren Young, 1976. Out of print.
9 *Penal Policy-Making in England*, edited by Nigel Walker with the assistance of Henri Giller, 1977. Out of print.
10 *Problems of Drug Abuse in Britain*, edited by D.J. West, 1978. Out of print.
11 *Pressures and Change in the Probation Service*, edited by J.F.S. King, 1979. Out of print.
12 *Sex Offenders in the Criminal Justice System*, edited by D.J. West, 1980.
13 *Women and Crime*, edited by Allison Morris with the assistance of Loraine Gelsthorpe, 1981.
14 *Crime and the Mass Media*, edited by C.S. Sumner, 1982.
15 *The Future of Policing*, edited by T.H. Bennett, 1983.
16 *Controlling the Growth of the Prison Population: Implications for Criminal Justice*, collated by D.A. Thomas, 1983. Unpublished; available in the Radzinowicz Library, Institute of Criminology.
17 *Periodic Restriction of Liberty*, edited by Roger Shaw and Rita Hutchison, 1985.

Index